The Right to Play Oneself

(continued on page 313)

VISIBLE EVIDENCE SERIES, VOLUME 23

The Right to Play Oneself

Looking Back on Documentary Film

Thomas Waugh

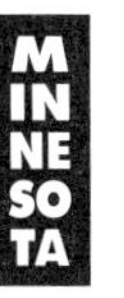

University of Minnesota Press

Minneapolis

London

See page 301 for publication information on previously published material in this book.

Published by the University of Minnesota Press
111 Third Avenue South, Suite 290
Minneapolis, MN 55401-2520
http://www.upress.umn.edu

Library of Congress Cataloging-in-Publication Data

Waugh, Thomas.
    The right to play oneself : looking back on documentary film / Thomas
Waugh.
        p. cm. – (Visible evidence ; v. 23)
    Includes bibliographical references and index.
    ISBN 978-0-8166-4586-2 (hc : alk. paper) — ISBN 978-0-8166-4587-9 (pb :
alk. paper)
    1. Documentary films—History and criticism. I. Title.

PN1995.9.D6W38 2011
070.1'8—dc22   2010032601

Printed in the United States of America on acid-free paper

The University of Minnesota is an equal-opportunity educator and employer.

17 16 15 14 13 12 11   10 9 8 7 6 5 4 3 2 1

In memory of Peter Adair, Artie Bressan,
Guy Hocquenghem, Curt McDowell,
Richard Schmiechen, Stuart Marshall, and
Marlon Riggs, who did make us queer
Harlan County, U.S.A.'s after all.

Contents

Preface

*Of Pulses, Panaceas,
and Parallel Universes*

Every two years I flee the snows of Montreal to participate in the
Mumbai International Film Festival for Documentary, Short, and
Animation Films (MIFF), and its eclectic showcase of both celebration
and self-flagellation keeps this "documentary expert" honest. MIFF
offers the usual panoply of new nonfiction work, as well as opportunities for taking the pulse of twenty-first-century documentary provided
by any large and bulimic international festival, opportunities heightened paradoxically by the festival's somewhat marginal orbit far from
the epicenters of Europe and North America. Dire prognoses for the
future of documentary are usually rampant, and astute insights into its
crises—whether financial, aesthetic, ideological, or ontological—are on
offer at every tea-and-samosa stall. But there are also the reassurances
to be gleaned unexpectedly from bold new small works from grassroots energies and unknown makers—and also works recycled from
the past seen in a strange new retrospective light (for example, the
2008 revival of Flaherty's *The Land* [1942] took on never-noticed resonance in a place with its own dire agrarian crisis seventy years after
the American one). The Mumbai festival serves a sometimes erratic
menu of choices, tastes, voices, and formats—and unfortunately levels
of quality—unavoidable with any event that can't afford to compete
with the prestigious documentary gatherings in Amsterdam, Toronto,
and Yamagata. But this was the price we gladly pay. At least MIFF
isn't as overwhelmed by fifty-two-minute television documentaries
as the North American festivals (a situation I've described elsewhere
as "the nefarious influence of television cable windows on the current state of documentary . . . the polite strangulation of authorial
subjectivity, point of view, and aesthetic resourcefulness."[1]). On the
other hand, the festival increasingly evidences a slight slowdown in the

Indian activist documentary that I had discovered and celebrated in the late eighties (see chapter 9). Whether digital technology has a hand in the slowdown of a trajectory launched almost singlehandedly in the mid-seventies by Anand Patwardhan in defiance of the "Emergency" dictatorship, whether the ideological tide has finally run up against triumphant globalization or whether this is a temporary phenomenon, I have no idea.

Documentary festivals are obsessed with "pitches," and at the 2008 Mumbai festival forum, a representative from the world's largest docfest, the International Documentary Festival Amsterdam, gave a presentation on the now standard institution of seven-minute presentations by artists to TV-commissioning editors. She cast this bizarre ritual, which cross-fertilizes Donald Trump's *The Apprentice* with Kafka's *The Trial*, not so much as the state of the marketplace (which it is) but as the state of the art (which it is not): "[Pitches are] how things are . . . [pitches are] reality." I have nothing but gratitude for the way producers from publicly funded channels in Europe, Canada, and Australia have sustained and stimulated the documentary scene, but the Amsterdam pitch felt too much like a very intimidating reproduction of imperial condescension. It took the outsider's vantage point offered by Mumbai for it to sink in how the proliferating network of documentary festivals is complicit in a boom that has too often left behind documentary's historic roots in the local.

In another intervention from the opposite end of the ideological spectrum, one of India's most respected political documentarists decried the crowding of the documentary field by first-person and autobiographical work, swamping "real" political discourses with their adherence to the commoditized cultures of public confession and reality TV (which raised my eyebrows, given my conviction of the political value of first-person work and my observation two decades ago that Indian documentary had so far proven immune to such discourses [see chapter 9]). Coming from another angle and addressing the Indian context, yet another voice, another leading Indian documentarist, exploded decades of frustration over the publicly funded infrastructure of documentary in India (the state television network Doordarshan and the Films Division, a National Film Board–like state studio in place since Independence). He denounced generations of bureaucracy, indifference, and political interference with social issue and independent documentary and advocated the total boycott of the public sector. This was the equivalent of heresy for European and Canadian observers, for whom governmentality is mother's milk. Call it the heritage of the liberal state, if you like, but the fight to maintain the principle of public arts funding is as fundamental to oppositional documentary as it is never ending. Maybe the documentarist's fantasy of extreme privatization was simply a Swiftian proposal, but I offered the cautionary rejoinder that in fact there is a growing dependency in India on NGOs such as the Ford Foundation and the Bill and Melinda Gates Foundation as documentary financing frameworks. This dubious panacea is not necessarily an improvement on home-grown governmentality and needs-focused assessment.

Awards night arrives at the end of every MIFF, and the raft of juries always makes the same provocative and principled recommendations for improvements—better research, planning, networking, and transparency. Too bad everyone knows that such recommendations soon join a dozen other sets of recommendations on the shelf. Nevertheless, lively debates by artists, distributors, and producers as well as jurists—about aesthetics, financing, outlets, and audience—at least reveal the throbbing pulse that belies the exhausted cynicism of the market. Among the prizewinning films in 2008 were a welcome U.S. feminist take on Afghanistan, *View from a Grain of Sand*; a hard-hitting U.S. exploration of the global politics of water, *Flow: for Love of Water*; an Egyptian feminist essay on cultural hybridization, *House Salad*; *One Day in People's Poland*, a Polish compilation work that reveals the huge untapped scope for working with Soviet-era archives; from India, an activist update on community challenges to groundwater depreciation by the Coca-Cola Corporation in Kerala, *Thousand Days and a Dream*; and a performance-based essay on transgender culture and politics in Tamil Nadu, *Our Family*. This momentum and diversity confirm that the perennial patient is still alive; such contradictory signs of cardiovascular health are as good as it gets in the documentary world.

One of the reasons for a slight disorientation I feel in Mumbai— other than the fact that this *documentary* event is held in a very posh center for the *performing* arts—is that it is usually positioned, in my mind at least, in tandem with the annual Visible Evidence (Viz Ev) documentary conference. Film festivals and film studies conferences are parallel universes on different frequencies. Yet aside from my usual complaints about the ahistoricity of such conferences, their cultural centrism, and all the usual gaps, Viz Ev also testifies in its way to the health of the documentary environment. The conference is rich in productive interdisciplinary encounters—of documentary practitioners and academics (and within the latter category, humanists with social scientists, communicationists with fine arts specialists, and emerging scholars with established ones). Several of the twentieth century's holocausts are always on the agenda through the filters of documentary evidence (World War I, the Shoah, and the Khmer Rouge genocide were spotlighted at the 2007 Bochum, Germany, conference), confirming, whether in keynote addresses, in papers, or in screenings, that historical trauma and the archive are solidifying as major problematics of documentary studies (joining "diaspora," "new media," "first-person," and "neoactivism" in the stampede to immortality). Like MIFF, Bochum had a performance tie-in, a keynote presentation by art world performance star Marina Abramović, who parachuted in to demonstrate once again that the art world is its own further parallel universe and blithely (mercifully?) not even on a frequency adjacent to that of the documentary world. Viz Ev panels that directly address the issue of the intersection of documentary culture with the gallery universe are typically uneven, veering among unshared presuppositions and experiences without the interdisciplinary productivity that marks the sober rigor of the other conference events. Similarly, artists' video, whether linear or installation centered, despite occasionally rearing its head at Viz Ev and receiving some fruitful attention since the mid-nineties,[2] has scarcely extended its toehold as an object within the documentary studies canon.

The Bochum screening of a superb recent German documentary, *The Halfmoon Files* (Philipp Scheffner, 2006), an exquisite essay on contact across epochs and across cultures (World War II and the twenty-first century in India and Germany), provoked much excitement with the way it shuffled the sound-image and archive-actuality equilibrium—at least in my corner of the conference reception that evening—but seemed forgotten for the rest of the conference. This was a reminder of how whimsical, uneven, and unreciprocated the love affair between the documentary studies universe and the production sector can be. The ebullient worlds of nonfiction production, programming, and distribution sure don't give much heed to the "parasitic" discourses of academic study and criticism, but many distributors depend on academic sales and rentals to thrive. Film scholars in turn often look down their noses at the triumphs of the marketplace, often preferring the fertile esoterica that institutional procedures seem to prefer. We often also raise concerns that not only makers but also audiences do not share—even the highly literate lay audiences targeted by documentarists. This is perhaps not an unhealthy situation— at least I often think as much in postscreening Q & A's when all the urgent questions hone in on content and characters, even sometimes at Viz Ev, and often give short shrift to form or art form. Yes, that is the specificity of documentary, speaking to the world, grabbing an audience engaged with that world, and making it momentarily skip over questions of rhetoric and referentiality.

The twenty-first-century revival of mainstream documentary is as interesting as it is precarious. For many the revival of documentary culture may be most conspicuous in the still-churning turbulence of reality TV genres or the Internet revolution, but its most encouraging manifestation may lie in the renewed viability of theatrical exhibition. Symbolized by Michael Moore's Oscar for *Bowling for Columbine* (2002) and his Palme d'Or for *Fahrenheit 9/11* (2004), the phenomenon has been corroborated by parallel sensations that ranged from *The Corporation* (2003) to its uncanny antithesis *March of the Penguins* (another Oscar in 2005), and the out-of-left-field lecture *An Inconvenient Truth* (2006—a third Oscar makes a trend!). The Academy's sudden interest in documentaries that not only are actually *seen* but also make money, enthroning arguably the first pop picks since *Woodstock* (1970), is not surprising. However cynical we must remain, such mainstream breakthroughs certainly mean more than a transformed marketplace—they also engender optimism about the range of new venues and possibilities opened up by technological advances, in particular the expansion of digital formats and distribution platforms, all with their two-edged potential for both consumer cooptation and subversion of authority. The breakthroughs really do seem to have some kind of synergistic connection with the reinvention of small-scale, personal, and grassroots nonfiction in a dozen different settings other than the movie theater and television—from cyberspace to the art gallery to the archive to the myriad possibilities of digital distribution, even to the storefront—and in genres other than first-person grandstanding—from diaristic forms to community agitprop to ethnographic film to nature docs to musicals to compilations to nonindexicality (e.g., animation) and even to filmed lectures (other than Al "Keynote" Gore's). Ultimately, documentary may well be chic at the moment, but I've seen enough cycles of style ebb and flow since I wrote my earliest entries in this book that I know that this roll will not last, apocalyptic views of the threats to our planet notwithstanding.

Books about documentary are another parallel universe I guess, essential to preserving what may be an ephemeral cycle of revival. They are also of course tied in with our concerns as academics around research productivity and pedagogical applications (for example, the apparently lucrative textbook market), too often at the expense of real-world stakes and historical perspective. To at least perform a historical referentiality, this book is organized into ten chapters sequenced in roughly chronological order according to subject matter, rather than in the order in which they were written over the past thirty-five years. I hope this will allow a somewhat meaningful scan of documentary film history as the axis of my analytic and critical interventions. Beginning with a manifesto-like overview of the field of "committed" or "radical" documentary, we shall then move chronologically from Vertov and the Bolshevik pioneers of the silent and early sound eras on to the interwar Popular Front and its testing ground in Spain. In chapter 4, starting with the Popular Front, I then take up the postwar dynamics of evolving technologies and aesthetics, especially as concerns the evolution of documentary idioms of performance. This sets the stage in chapters 5 and 6 for the extraordinary impetus of the New Left in the sixties and seventies, personified by de Antonio and the Canadian grassroots activist program Challenge for Change/Société nouvelle, respectively. Then we proceed into two chapters dealing with the emergence of identity politics as a determining motor of northern documentary in the seventies and eighties—specifically LGBTQ identities, or "lesbian and gay" as the nomenclature went in those decades. Next comes a targeted glimpse of political nonfiction work at the end of the eighties in the "South," notably India, before I conclude with another historical overview of radical documentary across many decades, this time with a genre-based and textual perspective as the base of its political vision. This rough chronology framing my ten essays should of course not be read as teleological, for documentary history has too often consisted of interrupted chains and isolated moments and breakthroughs, followed by clampdowns and hydraulic eruptions in the least expected places.

The twenty-first-century eruption of a revived theatrical documentary may be the backdrop for the publication of this book, but unfortunately it cannot fall within its scope. Reflections on the history of an art form are its primary mission, with hopes that this will qualify the presentist giddiness around *An Inconvenient Truth* (the first film to get its director the Nobel Peace Prize?). Moreover, readers are warned that the conventional canon of documentary history is sometimes lost sight of. Yes, Vertov, Ivens, the National Film Board of Canada, de Antonio, and Patwardhan are given their due to be sure, while Grierson, Flaherty, Leacock, Chris Marker, Trinh T. Minh-ha, and Michael Moore are all referenced (and as I am writing from Montreal, the ghost of Grierson especially is peering over the shoulder of this entire collection). There is admittedly a heavy dose of attention on the U.S. canon (unavoidable given the four years my impressionable young mind spent at graduate school in Manhattan in the mid-seventies), but there is nary a Maysles brother or an Errol Morris or the other old reliables of the current term-paper and conference mill, despite all their poignant ambiguities and analyzable self-reflexivities. (Albert Maysles was greeted at the Film and History Conference devoted to the "Documentary Tradition" [Dallas 2006] like Al Gore, and Viz Ev

Bochum offered the four hundredth conference paper on *Grey Gardens*
since 1975.)

My topics rather may seem almost random and eclectic, responding
to invitations and inspirations, hooks and opportunities along the way,
shaped by my frequent impatience with a canon of documentary studies
that is too often myopically North-centric and ahistorical. I have pushed
this canon somewhat to the side in favor of Rosa von Praunheim, Jean
Carlomusto, and Manjira Datta. If the corpus is not exactly a coun-
tercanon of documentary history, it's at least a slightly nonnormative,
hopefully eccentric one, with the urgent marginalities of the Left, the
queer, and the subaltern (and the Canadian) encroaching on the usual
assumed centrality of the mainstream (though of course the notion of the
"mainstream" with regard to documentary culture itself is complex if not
problematical). In some respects the corpus is also ideologically inclusive,
but you will encounter of course a decided tilt toward the left: the privileged place of documentary in the arsenal of the socially transformative is
what lured me into the field in the first place, and I shall never repudiate
this special vocation.

The other thematic thread is the sustained interest in performance
and mise-en-scène within the documentary lexicon throughout the generations. I hope that my title, *The Right to Play Oneself*, with its fused echoes
of both Benjamin (see chapter 2) and Ivens (see chapter 4) successfully
captures both my Left political preoccupation and this element of performance. Otherwise what all ten essays have in common methodologically is
their preoccupation with the text, what is on the screen. Though this book
reflects interviews with Ivens and de Antonio as well as with networks of
Canadian and Indian documentarists, the works themselves have always
seemed more important to me than what the makers say or don't say
(especially those makers who were interviewed far too much for their own
good). This attachment to texts that begin and end, to objects, may seem
old-fashioned in the age of Internet flow and flatulence, but that is all the
more reason to insist. For the same reason, my essays may seem resistant to
theory, but if that is so blame it on the tenacious real-world reference that
I keep coming back to rather than the allegation (in a review of my recent
book *Romance of Transgression in Canada*) that the author is "happily
unburdened by psychoanalytic knowledge" (Perovic 2007).

The ten essays emerged every few years or so, spread out more or less
evenly over a career that has spanned more than three decades of documentary history—from the 16mm heyday of the mid-seventies (abounding
in topical references to Vietnam and Watergate) to the Internet panacea of
2008 (with the never-ending HIV pandemic, war on terror, and global

warming as its dire context). As such the following ten essays represent focused scrutiny or horizon scans from ten small, punctual moments. All have been previously published except two—one of the earliest (on Vertov) and the most recent (on sixties Canadians' endeavor to update Vertov's kinok network with "Challenge for Change"). But they appeared in the mostly marginal forums that I have always prided myself in feeling drawn to (again, Canadian, queer, or Left but not so much subaltern I am afraid) and not a single one in *Film Quarterly* or *Screen*, not a one ever blind peer reviewed. Several were vigorously edited by fine conscientious editors, but none was ever vetted by the protocols of academic "quality" and scientific authority. I'd like to think this was systematic rebellion against the ivory tower, but it was perhaps accidental. How did I ever get tenure?

The task of assembling this book has forced me, not necessarily willingly, to look back at this question and others, via almost thirty-five years of intense critical and historiographical writing on documentary. At the risk of feeling and presenting myself caught up in the testamentary melancholy shown by Emile de Antonio in *Mr. Hoover and I* (see chapter 5), I am aware that changes in political convictions, in cultural and scholarly approaches and assumptions about documentary and about film in general—and perhaps most dramatically in writing style—will strike the reader. But I think for better or worse there has been no major paradigm shift in the trajectory from gung-ho and wet-behind-the-ears doctoral student to somewhat complacent and extraordinarily privileged preretirement baby boomer. In the earliest pieces, my New Left fervor, fanned by such impassioned discoveries as the early Stuart Hall volume, *The Popular Arts* (with Paddy Whannel, 1965), the anticipation of Bourdieu in my Columbia teacher Herbert Gans's *Popular Culture and High Culture: An Analysis and Evaluation of Taste* (1975), and of course my negative reaction to the claims of modernism, political or otherwise (see chapters 1 and 2), led me to constantly ask questions around cultural capital and audience. Meanwhile, as I was undertaking my doctoral studies in 1974 several founding moments in documentary studies were happening all at once, at least for the English-language tradition. The birth of *Jump Cut* that year provided a steady scholarly vehicle for the development of the hundred flowers of New Left–shaped documentary criticism and theory, while the publication of my mentor Erik Barnouw's *Documentary: A History of the Non-Fiction Film* demonstrated the urgent need for meticulous historical research as well. Bill Nichols finished his doctoral dissertation on Newsreel in 1975, demonstrating the pertinence of a radical object for a radical methodology, but it was "Documentary Theory and Practice," his 1976 article in *Screen* that consolidated the parameter shift that we are still living with today, the application of "scientific" film studies methodologies in their complexity and sophistication (including rhetoric and semiotics) to a field that had hitherto been most often the province of moralism, journalism, and advocacy (none of which should be thrown out with the bathwater, by the way). I was riding this crest, and other influences are palpable along the way—from Vertov, Grierson, and Rouch to Chuck Kleinhans and Julia Lesage to Richard Dyer and later Larry Gross and Jane Gaines.

However, the surfacing of lesbian and gay studies in the eighties and queer theory in the nineties may be the most obvious next shift. The "two solitudes" of my career, the poles of Left documentary and queer identity politics, seem irreconcilable in the early chapters—the latter even subterranean—but they come together in chapter 7, written in the mid-eighties. By the following chapter, written in the late nineties, the two rivers seem inextricable, even unproblematical in their convergence—and what is more they point to tiny fissures in my early treatment of such heterosexual icons as Vertov, Ivens, and de Antonio.[3] Who would have thought? All too felicitously these two poles bring together Nichols's sobriety and Renov's desire, separated at birth and together at last—with Gaines's synthesis of the two poles in her feminist-materialist exploration of affect and genre.[4] This inextricability is not solely an index of how queers have moved into the domain of documentary: It may be the case that there is still no queer *Harlan County, U.S.A.* (as I remember lamenting in chapter 9), but the documentary canon now comfortably embraces *Portrait of Jason, Word Is Out, The Times of Harvey Milk, Bright Eyes, Looking for Langston, Tongues Untied, Forbidden Love: The Unashamed Stories of Lesbian Lives, Silverlake Life: The View from Here, Paris Is Burning, Sea in the Blood,* and *Tarnation.* That these examples all are feature-length works and all from within the English-speaking world speaks to the lingering culture-centrism of syllabus planning of course (as well as the still-unresolved issues around the translatability of documentary). But canons aside, the twenty-first-century inextricability of queer perspectives and Left perspectives within the interdisciplinary documentary studies field is more about two marginal parallel universes slowly converging, again the fusion of sobriety (the first four chaste titles in my table of contents) and desire (the last seven). The fruitfulness of this fusion I hope is much in evidence to the reader throughout this book, even in its most chaste moments, but I wonder if at least some readers will agree that the lewd pulling out of all stops (to use an organ metaphor) in the "Cumming Out" section of chapter 8 may be among its most inspired.

(Those same readers will have detected a slight tongue-in-cheek aura around this book's title, where the intended evocation of political rights and documentary performance/performativity masks a subtextual allusion to playing *with* oneself, an acknowledgment of at the very least my sensitivity about the potentially perceived narcissism in republishing ten of one's essays in such a personally framed compendium, and at most a declaration of the foundation of desire, of self-esteem and self-pleasure, within documentary culture and spectatorship.[5]) In any case, at the very least Left versus queer is one of several dialectical tensions that I hope energize the book—the others being 16mm versus video, "life caught unawares" versus performance, metropolitan versus marginal, and direct versus vérité.

Speaking of the last-mentioned binary, a cautionary note is necessary on the fluctuations of terminology since the early seventies. Readers should brace themselves for a certain inconsistency in my use of the terms "direct cinema" and "cinéma vérité" in my discussions of documentary history. At the time I embarked on the earliest essay in this collection, chapter 5, I was fresh from my 1974 MA thesis on Quebec documentarist Pierre Perrault, famous for his application of Flaherty's catalytic process, hybridized with Rouch's interactivity, to the resurgent Quebec nationalism of the sixties' Quiet Revolution. For Perrault, as for francophone film studies in general, from Marcorelles (1970) and Marsolais (1974) to Gauthier (1995), "direct cinema" is a huge umbrella category that included the American subgenre naively called "vérité." (For about twenty minutes in 1960, the French followed Rouch and Morin in toying with the moniker "cinéma vérité" for their self-reflexive, interactive documentary method—a tribute to Vertov—and this unfortunately caught on across the Atlantic like foie gras, with some critics and practitioners taking it up and some not, and some taking up the more logical "direct cinema" and some not.) I wish we'd had Nichols's distinction between "observational" and "interactive" documentary at the very beginning instead of only with *Representing Reality* in 1991, for this nomenclature is clear and definitive (even his complicated 1976 advancement of the "direct discourse" and "indirect discourse" dichotomy would have helped). We didn't, and I had not yet discovered what a quagmire this had already become for historians and critics of the documentary as I started publishing. At a certain point in the eighties I would give up my crusade to convert American film studies to a historically correct signification of "direct" and "vérité," and simply switched to Nichols's "no fuss no muss" distinction, "observational" versus "interactive."

Less about fluctuations than a deluge, what about the specter of the digital, and is it haunting the way we look at the history of documentary?

With all due respect to Manovich and Feldman, the republication of these essays dares to answer no, or at least "somewhat." In this respect, my colleague Daniel Cross's interactive archive of the homeless (http://www.homelessnation.org, a kind of Wikipedia for Canada's homeless) may well be a remake of *Three Songs of Lenin*, a reframing of the perennial Benjaminian claim of everyone to be reproduced (see chapter 2). Or it may be the tip of a shifting culture around truth value and nonfiction, the interactive Web site only one of the myriad new genres that new technologies have spawned, an index of the increasing and fundamentally different role the digital is playing in a globalized political climate. This collection, a summary of a period of documentary history that ends with the swan song of the analog, cannot and does not purport to answer such questions—except insofar as a strong sense of documentary history, a century of evolving technologies, aesthetics and nonfiction cultures and politics, is indispensable to this task. Suffice it to say, the era of the social documentary is not over, far from it. Nor is the problematic of the truth value of documentary. Our research team in the Concordia Documentary Centre, in which I was joined by Marty Allor, Dan Cross, and Liz Miller, reflected on whether and how the culture of trust and belief, built up by the witnessing and indexical vocation of documentary film, journalism, and photography over the decades, has been eroded and transformed into a culture of distrust and lies in the age of digital manipulation and reality TV. But as I've said, I know the provisional answer already: "less than they claim." The crux of the matter is not lies but truth—the truth of social worlds, the truth of artist–subject–audience relations, and the truth of artistic visions of those worlds and relations, by artists as well as by subjects—and this despite the postmodern collapse of indexicality; the death of the author; the birth of *Survivor*, *Loft Story*; and all the rest. Will ten essays on the right to play oneself act as a modest corrective, as an incitement to truth? Truth in representing the world? Truth in inhabiting the world? That is for the reader—and the viewer, the subject, and the artist—to decide.

Acknowledgments

Heartfelt thanks: to my research assistants Alain Chouinard, Leanne Ashworth, Zoë Heyn-Jones, Marie-Ève Fortin, not to mention their predecessors since 1976, too numerous to mention, and above all to Robert Vitulano, for dedication, resourcefulness, and efficiency in putting together this volume; to the folks, past and present, at the University of Minnesota Press, Andrea Kleinhuber, Richard Morrison, and Jason Weidemann, for their confidence and patience; to Concordia University's Faculty of Fine Arts and the Humanities and Social Sciences Research Council of Canada and the Canada Council for the Arts for funding support without which this book would not have been possible; to original publishers of these essays, Scarecrow Press, *Jump Cut*, Cornell University, Oxford University Press, University of Minnesota Press, *CineAction*, and Amsterdam University Press, for their original support and reprint permission; to Sara Halprin, Kathleen Vernon, Carole Zucker, Chuck Kleinhans, Julia Lesage, John Hess, Larry Gross, Chris Holmlund, Cynthia Fuchs, Kass Banning, and Kees Bakker for their original support for these publications; to Kay Armatage, Maurice Bulbulian, Jean Carlomusto, Manjira Datta, Emile de Antonio, JoAnn Elam, Barbara Hammer, Dorothy Todd Hénaut, Joris Ivens, Alison Burns and Trish Kearns, Bonnie Sherr Klein, Jay Leyda, Mike Mitchell, Ranjan Palit and Vasudha Joshi, Anand Patwardhan and Simantini Dhuru, Adam Symansky, Rosa von Praunheim, Nettie Wild, and any other media artists inadvertently omitted whose collaboration with my research on their work was indispensable in the original production of this writing; to rights holders for permission to publish illustrations (we welcome hearing from any rights holders whom we were not able to trace); to Mike Baker, Jane Gaines, Ross Higgins, Chris Holmlund, Jonathan Kahana, Chuck Kleinhans, Liz Miller, Ezra Winton, and Greg Youmans for precious feedback; to my husband, Francie Brady, for unflagging loyalty, provocation, and confidence.

[**1**] *Why Documentary Filmmakers Keep Trying to Change the World, or Why People Changing the World Keep Making Documentaries (1984)*

How does this essay written a quarter century ago and published at the height of the eighties look now to an author who shudders when his students invite him to "eighties revival" parties? Well, actually, despite the dreadful costumes and music not to mention more profound global traumas associated in my memory with the decade of Reagan–Thatcher–Mulroney—from the Contras to AIDS—this introduction to my first book, "Show Us Life": Toward a History and Aesthetics of the Committed Documentary, *doesn't cause as many shudders as I expected. It hopefully works as a stand-alone piece all of these years later, both as a historical document of a fraught and embattled decade and as still-pertinent reflections on a still-resilient genre of activist documentary in the decade of Al Gore and Michael Moore.*

How will my eighties revivalist students, born during the first Bush presidency, deal with all the signposts of the much-mythologized decade of their birth? Will they understand the charged atmosphere around the brief utopian glimpse of the Sandinista revolution and its treacherous American sabotage or around the invocation of the minimalist British documentary about domestic work, The Night-cleaners *(1975), now unjustly forgotten but then the ultimate symbol of the "Screen theory" model of political modernist documentary practice, so rigorously minimalist that it makes Straub and Huillet feel like Minnelli? They'll be creative, I think.*

Speaking of "political modernism," one reference to "redistributed signifiers" in the "Toward an Aesthetics of Committed Documentary" section of this essay bears a gloss and reminds me of the antagonism I felt at the time toward the avant-garde, whether cultural or political, ingrained since my four-year Manhattan

*immersion of the mid-seventies. (See also chapters 2 and 5.) The
echo is of Noël Burch, whose influential* Theory of Film Practice
*([1969], 1973), along with its introduction by Annette Michelson,
I found more obnoxious than any other text in our discipline,
despite—or no doubt because of—our shared Marxist sympathy.
I simply could not stomach its prescriptive modernist gospel of
cultural hierarchies and fetishization of European art cinema. The
positing of "redistributed signifiers" as a sole criterion for aesthetic
validity comes from a slightly later Burch text, a text redolent
with such intolerable (to me) dogmatisms as "the refusal to see an
aesthetically decisive discontinuity between the practices of, say,
Bresson and Preminger is a flagrant case of 'false consciousness'"
(Burch and Dana 1974, 42).*

*As I write this introduction for this chapter (once itself an
"introduction"), I feel befuddlement at my diagnostic of the state
of committed documentary evidenced every two years at MIFF
(see preface), where a few activist documentaries typically hold the
fort—here a generic denunciation of child labor in Kashmir, there
a generic exposé of multinational mining corporations' devastation of environments and indigenous cultures in eastern India—but
otherwise there is a slight lull in the earlier bushfires. Pioneering
independent activist Anand Patwardhan is now the greybeard dean
of the entire Indian documentary movement, without a release
since 2002, and the new generation is prolific but lacks sustained
momentum. Meanwhile, another household name of the New Left
documentary generation highlighted in the following essay and
the book it introduced, Fernando Solanas has long since returned
to Argentina (and dragging his feet, if I can be frank, in terms of
enabling a much-needed DVD version of* Hour of the Furnaces*).
As for my 1984 dedicatees, Kleinhans, Lesage, and Hess, they
have all retired but remain active. Their legendary journal* Jump
Cut *forges onward, as scrappy and rich as ever, now online of
course, with their entire bountiful archive also available to the post-
Reagan–born at the click of a mouse. Its treasure hoard of debates
and critiques on often "disposable, ephemeral, topical, direct,
immediate, instrumental, collectively or anonymously authored,
unconventional, non-available and non-evaluable" documentary
work (to paraphrase my favorite of the following essay's many
lists), is finding permanent value among my students' generation.
Still, internationally speaking, the firebrand young digital video
(dv) activists have nothing to begrudge their predecessors of earlier*

eras, despite the many wheels being reinvented. As an example,
take a unique recent tradition in my home institution, where an
organization called Cinema Politica has now been filling a seven-
hundred-seat screening room every Monday evening for several
years now and has spread to other Canadian cities and even to the
United States and Europe, challenging a new public culture orga-
nized around an old-fashioned screening infrastructure with Q and
A's wherever possible and with lots of hardcopy flyers at the door
as if the Internet had never been invented, regaling the eighties-born
with everything from 35mm prints of Darwin's Nightmare *to* Liz
Miller's The Water Front *(2008), the latest North American digital*
doc on another water crisis. These films, and this public culture,
where rad docs intersect with grassroots organizing, global con-
sciousness, and hip vegan progressivism, seem to readily embody the
generic and ideological dynamics that I tentatively dissected so long
ago. Specific references to the 1984 book for which this essay was an
introduction have been smoothed over in this recycling to avoid con-
fusion for twenty-first-century readers of The Right to Play Oneself.

We realized that the important thing was not the film itself
but that which the film provoked.
:: Fernando Solanas (1969)

Afraid that the discussion was getting too political, another
of the censors said,
    We cannot show this film, c'est trop de réalité.
:: Joris Ivens ([c. 1942] 1969)

These people are seeing the cinema screen for the first or
second time, they still don't understand the taste of "cine-
spirits," and when real peasants appear on the screen
after the "sugary actors" of the drama, they all liven up
and try to look behind the screen. A real tractor about
which they know only by hearsay crosses the field and
ploughs it in a few seconds before the audience's eyes.
Chatters, shouts, questions. "The actors" are forgotten.
Now there are real things and people on the screen. There
is not a single false theatrical movement to unmask the
screen, to prove the peasants' trust. This sharp boundary
between the reception of drama and documentary was
noticeable whenever a first, second, or third film was
being shown—everywhere where the poison had not yet

Sixty-three years of film history have passed since Vertov's polemic in the third year of the Soviet Revolution, yet his distinction between "Petrushka" and "life" still rings true. Kisses, sighs, and killings still lure us into movie palaces, but in order to be shown "life" we go elsewhere, to the austere environments of classrooms, libraries, and union halls—and occasionally to art cinemas or to a public television network—to watch 16mm documentaries frailly unwind. Vertov would find today's mass audiences incurably contaminated (though one thinks he would recognize the very contemporary but equally ingenuous French or Japanese peasants referred to in *Show Us Life*) and would not be surprised that documentary has acquired this aura of dreariness, that the battle against "Petrushka" has long since been lost.

Yet the documentary can still set off a Vertovian sense of urgency and fervor in certain quarters, namely, wherever people are struggling against oppression.

Ever since Vertov first entered the Soviet newsreel initiative, activists on the Left have continued to use the documentary medium to intervene wherever they have been challenging the inherited structures of social domination. This continuous tradition of radical documentary flourishes more than ever today as the front of radical change broadens and retrenches at the same time and as technology becomes increasingly accessible. At a gathering of more than five hundred radical media activists from the United States and Canada in 1979 (U.S. Conference for an Alternative Cinema, Bard College, New York), over eighty-five films were screened. Of these, fully seventy were documentaries. This book is about the rich and complex tradition whose contemporary manifestation was so evident at Bard. It is about both its founders and its divergent branches in

the last generation and about the practical and theoretical questions posed
by these hundreds of films.

All the films in my 1984 selection set about the job implied by the
word "documentary," but they also attempt to do more. They attempt
to act, to intervene—whether as gut-level calls to immediate, localized
action or as more cerebral essays in long-term, global analysis. They are
all works of art, but they are not merely works of art (although some
have been reduced to this role); they must be seen also as films made
by activists speaking to specific publics to bring about specific political
goals. Furthermore, a good many of the films treated in this book were
made under an important additional assumption: If films are to be
instrumental in the process of change, they must be made not only *about*
people directly implicated in change but *with* and *for* those people as
well. This latter assumption is true of committed books as well, and a
vital part of the audience for such books must be found among people
using film in political struggles.

I am thinking particularly of "poor" and marginal filmmakers and
film users, both those working within the framework of the traditional
Left and workers' movements and those within the progressive mass
movements of the seventies and eighties: the women's movement; minority,
antiracist, and national movements; the environmental, antinuclear, and
peace movements; lesbian and gay liberation groups; and other resistance
movements enlisting prisoners, consumers, welfare recipients, immigrants,
the handicapped, the elderly, the unemployed, and others on down the
endless list of those disenfranchised under patriarchal capitalism. Filmmakers are working on fronts situated everywhere along this list, expanding
the tradition of committed documentary around each one of these causes
(though for reasons of space and effectiveness and to avoid the scattershot
effect of some anthologies, I have chosen to represent some but not all of
these fronts in the book). In addition to oppositional filmmakers, I would
like to reach also those filmmakers working within dominant media, for
their role is a crucial one too.

All of these film workers and their fellow activists in noncultural
fields then are part of the target audience of this book. Committed film historians, critics, and theorists not only must address other scholars but must
also speak clearly and directly to nonspecialists and activists in all spheres
of our struggle.

Before going further, I must narrow down to some degree what I mean by "committed documentary." I will try to elaborate both components of this double-pronged concept, "commitment" and "documentary," with some degree of concreteness.

By "commitment" I mean, first, a specific ideological undertaking, a declaration of solidarity with the goal of radical sociopolitical transformation. Second, I mean a specific political positioning: activism, or intervention in the process of change itself. To paraphrase Marx, a committed filmmaker is not content only to interpret the world but is also engaged in changing it. But Marx's utopian ideal is expressed through very pragmatic applications by the filmmakers discussed here. Few would disagree with the French radical collective Iskra's reminder that filmmakers themselves cannot make revolutions but can only provide "working tools" for those who can.

Filmmakers on the Left have always realized that film, like all cultural forms, is a bearer of ideology and that even films that aspire to change are produced through and within the dominant structures of belief. How then can committed filmmakers escape the entrapment of traditional ideological forms and work within a truly revolutionary ideology? Not by finding and repeating a "correct" line, obviously, but by rooting their work *within* actively ongoing political struggles: by making films, I repeat, not only *about* people engaged in these struggles but also *with* and *by* them as well, and through this process, and with full awareness of the contradictions in play, hammering out the shapes of an evolving new revolutionary ideology around those struggles. This third and final criterion for commitment, this "subject-centered" or "contextual" ideal expressed in my string of emphasized prepositions, is as essential an element of my notion of commitment as the first two: ideological principle and activist stance.

I like the way the complexity of this notion has been visualized and summarized by Miguel Littín, the Chilean filmmaker whose own commitment has been expressed on the boundaries of fiction and documentary:

> We have used a line from the poet Antonio Machado a lot in our political development: "Walker, there is no road / Roads are made by walking." But, concretely, in our country, cinema has to be the avant-garde of events, opening the way to the great revolutionary perspectives, clarifying what revolution is and at the same time being a witness to reality, but projecting it to future transformations . . . and without demagogy . . . There is a distinct

difference in attitude between one who speaks to the public from a balcony
and those who work with and among the people, with all the richness and
dynamics that this implies: we ourselves are being transformed. (Littin,
1971, 20)

This notion of commitment, so poetically expressed in the abstract, must
be given concreteness within specific historical conjunctures. Since the
twenties, commitment, with its revolutionary principle, activist stance, and
subject-centered base, has taken innumerable different concrete expressions. I am always moved by the concrete poetry of place names that have
come to symbolize for me this diversity: Fuentedueña, Sanrizuka, Santiago,
Detroit. The contexts in which committed films intervene vary as widely
as these place names and as the styles of the films themselves; they range
from the euphoric dynamism of the first decade of the Soviet revolution,
to the desperate tension within the crumbling fortress of postindustrial
capitalism, to fierce defiance on the Central American battleground. It goes
without saying that the range of ideological coloring represented by the
films is just as broad. They occupy virtually all the gradations possible on
the left side of the political spectrum, from the social democratic through
the Marxist-Leninist to the Left-libertarian. Some would undoubtedly find
my nonsectarian criteria too broad; others would see them as too narrow or skewed in other ways. I hope that the majority will agree that the
spectrum of *"Show Us Life"* is a provocative demonstration of the range
of history's opportunities and a confirmation that there is no simple rigid
formula of committed filmmaking that can be applied to every historical
problem. Let a hundred flowers bloom.

Obviously, not all the films in *"Show Us Life"* fulfill the complex goal
that I have set forward. History has seldom permitted the committed filmmaker the clarity of perception, which we in retrospect invariably enjoy,
and thus the committed filmmakers discussed in this volume have the retrospective privilege of error. Criticism of filmmakers of the Popular Front
on both sides of the Atlantic, for example, should be read in the spirit of
respect for their achievements and for the complex contradictions of the
historical situation in which they found themselves. At the same time, some
committed authors stop short of direct criticism out of courtesy or solidarity, motivations that are perhaps misguided.

Even where clarity of perception existed, without error, history has
not always permitted the committed filmmaker the full and unproblematic
chance to live up to each facet of his or her own vision. To realize a vision
of commitment at every stage of a film's trajectory has usually required a
miracle of personal tenacity and historical fortuity at the stage of a film's

production, at the stage of its photography, during editing and postproduction, and at the final stage of its exhibition and consumption (and during preservation, I add in 2011!). The reader will have no trouble finding examples of films discussed in this volume that were unsuccessful in expressing the filmmaker's vision at any one of these three stages. In fact, it would be very surprising indeed if most of the films in this anthology did not express in some way various limitations and contradictions at some stage in their trajectory. Most of the articles included here are preoccupied in important ways with these gaps between political intention and achievement. It is only by exploring how committed artists of the past have come to grips with—or failed to come to grips with—their historical contexts that we can learn how to act within our own. In discussing the contradictions posed by the filmmakers included in this book: one artist speaking from a balcony (to use Littin's image); another failing to break out of the ahistoric avant-garde aloofness by which bourgeois culture sidetracks the political artist; another relying on authoritarian, individualist, or sexist modes of film production; another deploying mystificatory or illusionist filmic discourse; or still another working within the "system" without a precise strategic justification—the point is to perfect our own practice as filmmakers/film users and activists by learning from their efforts and experience.

A further qualification of the notion of commitment is necessary. It is possible that the reader may have already inferred a further criterion from my emphasis on distribution, or from the fact that a significant proportion of my committed canon is aimed at popular audiences. A large number of films in fact attempt—and often succeed—to break out of the frequent bind of Left cultural work, the restriction of appealing to a small, already politicized audience. However, this criterion of popular appeal is not absolute: given the complex dynamics of political media activism within the repressively tolerant, image-overloaded, postindustrial cultural environment, there is no necessary correlation between the size of a film's public (nor, for that matter, the size of its grain, its gauge, or its budget) and its political effectiveness. This selection includes both an Oscar-winner, *Harlan County, U.S.A*, and *The Nightcleaners* (not even nominated!), a film whose defenders readily admit when questioned that it was "badly received," all the while dismissing many of the activist premises of the last few pages as "conventional notions of agitprop" and "a very functional instrumental notion of cinema" (Johnston and Willemen, 1975, 113–14). The debate over this issue of audience, scarcely changed since similar debates in the twenties and thirties, continues to be a very lively one.

"Documentary" is less elusive as an organizing concept than "commitment," though equally problematical. Since the twenties, "documentary" has been a mode of film discourse that is popularly understood, historically defined, and as readily assumed by filmmakers, film audiences, and film critics as it was unwittingly by Vertov's "uncontaminated" peasants years before the term was even coined. The commonsense understanding of the label "documentary" combines ideas of nonfiction and education with social seriousness, noncommercial or alternative or television distribution, and of course Grierson's "creative treatment of actuality," the elements of creative shaping and actuality both being always understood (though in varying proportions for different audiences and different periods).

This taxonomical consensus is more or less universal and in my opinion not especially problematical in itself: such a consensus of audience with practitioners (or as Bazin put it, a "common fund") must always be the departure point and basic object of genre studies (Bazin [1957] 1985, 257).[1] However, this consensus has been attacked in the last decade by theorists who, like Steve Neale, Paul Willemen, and Claire Johnston, anthologized here, quite convincingly demonstrate that documentary must forfeit its claim to a privileged access to truth (including "pravda" and "vérité"), reality, and objectivity (though the last of these aspirations has never been claimed by most of the practitioners discussed here in the first place). Documentary, such theorists have shown, relies no less than any other filmic genre on its own systems of codes, conventions, and cultural assumptions and mediations. An obvious corollary of this insight, for some, is that a documentary, which does not challenge the terms of its own combinations of belief, which does not subscribe to the aesthetic prescriptions of what has come to be known as "political modernism,"[2] is guilty not only of a fallacious realism but also of a political complicity. Thus, it is now commonplace to read in undergraduate term papers that documentary is no different from fiction (an assertion somewhat less subversive now than when Godard first called Lumière a storyteller and Méliès a documentarist in the sixties) or that *Harlan County* is guilty of the most heinous illusionism.

What are the ramifications for this tool of our new sophistication in looking at documentary, of its teetering on its ideological pedestal? Many, and at the same time, very few. The emergence of the view of documentary, as an art form without any special transparency (it is uncertain whether the commonsense understanding of documentary will ever change that much), necessitates the alteration and enrichment of critical terms of reference, to be sure; they have been long in need of a tune-up in any case. Also on the agenda is a toughening of the standards of documentary historiography, long in need of antidotes to the "venomous sweetnesses" of the Riefenstahl/Flaherty/Grierson cultists (Bert Hogenkamp and Russell Campbell are only two historians who have made important advances in this direction). Perhaps more important, it is already apparent that the new theoretical awareness has enormously expanded the vocabulary of documentary filmmakers themselves. This expansion of documentary vocabulary has come, in fact, just in time to offset its impoverishment following, on the one hand, the enshrinement and then decline of the vérité movement, and on the other hand, the mass immunization against that same vérité spread by television newscasting. Filmmakers as different as John Berger (*Ways of Seeing*), JoAnn Elam (*Rape*), and Emile de Antonio (*In the King of Prussia*) testified in their experiments with self-reflexivity or mixed modes to the most impressive addition to the documentary repertory since the advent of vérité. Their success has also hinted encouragingly about an availability and accessibility of the new image theory for the documentary public, just about the time that progressive and popular fiction filmmakers seem to have given up.[3] The sixty-year legacy of documentary activism that is the subject of *"Show Us Life"* is enriched rather than dissipated by our better understanding of the workings and the risks of documentary discourse.

On a broader scale, the new documentary theory has never even threatened to dislodge documentary as an important and discrete arena of committed film practice. The new skepticism has not led radical film activists to abandon documentary in favor of Godardian introspection: far from it. As evidenced by the interview with Paris's Iskra Collective (Hennebelle 1984) and other entries in *"Show Us Life,"* it has instead led them toward a greater precision about, and willingness to experiment with, political goals, target audiences, textual practices, and contextual relationships with subjects—in short, toward a fuller artistic maturity. In any case, documentary continues to be a privileged medium—indeed, the privileged medium—for committed artists and their publics, and a resource of first priority for the political activist. John Ramirez's intriguing piece on Nicaraguan cinema indicates that revolutionary societies today turn to documentary as an instrument of social construction no less enthusiastically than did the Soviets around 1920, the Chinese around 1950, and the Cubans around 1960. Lenin's dictum about the cinema as the most important of the arts seems to be taken up just as eagerly by the new societies of the Third World as it was by Vertov. This is equally true for Lenin's more detailed prescription for state film policy, the Leninist Film Proportion, a recommended ratio of fiction to nonfiction films for the early Soviet film industry. Thus, it is fitting that the Soviet experimentation with the new art form begins *"Show Us Life,"* just as it is that our accounts of new documentary activity in the Third World end it.

The cycle begun in those mobile agit-train editing rooms along the Volga and renewed in makeshift outdoor screening areas in the liberated zones of El Salvador, demands comprehensive historical and theoretical study. This long-standing demand is heightened rather than undermined by the recent theoretical refinements in film studies: it would be foolhardy to deny that the committed canon remains a coherent, authentic, and largely untouched corpus for scholarly, ideological, and political examination.

A few other remarks about documentary are also in order. My focus on documentary does not mean that I deny the political potential of all other cinemas, notably of fiction. On the contrary, I certainly vouch for the potential of committed fiction. Indeed, Littin is only one among many filmmakers who have ultimately opted for committed fiction. (Is it incidental, however, that most of the healthy traditions of committed fiction display strong documentary influences—the Cubans, the early Soviets, the Italians from Zavattini to Rosi, filmmakers here in Quebec?) I accept without reservation such filmmakers' provable interest in fiction's ability to reach and move large numbers of people and to introduce political concepts into mainstream culture. All the same, committed fiction raises entirely different historical, theoretical, and tactical questions from those raised by documentary. It is thus quite outside the scope of a volume that has already been forced for reasons of space to leave large geographical, historical, and political domains of committed documentary unrepresented. Some readers may even wonder whether Jean Renoir's *La Vie est à nous* should be thought of as a committed documentary, with its didactic hybridization of agitprop fiction, newsreel documents, and Party oratory, the ensemble undeniably weighted toward the first of these.

One further precision: by emphasizing analytic and activist documentary by my editorial selection, I do not mean to belittle the special power of those documentaries, which reflect or observe the world without either the desire or the capability to engage in a direct strategy of changing it. Scientific study is, after all, a key precept of Marxist thought: many observational documentarists in the traditions of cinéma vérité and direct cinema will continue to make important contributions by providing raw material for such study, as well as by gaining entry to media channels where radicals have no access. I am thinking, for example, of filmmakers, like Frederick Wiseman, whom early Marxist theorists might have called "critical realists" and who deserve our careful consideration. Though I do not dismiss Wiseman, none of the filmmakers I would select as models for political practice is content to remain at the observational level of Wiseman's work. Each one, in his or her way, endeavors to move beyond observation and all of its inherent liabilities: humanist ambiguity, fake objectivity, liberal empiricism, and the complicity of spectacle. They undertake rather to accede to the level of intervention, using Wiseman's language (if at all) only as an ingredient, which other cinematic strategies must expand, transform, or deconstruct.

On the other hand, finally, compilation documentary, a prolific and creative radical tradition, founded by Esfir Shub, and some of its most interesting practitioners of the last twenty years, primarily from Latin America, belongs at the center of the committed canon. Admittedly, my "subject-centered" ideal, expounded at the outset, has no obvious direct application to the admirable work these artists accomplish on their own terrain: the stock footage library and the editing room. Yet their project of radical historiography is second in importance to none and, led by the work of Emile de Antonio, has been a major influence on radical documentarists since the seventies.

Toward an Aesthetics of Committed Documentary

"Show Us Life" appears at a time when documentary studies is finally entering its own within the discipline of film studies. It is no longer possible to complain, as Bill Nichols did in his seminal 1976 essay, "Documentary Theory and Practice," that the theoretical examination of the formal structures of documentary, its codes and units, is "scarcely begun." Since then, there has been a small flood of new entries in the field, inaugurated in many ways by Nichols's work. The best of the new entries confront documentary in terms of the new methodologies developed in the seventies: semiotic or structuralist analysis; psychoanalytic approaches; formal(ist) analysis; ideological, industrial, exhibition, and audience history. The once bleak picture now looks very lively, building expansively on the work of the pioneers of documentary studies, Erik Barnouw, Jay Leyda, and Lewis Jacobs.

As for political film itself, both fiction and nonfiction, its study is just as healthy, thanks largely to the unpaid periodical work of the last few years (rather than to the grace of the publishing industry). Too often, however, criticism of political film is still dominated by ad hoc critical principles, outdated conceptual models, and the all-too-frequent substitution of ideological fervor or indignation for solid analysis. The notable achievement in this area has been in the feminist camp, whose intellectual acuity and diversity, as well as enviable political strength, the reader will find well represented in *"Show Us Life."*

As for the hybrid field of political documentary proper, outside the feminist area, there has been a tremendous gap, which I hope this anthology will help fill. We have still to muster a set of critical and theoretical principles for dealing with the aesthetics of a genre, political documentary, which refuses to meet any of the expectations of bourgeois aesthetics, modernist or otherwise. Instead of meeting the criteria of durability, abstraction, ambiguity, individualism, uniqueness, formal complexity, deconstructed or "redistributed signifiers," novelty, and so on, all in a packageable format, political documentaries provide us with disposability, ephemerality, topicality, directness, immediacy, instrumentality, didacticism, collective or anonymous authorship, unconventional formats, nonavailability, and ultimately nonevaluability. No wonder we keep running into baffled dismissals such as that of Andrew Sarris in the face of the French collective work, *Far from Vietnam*: "Zero as art." (Sarris 1971, 317). How then do we talk about films whose aesthetics consist in political use-value? What does the concept of an aesthetics of political use-value mean, beyond the fact, say, that *The Spanish Earth* raised enough funds to send eighteen ambulances to the Spanish front? *"Show Us Life,"* (and *The Right to Play Oneself*, I hope in 2011), will advance us considerably in our search for an alternative, political aesthetics. It will also, I hope (and this may mean the same thing) occasion a certain recycling of many of the films covered, films whose original political context and thus "use-value" have lapsed but that may find new uses and engage new aesthetics in new contexts.

▶ ──

Patterns of Change and Continuity

"Show Us Life" is organized into two historical blocks. This roughly chronological, historical arrangement seemed natural for a film genre whose roots in specific historical conjunctures are more evident (though perhaps not more determining) than for any other genre. The first and shorter block deals with the achievements of the pioneers of the committed documentary of the period between the Wars, in the Soviet Union, in Western Europe, and in North America. The second consists of a survey of contemporary work from the West and from the Third World (except for one entry, the "Second World" is conspicuous by its absence), from between approximately 1960 and 1984. This has been a period when the

simultaneous resurgence of three only partly connected phenomena set off a renewal of the committed documentary whose abundance, diversity and fervor world surpass the legacy of the first period: (1) the entry of the Third World as a fully enfranchised player on the geopolitical scene, (2) the emergence of the New Left in the "First World," and (3) the explosion of cinéma vérité/direct cinema in the domain of documentary technology.

Two questions. First, why the gap between the two chronological blocks? It is not that committed documentaries disappeared for a decade or two during the war and the Truman–Eisenhower era. Far from it: their participation (some would say submersion) in the Allied wartime propaganda effort was a distinguished one, as was their intermittent but by no means inconsequential achievement in the Dark Ages that followed in both East and West. These subjects have been neglected and merit careful study (two of the most celebrated figures of this period, Leo Hurwitz and Joris Ivens, are known in terms of earlier work, and others, Andrew and Annelie Thorndike, the East German compilationists, as well as the Americans Sidney Meyers and Herbert Biberman, are sometimes invoked in passing); my leap over this fascinating period, however, results only from the relative shortage of film historians working in the area. The task of defining the unbroken continuity between the thirties and the sixties is high on the agenda for the future.

A second question is about what tentative conclusions may be reached from such a juxtaposition of two distinct historical bodies of similarly motivated film activism. Though it is ultimately up to the reader to determine the fundamental continuities and ruptures between the two periods and to draw the appropriate lessons from them, it is perhaps useful for the editor to sketch some of the more obvious contours in this introduction. The most basic pattern is that the three-part typology that I establish at the beginning of my essay on *The Spanish Earth* is quite constant throughout the entire scope of *"Show Us Life."* I am referring to three distinct categories of interaction of historical context, political goal, and audience dynamic: (1) films of information, agitation, and resistance whose primary audience is situated within the same prerevolutionary political context as that depicted (*Native Land* and *Hour of the Furnaces* may be considered prototypes here); (2) films of information and international solidarity depicting pre- or postrevolutionary situations for audiences outside of the context depicted (of which *The Spanish Earth* and *The Battle of Chile* may be considered self-reflexive interrogations); and (3) films of information and exhortation for audiences within the same postrevolutionary situation as that depicted (Vertov's *Kino Pravda*

series and the contemporary Cuban and Nicaraguan films entering this
category). Of course, hybrids appear as often as the pure examples, and
films shift from one audience category to another in the course of their
careers, as is vividly documented by Anand Patwardhan in his discussion
of his own work (Patwardhan 1984).

Yet for all the apparent continuity in these three basic types of contextual political dynamics in the work of our two generations of committed
documentarists, their films, obviously do not look at all alike. Here is
where the three determining factors I have mentioned come in: the enfranchisement of the Third World, the emergence of the New Left, and the
explosion of cinéma vérité. All have become interconnected to change
the face of the contemporary committed documentary, with the technical
transformations of the third factor often mirroring the significant ideological and thematic shifts occasioned by the first two. For example, the new
lightweight cameras encouraged filmmakers to go beyond their traditional
observational modes toward modes of participation and even of collaboration, intervention, and social catalysis. New stocks permitted new
environments to be added to the documentary arsenal, for example leading feminists to add the iconography of kitchen-table rap groups to that
of classical street corner demonstrations, enabling them to translate into
filmic practice the political practice of intervening in the personal sphere.
On another level, new accessibility of film and video hardware dramatically multiplied forms of collective and grassroots authorship to match
the democratic aspirations of the new political movements. At the same
time, increased access to the mainstream media added to the resources of
compilationists; this enabled, on the one hand, filmic applications of new
modes of social historiography (for example *Before Stonewall*), and on the
other, new possibilities for montage subverters of the mainstream media,
matching our increasing sensitivity to cultural aspects of domination (from
Millhouse to *The Atomic Café*).

Perhaps most striking among the technical transformations was the
new sound. The first generations of sound documentarists had neither the capacity for on location recording and subject interviews nor
the ideological aspirations that have come to be connected with these
tactics. Working within or alongside a centralist party formation, they
were also constrained for the most part to make do with silent films or
with voice-over narrators that seemed to mimic the hierarchical political
organization. The era of the portable sound recorder, the Nagra, allowed
filmmakers, virtually for the first time, to listen to and record their
subjects in their everyday situations, an enormous potential leap toward
the subject-centered ideals and rank-and-file agendas of contemporary

liberation movements in both the First and the Third Worlds. The potential for "letting the people speak," has led to excesses, correctly criticized by Guy Hennebelle and admirably defended by Barbara Halpern Martineau (1984). All the same, a general tendency of contemporaries has been, despite the "workerist" or populist trap, toward antidogmatic, discursive, more open-ended, more flexible, and more democratic forms in a very literal sense, bringing political ideals of contemporary radicals much closer to the reality of filmic practice. (Julianne Burton provides a thorough and provocative chronicle of this tendency in Latin America.) The authorial voice has not disappeared, but it is now most often more collaborative, more sensitive, more intermittent, less prescriptive, and less self-righteous.

Thematically, our two blocks of films in *"Show Us Life"* reflect, as might be expected, a certain evolution in the concerns and struggles of the Left since the twenties. The early films express the preoccupations of classical Marxism: exploitation and oppression under capitalism; the crisis of capitalism; and the production, organization, struggles, and victories of workers. Strikes and demonstrations are at the dramatic and visual center of these works. During the Popular Front of the late thirties, the same themes are still central but have become modulated toward more conciliatory imagery, the utopia of workers' revolution having been postponed by the more immediate job of forming alliances in the struggles against fascism. The theme of the People's War enters the documentary repertory at this time, resurfacing in our own era, with fascists now replaced by neoimperialists, whether in Latin America or in Indochina, Africa, and the Middle East. All the classical themes continue to preoccupy our contemporaries, of course, as *Harlan County, U.S.A.* and other films testify. At the same time, however, the taking up of the camera by Third World filmmakers and by nontraditional radicals in the First World, from feminists to antinuclear activists and gay liberationists, has resulted in a staggering proliferation of new thematic interests in the contemporary committed documentary. From neoimperialism to health care, from sexual violence to popular culture, each new theme is linked to a more general global analysis and comes out of the political practice that is the focus of *"Show Us Life."* Interestingly, one theme omnipresent in the films of the pioneers (either explicitly or by conspicuous omission, as in the case of many Popular Front artists), the presence of the Party has all but disappeared in contemporary work, with the only exceptions appearing in those situations where electoral politics is still on the agenda on the Left, as in France, or in a certain subgenre of

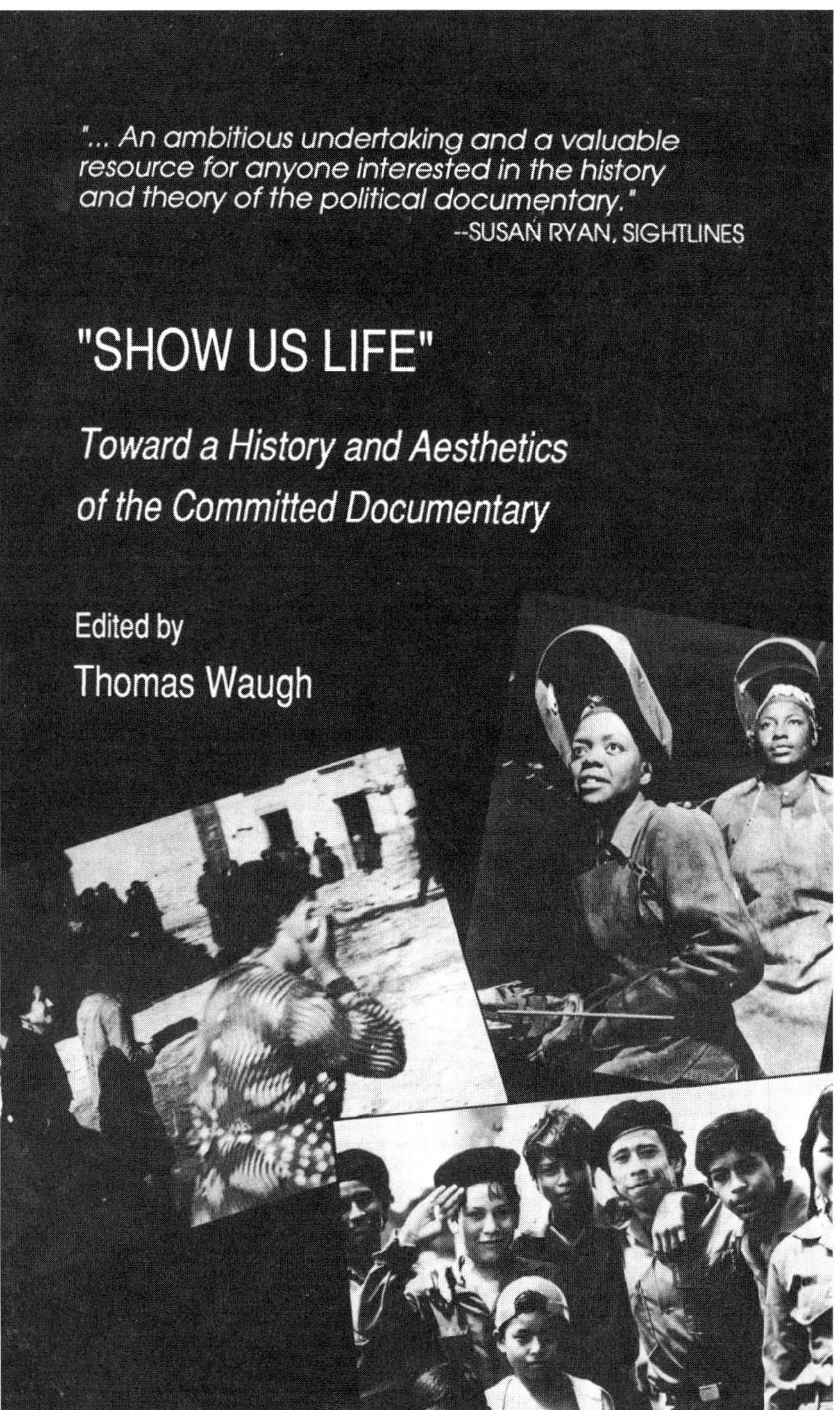

In 1984, halfway through an embattled decade, *"Show Us Life"* collaged iconic images from earlier decades on its cover and recharged a sixty-year tradition of radical documentary.

compilation work, not without traces of nostalgia, pioneered chiefly by the New Day Films (*Union Maid* and *Seeing Red: Portraits of American Communists*).

One final note: "*Show Us Life*" is dedicated to *Jump Cut* founders Julia Lesage, Chuck Kleinhans, and John Hess, who have demonstrated that political film criticism is an integral part of political film practice.

[**2**] ## Dziga Vertov, *1930s Populism, and*
Three Songs of Lenin *(1975)*

*It takes a certain chutzpah to include a term paper from a doctoral
seminar in such a collection as this, but there is so little published to
this day on Vertov's 1934 masterpiece* Three Songs of Lenin,[1] *that
I have decided it is worth the risk. This article was written in 1975
and is published here for the first time, more than three decades after
it was originally written for a seminar on Dziga Vertov offered at
New York University (NYU) by Annette Michelson. Doing my doc-
torate in Columbia's moribund doctoral program, I was going stir
crazy on the Upper West Side and jumped at the chance to take two
seminars with Michelson downtown at NYU, one on Soviet cinema
of the twenties and the other on Vertov, held at the Anthology Film
Archives, then on Wooster Street. The seminars were invaluable and
have remained with me to this day, testimony to Michelson's impact
as a teacher and an intellectual. I consider one index of her pedagogical effect to have been its incitement to revolt, and this article is
the embodiment of my revolt.*

*The essay reflects most saliently my discovery in the two Vertov
seminars I took (Michelson's as well as Erik Barnouw's at Columbia) of the 1972 French edition of Vertov's writings—*Articles,
journaux, projets, *based on a 1966 Soviet revival at the peak of the
Thaw period—which appeared twelve years before the long-time-
coming English edition edited and introduced by Michelson in 1984.
It influenced me more than almost any other book at the time and
easily replaced the volume of Grierson's speeches and articles that
had been my Bible during my master's program (good Canuck that I
was). This essay registers among other things my shock at the fundamental disconnect between what I was reading in Vertov's writings
in my far-from-perfect French, what I was seeing on the screen[2]*

*and what I was hearing in Michelson's seminar. More generally
these interpretations and arguments reflect my New Left inspiration, as I was beginning to develop my dissertation on the Old Left
pioneer Joris Ivens and wrestling with problems of ideology and
documentary form, above all with issues of audience and cultural
capital—a tough fit with documentary studies, then as now. This
article also expresses my dismay at the way Vertov's standing was
being stretched and pulled in various directions during the seventies,
in particular at the canonization of* Man with a Movie Camera *at
the expense of his other works. One symptom was the way his films
were being projected at that point only in Jonas Mekas's Anthology
Film Archives, without English subtitles, as if the filmmaker's discursive apparatus that I found so enthralling was of little consequence
alongside his visual virtuosity.*

*Michelson is a still-prolific pioneer of our discipline who gra-
ciously accepted our honorary degree at Concordia a few years back,
and I wonder if it is fundamentally uncollegial to offer this public
critique? Perhaps. But it is not for me to decide this or whether there
is some irrepressible oedipal mechanism at work here, an overstated
diss served cold, and I must proceed. Perhaps my strongest memory
from her seminar has to do with a scene from Kino-Glaz, shot at an
asylum, in which Vertov dwells on a deranged female inmate acting
out her palpable pain in front of the camera. Summoning my courage, I asked Michelson what she thought of the scene in terms of
issues of documentary ethics. Looking at me as if I was speaking
Klingon, she paused and then with pontifical froideur pronounced
that the early twentieth-century modernist avant-garde no longer
accepted earlier conventions around appropriate subject matter (my
concern was so totally pre-Raphaelite apparently) and embraced
the full spectrum of human experience as subject matter, witness
Duchamp's urinal, and so forth. I should have argued, but didn't,
that modernist hoo-ha did not absolve anyone, artist or not, of fundamental ethical obligations as citizens, whether of a revolutionary
state or not, and as human beings. Michelson had a legendary
status as a seminar terrorist who would pounce on the unwary, the
unprepared, and simply the unfortunately placed around the table,
wielding tongue-lashing and public humiliation, and one did not
talk back. And I was not secure enough to offer myself as that day's
sacrificial lamb. I think now that neither "documentary" nor "ethics" were part of her lexicon.*

At the end of term I dropped this paper and ran. I will never forget a long time later being called downtown to Michelson's office for her feedback, aware that I was clearly being singled out by this summons. She archly informed me that she had received several good papers from the seminar but that my paper was not among them and asked for whom I had written the piece, apparently concerned that this "attack" was going to be published. One other thing I remember from this meeting was that she had just washed her famous blond hair, and it was frizzy and wet, which somehow added to the theater. More important, she not so obliquely accused me of being a Stalinist—a perhaps normal response from someone with so much investment in the perspective I was critiquing, and so much at stake in whatever reckless rehabilitation of socialist realism I seemed to be advocating.

I cannot deny however, despite this mentorcide melodrama, Michelson's strong influence on my work of the day, positive as well as negative. It is palpable in much of my language, as well as in my analytical framework. Other mentors are present as well, of course, but less conspicuously. It is not hard to detect my muted admiration for Michelson's colleague Jay Leyda, who was being a supportive resource person for my new research on Joris Ivens (and who as it turned out had been Ivens's ghostwriter for his autobiography). My brief citation from his Kino, *I think, corroborates my account of Vertov's work. There is also an even more discreet tribute to my uptown professor, Barnouw, who saw his seminar in Vertov and Flaherty as a collegial collective exploration rather than a podium. Finally, my interest in populism had been sparked by yet another teacher, Raymond Durgnat. This essay languished for literally a couple of decades in* Jump Cut *drawers, awaiting a special section on Soviet cinema that somehow never seemed to materialize (no doubt the ball was in my court the whole time, while I was distracted by Vertov's queer antipode Sergei).*

Almost nothing has been changed in this text since 1975, except for a few necessary footnotes acknowledging more recent advances in Vertov scholarship, and a shortening of some of the citations (though this will not be evident to twenty-first-century readers who may still find them excessive). For example, I have retained such concepts as "bourgeois" and "formalism," since they reflect my excited discovery of Brecht and the Frankfurt School during my graduate studies, but I don't use them much any more despite their occasional usefulness.[3] *Otherwise, it was a tough call not to incorporate more than three decades in advances in Vertov scholarship, by Seth Feldman,*

James Roberts, Richard Taylor, John MacKay, Aleksandr Deriabin, Malcolm Turvey, and Yuri Tsivian—which have helped defuse the issues I was railing against.[4] A full update would have caused the entire thrust of my mid-seventies polemic to evaporate, though I have the effrontery to hope that these advances by and large are in sync with my original arguments—all the more so since Vertov's sound films have received relatively short shrift over the years. And I hope I am not deluded in standing by my synthesis of the three "readings" of Vertov that I delineate at the outset, and most importantly by my focus on "affect," or what Leyda calls Vertov's "synthesis of fact and emotion" (Leyda 1973, 179), my exploration of his relationship with his audience and his subjects, and his kinship with the international currents of populist documentary of the thirties. I have restrained myself from toning down any rhetorical excess that is present; more significantly I have not covered up any embarrassing blind spots that will seem evident in hindsight in relation to either postcolonial politics or ecological politics, the former in terms of Soviet expansionism in central Asia and the latter in terms of catastrophic fallout of the Soviet ideology of industrial development—from which the planet may never recover.[5]

A final penance. This past year I received a term paper from a graduate student entirely focused on undermining the basic premises of my magnum opus on Canadian cinema, ten years in production, as well as the basic methodological incorporation of sexual identity and queer theory that I had been developing in my scholarship throughout my career. The student, a gay man whose boyfriend had allegedly failed to wake him for the meeting in which we were going to discuss his term paper topic in advance—hence my great surprise—was born the year that his home province had finally added, after years of struggle in court and in the streets, sexual orientation to its charter of human rights (as I did not fail to point out to him in my feedback). I called him in to meet with me, and washed my hair in preparation, but he declined. I gave him what I think was an objective grade. I don't recall what grade Michelson gave me for this paper that follows, but I think I now know how she may have felt when she read it.

The rediscovery of Dziga Vertov has hardly been characterized by unanimity regarding the exact nature of that artist's historical role and artistic stature. The scarcity of historical documentation, which usually hampers our estimation of early Soviet cultural figures, is much more severe in this case; and Vertov, bestriding the ambiguous border areas of art and politics, is more susceptible than most to sharply contradictory interpretations of his work. Vertov's admirers have grouped into a number of seemingly incompatible camps, each one defensively claiming sole legitimacy and determinedly confining Vertov's scant artistic legacy and personal records to its own predetermined procrustean conception. One tradition, most persuasively articulated by Annette Michelson, places Vertov solidly within the avant-garde tradition of bourgeois high art, interpreting the Soviet artist with the formalist idiom and the individualist ideology of conventional Western academic art criticism. A second tradition looks at Vertov from the perspective of the history of the documentary film, for the most part depoliticizing the Vertovian legacy as thoroughly as the first group. Most commonly this perspective locates Vertov as the precursor of direct cinema, the dominant documentary idiom of the sixties. Georges Sadoul, for example, sees Jean Rouch as Vertov's chief descendant (Sadoul 1971), although Vertov has also been evoked variously as the mentor of the British Free Cinema movement, the American cinéma vérité movement, and even contemporary television journalism, all with some degree of truth. Yet a third position, articulated by the editors of *Cahiers du cinéma* in their preface to the 1972 French edition of Vertov's writings, sees him as a pioneer of Marxist-Leninist praxis in the specific historical context of the Soviet revolution.

The purpose of this essay is not to propose a new revision of Vertov's reputation, but more or less to synthesize whatever is valid in these existing orthodoxies of Vertov scholarship, and incidentally to point out their more striking limitations. Above all, I would like to explore one or two areas of Vertov's oeuvre that have been underemphasized as the various devotees have rushed to venerate the idols of their own making.

Specifically, *Three Songs of Lenin* (1934), the last of Vertov's films to be known in the West, his seventh feature, is a much neglected and misunderstood work. The avant-gardist camp concentrate primarily on earlier works, preferring their structural intricacy, connotative ambiguity, and analytical postures to the directness and the hagiographical simplicity of this utterance; the direct cinema enthusiasts seem to resist the self-consciousness and apparent lack of spontaneity that make this last great work unique among the films of Vertov; the *Cahiéristes* probably prefer the more explicit hymns of socialist labor and more direct propagandistic orientation of earlier films to *Three Songs*'s subdued religiosity.

Yet *Three Songs* is an achievement of great power and beauty. To recognize it for its own merits and historical significance must inevitably

First publication in the West of Vertov's collected articles, diaries, and film proposals (Paris, 1972): the pioneer of Marxist-Leninist praxis?

enrich and heighten our view of its author. The recognition I would
propose is simply its recognition as a populist film, a film profoundly
and committedly popular in its sources and inspiration, in its form, and,
equally important, in the direction of its appeal. It represents the culmina-
tion of a movement evident in the thought and the art of Vertov's entire
career, a movement often tentative and perhaps unconscious, toward a
popular humanism that is very remote indeed from the futurist influence
that exerted itself upon the origins of that career. Just as Vertov's futurist and constructivist interests of his early artistic life firmly connect him
to the avant-gardes of the postwar decade in Russia and elsewhere in the
West, in the same way the populist preoccupation represented by *Three
Songs of Lenin*, the inspiration that is in increasing proportion at the root
of Vertov's entire career, demands that a whole new catalog of artists be
considered alongside Vertov's name, artists such as John Grierson, Joris
Ivens, the mature Cavalcanti, Pare Lorentz, Robert Flaherty, Willard van
Dyke, Basil Wright, Paul Rotha, Henri Storck, Roman Karmen, and those
expressing similar inspiration in the fiction film and other media, such as
Jean Vigo, René Clair, Marcel Pagnol, Jean Renoir, King Vidor, John Stein-
beck, John Dos Passos, Dorothea Lange, and Walker Evans, to name a few.
These are voices of a much richer and more fertile current than that of the
various artistic elites of the twenties, a movement of populism in culture
and politics concurrent to and in interaction with that Soviet movement
of which Vertov is a representative. It is a perspective of Vertov that is a
necessary complement to any other that has been proposed and arguably
one that supersedes the partial visions already indicated.

However, before returning to *Three Songs*, let us digress momentarily
and briefly examine the avant-gardists' conception of Vertov, since it is this
conception that most persistently ignores the populist current of Vertov's
work, refusing to ask the most basic questions regarding the dynamic
of documentary artist, subject, and audience. The single most creditable
expression of this limited apprehension of Vertov is Annette Michelson's
celebrated article, "*Man with a Movie Camera*: Magician to Epistemologist" (1972). Insisting on the 1929 silent film as Vertov's masterwork,
Michelson asserts the film's theme to be the "cinematic consciousness,"
and its effect to be "a revelation, an exposure of the terms and dynamics of
cinematic illusionism." Relying on the strategy and vocabulary of formal
analysis, the liturgy of contemporary bourgeois art criticism, Michelson
traces the mode of the film's "epistemological enquiry," not incorrectly
seeing constructivist influence in its concern with the technique and the
material of the cinematic experience. She also traces the film's celebration
of the mechanical perception afforded by the camera to the young Vertov's

futurist-inspired manifestos of the first years of the Revolution and to
the tentative probing of this theme in Vertov's first feature, *Kino-Glaz*
(1924). The article also lists a number of the aesthetic strategies of the
film (including a provocative though somewhat pedantic suggestion that
many of these are in fact filmic equivalents of classical rhetorical devices).
We hear the same analytic language as that used by Michelson and others
in championing the so-called "New American Cinema," a language that
when applied to Vertov seems curiously disrespectful (Michelson 1973). To
approach an artist vitally concerned with the mechanics of social practice
in an era of socialist construction with the same vocabulary and presuppositions employed in the criticism of a small avant-garde largely indifferent
to the possibility of communicating with a significant public in an era of
postindustrial capitalism, is a callous disservice. Vertov, as we shall see,
was consistently preoccupied with the substance of his images and with
the social dynamic of their inscription and their consumption; to ignore
such a preoccupation in our reading of his films is dishonest and facile. If
we impose an epistemological project upon his work without questioning
the possibility of that reading by the artist's contemporary audiences of
workers and peasants, we are dealing with a film only in the abstract, a
theoretical film, not the historical artifact constructed for a specific purpose in the year 1929.

Michelson's article ignores the relevance of the film to Vertov's constantly repeated goal of socialist edification and for all her research offers
no evidence of whatever the contemporary reception to the film may have
been. And her own personal reading of the film simply treats too ponder-
ously what is in fact a film of captivating playfulness. Its predominant
effect on an audience that has not devoted its life to an exposition of
surfaces and planes and color fields must surely be one of capricious innocence, baroque decorativeness, and rather palatable didacticism. In short, it
affirms the man with a movie camera as most essentially a magician rather
than an epistemologist, at least for ordinary audiences. And the common
response to the film must have been similar to that of the children in the
film as they watch the tricks of the Chinese magician, a mixture of puzzle-
ment, fascination, and delight.

In terms of Vertov's entire career, Michelson's emphasis on *Man with
a Movie Camera* as the masterwork of the oeuvre is equally misplaced.
In many ways, *Man with a Movie Camera* is the least typical of all the
films, the one that stands out the most as a temporary departure from
the evolution in cinematic and social consciousness manifest in the other
films as they unfold one by one, and in the artist's writings, both public
and private, as they are now available to us. Vertov's most personal film, it

seems almost like an aside, a momentary self-indulgence perhaps in some way associated with the mysterious exile to the Ukraine that Vertov and his brother had experienced a year or two previously. Rather than the apex of his career, *Man with a Movie Camera* seems more like a pause before the artist continued his more serious projects of socialist edification of the masses and the development of the documentary form. With *Man with a Movie Camera*, the grand mythologizer of the labor of others, meditates for a moment on his own labor, delivers a playful *apologia pro sua vita*, if you like. The film is a combination of one dominant genre of the late silent cinema, the city film, one pioneered by Vertov himself, with yet another substantial subgenre, the film about filmmaking (pursued as intently in Hollywood as elsewhere). And a predictable overlay of the mythology of socialist construction is present as well. Compared with the immediately preceding and the following films in his filmography, *The Eleventh Year* and *Enthusiasm*, both paeans to the gargantuan construction projects of the post-NEP period (New Economic Period), *Man with a Movie Camera* seems curiously frivolous and inarticulate. It is certainly the one film by Vertov that is most amenable to the apolitical descriptive language of bourgeois art criticism. It is no wonder that contemporary New York art critics, weaned on an avant-garde tradition whose very essence is frivolity and inarticulateness, should choose this film above all others of Vertov's oeuvre to defuse with their insidious, formalist bombast.

If the exclusive focus on the epistemological and formal experimentation of Vertov's works is decidedly unrepresentative of their richness and gradual variations in focus over the years, the writings and speeches of Vertov chosen by his New York admirers to support their one-sided view of him are equally unrepresentative of the great range of the body of utterances, both formal and informal, that have been preserved for us. *Artforum* and *Film Culture*, the two organs of the New York school of Vertov criticism, have both relied disproportionately, in their reprints of various Vertov texts, on the manifesto-style declarations from very early in his career (*Film Culture* 1962). The thinking of the impressionable young man who had not yet made a feature film undeniably shows a decidedly futurist influence, for example in its polemical tone and in its utopian celebration of the superiority of mechanical perception of the world. But another Vertov, present all the while, slowly emerges and by the mid-twenties the futurist cant that so fascinates the Mekas generation has virtually disappeared from both the speeches and the journals. The other more pragmatic Vertov was always in evidence in the artistic output during the early years as editor and producer of newsreels, those sober, factual efforts on behalf of the consolidation of the new regime. In fact the early utopian vision of the manifestos during those years seems completely at odds with the more telling testament on film. The early theoretical utopia is gradually replaced by a newer, patently more sincere utopia of pragmatic, humanist socialism. The decidedly earthbound and untheoretical task of national cinematic strategy becomes a more urgent challenge than titillating the perceptual faculties of hypothetical spectators. Yet most of the references to Vertov's writings and theory in the avant-garde journals point to the early immature period (often the 1922 manifesto *We,* issued two years before the release of his first feature) or to later recapitulations of these early ideas culled from an overwhelming preponderance of other more pragmatic concerns.

An example of such editorial manipulation occurs in a selection of extracts from Vertov's journals that follows the Michelson article in *Artforum.* One text is from a 1926 entry that included comments about the diarist's recently having seen René Clair's Paris *qui dort.* In the reprinted section of this entry, Vertov regrets that Clair should have been able to make a film that coincided with his own aspirations of long standing, and complains against the bureaucracy and the inertia of the Soviet film industry that necessitates such a gap between conception and execution. The text also reflects the artist's pride in three recent victories of his kinok movement: a tentative commercial success, an artistic coup reflected by the burgeoning exodus of dramatic film-workers over to the documentary side, and a popular victory, based on increasing response from the public and from film groups. However, at this point, *Artforum*'s reprint omits a large section of the original entry (without notifying the reader even that anything is missing). The part so discreetly withheld proclaims the edification of the peoples of the Soviet Union as the principal, permanent task of Vertov's art and asserts Vertov's three most recent films to be parts of this single huge job to be done. The omitted passage goes on to describe the substance of *One Sixth of the World,* his latest film at this point, in terms of this task:

> If in *Stride, Soviet!* the viewer's attention of the spectator is focused on the capital, on the center of the USSR, then *One Sixth of the World* (as if in continuation of the first film) acquaints us with the vast expanses of the USSR, the peoples of the USSR, the role of state trade in drawing even the most backward peoples into the construction of socialism (here, in the last two reels, we deliberately bring together the goals of state trade and those of the cooperatives, aiming toward the gradual replacement of the former by the cooperative system). At the same time, we pour all the picture's "streamlets" into the channel of our country's industrialization; and while strongly emphasizing the theme "machines that produce machines," we attack along the lines of "our economic independence" and "we ourselves will produce the machines essential to us."

From there, by "uniting our industry with our peasant agriculture" (the cooperative system), by drawing millions of peasant farms (the cooperative system) into the building of socialism, we arrive at the conclusion: "We are becoming the center of attraction for all other countries that are gradually breaking away from international capital and are flowing into the channel of our socialist economy." (Vertov 1984, 163–64)[6]

This passage, with its exultation in the prosaic and the pragmatic details of economic development, its matter-of-fact pride in the successful transmission of a message to an audience and in the author's willing subservience to the primacy of that message, scarcely supports the image of Vertov as individualist modernist that we are asked to swallow whole.

Similar examples of such selective editing are found within the Michelson article itself. For example, Michelson asserts that the 1924 film *Kino-Glaz* "articulates in a remarkably subtle and complex manner a polemical statement made the very same year," which she proceeds to provide in undocumented form for the reader (an example of Vertov's more strident manifesto style that virtually disappears from his papers after this date):

> We oppose the collusion of the "director-as-magician" and a bewitched public.
> Only consciousness can fight the sway of magic in all its forms.
> Only consciousness can form a man of firm opinion, firm conviction.
> We need conscious men, not an unconscious mass submissive to any passing suggestion.
> Long live the class consciousness of the healthy with eyes and ears to see and hear with.
> Away with the fragrant veil of kisses, murder, doves and sleight-of-hand.
> Long live the class vision.
> Long live Kino-Eye. (Vertov [1926] 1984, 66, citing "a kinok proclamation")

Michelson uses the chronological juxtaposition of *Kino-Glaz* with this rather abstract text to support her view of that film and of Vertov's oeuvre in general as a development around a "complex central core," the "thematic interplay of magic, illusion, labor, filmic techniques, and strategy, articulating a theory of film as epistemological enquiry." The contrived nature of her argument becomes immediately visible when we consider all of Vertov's writings during that prolific year and find this vision of the cinema as epistemological consciousness-raising as only one of a wealth of ideas, richly contradictory and heterogeneous, which dominated his thinking that year, all of which can be seen to be reflected in *Kino-Glaz*. We find, for example, the preoccupation of an anxious propagandist with the distribution of his films to as wide an audience as possible. We see him alternately in great despair over the critical consensus that saw *Kino-Glaz* as "cut-up" and in great jubilation over the film's reception in young people's and workers' clubs. He continually expands his notion of "consciousness" in terms of its concrete revolutionary implications, repeatedly arriving at new formulations of his "task" as the year progresses:

> To see and hear life, to note its turns and turning points, to catch the crunch of the old bones of everyday existence beneath the press of the revolution, to follow the growth of the young Soviet organism, to record and organize the individual characteristics of living phenomena into a whole, an essence, a conclusion—this is our immediate objective.
>
> It is an objective with importance and far from merely experimental significance. It's a general checkup on our entire transitional time and, at the same time, an on-the-spot checkup, among the masses, on each individual decree or resolution.
>
> Our basic, programmatic objective is to aid each oppressed individual and the proletariat as a whole in their effort to understand the phenomena of life around them.
>
> The establishing of a class bond that is visual (kino-eye) and auditory (radio-ear) between the proletarians of all nations and of all lands, under the communist decoding of the world—that is our objective. ([1925, published January of the following year], 49–50)

In addition to considerable attention to the mechanics of this network of communication among the peoples of the Soviet Union and the world, is the frequent affirmation, with a solidly Marxist bent, of the historical and social meaning of the phenomena of the world, and of the primacy of this meaning as the logical material of the filmmaker. Vertov's 1924 writings, as is well known, reflect his contempt for commercial dramatic filmmaking, but they also reveal his impatience with the contemporary artistic avant-garde in the Soviet Union. In particular he seems to relish the metaphor of the perfumed veil of kisses and prestidigitation already quoted as an image that expresses this impatience, for he repeats it in a text from early in 1924, clearly alluding to the theatrical experimentation that was characteristic of the period, and even pointedly referring to the theatrical efforts of the constructivist movement, with which he is so often linked by his latter-day devotees. His apparent equation of these efforts with the tricks of the cinematic illusionists, and his championing of his own anticipation of socialist realism in preference to them are most telling:

> But since this influencing is done through facts, not through acting, dances, or verse, it means we devote very little attention to so-called art.
>
> Yes, comrades, as many of you know, we relegate "art" to the periphery of our consciousness.

And this is wholly understandable. We place life itself at the center of
our attention of our work, and by the recording of life we all understand
the recording of the historical process; therefore, allow us, the technicians
and ideologists of this work, to base our observations on society's economic
structure, not screened off from the viewer's eye by a sweet-smelling veil of
kisses and hocus-pocus, constructivist or not as the case may be. (1925, 50)

When we also recall Vertov's hostility, expressed throughout the
decade, to the theatrical experiments of the futurists whom he had once
echoed so vehemently and even to such sacred cows of modernism as
Meyerhold, whose biomechanic theory he ridicules in 1923 (1984, 20), the
image of Vertov as a fellow traveller of the NEP avant-garde becomes even
more untenable. Accordingly one can only marvel at Michelson's comparison of Vertov's work to Tatlin's model for the monument to the Third
International, that aborted artifact of constructivist idealism that Vertov
does not dignify with a single reference during his entire career. If we are
to link Vertov's career to concurrent cultural trends in this period, we must
not be so disrespectful to Vertov, the pragmatic socialist, as to focus on
Tatlin's projected monument, which according to his contemporary El Lis-
sitsky was not even based on technical competence (Lissitzky 1968, 334)
and which was soundly condemned by Trotsky for its uselessness.[7] Instead,
we must look at those constructivists who, like Vertov, applied themselves
to productive, pragmatic endeavors, not gestures, and found inspiration in
the needs and the folk traditions of the revolutionary classes—weavers and
textile designers who worked in villages, poster makers and sloganizers,
experimenters in the decorative arts, and so on.

Or else we must look at the totally different current in journalism,
literature, and the drama, of "factography," that forms a striking parallel
to the career of Vertov in its orientation toward documentary representation of the "facts" of the great achievements in socialist construction. This
movement must certainly have derived much inspiration from the kinok
impulse that preceded and accompanied it into the era of socialist realism.
And it is surprising that Vertov has never been linked to this current, much
less been seen as one of its most eminent and original practitioners. After
all, the affirmation of the "fact" as a primary material of the artist was one
of the most often repeated themes of his writing, the year of *Kino-Glaz*
and every other year of his productive life as well. Michelson's exclusive
focus on one aspect of Vertov's oeuvre seriously distorts the range of its
impact and the diversity of its sociocultural context.

In fact, the most serious omission from the *Artforum* image of Vertov
is a true sense of the personal artistic and political growth that characterizes the accumulation of his works and his writings over the two decades

of his productive life. From the brash utopian polemicist, whose utterances
are strangely incongruous with the prosaic tone and utilitarian sobriety
of newsreels he was producing at the time, there emerges a more pragmatic, political individual, one more inclined to conciliate than repudiate,
to convince than offend. From the rigid hard-line purist, intolerant of
any deviation from his prescription for the future of the cinema, we see
developing a more discreet, concessive person, one eager to recognize the
legitimacy of a pluralist cinema and constantly willing to regret and even
retract the overzealous errors of his youth. Vertov the theoretician gradually becomes a concerned practitioner of public policy, more preoccupied
with the details of the vast network of kinok cells that he envisioned, a
kind of Griersonian alternate production and exhibition system, than with
the jargon and rhetoric of his futurist-inspired days. Like many of the late
tsarist intelligentsia who chose to support the revolution, Vertov gradually
balanced the romantic, individualist presuppositions of his youth with a
growing concept of his art as collective and utilitarian (and both of these
radical conceptions of art are totally foreign to Vertov's current American
exegists, who consequently ignore them). Like the artists who devoted
themselves to textile production and design or the poets who anonymously
churned out the slogans of socialist construction, Vertov set aside his
notions of the artist as "priest of perception" and buried himself in the
mechanics of agitprop for the new revolutionary state, accepting projects
from public bodies like the Moscow Soviet or Gostorg, the state commerce organization, promoting the great electrification schemes of the NEP
period and the gargantuan industrial projects of the first Five Year Plan.
Above all, the antihumanist tinge of the early rants about the perfection of
the machine becomes immersed from the mid-twenties on, in the deeper,
more compassionate humanism that radiates from the best moments of
his films. From the early emphasis on analysis of the world of visual phenomena, Vertov turns by the early thirties to a fascination with an interior
universe. It is a fascination with emotions and behavior, with "the human
being without the mask" as Vertov repeatedly puts it, that is expressed
with increasing sensitivity and more systematically in the films of the thirties and that is acknowledged explicitly in the writings of that period. The
early impatience with the human being as an object of the camera, the irritation that a person cannot control his own movements, become radically
modified so that by the time of *Three Songs of Lenin*, the human universe
becomes the exclusive preoccupation of the camera. The human as object
becomes the human as subject. Human vision, once repudiated as "myo-
pia," becomes affirmed and celebrated. The revelation of "unconscious
optics," as Walter Benjamin accurately puts it ([1936] 1969, 237), becomes

superseded by the revelation of unconscious community, unconscious social reorganization. The luxurious lingering pans, in extreme close-up, of the faces of *Songs*'s Uzbek women, in mourning for a leader whom they had never seen, are microcosms of this new, *post*modernist,[8] humanist, and populist sensibility.

The growth of the artist from modernism to postmodernism is vividly chronicled in the intricate fabric of film and text that constitutes Vertov's legacy. It is a growth arising from the dynamic interaction of an artist with a popular audience, a process that we never associate with the avant-garde, by definition, but a process that is clearly visible as the informing impulse of Vertov's career. Despite the sparseness of the documentation, the picture of the filmmaker implied by the conjunction of film and text is poignant and detailed. The suggestion of an oeuvre being molded by Vertov's response to feedback from a critical and popular audience is present from the earliest stages in his career. For example, one wonders whether the hostility to the fragmentary cutting of the later "Kinopravda" newsreels referred to several times by Vertov, or whether the self-criticism evident in his admonition to his fellow kinoks to avoid the usual newsreel repertory of funerals and parades, led him to attempt a solution to these problems with his first feature *Kino-Glaz* in 1924. Certainly the sense of thematic and structural coherence arising from *Kino-Glaz*, and the indulgent

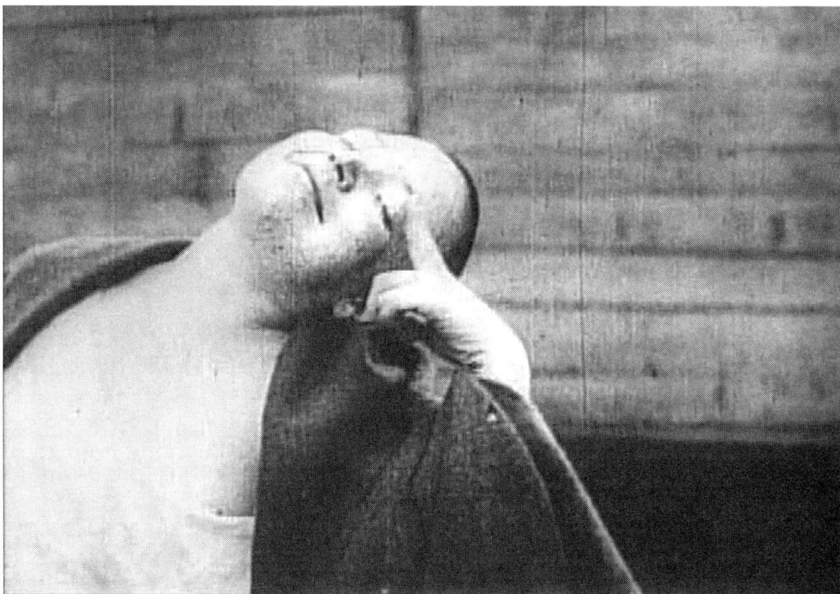

Kino-Glaz (Dziga Vertov, 1924): Against the grain of a film notable for mise-en-scène, this exceptional unrehearsed scene of inmates in an asylum raises issues of documentary ethics for twenty-first-century viewers.

use of mise-en-scène, the most conspicuous presence of semidocumentary arrangement of material in any of his silent films, both seem to be responses to the limitations of the newsreel form as he articulated them.

By the same token, an article by Vertov assessing the faults of *Kino-Glaz* (published in 1926) implies a connection between this kind of self-evaluation and the radical structural and thematic evolution of subsequent films. It is an article whose basic theme is the enormous growth experiences by the artist as a result of his experiment with the feature film, and the lessons learned from its exposure to the public. The inference is that the central problem with *Kino-Glaz*, aside from the lack of cooperation from exhibitors, was its inaccessibility to its audiences. Vertov worries about alienating his audiences through exhaustion, and regrets both the complexity of the subject matter and the superficiality of his treatment of it; he then resolves to avoid these defects in his next work:

> The field of kino-eye is a new one, and the option being served to the viewer should be increased cautiously to avoid tiring him and shoving him into the arms of the art-drama.
>
> Hoping to break into the big movie theaters, we yielded to the demand to provide a six-act film and made a mistake; this has to be admitted. We must correct this mistake in the future and make small objects of various types that can be shown individually or in a group program as desired.
>
> The overly broad sweep of Part One, the excessive number of themes interconnected at the expense of the deepening of each single one, can also be considered shortcomings.
>
> I mention only these shortcomings—not that there are no others, but because we need to give first consideration to the already mentioned defects and mistakes and to draw appropriate conclusions for future work. ([1926] 1984, 76–77)

Vertov at this point proceeds to outline, exultantly, the growth of the concept of Kino-Eye, and then concludes with a defiant affirmation of his "responsibilities to the spectator."

The practical benefits of this lesson are reflected in the feature that follows in 1926, *Stride, Soviet!* Its hortatory tone, its heightened formal unity effected through transitional dissolves and a unitary, climactic arrangement of the theme, and its reliance on more conventional narrative and dramatic units (rather than the associational clusters that predominate in *Kino-Glaz*), all contribute to a simpler, more accessible work that is in striking contrast to the previous feature. Two intervening short films, which appeared just before *Stride*, evidently display the same orientation toward a greater accessibility for popular audiences. According to Jay Leyda, these two shorts rely on an emotional appeal that we associate with *Three Songs of Lenin*:

Two shorter films, *Leninist Film-Truth* and *October without Ilyich*, both of them finished and issued in January 1925, should be mentioned here because they introduce a far from objective and apparently non-Kino-Eye pathos that was afterward to be laid aside until 1932 when Vertov made his *Three Songs of Lenin*. This later film not only revives the forgotten pathos of the earlier films, but recovers the themes and methods used in 1924, expanding these to further breadth of material and depth of emotion. *Leninist Film-Truth* (issued as no. 21 of the series *Kino-Pravda*) uses a main structure of Lenin's funeral, developing from it parallel sequences of sorrowing peoples, and followed by a paean of pride in the accomplishment of Lenin's directives—in industry, in agriculture, in culture, in social life. *October without Ilyich* has much the same Mayakovskian quality, using the annual celebration of the October Revolution as a base upon which to build both memories of Lenin's life and funeral, and to show his inspiration continuing after his death. As anyone will realize who has seen *Three Songs of Lenin*, this approach is almost identical, but none of his work between the two dates, as we shall see later, attempted this successful synthesis of fact and emotion. (Leyda 1973, 179)

The other striking example of this basic pattern of experiment followed by feedback and then reformulation of goals is more pertinent to the theme of this paper. It is of course the transition from the exuberant modernism of *Enthusiasm* (1931) to the populist lyricism of *Three Songs of Lenin*: the dramatic interaction of artist and public that at least partly accounts for this the most radical contrast between any two successive films in Vertov's entire career. Vertov's own survey of the hostile reception that met *Enthusiasm* is extremely informative. In one text, he outlines the variations of this response: he refers to those critics who, baffled by the overwhelming innovativeness of the film's soundtrack, either branded it as unredeemed cacophony or ignored it altogether, and also mentions critics who denounced the film as a formalist exercise on the one hand, and those who extolled it for the same reason on the other. Equally striking is a reference in a 1934 publication to a criticism of the film for being too concrete, presumably because its wealth of minute detail cumulatively resulted in an abstraction that obscured the articulation of its basic theme. The same article, interestingly enough, contains a repudiation of the earlier self-conscious mode of expression that constitutes, according to Michelson, the central fabric of Vertov's work: "In previous work, I frequently presented my shooting methods outright. I left the construction of those methods open and visible, Meyerhold style. And I was wrong. However, whatever I did, I acted as I had that first time when I leaped from the roof" ([1934] 1984, 125).

An unpublished article of the same year heavily stresses the aesthetic ideal of clarity and simplicity, a frequent theme of the writing of that decade. Even if we assume some degree of political motivation—even opportunism—for this emerging emphasis on simplicity (the reference to Meyerhold seems more than a coincidence), it is by no means unwarranted to infer that the widespread incomprehension that greeted *Enthusiasm* is responsible in a significant way for the shift in emphasis away from technological experimentation toward a consolidation of present technological capacity in subservience to an easily understandable populist theme. It is also a shift between two contradictory universes of twentieth century art, a movement away from the analytic, self-conscious, alienating mode of the modernist impulse, toward the absorbing, mythopoeic simplicity of populist and popular art. The dramatic deemphasis of the so-called "trick" photography that had characterized most of his work up to this point, the laying aside of almost all the alienating, disjunctive editing strategies of his other films, represents a radical new departure for this artist at the peak of his creative powers. Although it is anticipated by major themes and subtexts in all of his previous works, this departure seems to be a reevaluation of the modernism that had informed so much of his artistic output but that had never inflamed the proletarian roots of Soviet culture as he had so fervently planned. And it also seems to be a repudiation of that modernism in favor of the populist hagiography that later in the decade becomes a major current of Soviet culture and that, significantly, characterizes the artifacts of other populist film movements of the era from *Industrial Britain* (1933) and *Man of Aran* (1934) to *Young Mr. Lincoln* (1939). However, in the meantime, let us approach this great film from yet another direction.

In 1934, Vertov wrote two entries in his diary about the poet Vladimir Mayakovsky (1892–1930). The first recalls the occasions the two artists had met and expresses the gratitude Vertov felt for the encouragement he had received from the poet. The text concludes by describing one last rendezvous that Mayakovsky had not kept, two weeks before his suicide. The second entry attempts to discuss Mayakovsky's cultural significance, positing him as an exemplary figure because of his popular accessibility and appeal. Vertov then reflects on his own most recent film, *Three Songs of Lenin*, in terms of the ideals offered by his famous friend's career. The attitudes expressed in this entry offer us, of course, less insight into Mayakovsky than they do into Vertov's own importance as an artist, and specifically, into the inspiration for *Songs*. The comments shed light on two aspects of Vertov's self-image as a popular and populist artist, his emphasis on teaching a large popular audience, and his newly articulated but long maintained interest in using the folk and popular arts of Soviet peoples as the source of his filmic art. Here are relevant passages from this long and intimate essay:

My love for Mayakovsky's work did not in any way conflict with my attitude toward folk creation.

I never considered Mayakovsky unintelligible or unpopular. One must distinguish between popularity and trying to be popular.

Lenin, in his note "On the journal *Freedom*," talks quite well of this: "The popular writer leads the reader to deep reflection. To depth in study, by proceeding from the simplest common knowledge through the use of simple arguments or well-chosen examples, pointing to chief conclusions to be drawn from those data, spurring the thinking reader on to ever further questioning. The popular writer does not assume a reader who does not think or who does not want or know how to think: on the contrary, he assumes the serious desire of the undeveloped reader to use his head, and he helps him in this serious and difficult work, he guides him in his first steps and teaches him to proceed further on his own. The vulgar writer assumes a reader who does not think and is incapable of thinking. He does not spur him on to the first rudiments of serious science but serves up the conclusions of a certain teaching 'ready made' in a deformed oversimplified form, salted with jokes and witty sayings, so that the reader doesn't even have to chew; he has only to swallow this mush."

Mayakovsky is intelligible to everyone who wants to think. He does not assume a totally unthinking reader. He does not try for popularity at all, but he is popular . . .

The unity of form and content—that is what strikes one in folk art, and that's what strikes one in Mayakovsky as well.

I work in the poetic documentary film. That's why both the songs composed of the people and Mayakovsky's poetry are very near and familiar to me. The fact that a great deal of attention is now being paid to Mayakovsky as well as to folk creation tells me I've chosen the right course in my field of film poetry. Actually, *Three Songs of Lenin* was only a first significant attempt in that direction. But our party's central organ confirms this: "Despite the great difficulty of the conception, the attempt has succeeded. A truly remarkable picture, a picture of great force, infecting the viewer-listener with deep feeling." In an unsigned editorial article, *Pravda* calls *Three Songs* "the song of the whole country."

We know from letters and critics that the whole country, from Vladiovostok to Leningrad, expresses, through the voice of the mass of viewers, confirmation of *Pravda*'s view. The reception the film got this time, not from ten thousand, but from millions of viewers, has shown that I stand on the threshold of the right, clearly indicated path. ([1934] 1984, 182–83)

Vertov goes on to talk about Mayakovsky's experiences with the cinema, railing against the bureaucrats who prevented him from applying his genius to the screen and thus launching a more personally motivated tirade against his own bureaucratic obstacles, above all the demands for preproduction scenarios in a kind of film where this is by definition impossible. Then in a rather deft maneuver, Vertov twists the definition of his old

bugbear, formalism, to mean any compromise to such red tape. There then
follows the profession of a burning, insatiable desire to create, which is
among the most moving passages in his diary and one that sets the tone of
his writings over the next two decades until his death. He concludes with a
note of pride and determination:

> I managed (to a considerable extent) to make *Three Songs of Lenin*
> accessible and intelligible to millions of viewers. But not by sacrificing film-
> language. Not by sacrificing the techniques I'd found earlier.
>
> The problem lies in not separating form from content. The problem is
> one of unity of form and content. Of not permitting oneself to confuse the
> viewer by showing him a trick or technique not generated by the content and
> uncalled for by necessity.
>
> And there's no need even to set your heel on "the throat of your own
> song." In 1933, I decided, in thinking about Lenin, to turn to the sources of
> folk art. And as the future was to show (recall Gorky's speech at the Writers'
> Congress), I was not mistaken. The objections to this approach of mine were
> wrong. I was not mistaken; I foresaw things correctly. ([1934] 1984, 187)

I want to pursue this direction further.

Whether or not we interpret this long impassioned essay as being
astutely political in its design (the invocation of the safe authorities of
Lenin, Mayakovsky, Gorky, and *Pravda* is a common tactic of Vertov's
later writings and by no means limited to Vertov's use alone), there is no
reason to doubt its sincerity, since *Three Songs of Lenin* is an affirmation of its ideas. And *of course* the evolution of such attitudes is visible
throughout all of Vertov's writings, both personal and public even from the
earliest years. Vertov always had verified his work through evaluating audience response (at one point in 1926 he states that a seventeen-meter long
sequence from *Kino-Glaz*, constructed from fifty-three shots had been verified as not being fatiguing by a workingman spectator); his greatest defeat
was always to be separated from that nourishing contact with the public.
As we know, Vertov's lifetime of contact with the urban and rural masses
of Soviet society began during the civil war with his first work as editor
with the agitprop trains on both the Eastern and Western front. One of his
more vivid recollections of this period describes the attitudes of peasants
toward certain decorations on one of the agit trains, their inability to penetrate whatever symbolic meaning was intended by the design. The peasants
were preoccupied instead with a detail that contradicted the concrete
reality of their daily lives, in this case a horse improperly shoed. Vertov's
recollection of these peasants mocking "artistic" endeavors permanently
colored his conception of his proletarian audiences; their suspicion and
incomprehension of artistic pretense became a central argument for him

against the theatrical films that he repudiated so vehemently. He admired the peasants' rejection of romanticized spectacle and their down-to-earth insistence on the facts of reality. The aesthetics and politics of the Kino-Eye movement, as well as the "factographic" and documentary orientation of his career, were based on this perception of popular attitudes. He describes a 1920 rural screening of a film program containing both dramatic and documentary material, rejoicing in the contrasting audience responses to each, and extolling the peasants' desire to be shown, not "Petrushka" but "life."[9] Such an audience continues to be a major reference point for Vertov's thought, whether he is preoccupied abstractly with perceptual and cognitive expansion or specifically with the task of propaganda. If his early image of illiterate peasants as the targets of futurist-inspired perceptual experiments is disarmingly naive, his youthful idealism is less risible if we recall that it was accompanied in the realm of praxis by the newsreel series, an achievement not approached by various of Vertov's contemporaries in the Russian intelligentsia who were never to graduate from the pre-October world of aesthetic theory into a truly revolutionary application of their ideas. And the proletarian audience was always the focus of this praxis. At a 1923 meeting of the Association of Revolutionary Cinema Workers, Vertov felt constrained to defend himself against charges of being inaccessible to the masses that were apparently already being circulated by his numerous enemies. He uses a reference to Lenin in a way that is already familiar:

> One of the chief accusations leveled at us is that we are not intelligible to the masses.
>
> Even if one allows that some of our work is difficult to understand, does that mean we must not undertake serious exploratory work at all?
>
> If the masses need light propaganda pamphlets, does that mean they don't need the serious articles of Engels, Lenin? The LENIN of Russian cinema may appear in your midst today, but you will not allow him to work because the results of his production will seem new and incomprehensible.
>
> Our work is not in that situation, however. We have not in fact created a single work more incomprehensible to the masses than any given film-drama. On the contrary, by establishing a clear visual link between subjects, we have considerably weakened the importance of intertitles; in so doing we have brought the movie screen closer to the uneducated viewers, which is particularly important at present.
>
> And as if in mockery of their literary nursemaids, the workers and peasants turn out to be brighter than their self-appointed nursemaids. ([1923] 1984, 37–38)

The illiterate spectator was always the object of the concern demonstrated above. It is interesting to contrast Vertov's search for a titleless film form, motivated at least partly by a desire to communicate with illiterate spectators, with a similar search on the part of bourgeois filmmakers in the West, such as Murnau, whose own motivations can hardly be considered to be founded on such realistic social perceptions as Vertov's. Even in the early films, up to *One-Sixth of the World*, in which intertitles play an organic role, Vertov's highly individualistic treatment of them is clearly related to his concern for illiterate audiences. The emphatic arrangement of phrases and key words, spatially, typographically, and sequentially; their frequent repetition; their frequent literal overlap with the content of the following image (titles such as "on the tundra" and "on the ocean" from *One-Sixth of the World*, followed immediately by the appropriate image)—all such devices must certainly have functioned as highly sophisticated teaching aids, particularly when we remember that Soviet audiences in the preliteracy era, like their counterparts elsewhere in the modernizing parts of the world such as India, frequently must have made use of informal, volunteer readers to help the audiences with the intertitles.[10]

A major theme of Vertov's thought during the twenties is what he calls the "cine-liaison" among the peoples of the Soviet Union. This concept is an extension of his basic concern with communicating with a wide audience, but also incorporates the idea of people exploiting filmic technology to reach each other. Thus the proliferation of the kinok circles that occasions Vertov so much consolation during the twenties (perhaps premature) is central to this vision. As we know, several of Vertov's films contain an elegant visual correlative of the concept of cine-liaison, an audience synthesized through the magic of Kuleshovian shot–countershot, grouped around a loudspeaker in the silent films and, in the sound films, a radio transmitter, concrete symbols of technology's capacity to unite people from disparate areas of the country. It is not surprising that by the early thirties, this concept should have grown to include an emphasis on the popular inspiration that would naturally be the source of any genuine cine-liaison among peoples, thus the great interest in popular art forms in Vertov's comments about Mayakovsky that we have already regarded. And the pride Vertov reveals in that passage is quite justifiable; he quite rightly claims to have anticipated the concern with the popular and folkloric roots of proletarian art, which became official cultural dogma at the 1934 All-Union Congress of Soviet Writers. As Vertov mentions several times, it was Gorky's contribution in particular that inspired this new theme in cultural policy. A later, 1936 reference to the same event points out not only *Three Songs of Lenin* as a manifestation of popular expression but also such an interest as an aspect of Vertov's career from its earliest point:

In a speech to a plenary session of the Central Committee of the Workers in the Arts, Comrade Kerzhentsev advised Shostakovich, the composer, "to travel through the Soviet Union collecting the songs created and preserved by the people." He would thus make contact with the very rich stream of folk art and find that base "on which he might develop creatively."

At the Writers' Congress, Gorky spoke of turning to folk art.

My experiment in this area was done in 1933 when I began work on *Three Songs of Lenin*. Except for the collecting of *chastushki* in which I was absorbed after my grade school years, I was a novice in this field. At this time almost no one collected songs. And my attempt as a film director to acquaint myself with the work of anonymous poets caused surprise and sometimes pity (at that time few people anticipated that folk art would soon become the center of our attention). ([1936] 1984, 195–96)

Vertov goes on to tell how his sound engineer and he went about recording popular and folk songs from the peoples of Central Asia for *Three Songs of Lenin*. He praises the simple power of the songs and their great impact on him personally, having felt reawaken in him what had inspired him to collect the *chastushki* so many years previously. Given the paranoid political atmosphere surrounding this entry in the diaries (1936 was the year of the first Moscow purge trial and saw the height of the denunciations in the cultural realm as well), one can excuse Vertov's modesty and/or shortsightedness in claiming to be a novice in such a field. Certainly the foundation of the documentary ethic as he had developed it had been the impulse to record the expression of the popular consciousness, albeit in perhaps more contemporary and relevant ways for the Soviet people than in obsolescent folkloric forms.

A glance at the pronouncements of Gorky referred to by Vertov clarifies the direction of the new official interest in popular culture and art, and clearly reveals Vertov's oeuvre as the incarnation of such an inspiration. The Gorky speech asserted that the theme of popular culture in its historical development had always been the struggle of labor and survival. His prescription was that the continuation of such a theme be the official theme of the new Soviet mode of aesthetic expression, socialist realism. Gorky's conception of mythology in both its traditional and its newer revolutionary context is particularly illuminating in regard to Vertov's vocation as propagandist (or mythologist) of the Soviet revolution:

The true hero of all our books should be labor; in other words, men formed by the processes of labor, which in our country is armed with all the resources of contemporary technical progress, men who in their turn work to make labor both easier and more productive and whose goal is to raise labor to the level of an art. We must learn to look upon labor as a process of creation.

Socialist realism looks upon being as doing, and regards existence as a
creative development of the most valuable individual gifts of men in order
that they may conquer the forces of nature, achieve health and long life and
enjoy the great good fortune of living on an earth which man, in conformity
with the incessant growth of his needs wants to exploit in its entirety as the
magnificent dwelling place of mankind united in one great family. (Gorky
[1934] 1946, 133)

It is striking how Vertov's oeuvre parallels Gorky's prescription so
closely. As epitome of the new Soviet mythology it is clearly a reflection
of the struggle for survival of the new order, a heroicization of the labor
whereby that struggle was fought, and the creative expression by working
people of that mythic process. Certainly Vertov shared Gorky's conception of labor as the ultimate creative activity and by devoting his artistic
energies to the recording of the labor of the revolutionary classes, he had
already turned to popular self-expression as the source of his art, long
before he did so self-consciously and explicitly with *Three Songs of Lenin*.
A 1924 notebook entry set the tone for an entire career:

Everyone has something of the poet, artist, musician.
 Or else there are no poets, artists, or musicians.
 The millionth part of each man's inventiveness in his everyday work con-
tains an element of art, if one must use that term. ([1924] 1984, 162)

In similar vein we find constant references to "the creative joy in each
creative job," to the film *Stride, Soviet!* as a "symphony of creative labor,"
or to the task of the artist as the revelation of the life of "Man with his
right to creation, with his rich productive development, with his mastery of
technology, science, literature, art" ([1936] 1984, 137).

To the Marxist view of labor as the essential human activity, of labor
as the essential means whereby man expresses and defines himself, and
creates his own world, Vertov adds the corollary that art is the servant of
working peoples and that the artist's vocation is to record and inspire this
creative activity. The filmmaker's task in the era of socialist construction is
to show the worker an image of himself, of the creativity, the wholeness,
and the dignity of his own work and of the work of his comrades, to correct the alienation of men from their labor inflicted by capitalism:

In disclosing the origins of objects and of bread, the camera makes it possible for every worker to acquire, through evidence, the conviction that
he, the worker, creates all these things himself, and that consequently they
belong to him . . .
 The textile worker ought to see the worker in a factory making a machine
essential to the textile worker. The worker at the machine tool plant ought
to see the miner who gives his factory its essential fuel, coal. The coal miner

ought to see the peasant who produces the bread essential to him. ([1925] 1984, 34, 52)

A film of people working is not simply the artistic expression of a personal world-vision, nor is it simply an agit-prop commercial for the Soviet state. As a record of real individuals at work, engaged in the most important means whereby individuals in the age of revolution can express themselves and exert control over their environment, the work of art transcends its traditional individualist framework. The artist transcends his or her traditional isolation from society and enables the masses to express their right to be artists themselves. Vertov brings modern technology to workers and peasants, shares his skill with them, and allows them to participate in a uniquely contemporary folkloric expression.

Georges Sadoul is right in proclaiming Vertov's place as the first pioneer in a tradition of filmmakers who subject the medium to the self-expression of others (Sadoul 1971). Vertov is indeed a major precursor of Jean Rouch and countless anonymous others for whom technological strides have altered the form and the intensity of film's role as a medium of folk expression far beyond its potential during Vertov's career (see chapter 6). Vertov's efforts were probing and often distracted to be sure, but all the same the continuity of inspiration is remarkable, and the same implication of the ultimate disappearance of the professional artist is present in both cases.

With Vertov, the frequently elaborated schemes of circles of kinoks and Komsomol film leagues, and so forth, with their accompanying networks of cine-stations and exhibition facilities, were to be the organizational means of expanding this ideal into reality. Parallel movements to Vertov's, frequently more successfully realized, included Medvedkin's agit-prop trains in the Soviet Union in the late twenties, or Grierson's schemes for alternative exhibition systems in Britain and Canada on remarkably similar lines to those suggested and partly realized by his Soviet contemporaries. With Rouch and his contemporaries, whether in urban video centers or other neo-Griersonian networks, the ideal is of course much more within reach than with the underdeveloped documentary technology of the interwar years. Partly for technological reasons and partly for political reasons, Vertov's vision of a "universal cinema" manned by an "army of kinok-observers" in the service of the classes of workers and peasants fell tragically short of permanent realization. Yet Vertov's oeuvre remains a stirring testimony to the possibility of all people being artists (and as such it profoundly challenges the individualist premises with which it is unquestioningly approached in contemporary Western critical circles):

Specifically, all groups of kinok-observers will be drawn into the production of future Kino-Eye series. They will be author-creators of all subsequent film-objects. This departure from authorship by one person or a group of persons to mass authorship will, in our view, accelerate the destruction of bourgeois, artistic cinema.([1926] 1984, 70–71)

Walter Benjamin, in "The Work of Art in the Age of Mechanical Reproduction" (a work justly celebrated by Michelson for its striking confirmation of Vertov's feelings about the cinema's aptness for expanding perceptual horizons), also confirms the new possibility, offered by technology and first probed by Vertov, of mass artistic expression. It was commonplace during the first decades of the history of the cinema for cultural critics to respond to the mass appeal of this new art form and often to lament the inevitable decline in cultural standards that mass art supposedly pointed to. (Benjamin quotes Aldous Huxley as an example of such anachronistic snobbery.) However, the insight that the new technology permitted mass participation in new and positive cultural directions in addition to mass consumption was relatively rare, Vertov in practice and Benjamin in theory being two exemplary visionaries in this respect. Benjamin elaborates:

> It is inherent in the technique of the film as well as that of sports that everybody who witnesses its accomplishments is somewhat of an expert. Similarly the newsreel offers everyone the opportunity to rise from passerby to movie extra. In this way any man might even find himself part of a work of art, as witness Vertov's *Three Songs of Lenin* or Iven's *Borinage*. Any man today can lay claim to being filmed. This claim can best be elucidated by a comparative look at the historical situation of contemporary literature. For centuries, a small number of writers were confronted by many thousands of readers. This changed toward the end of the last century. With the increasing extension of the press, which kept placing new political, religious, scientific, professional and local organs before the readers, an increasing number of readers became writers—at first occasional ones. It began with the daily press opening to its reader space for "letters to the editor." And today there is hardly any gainfully employed European who could not, in principle, find an opportunity to publish somewhere or other comments on his work, grievances, documentary reports, that sort of thing. *Thus, the distinction between the author and public is about to lose its basic character . . . In the Soviet Union, work itself is given a voice.* To present it verbally is part of a man's ability to perform the work. Literary license is now founded on polytechnic rather than specialized training and thus becomes common property.
>
> All this can easily be applied to the film, where transitions that in literature took centuries have come about in a decade. In cinematic practice, particularly in Russia, this changeover has partially become established reality. Some of the players whom we meet in Russian films are not actors in

our sense but people who *portray themselves*—and primarily in their own work process. In Western Europe, the capitalistic exploitation of the film denies consideration to *modern man's legitimate claim to be reproduced.* Under these circumstances, the film industry is trying hard to spur the interest of the masses through illusion-promoting spectacles and dubious speculations. (Benjamin [1936] 1969, 231, my emphasis)

It is striking that Benjamin's choice of an example of the trends he was describing should be *Three Songs of Lenin.* It is a rare and fitting homage to an artist by one of his most distinguished contemporaries, a recognition of Vertov for his real value and valor, undistracted by mere formal innovation. And *Three Songs of Lenin* was the best choice Benjamin could have made, since it represents the peak of the development of Vertov's own recognition of the implications of the aesthetic revolution of which he was at the center.

During the silent period Vertov consistently emphasized the importance the advancement of technology would have in the realization of his vision (the 1926 text already quoted insists on the urgent need for film of greater sensitivity, smaller, extralight cameras, and more portable lighting equipment). It is thus not surprising that the advent of sound, the major technological stride of Vertov's career, radically expanded the potential for public participation in his art form as Benjamin implies (just as thirty years later a technological revolution along the same lines that Vertov had desired in 1926 facilitated the even further achievements in the same direction of his direct cinema descendants on both sides of the Atlantic). Interestingly, in the silent years, the development of technology actually resisted Vertov's and his brother's frequently stated goal of shooting with a hidden camera that was based on the ideal of recording "life caught unawares." Because of the bulkiness of the equipment, and presumably for other reasons as well, only a fraction of the material used in the silent films could be said to have achieved that ideal. The rest is composed of a wide range of various styles, or rather of various degrees of mediation of reality by the camera. Very little of the material of this period has the rawness and the spontaneity that we associate with the direct cinema of the sixties. The rest depends on various degrees of cooperation by the subjects, often performance, in fact on what Sadoul terms a documentary equivalent of mise-en-scène (Sadoul 1971, 113–14). It is true that the most blatant betrayals of subjects' self-consciousness seem to have been edited out (in keeping with Vertov's frequent irritation at people's inability to behave properly in front of the camera), but otherwise, the dialectic between "life caught unawares" and life deliberately expressing itself for the camera is as pronounced in Vertov as it is in, say, Flaherty or Ivens, who were both certainly more disposed to admit to the necessity of reconstructing reality than was their Russian contemporary.

In any case, we have on the one hand the Pioneer children of *Kino-Glaz* obviously following the instructions of the filmmaker as they march through the countryside and the film. And there are scenes such as the rescue of the asphyxiated janitor in the same film or the decadent party of the NEP-men in *One Sixth of the World* where, according to operator Mikhail Kaufman, the presence of the camera was known but was ignored (although in the case of the latter the activity is observed at such close quarters that the active cooperation of the revelers must have been required [Sadoul 1971, 113–14]). Apparently in the same category are the innumerable sequences of individuals and small groups at work in factories or fields, in which camera perspectives and shot distances are varied regularly, often with the precision of the most controlled studio shooting, and these could not have been achieved without the cooperation of the individuals involved (not to mention mining sequences shot in low-ceiling tunnels with artificial lighting that must have resembled studio shooting, albeit very difficult, rather than documentary reportage). We also have the somewhat diluted form of mise-en-scène involving parades and processions, for which Vertov certainly had a fondness, which presumably involved foreknowledge of the details of the action to be filmed and consequently permitted a degree of preparation not usually afforded by more unpredictable events. There are also the obvious sequences where the attention of a subject has clearly been distracted by the cameraman and his image is recorded during his moment of distraction. The most famous instance of this is the scene with the Chinese magician in *Man with a Movie Camera* (in fact a repeat from *Kino-Glaz*) in which the children's natural inclination to stare at the camera has apparently been overcome by the fascination exerted by the magician. And of course there is also the rare occasion when a subject is clearly unwilling to be filmed, and an angry gesture of refusal or a hostile glare is recorded. Perhaps most interesting because they are quite common are the scenes where a subject reveals his complicity with the cameraman, most often a mere flicker of recognition or a glance of curiosity, but also such situations as in *Man with a Movie Camera* where a female subject of a long tracking shot flirtatiously mimics with her hand the cameraman's rotation of his camera handle. In short, in the bulk of Vertov's work in the twenties, the ideal of catching life unawares was clearly inoperable, at least in dealing with the human universe within Vertov's preferred range. And it seems that Vertov, although at first frustrated by the necessity of relying on the cooperation of his subjects, gradually came to accept this exigency, even so far as to make a virtue of such a necessity, just as Flaherty was doing at the same time. Accordingly, just as a formal portrait in still photography usually incorporates as much of the self-image of the subject as it does the personal expression of the photographer, in Vertov's silent films we have the same double layer of self-expression, that of the artist to be sure, but also that of the subject, based on the necessity of presenting one's image to the big, noisy mechanical black box with the rotating handle and the tripod. It is this aspect of Vertov's art, its reliance on the self-expression of the subject, which the coming of the sound technology with its increased rather than lessened awkwardness and immobility had the effect in live recording situations of magnifying and accentuating.

It is interesting how *Man with a Movie Camera*, notable for its anticipation of sound in many ways, also anticipates the increased complicity of subject with filmmaker, the heightened element of personal expression of the subject, which the sound documentary was to require. This film relies on mise-en-scène perhaps more than any other of the silent films, with the possible exception of *Kino-Glaz*. Its central mediator-protagonist, the man with a movie camera, Mikhail Kaufman at his most versatile, is certainly a performer of great self-consciousness, agility, and bravado. He constantly poses for the camera with as much aplomb as the camera itself seems to exhibit in the famous pixilated scene in which the apparatus struts around on the tripod, displaying its dexterity, and bows to the audience. The cameraman, epitome in this film of the Soviet worker as well, proudly displays the vocation through which he expresses himself, offering a record of his contribution to socialist construction to the audience. In this the cameraman is typical of the role of workers in Vertov's films, particularly those in the sound films who are given a voice; they proudly and energetically perform their task for their countrymen and for posterity, contributing their cooperation and their sweat to the concept of cine-liaison. They continue their jobs, no doubt obeying the filmmakers' instruction to pretend to look away from the camera, and even obediently smiling when he jokes or perhaps admonishes them to look cheerful; and they do so with all the simple rectitude and self-importance of a caveman painting his latest hunt on his cave wall, or of a medieval peasant carving an image of the animal who draws his plough, offering this record of the creative labor of survival to the immortality ensured by art. The Stakhanovite cigarette-girl of *Man with a Movie Camera* does the same, feverishly continuing her tedious work, participating in the process of the democratization of the arts identified by Benjamin, exercising her claim to be reproduced and smiling obligingly as the cameraman readjusts his apparatus to focus in on her hands in close-up and then returns to her beaming face. Another "character" in the film, Vertov's editor and partner, Yelizaveta Svilova

(1900–1975), expresses herself in the same way in the sequences in which she displays the mechanics of editing, studiously avoiding the camera and the lighting paraphernalia as she carries on her job for the wide audience of her fellow workers that modern technology permits her to reach.

With *Enthusiasm* (1931), the sound film conclusively demonstrates the even greater disinclination of the camera to catch life unawares and its heightened sensitivity to the self-expression of its subjects. For one thing, we have for the first time the abandonment of the strategy of editing out obtrusive self-consciousness on the part of subjects of the camera. Whether it is simply a coincidence that this is Vertov's first film without the collaboration of his brother is perhaps an unanswerable question; but it has been speculated by both Sadoul and Barnouw that it was largely Kaufman who was responsible for the preponderance of the theme of "life caught unawares" in Vertov's rhetoric in the twenties (Sadoul 1971, 109; Erik Barnouw, seminar discussions, 1975). In any case, *Enthusiasm* is full of shots of people acknowledging the camera and indeed even celebrating it. There are crowd scenes with whole portions of an assembly staring into the lens. As columns of workers pass the camera, many of them casually acknowledge its presence with a matter-of-fact glance. At one point a whole cartload of children excitedly wave at the lens. Even Nikita Khrushchev, in his early role as a union organizer in the Ukraine, appears in glowing close-up and acknowledges the camera with a grin. There are also the vagrants and drunks ineffectually threatening or avoiding the camera, a few of the devotees at the icon anxiously realizing that their genuflections have been recorded, and even a few glimpses of a sound person unaccountably appearing on screen microphone in hand. And in a somewhat different category are the brilliantly orchestrated sequences of the bands, whose members are already engaged in public performance but for whom the sight of the tracking camera and sound apparatus no doubt multiplies their consciousness of their role. The serious young cymbals player, soberly facing the camera head-on in medium close-up, does not miss a beat as he takes advantage of the newly increased potential of the cinema for honoring his claim to be reproduced. This is not to mention the role of the young radio-listener who takes over the role of the cameraman in *Man with a Movie Camera* as the chief mediator-persona of the film, a role in this case primarily realized through conventional mise-en-scène.

But as in the case of the boy playing the cymbals, it is sound that is the specific instrument for the most radical expansion of popular expression. Sound becomes the crucial factor in the achievement of Benjamin's vision of the democratization of art, of the technologization of folk expression. And the soundtrack celebrates not only the musical self-expression of the cymbals player but also records their voices both collectively, in group singing, orchestrated cheers, and production pledges, and individually, as cheerleaders, as narrators, and most significantly as ordinary citizens. Admittedly, the short speeches of the shock workers and of their leaders who address them are stilted and self-conscious, but the impression of integrity is still as strong as or perhaps stronger than comparable speeches with the nuances of simulated naturalism might have been. As a shock worker recites his pledge "to help in the delivery of over 202,030 tons by the end of the year," the detail of his face in sunlit close-up and the stiff self-conscious quality of his voice definitively captures both the representativeness and the specificity that had often only been suggested in the silent films.

The progression toward this new specificity entailed by sound is no doubt reflected in the changing forms of the verbal themes of the silent films. The impersonal, narrative tone of *Kino-Glaz* (primarily third person in its attitude to the events it is describing) is intensified into the hortatory, first-person plural sensibility of *Stride, Soviet!* ("*We* fight disease, *we* fight dirt . . . Build Soviet! Stride, Soviet!") *One Sixth of the World* modifies the cinematic perspective once again in its summation of revolutionary achievements: now the audience is addressed in second person plural and its success is described ("*You* are all the masters of the Soviet Land!"). If the subject of the discourse of *The Eleventh Year* is a unanimous collective "*We*" ("We are building blast furnaces,"), and if the subject of the discourse of *Man with a Movie Camera* is an implied demonstrative "He," the coming of sound dictates its own specific syntactic sensibility. *Enthusiasm* introduces the first person singular with the pledges of the shock workers and *Three Songs of Lenin* confirms this direction by stressing this tone in the argument of its first song, "*My* sovkhoz, *my* country, *my* land," and so forth.

In addition, the film relies on the specificity of the spoken word as a major modality of its expression. If *Three Songs of Lenin* is from one point of view a collective elegy, an expression of public, anonymous feelings, it also at the same time includes the most vivid, personalized portraits of Soviet citizens in the entire oeuvre. And it is of course the power of the spoken word that endows these portraits with their concreteness and their credibility. In this film, the voices of Soviet workers, already tentatively captured in the previous film, are now recorded with authority and finesse. And it is significant that the mode of this record is the continued reliance on the self-conscious interaction of subject and camera that was a major condition of the silent work. In the third song, the concluding movement of the film that mingles the themes of the liberation of Asian women and

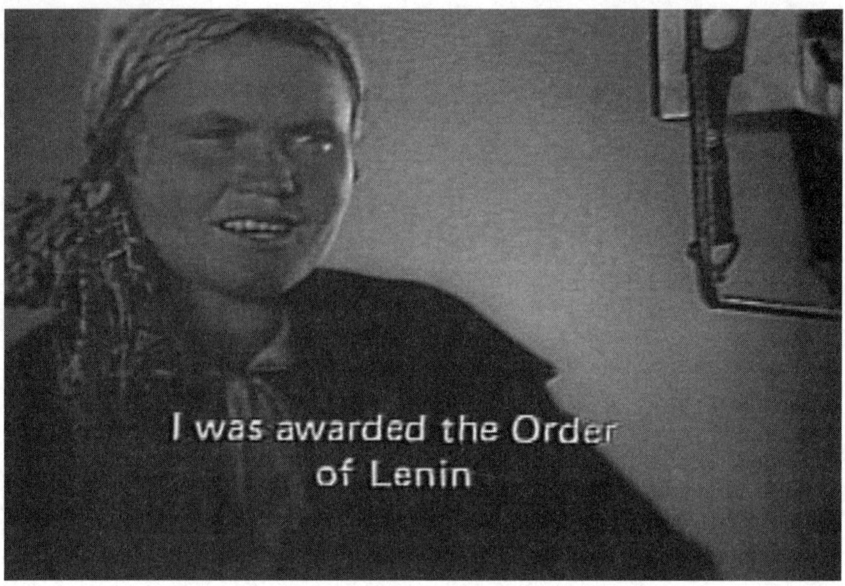

Three Songs of Lenin (Dziga Vertov, 1934). The Dneprostroi shock worker telling of her labor confirms the potential the new sound technology brought to Vertov's evolving populist aesthetics and politics of the thirties.

of the legacy of Lenin with a survey of the challenges of the present, the tasks of the Five Year Plan, we have a series of portraits of Soviet workers, two decorated with the Order of Lenin for their contributions to the goals of the Plan. Each confronts the camera in turn and gives a personal account of his contribution. A woman shock worker on the Dneprostroi project shyly and somewhat stiffly describes how she averted a near accident with some concrete tubs; an engineer connects the hydroelectric power station he has designed with Lenin's original vision of the need for electrification, his delivery halting and awkward; an elderly male kolkhoz-worker, bearded and fur-hatted, recalls an earlier exceptional harvest and praises the current generation's industry; and finally, most memorably, a female kolkhoz worker chats rather distractedly about the role of women in her kolkhoz. Each testimony has an authentic ring to it, despite the possibility that scripts may have been provided for them in part. The speech of the kolkhoz woman in particular is convincing, and extremely moving at the same time, as she progresses from her initial, rather stiff composure to her more natural volubility with its dramatic and graceful gestures.

The importance Vertov himself attached to this strategy as a means of nearing his long-sought ideal of "truth" is clearly revealed in the several references to this sequence in his writings. In a 1934 article he stresses the authenticity of these personal testimonies despite the artificiality of their setup:

It is possible, by means of the kino-eye to remove a man's mask, to obtain a bit of kinopravda. And it was the revelation of just this truth, by all the means available to me, that I designated as my entire future path in cinema.

Speaking symbolically, can't we find a similar "leap" here in *Three Songs of Lenin*? Yes. It's present if only in the woman shock-worker. Why does she have an effect? Because she's good at acting? Nothing of the kind. Because I got from her what I got from myself during the jump: the synchrony of words and thoughts.

If a shock-worker is addressing a congress and speaking words that he has memorized, or if he's thinking about something else at that time, you won't feel that synchrony of word and thought. ([1934] 1984, 124)

The inspiration for this innovative strategy, such an uncanny anticipation of the repertory of the direct cinema of thirty years later, clearly has for Vertov the same place as a milestone in his aesthetic growth as the famous leap referred to above, the moment shortly after the Revolution when a jump from a roof onto a Moscow street, when relived on film, revealed to him the extraordinary potential of the cinema as a means of heightening our perception of the world. Now the technological advances of what is virtually another era occasion a similar revelation, this time of the power of the sound cinema to probe the interior human universe.

A later reference in an article published posthumously, apparently written during the years of his despair, recalls the same sequence as emphatic proof that the documentary sound film is capable of expressing the human personality; after quoting the old kolkhoz worker's speech, her image returns to him as well:

And indeed, real, nonacted tears start to appear in the woman's eyes, while her face is smiling; and we think of a rainbow. The absolute, genuine sincerity, the 100 percent synchronization of thoughts, words, image is astounding. It's as if we are seeing the invisible—seeing thoughts on the screen. ([1958] 1984, 149)

It is in this light that we must see Vertov's view of the film as a "symphony of thoughts," as opposed to *Enthusiasm*, which was for him a "symphony of sounds." And one cannot help but reflect upon the irony of this apparent discovery of a mode of expressing thought upon the screen, when the search for such a mode had preoccupied Vertov's confrere, Eisenstein, during most of his career up to this point (and the even greater irony that this discovery was not to be confirmed and extended by either of these two great innovators of the cinema).

Apparently, the discovery of this strategy had been anticipated not only by the fragmentary personal declamations in *Enthusiasm* but also, according to Sergei Drobachenko, the leading Soviet authority on the subject, by Esfir Shub (1894–1959) in a 1932 film titled *Komsomol: Leaders of Electrification*, apparently released during the work on *Three Songs* (Drobashenko c. 1966).[11] The question of whether Shub was inspired by the tentative experiments in this direction in *Enthusiasm*, or of whether the chain of influence proceeded in the opposite direction, as well as other related questions pertaining to the interaction of the two leading exponents of the Soviet documentary, cannot be resolved on the basis of the information now available to us in the West. Of course, the issue of influence emanating from *Three Songs of Lenin* is another matter: the strategy of interview-style spontaneous declamation by film subjects finds a striking echo in John Grierson's *Housing Problems* two years after the release and exhibition abroad of *Three Songs*. The suggestion of Grierson's reworking of Vertov's idea is highly persuasive in this famous work, the highlight of which is a sequence in which a garrulous slum housewife tells the camera of her problems with rats. It is ironic that this highly successful experiment as well was not consolidated by inclusion in the cinematic lexicon until the age of direct cinema, television, and Godard.

The four dramatic and personal portraits that appear in the third movement of *Three Songs* are balanced throughout by less innovative but equally successful uses of sound in the service of the personal self-expression of the film's subjects. This is achieved primarily through the mediation of music. There has already been allusion made to the dialectical juxtaposition of collective, anonymous expression of communal feeling, and individual personal self-expression that forms a fundamental rhythm and structural principle of the film. Music functions as a primary agent of this dialectic. On the one hand we have the conventional, familiar classical themes from Chopin, Beethoven, Wagner, and Tchaikovsky, as well as the irresistibly magnetic Russian marches for which Vertov had already demonstrated a passion in *Enthusiasm*. These seem to express the theme of public, communal bereavement; and the choral music (patriotic cantata style) that surfaces during the concluding sections of the film reinforces the concluding theme of collective response to the challenge of socialist construction. In vivid contrast are the sections of Asian music on the soundtrack, most often conveying an impression of much greater intimacy and spontaneity than the solemn, funereal Russian music. And this impression is repeatedly confirmed by the inclusion of the image of the performance as well as the sound. For example, early in the film, a shot of a man playing an Asian stringed instrument and then a longer, more frontal view of a woman playing the same instrument are intercut with the sequence of the Muslim woman learning to read at a club, their music being the uninterrupted accompaniment to the entire narrative unit. In another case, we are presented with a recital of a spirited native dance by a young Asian Pioneer girl, with a captivating song, also by a young girl, accompanying it on the soundtrack in strict synchronization. This and a segment of another Asian folk dance are juxtaposed to two other kinds of choreography with striking effect, one being panoramic views of Red Square–style mass gymnastics by Young Communists in white (set to music from the Nutcracker Suite), and the other being ground-level images of parallel streams of water flowing through irrigation channels in an amazing "ballet concret" that is no less in time to the music than the gymnastics. This confluence of contrasting styles and qualities of music and dance is a striking microcosm of the central dialectic of the film.

Numerous other recordings of Central Asian vernacular music (including one selection with an apparently more contemporary origin, a song delivered presumably by school children or Pioneers to piano accompaniment), and even a prayer call, have their place on the soundtrack, both vocal and instrumental. One sequence that unites both the Asian inspiration and the Soviet theme displays an entire symmetrical chorus of tractors proceeding down a field driven by Asian women in their local finery, to the accompaniment of one of the stirring Moscow marches; if Busby Berkeley had been interested in socialism and irrigation, he might have been envious. In any case, the musical and choreographic self-expression of the Asian women and children, along both traditional folk-cultural lines and more contemporary ones, is a brilliant addition to the film's other currents of popular expression. According to Jay Leyda, this element was to have had an even greater role in the film according to Vertov's original conception (one Tajik melody in particular was to have dominated the second song [Leyda, seminar discussion, New York University, May 6, 1975]). And the intrusion of the ethnic, vernacular element into the popular expression captured by the film, adds an additional richness to its fabric of dialectical opposites; to the basic antimonies of the collective and the individual, the capital and the hinterland, the present and the past, the presence of Lenin and his loss, film actuality and film artifact, the additional antimony of Russian and non-Russian is added with all its highly charged implications of internationalism.

This is all not to mention the central structuring principle of the film, the three songs referred to by the title. These three lyrical expressions of collective grief each constitute a movement of the film. The fact that Vertov chose to call this new form a song (he had at one point called *Stride, Soviet! a symphony* and at another had referred to *One Sixth of the World* as a film-poem) is significant not only of its use of sound but also of its structure. *Enthusiasm* had been subtitled "Symphony of the Donbas" and

Three Songs, as a sound film, is as different from that earlier sound film as a song is from a symphony. All the implications of this distinction are relevant here, the strategic verbal dimension of a song, the reliance on simpler structural and melodic configurations, the predominantly mythopoeic orientation of song as opposed to the potential analytic bent of symphony, and of course the sociological implications of the distinction as well. The result is no doubt less challenging a work than *Enthusiasm*, if we assume the cinema to be only a mode of intellectual discourse. Otherwise, there is no comparison. It is a masterpiece of simple and straightforward elegance, of often monophonic beauty like that of the folk songs that are its substance.

The first song movement reflects a personal and private perspective of Lenin's role in terms of the liberation of a single Muslim woman from "her tower of darkness," the black veil and the oppression that it signifies for Vertov and his generation of atheist Bolsheviks. It is composed on the visual level of footage primarily from the Asian republics, contrasting traditional folkways with new achievements in agriculture, education, and industry. This song is unified by the point of view of the nameless Muslim woman whose efforts to learn to read we follow intermittently and whose face is an important visual motif of the first song.

The second song presents a more public, communal emotion, a eulogy of Lenin's historical role. Here the primary visual material is an assemblage of the newsreel footage of Lenin's life and funeral that Vertov prized so highly. The mourning passages of this material intercut with dark, luxurious pans of contemporary Asian women in extreme close-up—another of Vertov's synthetic audiences but this time bridging the gulfs of time and consciousness as well as of geography. The conclusion of the song returns briefly to the style of *Enthusiasm*, creating an impressive semiabstract dirge from a rhythmic accumulation of auditory elements such as factory sirens and cannon salutes together with diverse visual motifs—contrasting landscapes from all over the Soviet Union, more industrial material, newsreel clips, and additional contemporary footage of workers and mourners, and so on.

The third song moves from a contemplation of the "stone tent" where Lenin is buried to a contemporary summation of the achievements of the Revolution ("If only Lenin could see our country now!") and a prospectus of the challenges ahead. Here the visual elements, including portraits of workers and the dancing already described, rely on material more representative of Vertov's customary repertoire, forceful phrases built around industrial and agricultural projects (many reconstructed as usual from footage used in previous films), and even a return to the Lenin-as-icebreaker motif of several earlier films.

Vertov describes how he gathered the folk songs that form the material of this film:

> In Azerbaijan, Turkmenistan, Uzbekistan our group tape-recorded folk songs about Lenin. Their authors are mostly anonymous, but the songs are transmitted by word of mouth, from *yurt* to *yurt*, from *kishlak* to *kishlak*. We included several songs of the Soviet East in the film. Some songs are present on the sound track, some on the image track; still others are reflected in the intertitles. These are songs about the October Revolution, about a woman who has taken off the *yashmak*, about Ilyich's light bulb coming to the desert, about the illiterate who have been educated. ([1934] 1984, 117)

Perhaps the supreme irony of this extraordinary film is that it combines the most recent cultural technology with the most ancient, oral-formulaic and musical technologies for the transmission of culture. And yet there is a striking similarity between the new technology as Vertov pioneered it, as a means of contemporary folk expression, and the ancient technology that fascinated him so much. This film, the peak of this particular line of development of cinematic technology as an instrument of popular expression, is an extremely rich one, assimilating as it does the ancient forms of folk expression, song and dance, with contemporary Soviet forms, labor, filmmaking, factography, and revolutionary hagiography. Its potential in terms of the democratization of art and culture as seen by Benjamin and Gorky was very great indeed, but, as we know, it was a potential that was stifled by the weight of history.

Vertov, always somewhat of a political naïf when it came to dealing with the officialdom above him, can be forgiven for refusing to believe its potential could not be realized, even as project after project met with refusal, and humiliation and demotion became his only future. His chosen medium of expression did not permit him to avail of the refuge of Aesopian language, the way it did children's writer Yevgeny Shvarts (1896–1958), or the refuge of epic history, as with Eisenstein. His conscience refused to consider the alternatives of exile or silence as with writers Yevgeniy Zamyatin (1884–1937) or Isaak Babel (1894–1941). And his political acumen was not such that he could survive the years of Zhdanovism with the relative dignity retained by Ilya Ehrenburg (1891–1967), Mikhail Sholokhov (1905–1984), and Dmitri Shostakovich (1906–1975). The path of continued idealism, effort, and frustration reflected in the writings of his last fifteen years was perhaps the most difficult of all. The silence that followed *Three Songs*, or more precisely the silence signified by the triviality of the assignments to which he devoted the rest of his life,[12] is not only the tragedy of individualist dissent and of the modernist

avant-garde being crushed by the Stalinist state. It is also the tragedy of
continued political idealism and conviction in support of that State and
the ideals and the potential achievements it represented, and the tragedy of
that idealism being unrecognized and misunderstood by the very forces it
sought to aid.

[3]

Bread, Water, Blood, Rifles, Planes

Documentary Imagery of the Spanish Civil War from the North American Popular Front (1990)

The conference at Cornell University convoked by Kathleen Vernon to mark the fiftieth anniversary of the outbreak of the Spanish Civil War through a focus on the visual arts was an eye-opener to me. I had never encountered the kind of historiographical neutrality that was quite conspicuous among the interdisciplinary band of scholars participating. I am as troubled by the "both sides were bad" gang as I am by those who "objectively" can discuss Leni Riefenstahl (as a recent student who attempted to do so found out in my evaluation of her paper). I'm sorry, but one side in the Spanish conflict, the side that lost, was right . . . er, left . . . and the other side was not. In film history, such political morality can usually be corroborated by textual analysis, and the thirties provide a prime laboratory for this principle. In retrospect I think I accomplished my goals of demonstrating this in this piece, as well as providing a compact capsule of my epic research on The Spanish Earth. *My objective was also a kind of deauteurization of the film at the same time, to see the two American solidarity films as products of a Left generational subculture and a historical conjuncture, rather than of the stamp of individual creative genius. I hope that this renewed attention to the sadly overlooked* Heart of Spain *will attract the attention of the DVD market, for this fine film has the bonus of including rare and stirring footage of Canadian Communist doctor Dr. Norman Bethune innovating his mobile blood transfusion clinic in the heat of the Spanish front. As his statue in front of my Concordia University gets refurbished as I write, in preparation for its next generation of service at the center of Place Bethune, it is time to restore and recirculate* Heart of Spain.

The fifty-year anniversary of the art of the Spanish Civil War must be more than an occasion for a neutral historical retrospective of an epochal cultural moment. We should also celebrate that moment and the valor of a people who struggled to take charge of their history and who saw culture as an integral weapon in that struggle. The commitment of our own ancestors as North Americans to the Spanish cause is also to be celebrated; their integration of their art and their politics was also a stirring example to their generation and our own.

As part of this tribute, this paper reflects on two 1938 documentary films, *The Spanish Earth* and *Heart of Spain*. These two works of art, offered by the American Popular Front to the Loyalist effort, were fashioned both as artistic testimony and political support for a struggle toward which the official U.S. neutrality was morally and politically unacceptable. This paper is not meant to replace the excellent and comprehensive studies by William Alexander and Russell Campbell of the films' artistic and ideological aspects nor to replace my own more detailed studies of *The Spanish Earth* and that film's key place in the trajectory of both the political documentary film and the career of its author (Campbell 1982; Alexander 1981; Waugh 1981; Waugh 1984; Waugh 1982). Rather I will briefly examine the imagery of the two films and the sources of that imagery in the cultural and political currents of the day. I will conclude by reflecting on the centrality of these images of Spain in the political and cultural consciousness of the North American Popular Front at a turning point in the cultural and political history of our century.

The Spanish Earth by Joris Ivens and *Heart of Spain*, which was directed by Herbert Kline for Frontier Films, were released in New York in August and September of 1938, respectively. That they were produced in a collaborative spirit is evident: Not only were they edited in adjacent editing rooms in the spring of 1938, but the second film made use of some of the first's outtakes, even repeating some of the shots used in *The Spanish Earth*.[1] *The Spanish Earth* and *Heart of Spain* should be seen as companion films for other reasons as well. They were shaped by complementary strategic goals and topical emphases within the general vocation of solidarity with the Spanish Republican cause. They arose out of the same political-cultural milieu—the New York communist-sympathetic intelligentsia—or rather from adjacent corners of that milieu. Ivens's star list of fellow-traveler contributors from mainstream cultural quarters—Lillian Hellman and Herman Shumlin from Broadway, Dorothy Parker, Ernest Hemingway, and John Dos Passos from the literary firmaments—was consistent with his coalitionist political program of explaining the Spanish military front in terms of the democratic ideals of a broader civil revolution. Kline's crew—Paul Strand,

Leo Hurwitz, Ben Maddow, Geza Karpathi, and Jay Leyda—focused on the narrower, more pragmatic goals of medical relief and recruitment for the International Brigades, a mission consistent with the activist past most of them had within the Film and Photo League.

Adjacent editing facilities do not entirely explain the two films' most striking formal resemblance, their key use of similar editing structures. A climactic montage trope reprises in each case the visual terms of the basic argument and offers a final rhythmic manifesto of defiance and support.

In *The Spanish Earth*, Ivens intercuts his poetically representative villagers completing their new irrigation ditches with shots of military trucks surging along the successfully defended road to Madrid, then with closer shots of water rushing through the ditches, all punctuated with a close-up profile of a lone unshaven soldier firing a rifle. The last image is of water sinking into the earth that was "dry and hard" at the outset. The finale of *Heart of Spain* is no less metaphorical: the film's basic images of a village dance, marching squadrons, and artillery fire are intercut with images of blood transfusion, capped by the brilliant visual equation of the fist of the blood donor with the fisted salute of the Spanish people.

Ivens's summation equates by means of montage two dissimilar image-concepts, military defense and social revolution, and thereby arrives at their fusion, a profound visual statement of the link between civil war and social revolution, the quality of life fused with its defense. The viewer knows that the newly irrigated fields will produce the fine union bread already seen in close-up in the film, bread that will belong to the whole village as well as feed the besieged capital. Kline leaves the question of social revolution to Ivens, addressing it only obliquely through the convergence of medical relief and military defense. In his film, civilian blood becomes the resource underlying the military defiance, these two thematic threads having already been united in the meeting of Hero Escobedo, the motherly blood donor, with the injured soldier who has received her blood. Through images of water and blood, each film and its summation encapsulate the concept and the reality of the People's War, a concept to which I will return.

Such stirring montage summations were favorite devices of Popular Front filmmakers. One thinks not only of Frontier Film's *People of the Cumberland* from the following year but also of the Farm Services Administration's *The River* (1937) and *The Land* (1942) and, further afield, of Jean Renoir's 1936 electoral film *La Vie est à nous* (for the French Communist Party). The formula would eventually degenerate into a cliché of wartime propaganda such as in the U.S. Army's *The Negro Soldier* (1944). Whether or not the montage perorations can be traced back directly to Dziga Vertov's strikingly similar finale in *The Eleventh Year* (1928), with its highly kinetic montage of agricultural machinery, columns of marchers, a hydroelectric dam, and a metaphor of water as revolution, it is undeniable that the Soviet cinema's development of the trope in its pioneering documentary features of the late twenties and early thirties provided a general model of inspiration. More than one contributor to the two American films had seen Vertov's dazzling climaxes in *Enthusiasm* (1931) and *Three Songs of Lenin* (1934) firsthand in the Soviet Union, and Eisenstein's experiment with the form in *The General Line* (1929), a choreographed tractor variation, was widely known.

My invocation of Eisenstein and Vertov should not lead to the inference that the two American films are compendiums of modernist aesthetics derived from the Soviet revolutionary avant-garde of the twenties. It must also be remembered that Ivens's mentor was the Romantic Pudovkin rather than the constructionist Eisenstein, and that his works echo Dovzhenko's pastoral lyricism more than Vertov's playful fragmentation. In general Ivens's and Kline's stirring finales reflect their generation's will to orchestrate through emotional and poetic means popular understanding of and commitment to the political imperatives of the day. The conciliatory rhetoric of the Popular Front was in sharp contrast both to the more contestatory tactics of the proletarian documentarists of the earlier years of the Depression and to the uncompromising flourishes of the even earlier avant-garde, which included the anarchists of the West (such as Buñuel and Vigo) and the Bolshevik intellectuals of the East. In short, Ivens and the Frontier group were following the general Popular Front strategy of streamlining and popularizing the earlier achievements of the avant-garde.

At the same time, Ivens must be seen as chief interpreter in the West of another Soviet aesthetic, the somewhat later, more populist, and much maligned doctrine of socialist realism. Situating him, and to a lesser extent Kline, in this light should contribute to the current, long overdue reevaluation of socialist realism that may finally be happening in the West (Robin [1986] 1992). *The Spanish Earth*'s positive exemplary hero and its utopian, virtually allegorical images of social transformations, not to mention its populist audience strategy, are reminders that Ivens was in the Soviet Union at the time when socialist realism was being consolidated as the official aesthetic of the Soviet arts. Ivens's 1932 film for Mezhrabpom, *Komsomol*, had been part of a movement away from the more intellectual and allegedly inaccessible configurations of the twenties toward the rounded flesh-and-blood characterizations of the rose-tinted thirties. As he was making *The Spanish Earth*, the post-1934 wave of populist entertainment films from the Soviet Union was catching the New York

Leftist intelligentsia by storm: *Chapaev* (1934), *Youth of Maxim* (1935),
Childhood of Maxim Gorky (1938), and so on. This audience saw nothing contradictory in their simultaneous delight in the new work and their
somewhat foggy nostalgia for Eisenstein and the earlier avant-gardists. The
same constituency were also big fans of Hollywood, or more precisely of
Warner Brothers biopics like *The Story of Louis Pasteur* (1936), *The Life
of Emile Zola* (1937), and *Juarez* (l939), which after all were simply individualist New Deal versions of socialist realism.

The reader may observe that flesh-and-blood characters are not
exactly what appear on the screen in *The Spanish Earth* and *Heart of
Spain*, but it was not for want of trying. Ivens's and Kline's struggle to
construct such characters in the adverse conditions of low-budget frontline
silent filmmaking is clearly imprinted in the works. Ivens used to call this
enterprise of introducing characterization into documentary "personalization," and for him this individuation of dramatic characters within the
documentary format was highest priority if political documentary was to
gain the popular audiences so desired by the Left:

> For several reasons, it is important to personalize the documentary. We
> would never break into commercial distribution without it. For years and
> years we tried, only to meet with the same complaint from movie theater
> owners; if you just pointed to one or two persons, the film could be a story,
> not necessarily a love story, but some little story. (Ivens 1969, 210–11)

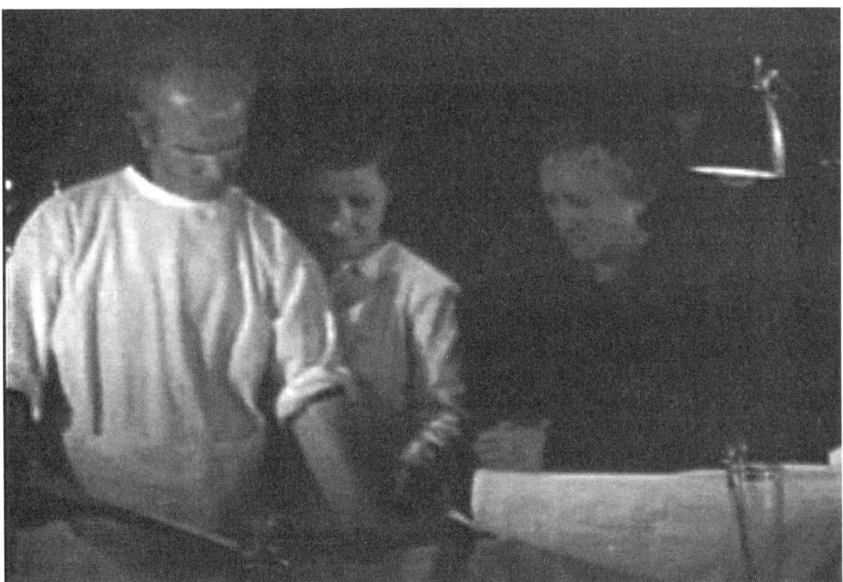

Heart of Spain (Herbert Kline, 1938). Dr. Norman Bethune (left), nurse, and
Hero Escobedo, the exemplary blood donor, on the Spanish front.

It was easier said than done. *The Spanish Earth* presents the rudimentary prototype character of Julian, the pleasant enlistee who was to disappear on the front and thus never return to the shoot to complete his persona. The existing material was valiantly stretched in the image editing and commentary, but to uncertain effect. *Heart of Spain* was perhaps somewhat more fortunate with the characters of the photogenic blood bank pioneer Dr. Norman Bethune and above all donor Escobedo. These individual characters, together with other vignettes involving minor characters were intended to dramatize as well as humanize the profound structures and dynamics of the Spanish Revolution and the war—in *Heart of Spain*, the North American intermediaries such as the black nurse are especially memorable in the best Hollywood tradition of recognizable mediators for exotic conflicts.[2] Later projects for Ivens and the Frontier group, closer to home base, would succeed better in going beyond "hasty and attempted identities now and then walking through a documentary." The formula would be elaborated before too long by a whole generation of documentarists, during World War II and afterward, until with the advent of direct cinema around 1960 the technological potential for fully fleshed portraiture was taken as far as it might be conceived to go, well within range of the dangers of individualist excesses lurking within sixties and seventies American liberalism.

Having evoked a certain kinship between the two documentaries and cultural currents in the Soviet Union, as well as the lure of the American box office, I must now touch upon certain other North American sources and inspirations. Spain may have catalyzed the international commitment of a whole generation of artists, but it also crystallized decidedly domestic cultural concerns. After all, Ivens's choice of the concept of village as microcosm of the Revolution was already decided before the crew left New York. In fact, I would argue that the agrarian imagery that dominates *The Spanish Earth* in particular corresponds very closely indeed to the Dust Bowl iconography of the American documentary movement of the same period. Ivens's Fuentedueña peasants are first cousins of the exploited sharecroppers and drought refugees that people the photographs of the Farm Services Administration and the exposé photo-essays of liberal journalistic media of the day. As early as 1934, Ivens's Hollywood friend King Vidor had in *Our Daily Bread* crafted the West Coast prototype for *The Spanish Earth*, complete with collectivized workers improvising an irrigation system and a coda showing water rushing across the dry earth! The project was considered fairly audacious *that* early in the New Deal, and Vidor had to finance the film independently despite his proven track record.

Hemingway's carefully worded 1937 narration of land appropriation from absentee landlords now seems a genteel retread of Vidor and in general echoed the agrarian agenda of the American Popular Front with its mythic roster of noble sharecroppers and anonymous bankers. Some of the collectivist references like Hemingway's "they held us back" and "the common good" or the shot of the union stamp carefully shown on the village loaf had specific domestic resonance. Yet the filmmakers made sure that the Leftist agenda of unionization and land reform was gentle enough to be recuperated by spectators situated anywhere to the right in terms of universal humanism, as *Time* magazine's reading of *The Spanish Earth* testifies:

> Not since the silent French film, *The Passion of Joan of Arc*, has such dramatic use been made of the human face. As face after face looks out from the screen the picture becomes a sort of portfolio of portraits of the human soul in the presence of disaster and distress. There are the earnest faces of speakers at meetings and in the village talking war, exhorting the defense. There are faces of old women moved from their homes in Madrid for safety's sake, staring at a bleak, uncertain future, faces in terror after a bombing, faces of men going into battle and the faces of men who will never return from battle, faces full of grief and determination and fear. (*Time* 1938)

Personalization had the convenient ideological property of being open to readings of the human soul and of the proletariat at the same time. (Not that the Spanish industrial proletariat was conspicuous in either American film, for their communist-sympathetic directors were geographically and ideologically too far from anarchist Barcelona for them to record this essential factor in Spanish politics, and industrial workers were in any case too far from American preconceptions of Spain—but that is another story.) The music of the two films rounded out the picture, with their anthologized Spanish folk scores echoing folk scores of Pare Lorentz's *The Plow that Broke the Plains* (1936) and *The River* (1937), the major nuance of difference being that the discourse of agrarian exoticism in the Spanish films replaced the discourse of agrarian nostalgia in the Lorentz films.

Where Ivens and Kline made an essential departure from the aesthetics of Dorothea Lange and Lorentz, however, was their grafting of Socialist Realist optimism onto homegrown eloquent despair. Instead of the apathy, immobility, and gaunt tragic dignity of their American counterparts, Spanish villagers are vigorously undertaking the solution, cheerfully taking possession of their land, and digging ditches across it to feed themselves and Madrid.

Having briefly discussed an iconography of social construction and peace—bread, water, blood, and earth—I must conclude by sketching the iconography of war and destruction to which Ivens and Kline made a haunting and decisive contribution. It is hard to overestimate the impact the new imagery of aerial bombardment of civilians had upon virgin audiences of 1938: *The Spanish Earth* has three devastating sequences, *Heart of Spain* two, all synthetically edited and highly fictionalized scenes, constructed in the editing, showing real bombs killing real children. These five cinematic Guernicas were crafted with all the auditory sophistication that synthetic sound recording technology was capable of in 1937— shattered glass, whining shells, screams, and above all eerie silences—and were situated as regular narrative crises for maximum rhetorical effect. Ivens's editor, Helen van Dongen, had just done an apprenticeship in Hollywood, and her newly acquired skill in the invisible editing of narrative illusion and identification perfectly matched the audience strategy of Popular Front cultural practice. The only traces remaining of Eisensteinian editorial confrontation were Kline's concise inserts of clips of Mussolini and Hitler puncturing his bombardment sequences.

It is hard to remember that this quantum escalation in the imagery of war these sequences represent was almost equivalent to that occasioned by Hiroshima eight years later. Of course Italian and Japanese bombers, followed eagerly by Western newsreel companies, had already been used in Ethiopia and China, respectively. But the new repertory of images from Spain—civilians running to air raid shelters, random and arbitrary violence and destruction, atrocity footage of corpses—really struck home with Western audiences for the benignly racist reason that white bookkeepers were among the victims rather than coolies, and urban apartments with still swinging lighting fixtures rather than grass huts were devastated. That both films used the same shot of an enemy plane being shot down is telling: The point of view belongs to the sympathetic victims on the ground, not helpless, but fighting back against the terror in the skies as neither the Chinese nor the Ethiopians had effectively been able to do. It is symbolic also that a rapid shot of a falling bomb, also from the victim's point of view, was in fact the reversal of a newsreel shot of an Italian bomb being dropped on Ethiopia *from the bomber's point of view.* The new antifascist documentary undertook a reversal, both literal and figurative, of the imagery of the complacent, sensationalistic, and reactionary commercial newsreel companies and indeed of the Western cinema itself, which had provided until this time the dominant audiovisual imagery of the world from the point of view of colonizer, exploiter, and aggressor.

Ivens's and Kline's bombardment footage was recorded differently of course from the studied images of the village construction or medical relief, with their tripod steadiness and collaborative mise-en-scène of exemplary personae. Captured improvisationally with small handheld cameras, the images of the bombings and their aftermath meshed with the mise-en-scène footage into a hybrid form well matched to the double goal of the films: the recounting and denunciation of the aggression and a profound poetic understanding of the calm courage of everyday life and the social transformation behind the lines. As Leo Hurwitz, coscenarist of *Heart of Spain* had written, the new documentary needed to become a mixed form of the synthetic document and the dramatic, a synthetic documentary film that would allow for material that recreates and fortifies the actuality recorded in the document and makes it clearer and more powerful (Hurwitz 1934, 93).

This hybrid structure facilitated also the concept of the People's War, since it enabled at the same time an eyewitness account of the violence and an interpretation, in collaboration with its architects, of the social foundation that made this war different from the conventional wars of kings, capital, conscripts, and mercenaries.

A special iconography of arms and arms-bearers belongs to this concept, as I have already implied. The bombardment of civilians being at its center, it is an iconography of flesh versus steel, rifles versus planes, the earth below versus the sky above. The high technology of a developed industrial culture imposes economic and political hegemony upon the muscle and grit of a traditional culture defending its livelihood with all its means and at every moment. As I've said, the battle is seen from below, and in both *The Spanish Earth* and *Heart of Spain* the enemy is kept visible primarily through their technology—and their corpses. On this matter the commentator Ernest Hemingway offers what might seem a self-parody were it not so appropriate to the image: "Before, death came when you were old and sick, but now it comes to all this village. High in the sky and shining silver it comes to all who have no place to run, no place to hide."

Resistance is mostly eloquently encapsulated in the image of the rifle. Both films make sure to show sophisticated artillery and antiaircraft weaponry, but the large machines don't have the cinematic quality of the lone rifleman of Iven's finale nor of his equally poignant image following the earlier village bombardment sequence of a single soldier seated in a doorway of the devastated village, calmly cleaning his rifle under the attentive gaze of two children.

Hemingway's poeticization of battle on the soundtrack of *The Spanish Earth* is well known:

The men move on in columns of six in the ultimate loneliness of what is known as combat. For each man knows there is only himself and five other men and before them all the great unknown. This is the moment that all the rest of the war prepares for. When six men go forward into death, to walk across a stretch of land and by their presence on it prove this earth is ours.

However effective this may be in cinematic terms over the less than spectacular footage of the Battle of Brihuega, it is clear that the emphasis on conventional military engagements tends to undercut the specificity of the Spanish Civil War and fails as well to grasp the general political relevance of Ivens's testimony of a People's War. The contradiction between Hemingway's soundtrack existential machismo and Ivens's happily predominant sense of the heroism and commitment of daily life and of the civilian front is responsible for much of the creative tension of the film. It is as heroic, in Ivens's terms as in Kline's, to get a haircut at the Enrique Lister barbershop as to confront the great unknown, to give blood as to spend blood. The filmmakers' insight is, as Walter Benjamin put it in another context, that "events are not changeable at their climax, not through virtue and resolve, but only in their strictly ordinary, habitual course, through reason and practice"; their skill was to endow the "smallest elements of behavior" with the dimensions of dramatic "action." (Benjamin 1934, 100)[3]

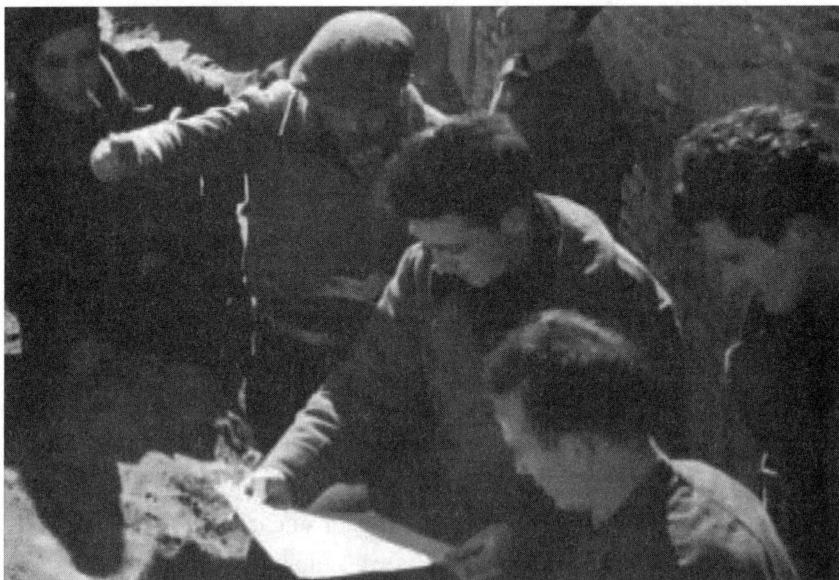

The Spanish Earth (Joris Ivens, 1937). Loyalist soldiers reading newspaper coverage of their fight against fascism: vividly human nonprofessionals "who were not trained in arms, who only wanted food and work."

In this sense, soldiering is depicted not only as combat but as everyday work, especially by Ivens, and soldiers are seen as vividly human individuals as they go about their jobs. They are presented as ordinary "little men," nonprofessionals who "never fought before, who were not trained in arms, who only wanted work and food." If in retrospect the propaganda value of an emphasis on nonprofessionalism may be called into question, particularly in view of the stereotype of the "undisciplined" Loyalist army perpetrated by the newsreel companies, it was an emphasis that spoke very strongly to its intended audience as well as to subsequent generations. Shots showing "unsoldierly" data were clearly deliberately retained—soldiers grinning at the camera, awkward drilling, and so on.

The contrast with Leni Riefenstahl's approach to military imagery in *Triumph of the Will*, made one year previous to Franco's uprising, gives a vivid sense of the evolving political context of the Spanish imagery. Her preoccupation is with mass uniformity, discipline, ceremony—in short, insofar as architectural formations of troops are repeatedly captured in her films, with inhumanity. It is significant that when Riefenstahl anticipates Ivens's strategy in showing troops and paramilitary groups at leisure in *Triumph of the Will*, their behavior is shown as giggling and boyish—as if adulthood can only be expressed in synchronized step and military formation. As for the trope of marching troops that would soon overwhelm world screens, Ivens and Kline present a very different picture from their Nazi counterpart. Instead of abstract kinetic formations, ballets of boots and banners proceeding with precision across the screen, we see irregular groups of confident, or nervous, clearly identifiable individuals. Loyalist soldiers are most often seen in small groups, often at medium range or closer, as in an informal circle of new recruits receiving rifle-loading instructions, rather than in large precise formations. These divergent cinematic practices seem to bear out Kracauer's famous observation about the ideological determination of the visualization of the crowd, his perception that the fascist aesthetic renders the mass as a symmetrical ornament whereas for the socialist aesthetic, exemplified by the classical Soviet cinema, the mass vibrates with raw vitality (Kracauer 1947, 289, 299–303).

Of the two films, *The Spanish Earth* and *Heart of Spain*, it is not surprising that the latter should provide an artistic vision of the conflict that is somewhat less commanding and clear than the other. The Frontier filmmakers had less means, less preparation, less time, less directing flight-time behind them, not to mention less of the individual personal control that Ivens was able to exert on *The Spanish Earth* collaborators. Despite its many merits, *Heart of Spain* is less authoritative in conveying an enduring understanding of the war, of the interaction of the civilian front and the military front, and even of the purposefulness of conventional military activity (which *The Spanish Earth* with its maps and charts does beautifully).

The Spanish Earth thus provides the more important prototype for a central tradition of cinematic understanding of our era that has endured to this day and of which the iconography and the politics have changed amazingly little. The prophetic image of the People's War occasioned by Spain would be elaborated once more by both Ivens and Frontier Films the following year in relation to the Chinese defense against the Japanese. The Allied propaganda outfits would thereafter make full use of the same full repertory of imagery during the ensuing World War. But the cinematic image of the People's War would come into its fullest use in the postwar generations of anti-imperialist struggle in the Third World, from Algeria to Vietnam to Cuba to Namibia and South Africa. Spain set off an artistic continuum in which the documentary film would continue to enlist on the side of liberation.

The ideological elisions, avoidances, and self-censorship of both *The Spanish Earth* and *Heart of Spain* have been amply discussed by Alexander and Campbell, and this is not the place to engage in the debate on the blunders and blindspots of the Communist Party in Spain or the United States that the present anniversary has revived. It is sufficient here, I hope, to suggest that Ivens's and Kline's ellipses as political historians were as determined by their films' vocation as popular mobilization as they were by the fragile alliances within the Popular Front. As Campbell and many other children of the New Left have argued, it may have been an error to follow the Communist Party platform, necessitated according to the wisdom of the day by the precarious nature of the antifascist alliance, that is, the strategy of keeping Communist Party presence and affiliations invisible, of blurring the political dynamics within the Spanish Revolution, whether of agricultural policy or regional differences or political diversity or tensions. It is interesting that of all the foreign filmmakers, perhaps André Malraux was most successful in conveying these dynamics, no doubt because his French audience would be better equipped to understand interfaction tensions within a Popular Front coalition. In any case, questions over whether Ivens's and Kline's adherence to the Communist Party policy was justified in view of the unquestionable threat of domestic censorship, whether their simplifications were justified in the interests of a common front in the face of the enemy, and whether a popular artistic medium can be a vehicle of nuanced political analysis at the same time as it is a weapon of mobilization and solidarity, are larger questions still being resolved on other fronts, fifty years later (and seventy-five years later, as well, I add in 2011).

     BREAD, WATER, BLOOD, RIFLES, PLANES

For this anniversary is occurring just as other Hispanic societies are attempting to appropriate their own history and are facing with no less courage a not dissimilar threat of fascist intervention. The anniversary of the Spanish Civil War is rendered all the more resonant by its analogues in Central America. As progressive filmmakers and other artists in North America and other Western countries rush to offer their images of solidarity with Nicaragua (not to mention Guatemala and El Salvador), the echoes are as uncanny as they are telling. In neither the romantic past nor the brutal present, however, could or can films of solidarity win the war. If one subscribes to the naive belief that films can save revolutions and win wars, then the Spanish Civil War provided a test that the artists of the Popular Front failed. Yet in focusing our commitment to a struggle other than our own, the art of solidarity, coming out of our own cultural and political context, reverberates back upon and challenges our own political wills in a way that is as useful and authentic as its record of exotic battles of Spain or Nicaragua.

The Spanish Earth and *Heart of Spain*, like the other artifacts discussed at this fiftieth-anniversary conference (1986) from Picasso's *Guernica* to Walter Wanger Productions' *Blockade* (1938), filter Spain and the world through the conscience and consciousness of outsiders. That is not to say that the films on Spain and Nicaragua will not buy ambulances or sway public opinion or policy, both worthy ambitions for any artist. But their primary effect must first be measured in the political and cultural context in which they are shaped, and in this sense *The Spanish Earth* and *Heart of Spain*, progenitors of a stirring cinematic tradition of solidarity, provide us with a priceless and enduring legacy.

As Alexander sums up this legacy, quoting Frontier filmmaker Sidney Meyers: "The documentary film found in antifascism its reason for being" (Alexander 1981, 165). In pioneering both a new documentary genre and an anti-imperialist cinematic tradition, the "solidarity film," in inaugurating this tradition of testimonies of exotic struggles abroad, *The Spanish Earth* and *Heart of Spain* participated in a social and cultural movement of resistance at home, providing a political opposition with an arm, a goal, and a conscience; formulating the political choices for a society in crisis; and stimulating Western political discourse with alternative social models, with challenges to its complacency, with utopias.

[**4**]   Acting to Play Oneself

Performance in Documentary (1990)

This piece was written for my colleague Carole Zucker who was putting together her 1990 volume on acting in the cinema, brought out with Scarecrow Press, my own publisher for "Show Us Life." Her only entry on nonfiction film amid much analysis of actors and auteurs, "Learning to Play Onself" is a trifle out of sync with the volume as a whole and is one of my less traveled articles. Though it perhaps requires more of a familiarity with the eighties documentary canon than is very common these days, I think it's less embarrassing than others of the decade's pronouncements, and I have been gratified on several occasions over the years when researchers have discovered it unexpectedly.

No doubt this is the moment to pay tribute to Scarecrow Press, that New Jersey book mill (now in Maryland), still going strong, whose contribution to the discipline of film studies has not been adequately acknowledged. Somehow staying in the black for more than five decades by giving previously unpublished young scholars, fans, cultists, list makers, anthologists, and independent researchers alike their first imprint when no one else would, Scarecrow may not have been as consciously political as Jump Cut *but served an analogous function for Carole and me and so many others.*

Speaking of lists, my inclusion of "trans" people in my list of "performers" who had served as privileged subjects for direct cinema documentary of the sixties, seventies, and eighties, got me into very hot water indeed two decades after it was written with a transman graduate student. He was of course right that my inclusion of his ancestors who had performed so memorably for the camera a generation or two ago among my long list of categories of "performing" subjects, from preachers to actors, could be read

In 1940, Joris Ivens, in the midst of finishing *Power and the Land* for
Pare Lorentz's U.S. Film Service, wrote an essay on "Collaboration in
Documentary" (which would later be modified for inclusion in his 1969
autobiography). It was time to summarize much of what he had learned
in the first fifteen years of his career. Much of the resulting manual of the
classical documentary concerns the challenge of working with nonprofessional subjects in "reenactment," one of documentary's "wide variety of
styles." As a lead-in to my reflection on the presence of performance within
the documentary film tradition it is worth excerpting this text at length:

> We come to the problem that has attracted and sometimes baffled us for
> many years: the handling of non-actors. In re-enacting a situation with a
> group of extremely pleasant persons, who for your purposes have become
> actors, the danger of letting them do what they like, of falling back on pleas-
> ant, easy naturalism, is even greater. And as your location work progresses,
> the non-actors become the central figures in your group, creating problems
> that temporarily force all the other problems out of your consciousness . . .
>
> Our farm film presented material that seemed to demand re-
> enactments . . . In choosing the people who were to play the roles (of
> themselves—the farmer as the farmer, his sons as the farmer's sons, etc.), the
> first visual impression is very important. Casting has its own difficulties too.
> A father and a son may work well separately, but not at all well when they're
> together in a scene. To get close enough to these people, to work with them, the
> director must be sensitive to these relationships. In general, I feel a knowl-
> edge of psychology is demanded of every member of the group, for all must
> watch and sense delicate situations.

The writer must employ his imagination to manipulate the real personal characteristics of the new actors—searching them with seemingly careless observations. He must learn thereby, for example that the farmer takes a special pride in the sharpness of his tool blades, and therefore suggest a toolshed scene which will make use of that fact. The key to this approach, I think, is that a real person, acting to play himself, will be more expressive if his actions are based on his real characteristics.

My experience has been that directives to non-actors who are playing together would usually be given them separately, so that a certain amount of unrehearsed reaction can be counted upon. To get natural reactions we played tricks similar to those Pudovkin has recorded, and some of them worked. For example: the father was filmed receiving a notification from the dairy that his milk is sour; he expected to unfold and pretend to read a blank piece of paper. But he read instead a startling message from me, complaining about his sour milk in no uncertain terms.

In general my method was to give precise directions to these non-actors but not to do it for them—simply to tell them what has to be done . . . The farmer will have his special way of doing it, whether it is entering a room or moving a chair, and it is usually a very good way.

I have come to believe it is best to have as few re-takes as possible. Repetition seems to have a deadening effect on the non-actor. If rehearsals are necessary, allow some time to elapse between rehearsals and shooting. Use yourself or anybody as stand-ins—to keep the non-actor from exhaustion or self-consciousness. On the other hand, if the period of filming a re-enactment is short or very rushed, there can be less care in humoring him, depending more on the camera's ability to break up the action into useful closeups.

The cameraman has to understand the special difficulties in working with non-actors ("What good is all this fooling with lights?") to render the length of time during light and camera adjustment tolerable to the non-actor. I don't believe in having long conferences before takes, while the non-actor waits. Keep discussions away from him. He begins to feel that these long, visible, but inaudible conversations are about himself and his acting—and he is usually right. We learned to use a code. Whenever the cameraman said, after a shot, "Very good" I knew he meant, "It's not so hot, try it some other way."

The surest way to avoid loss of time with re-takes is to know and anticipate the real movements of the man, to catch the regular rhythm of his normal action (which is far from re-enactment). The whole action should be watched (away from the camera) before breaking it up for filming. And the breaking up, and covering shots, should absolutely include beginnings of an action, endings of an action, and the places where the worker rests—not just other angles of the most exciting sections of his movement. Thus you get material for good human editing . . .

Overcoming self-consciousness is of course the greatest problem with the non-actor, no matter what his background. If you work for months with the same group of persons, you can gradually expect to find more consciousness of themselves as actors. They become more flexible and adaptable and greater demands can be made of them. They can even be taught something of the film's technique. When the father in the farm film couldn't understand why he had to repeat an action more than once while the camera was shifted about, I took him to see a Cagney movie at the local theater and pointed out how an action in a finished film was made out of long shots, medium shots and closeups. From then on he understood our continuity problems and gave very useful assistance in this way. But I don't think it wise to show them their own rushes. I waited until the last few days before showing our farm family themselves on the screen.

I advise not to fool with a man's professional pride. Don't ask a farmer to milk an empty cow, even though it's just for a closeup or the farmer's face. He fights such an idea because to him it is false—until he has been with the filming group for a long time.

Even as simple a rule as "Don't look at the camera" is bound up with the man himself. But this is such a basic necessity for the quality of your film that you must enforce the rule even though it hurts you to. (Ivens 1940, 30–42)

Ivens goes on to illustrate this last point with an anecdote from his Chinese shoot a few years earlier (for *The Four Hundred Million*) where he had to force himself to impose the rule of "not looking at the camera" on traumatized stretcher-bearers in a battle scene.

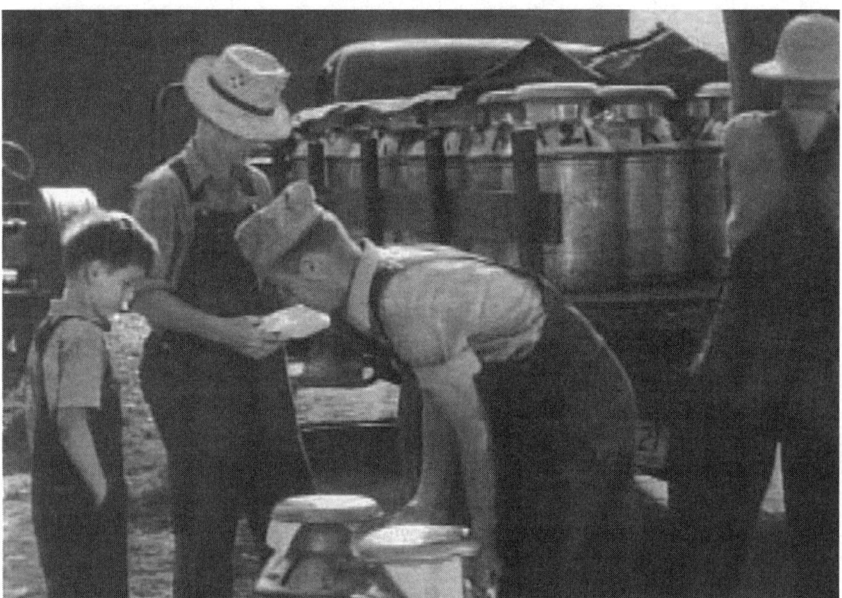

Power and the Land (Joris Ivens, 1941). The director has played a trick on his Ohio farm collaborator, who is unexpectedly reading a stern reprimand about his spoiled milk intended to spark a "natural" representational performance.

Acting Naturally in the Classical Documentary

Documentary film, in everyday commonsense parlance, implies the absence of elements of performance, acting, staging, directing, and so forth, criteria that presumably distinguish the documentary form from the narrative fiction film. Ivens's text helps focus a discussion of performance in documentary because it challenges the common understanding. It reveals how basic the ingredients of performance and direction are within the documentary tradition—certainly within the classical documentary as reflected in this 1940 document, but also, as I will argue, in the modern vérité and post-vérité documentary as well.

For Ivens and his generation, the notion of performance as an element of documentary filmmaking was something to be taken for granted. Toward the end of the thirties, as documentarists yearned to get out of the basements and into the theaters, semifictive characterization—or "personalization," as Ivens called it—seemed to be the means for the documentary to attain artistic maturity and mass audiences. Social actors,[1] real people, became documentary film performers, playing themselves and their social roles before the camera.

The decade's prevailing notion of documentary performance is reflected most in Ivens's terminology with its echoes of narrative studio-based filmmaking: "roles," "retake," "continuity," "covering shots," "rehearsals," "casting," and so on. His directing techniques, significantly, are borrowed from Pudovkin, a director notable for his work with professional dramatic actors. Documentary performers "act" in much the same way as their dramatic counterparts except that they are cast for their social representativity as well as for their cinematic qualities, and their roles are composites of their own social roles and the dramatic requirements of the film.

Ivens's term "natural" indicates a problematical concept and practice for the classical (pre-vérité) documentarist. By "naturalism" Ivens means a cinematography characterized not by "content value" (a concept he uses elsewhere in the article) but by a spontaneous textural or behavioral quality, a quality that the later vérité generation would transform into an aesthetic gospel. But he also refers to "acting naturally" in reference to "not looking at the camera," the code of illusion by which both extras, such as the Chinese stretcher-bearers, and principal (non)actors should "perform" unawareness of the camera. This clearly artificial code of "acting natural" is so rooted in our cinematic culture, then as now, that Ivens posits it unquestioningly as a basic axiom of "quality" cinema. The vérité school, in its American observational incarnation (Leacock, Wiseman), would share this axiom with Ivens and his generation however much they would repudiate the principle of "content value."

But the concept and the practice of acting naturally are more complex than either generation realized. Let us use "*representational*" to refer to Ivens's "acting naturally," the documentary code of narrative illusion, borrowed from the dominant fiction cinema. When subjects perform "not looking at the camera," when they "represent" their lives or roles, the image looks "natural" as if the camera were invisible or as if the subject were unaware of being filmed. This performance convention is by no means inherent in the documentary mode. Certainly in documentary still photography it is considerably less unanimous, for from August Sander to the Farm Security Administration to Diane Arbus, from Wilhelm von Gloeden to Robert Mapplethorpe, the convention of "posing" is much more the dominant tradition. In contrast, the convention of "representation" as found in, say, Henri Cartier-Bresson (whose influence on the direct cinema movement is of course not without interest), informs a vigorous but secondary countercurrent. The convention of performing an awareness of the camera rather than a nonawareness, of presenting oneself explicitly for the camera—the convention the documentary cinema absorbed from its elder sibling photography—we shall call "*presentational*" performance.

Although posing, the presentational convention of acknowledging the camera, never became the standard convention in classical documentary cinema, it did become an important secondary variant of documentary cinematic practice, particularly in the sound era. Whereas Flaherty's silent *Nanook* was depicted performing presentationally a few times—posing for the camera with a grin or a look—he for the most part performed naturalistically, "acting" or representing his daily life for the camera without explicitly acknowledging its presence. *Moana* similarly displayed some engaging moments of presentation—a subject displaying a captured tortoise to the camera, for example—but by and large Flaherty succeeded in getting his Samoan social actors to perform according to the codes of representation. By the time of his later features, *Man of Aran* and *Louisiana Story*, Flaherty was following the codes of representation obsessively—to the extent that they become abstract mytho-narrative mediations on exotic landscapes rather than social narratives rooted in the daily cultural contexts of those landscapes' inhabitants. These latter films are no longer able to bear, for contemporary eyes at least, the slightest pretension to ethnographic veracity, nor even, my students would say, the least claim to the documentary mantle at all—a point whose significance I will take up later.

Not all sound documentarists followed Flaherty's lead. During the sound era, the countercurrent of presentational performance in fact became quite visible—or rather audible. Inspired in part by radio, aural presentational conventions like the interview, the monologue, even choral speech, were experimented with in the thirties by Vertov, by Grierson's British school, by Frontier Films, and even by Flaherty himself in his project for the U.S. Film Service (slightly later than Ivens's), *The Land*. Traumatized by the devastation he "discovered" in his own backyard on this latter project, Flaherty somehow let go of the representational style he had perfected on Aran. Prominent in the film are curious silent/nonsync variations of aural presentational performances as well as several moments of silent presentational posing clearly inspired by Flaherty's fellow federal employees in the still photography business. For his part, Ivens was accustomed of course to "representing" far more traumatic devastation than nonelectrified farming in Ohio, as his Chinese anecdote reminds us. In *Power and the Land*, then, his representational skills were thus honed to their finest point, and the performances that spurred the manual excerpted at the outset of this article became milestones in documentary representation.

It is interesting that the two traditions intersect in the career of a single editor, Helen van Dongen. Ivens's longtime collaborator and a principal pioneer in the perfection of representational documentary editing, van Dongen edited both *The Land* and *Power and the Land*. I have always found odd her complaint about the "staged" quality of Flaherty's most intricate representational scene, in which a black farmhand moves about a deserted plantation and rings the plantation bell. In practice van Dongen sculpted this scene with all the representational precision and smoothness that she had just brought to *Power and the Land* and would later bring to *Louisiana Story* (van Dongen 1965, 4). Flaherty's uncharacteristic posing shots, however, were never brought up in her published notes about the editing, though they clearly disturbed the seamless continuum that was van Dongen's professional pride. The FSA-style posing shots she treated with an anomalous awkwardness, cutting them off with abrupt, haunting fadeouts before the intrinsic rhythm of the shot, and the dynamic of the spectator's encounter with the performers are fulfilled.

As for Flaherty's and Ivens's British contemporaries (and admirers), they pushed the cumbersome sound technology of the day much further than the Americans in the direction of both presentational and representational performances, achieving unintentional self-parody with the latter in *Night Mail* and groundbreaking revelation with the former in the legendary interviews and monologues of *Housing Problems*. In the Soviet

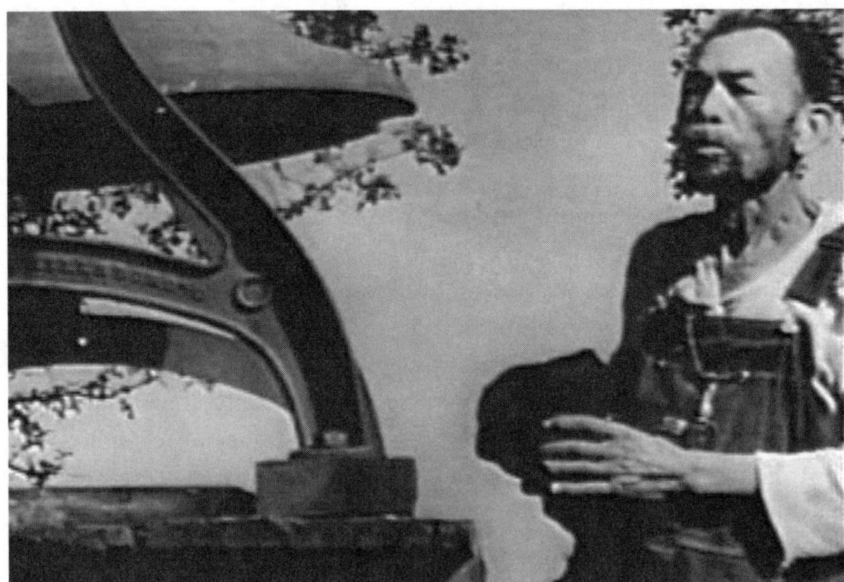

The Land (Robert Flaherty, 1942). Editor Helen van Dongen critiqued this "representational" scene in which a black farmhand rings a plantation bell as staged, but even more awkward "presentational" scenes about the agrarian crisis abound in this film.

context, such experimentation appeared even earlier. As early as 1931, the only Soviet documentarist of the sound period whose work is available in the West, Dziga Vertov, incorporated short production pledges delivered as monologues by shock workers in *Enthusiasm*, a film that must be considered his manifesto of the possibilities of documentary sound, despite the stilted and self-conscious effect of these first attempts. Three years later, *Three Songs of Lenin* offered vivid and personalized portraits of Soviet citizens by virtue of a more developed use of monologue performances: two of the portraits feature a woman shock worker as she shyly describes how she averted an accident with some concrete tubs in a construction project and a woman kolkhoz worker who chats with amazing informality and dramatic gestures about the role of women on her farm. The possibility of Vertov's influence on his Western European counterparts is a strong one since the Grierson group knew his work.

Yet despite the inspiration occasioned by Grierson's rat-plagued housewife holding forth to the camera and by Vertov's vivid portraits, the presentational style predominated only in the documentary vernacular of the commercial newsreel (as later in its descendent, television journalism) or the still rare campaign film (such as Renoir's *La Vie est à nous*, which incorporated Party oratory along with a range of representational

   ACTING TO PLAY ONESELF

sketches). Ivens's representational style of naturalistic acting and mise-en-scène was never edged from its hegemony within the hybrid repertory of the so-called artistic documentary vocabulary of the period.

In summary, now that we have returned to Ivens, performance—the self-expression of documentary subjects for the camera in collaboration with filmmaker/director—was the basic ingredient of the classical documentary. Most directors relied principally on a naturalistic, representational performance style borrowed from fiction, which some varied from time to time with presentational elements akin to the conventions of still photography and radio. The difference between representation and presentation is not that one uses performance and the other doesn't, but that the former disavows and hides its performance components through such conventions as not looking at the camera, whereas the latter openly acknowledges and exploits its performance components. This difference must now be explored.

▶

Presenting versus Representing

The distinction between representational and presentational performance is a very useful one for looking diachronically at documentary history. The pendulum of fashion and usage has swung back and forth between the two conventions, from one period to another, from one culture to another, and from the margin to the mainstream within one particular period and culture. I have already mentioned, for example, that presentational performance became visible, though not predominant, during the latter half of the thirties, during the first maturity of the sound documentary. At the same time proponents of the predominant representational element of the period's hybrid form often went even further than Ivens in availing themselves of the resources of fictional cinema: the use of studio sets (*Night Mail*) and professional actors (*Native Land*) during the thirties as a means of both overcoming technological difficulties and deepening the social perspective of Ivens's representational form did not attract any notice at the time, but would become anathema thirty years later during the heyday of vérité. During the war (*Fires Were Started*) and especially during the postwar decade, the representational convention evolved so much that the resulting docudrama format (*Quiet One, Strange Victory*, and the *Mental Mechanisms* series) seemed the unamimous style on the eve of the vérité breakthrough, although voice-over narrations by subjects sometimes superimposed a presentational level (*Paul Tomkowicz: Street-Railway Switchman* or *All My Babies*) on representational films from those years.

The first wave of vérité or direct technology, cresting in the early sixties, continued the representational mode of performance. At the same time, vérité radically revised its execution. The new technology was often able to dispense with mise-en-scène, though not with performance, to follow an event or performance without "setting it up." While much of the studio paraphernalia of rehearsals and retakes, and so forth, was no longer necessary, the code of not looking at the camera, whether implicit or explicit, was still in force—at least in the United States. The classical American vérité filmmakers systematically snipped out all looks at the camera in order to preserve the representational illusion. It didn't matter that even the most noninterventionist camera instigated palpable performance on the part of subjects, tacitly understood and enacted as part of the representational code: has anyone seen hospital workers or high school teachers as conscientious, flamboyant, and downright cinematic as those who performed their daily jobs for Wiseman? The subject in a Wiseman film, consenting to continue daily activity, to act naturally, and to perform the pretense that there is no camera or crew, consenting to show the putative audience their lives, is performing at a most basic level. The pretense, the disavowal of performance on the part of filmmakers, editors, and subjects, is at the heart of the basic contradiction of cinéma vérité—the contradiction between the aspiration to observational objectivity and its actual subjectively representational artifice. Small wonder that the best moments in Wiseman often involve highly histrionic individuals such as *Hospital*'s black "schizophrenic" hustler, fighting the system for his self-reliance while flirting with the camera operator, or the bad-tripping art student who waxes melodramatic indeed ("I don't want to die") amid the floods of vomit and the most attentive audience he has ever had. These social actors become such memorable film actors because their clearly inscribed awareness of the camera amplifies their performance and transcends the representational pretense of vérité observation.

Small wonder also that two important genres of vérité have outshone Wiseman's cold observational eye in the marketplace to this day, genres that by their subject matter bypass and compensate for vérité's disavowal of performance:

1. Films whose crews have established intimate relationships with subjects, such as *Warrendale*; *Grey Gardens*; *Harlan County, U.S.A.*; *Best Boy*; *Soldier Girls*; or *Seventeen*, leading to on-camera performances that are clearly enabled by, addressed to, and improvised enactments of that relationship, despite token adherence to the "don't look at the camera" code.

2. Films about subjects whose extrafilmic social role consists of
   public performance, including entertainers (*Jane, Burroughs,
   Comedienne,* and *Eye of the Mask*); musicians (from *Lonely Boy*
   to *Woodstock* and *Stop Making Sense* via *Antonia: A Portrait
   of the Woman*); prostitutes (*Chicken Ranch* and *Hookers on
   Davie*); politicians (*Primary, Millhouse,* and *The Right Candidate
   for Rosedale*); transpeople (*The Queens, What Sex Am I?* and
   Hookers on Davie); sexual performers (*Not a Love Story* and
   Striptease); guerillas (*Underground* and *When the Mountains
   Tremble*); bodybuilders (*Pumping Iron I* and *II*); artists (*Painters
   Painting* and *Portrait of the Artist—as an Old Lady*); teachers
   (*High School*); street kids (*Streetwise*); salespeople (*Salesman*
   and *The Store*); crusaders (*If You Love This Planet*); and clergy
   (*Marjoe*). In this group of films, special scrutiny is usually given
   to the dialectic of public and private, and the subject's identity
   is expressed by means of an onstage-offstage intercutting. The
   genre offers as one of the pleasures of the text the deciphering of
   borders between social performance, film performance, and so-
   called private behavior and the discovery that the borders are both
   culturally encoded and imaginary.

Interviews and Beyond

Now, of course, within North American documentary, we have been back in
a phase since the early seventies where presentational forms of performance
are very much in vogue. The seventies revived the interview in the documentary, thanks largely to the feminists, the New Left, and such individual
pioneers as Emile de Antonio. The eighties has witnessed a flourishing wave
of hybrid experimentation with these presentational modes as well as with
stylizations of representational modes, including dramatization, a wave that
has been termed, not surpisingly, "postdocumentary" (Pevere 1986, 39).
The current repertory includes a whole spectrum of performance elements,
usually incorporated within hybrid works, as often as not alongside vestiges
of earlier styles, from voice-of-God direct-address narration to observational
vérité to the interview and compilation conventions of the seventies. The
following is a brief tabulation, offered simply as a suggestion of the richness
and range of the evolving performance vocabulary since the sixties.

I. Presentational

- Social actors perform formal oral narrative, both fiction (*Story-telling*) and nonfiction (*When the Mountains Tremble*)
- Social actors perform daily life presentationally (*Rate It X* and *24 Heures ou plus*)
- Social actors explore geographical setting of their past at instigation of filmmaker (*Burroughs* and *The Life and Times of Rosie the Riveter*)
- Social actors present musical performances (*La Turlute des années dures*; *Before Stonewall*; *Silent Pioneers*; and *Bombay, Our City*)
- Interviews: social actors analyze present (*Not a Love Story* and *Dark Circle*) or remember the past in archival/historical format (*Union Maids* and *The Times of Harvey Milk*); also, marathon autobiographical format (*Word is Out* and *Portrait of Jason*)
- Social actors present monologues (*The Life and Times of Rosie the Riveter* and *Rate It X*)

━

II. Representational

- Social actors role-play or dramatize improvisationally real-life situation (*A Bigger Splash* and *Michael, A Gay Son*)
- Social actors perform or improvise fictive or "mise-en-présence" situation created by filmmaker (*Waiting for Fidel*)
- Social actors perform daily lives, representationally (*Seventeen, Streetwise, Québec-Haïti, and Mother Tongue*)
- Group discussions represented by social actors (*Rape* and *Pink Triangles*)
- Indecipherable mixture of real and professional actors in scripted improvisational situation (*Prostitute*)
- Professional actors reconstruct a real-life situation (*Le Dernier glacier*)
- Professional actors reconstruct an event (*In the King of Prussia*) with the help of social actors and transcript
- Professional actors in scripted historical reconstruction employ simulated documentary codes (*Edvard Munch*)
- Representational autobiographical personae perform in investigative documentary format (*Not a Love Story, Dark Lullabies,* and *Rate It X*)

- Social actors dramatize representationally their own social conditions, contextualized presentationally (*Quel numéro what number?* and *Not Crazy Like You Think*)
- Social actors dramatize representationally their collective history, contextualized presentationally (*Two Laws*)
- Composite documentary characterizations performed presentationally by actors (*What You Take for Granted*)
- Pseudo-vérité docudrama plus autobiographical voice of filmmaker (*Daughter Rite*)
- Professional and nonprofessional performers construct intertextual essay on sociopolitical situation, including elements as diverse as transcript-based dramatization and semifictional autobiographical improvisation (*Far from Poland*)

A timely intervention by Bill Nichols has pointed out a central problem of authority and voice arising from the seventies trend for interview films, namely those mostly historiographical texts reacting against vérité discourses, building on the de Antonio model and addressing feminist or New Left constituencies. The model is very familiar: representative subjects offer interview performances of personal reminiscences or present experience that figure large in a documentary investigation of a politically apt topic. Nichols's criticism is directed at those documentaries in which the authority of the filmmaker is diffused through, or uncritically hidden behind, the voices of the subjects. The best-known example of this risk is New Day Films' *Union Maids*, in which the evasions and nostalgias of the subjects' oral histories become the liabilities of the film as a whole. Although "interviews diffuse authority," Nichols argues,

> a gap remains between the voice of a social actor recruited to the film and the voice of the film . . . The greatest problem has been to retain that sense of a gap between the voice of interviewees and the voice of the text as a whole. [In *The Day After Trinity*] the text not only appears to lack a voice or perspective of its own, the perspective of its character-witnesses is patently inadequate . . . the text disappears behind characters who speak to us . . . we no longer sense that a governing voice actively provides or withholds the imprimatur of veracity according to its own purposes and assumptions, its own canons of validation . . . the film becomes a rubber stamp . . . the sense of hierarchy of voices becomes lost. (Nichols 1983, 265–66)

The problem of the disappearing voice, however, is not intrinsic to the interview performance mode—it may just as well be a condition of state funding for most of the films in question. In any case, it would be extremely foolish to disparage the tremendous advances in popular social history and the political enfranchisement enabled by the interview genre or to disallow filmmakers' choices to mute their individual voices in favor of providing a forum for a voice that has been suppressed, forgotten, or denied by media access. Nichols points to several films, such as *Rosie the Riveter* and de Antonio's works—in which the self-reflexive contextualization of interviews allows the filmmaker's analytic perspective to complement and coexist with, without drowning out, the voices of subjects. The disappearance of the voice derives less from the interview format than from a lack of focus in conceptualization, research, and political goals or from self-censorship triggered by funding from the Public Broadcasting Corporation, the National Film Board (NFB), or the National Endowment for the Humanities (NEH). It can also be derived from a fuzzy and sentimental populism leading to what Jeffrey Youdelman has described as an abdication of political leadership on the part of media intellectuals or to the absence of historical contextualization with which both Youdelman and Chuck Kleinhans have taxed *The War at Home* (Youdelman 1982, 8–15; Kleinhans 1984, 318–42). Ethics also enters into the picture whether it is a question of responsibility to the subject or to the spectator. The latter is certainly not served by the camouflage of the terms of the construction of the discourse: Does the spectator not have the right to know who is speaking; what the author's political relationship to the speaker is; and how, to whom, and to what end the film is addressed?

Nichols diagnoses this latter problem by focusing on corrective self-reflexive tendencies in much of the best current work. However, it is more pertinent to this article to focus on evolving performance styles in the same work, particularly on the very promising excursions into the presentational mode, which in any case have much in common with Nichols's prescription of self-reflexivity. In fact the self-reflexivity of some of the films he refers to, such as *Rape, Rosie the Riveter*, and *Atomic Café*, is constructed through the counterpoint of dramatized elements with other modes (though it is only in the first named that these elements are original live-action materials). The most visible and innovative pattern in the current decade is in fact the expansion of performance input by social actors that goes beyond the oral history format of the seventies to experiment with dramatic performance modes, both presentational and representational. The new visibility of dramatized and semifictional performance components constitutes a reaction against the "string-of-interview" orthodoxy. Dramatization is clearly a useful means of fleshing out the gaps left by the interview format, gaps of a technical or ideological nature, or gaps simply due to uncontrollable factors and tact (as in *Michael, A Gay Son*, in which a very tense "coming out" encounter with the protagonist's hostile family is conveyed through fictionalized role-playing). It is not surprising that the new "dramatized" documentaries (or "docudramas," as they are called in some quarters, misleadingly I think, since the term is used most commonly for fictionalized reconstructions like the U.S. television films *The Missiles of October* or *The Atlanta Child Murders*)[2] may be divided like all their forebears into the following:

1. Those whose emphasis or context is presentational (*In the King of Prussia, Far from Poland, The Kid Who Couldn't Miss, Two Laws, Not Crazy Like You Think*, or *Quel numéro what number?*—in fact films Nichols would call self-reflexive)
2. Those whose primary address is representational (*Michael, A Gay Son*; *What You Take for Granted*; *Journal inachevé*; *Democracy on Trial*; *When the Mountains Tremble*; *Le Dernier glacier*; *Caffé Italia*; or *The Masculine Mystique*)

Needless to say, the new expansion of the repertory into the terrain of dramatization has greatly multiplied the importance of performance in documentary as a whole and greatly expanded the opportunities for social actors to "perform" their lives in every format from semifictional improvisation to didactic sketches.

The eclecticism of the expanded hybrid repertory sharpens our sense of our relation to our documentary past. One useful observation is that the more presentational of these new elements formats are most in keeping with the traditional documentary genius for incorporating the presence and performance of social actors into the cinematic text. The more representational films seem inclined more toward the tradition of "docu-flavored" fiction (de Sica/Rossellini, Cassavetes, McBride, Loach/Garnett). From another point of view, the new repertory removes us yet another step away from the sixties: the small amount of work still appearing in an unadulterated vérité style (*Middletown* or *The Store*) seems purist indeed, even classical, and reminds us that the sixties is no longer the definitive formative training ground for today's documentarists but more and more yet another period style available for postmodern recycling. On the other hand, the new work looks back in a very vivid way to the years of the Popular Front, in particular the "wide variety of styles" that characterized such late-thirties films as *The Spanish Earth* or *Native Land*.

It is not surprising that the thirties are evoked more than any other period by the present work. For Ivens and his contemporaries were no strangers to several contextual conditions that have influenced today's alignment of a hybrid performance-based documentary style with an atmosphere of increasing political polarization and crisis and of cultural attrition:

1. Economic factors may have been predominant: after the late seventies and the arts funding crisis of the Reagan–Thatcher–Mulroney era, very few independents other than Wiseman, the National Film Board, and a handful of TV-funded artists have been able to afford the high-ratio budget of representational vérité (except perhaps in video). Sustaining the representational illusion is too expensive for the austerity of the eighties, and presentational elements offer filmmakers and subjects alike more control over the event in front of the camera and the budget. In the prewar period, for similar reasons, it was no accident that it was with the (relatively) luxurious state-supplied budget for *Power and the Land* that Ivens left behind the off-the-cuff hybridity of his earlier films for the graceful representational coherence of that film.

2. The fact that the new presentational performance modes were pioneered by political filmmakers, whether feminists or other progressives, is highly pertinent. In this regard, we've arrived once more back at Ivens, the Old Left grandfather of New Left political documentarists and their contemporaries. For Ivens, the protovérité style that he called "easy naturalism" precluded the organized communication of "content value," that is, the psychological or atmospheric texturing obscured the social text. Social documentarists generations later independently came to the same conclusion: pure representational vérité was often a medium of aestheticist psychologism that by itself often precluded the political explorations that such filmmakers sought to produce. I would like to look further at this issue in my concluding section.

3. Other factors in the current postvérité configuration must not be discounted, though they are decidedly minor. First, the critical acceptance of the presentational performance style was encouraged by the popularity of Brechtian theory in film culture persisting since 1968. A certain cross-fertilization may also have occurred with a presentational countertradition outside of Anglo-Saxon culture that predates the current phenomenon by a whole generation. This tradition, originating in France (Rouch and Marker) and in Quebec (Pierre Perrault and a national

documentary tradition known as the "le direct"), has never had
any commitment to representational illusion. Since the late fifties,
this tradition has accumulated a rich repertory of presentational
elements, elevating verbal and interactional performances to a
degree of exceptional expressiveness. Although Rouch is a household word among documentarists (and Perrault would be were he
from Paris rather than Montreal), this possible cross-fertilization
remains a subject for future research since the cross-linguistic
circulation of this cinema has been greatly hampered by its
privileging of speech and oral culture. Finally, the postmodernist
absorption and recycling of the presentational television vernacular is surely as important as it is hard to quantify as an element of
the new documentary performance style.

Performance and Collaboration

The title of Ivens's 1940 article in *Film*, "Collaboration in Documentary,"
is more than just a literal description of the relationship engendered by
the mise-en-scène of subject performance by filmmaker. "Collaboration"
also embodies a perennial ideal of the documentary tradition, the goal of
a changed, democratized relationship between artist and subject. The subject's performance for the camera becomes a collaboration, a stake in, and
a contribution to the authorship of the work of art. Performance becomes
a gauge of the ethical and political accountability of the filmmaker's relationship with subject.

Although Ivens's respect for the integrity of his cast is obvious,
his distance from the democratic ideal of collaborative performance is
problematical. He admits quite openly to manipulating and tricking his
"performers" into performing and of keeping them in the dark as to film
techniques and as to the results of their own performance. These less-than-
egalitarian terms of the collaboration were necessary, he claims (not unlike
some Method director who has terrorized his leading lady) to preserve
elements of freshness in the performance. Unwittingly, Ivens points to an
ethical liability of the representational mode during its classical phase, a
problem that surfaces perhaps even more acutely in the work of Ivens's
contemporary, Flaherty.

I mentioned earlier the dichotomy in Flaherty's work between his two
silent ethnographic features with their presentational elements and his later
mytho-narrative features based exclusively on representational performances. The issue of collaboration seems to be the crux of this dichotomy.

The absence of presentational elements in *Man of Aran* and *Louisiana Story* is surely an index of the same films' minimization of the input of the subjects and of their virtual embargo on the cultural textures and social realities of the Aran (West Irish) and Cajun communities, respectively. It is true that in both films rudimentary voice tracks gently ruffle the surface of the seamless representational unity: In the former, the performers improvise semisynchronized dialogue-commentary over the edited film, and in the latter, Flaherty's voice-over commentary is interpolated by a few awkward and static direct-sound sequences of an expository nature. But the verbal performances of the actors in either case do not constitute a qualitative heightening of their collaborative input—especially in *Louisiana* with the heavily scripted and heavily rehearsed feel of the dialogue. The representational web is ultimately as intact as the hegemony of authorial vision and control over ethnographic mission and subject input. The legendary contribution of "Nanook" to the film that bears his name is by now a distant memory and an inoperative ideal.

A decade after *Louisiana*, the introduction of direct sound technology into the documentary arena transformed the potential for subject collaboration as surely as it transformed the nature of subject performance. Vérité, as I have stated, failed to push this potential as far as it would go by retaining the representational mode of documentary performance. By the time the vérité movement had consolidated direct sound as the everyday vocabulary of the documentary, grassroots political movements were beginning to profit from the hitherto untapped political potential of the new apparatus. The New Left of the late sixties, and especially the women's movement a few years later, embraced speech and intercommunication as a political process, favored participatory and collaborative cultural forms, and privileged oral history as an essential means of political and cultural empowerment. It is not surprising then that their documentary cinema featured presentational performance elements from the simple interview and group discussion formats[3] of the early years to the more complex formats I have listed. Incorporating vocal performances into a film was a crucial strategy for an artist who wished to share creative and political control with subjects/social actors. Whereas vérité had by and large retained the Flahertian mystique of authorial control, the presentational modes of the New Left and the women's movement dissipated that mystique and permitted varying degrees of subject input into the finished documentary and subject responsibility for his or her image and speech. The ideal to which such filmmakers subscribed, to greater or lesser degree, was that the documentarist was the resource person, technician, or facilitator and the subject-performer was the real steward of creative responsibility (see chapter 6).

Such a prescriptive distinction between the political and ethical advantages of a specific formal strategy of course runs the risk of aesthetic idealism and political naiveté, not to mention the technological fallacy: the power of the filmmaker is such that ultimately no strategy is the automatic guarantee of collaborative process. Even the most presentational, collaborative performance is subject to ethical abuse in the editing room or exhibition context. Ultimately, the creative and political accountability of the artist is clearly the final guarantor against political and ethical abuses. However, this caveat having been registered, a concluding glimpse at two recent Canadian documentaries that focus on a similar subject clarifies the political dimension of the distinction between presentational and representational modes that I would like to insist on as a general guideline to the issues of the artist's accountability to subject performance and collaboration.

Bonnie Klein's National Film Board of Canada feature *Not a Love Story: A Film about Pornography* and Kay Armatage's independent short *Striptease* consider aspects of the sex industry through predominantly representational and presentational approaches, respectively. With *Not a Love Story*, the relationship between the on-screen filmmaker persona, embarked on her voyage of discovery of the pornographic night, and her guide, ex-stripper Linda Lee Tracy, is conveyed representationally through traditional vérité. Much of the criticism of the film centered on the manipulative appearance of this relationship between artist and collaborator. The narrative thread of the relationship includes two sex performance interludes set in representational frames (Tracy as a stripper on location in a Montreal club and as centerfold model in the studio of a *Hustler* photographer) and an ultimate conversion dénouement in which filmmaker and stripper discuss the latter's reformed vision of her past and future. This thread is intercut with interviews with feminist authorities on the subject. Caught up in the emotional charge of the subject, the audience may not notice that the distribution of representational and presentational roles in the film follows a certain hierarchy. The former sex worker Tracy is caught in a representational role, while the recruited intellectuals perform their role of analysis and polemics within the presentational interview formats. It is not difficult to conclude that the democratic ideals of feminism have been sacrificed in the process—are sex workers themselves less entitled than intellectuals to verbalize directly about the sex industry? Furthermore, the specter of voyeurism and visual pleasure is raised by the strong construction of observational discourse in Tracy's two principal representational scenes of sexual performance, with their assault on conventional

notions of tact and their inescapable flirtation with the pornographic
discourse that is the target of the film. To compare the *Hustler* posing
session, with its scandalous aura of brutality and complicity (the female
photographer applies "pussy juice" before the take) with, say, the similar
scenes from the improvised but fictionalized *Prostitute* where the sexual
performance scenes are lucid, controlled, and self-reflexive, demonstrates
the clear shortcomings of representational vérité and the great advantage
of dramatization in the domain of sexual politics.

Armatage's *Striptease* has surprisingly more clarity and complexity
than *Not a Love Story* despite its infinitely more modest means: strip-
pers and other sex-industry workers present themselves in interviews and
monologues and present their work in erotic dance performances constructed solely for the camera (in *Prostitute*, at the other end of the scale,
they perform semifictional dramatizations within a self-reflexive narrative,
collaboratively scripted, to similar effect). In *Striptease*, the sex industry
is not validated, but its workers are: as with *Prostitute*, subject-generated
performance, sharpened by its presentational mode, ensures that the
dignity and subjectivity of the subjects are respected along with their right
to present themselves and to define their images and their lives. As for the
problem of voyeurism, I suspect that the visual pleasure of the spectator

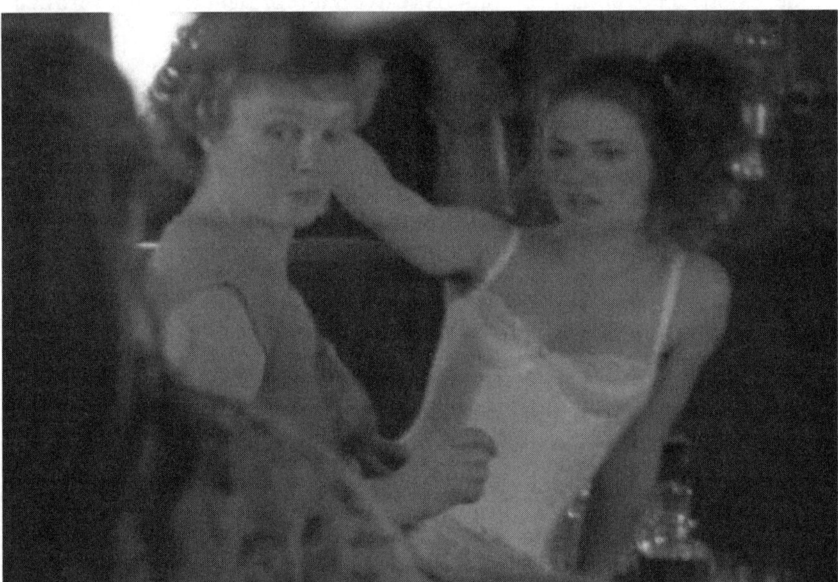

Not a Love Story: A Film about Pornography (Bonnie Sherr Klein, 1981). Ex-
stripper Linda Lee Tracy (right) "representationally" performs her posing session
for the *Hustler* photographer, but the film's feminist intellectuals perform "presentationally" elsewhere in the film.

is complicated by the explicit aura of control that characterizes the sexual
performance. It is no coincidence that a collective political solution is
thereby glimpsed (unionization) that makes Klein's ambiguous individual
moral solution all the more superficial.

▶

Voice and First-Person Performance

Not a Love Story has been criticized also for the autobiographical presence
within the diegesis of author Bonnie Klein. The first-person performance
seemed ineffectual both in terms of cinematic charisma presumably but
more importantly also in terms of the issue of authorial voice. As Nichols
puts it, this first-person presence lacks both the "self-validating, authoritative tone of a previous [voice-of-god] tradition" and "seem[s] to refuse a
privileged position in relation to other characters" (Nichols 1981, 265).
Submitting both to the authoritative testimony of the stellar lineup of
expert witnesses and to the grandstanding of her representational protagonist Tracy, the diegetic Klein serves rather as a timid, inconclusive, perhaps
faux-naïf guide throughout the pornographic nightmare. Similar problems
are posed by the whole tradition of autobiographical performance from
the first-person narrations of Flaherty (*The Land*) and John Huston (*The
Battle of San Pietro*) in the forties to the Me Decade's self-presentations
of everyone from Werner Herzog (*La Soufrière*) to the NFB's Derek May
(*Mother Tongue*) and Michael Rubbo (*Waiting for Fidel*, etc.). It seems
to me that the first-person format too often limits documentary to the
exploratory phase and pegs it at the level of political evasion, bewildering empiricism, and individual moral or metaphysical floundering. Even
where it is rigorously self-reflexive as with Jill Godmilow, the personal is
perhaps shown to be political, but the political often fails to rise above
the personal level. While the first-person performance does undeniably
provide a manageable dramatic entry to the enormously complex subjects
of pornography, Solidarity (*Far from Poland*), and the Holocaust (*Dark
Lullabies* or *Shoah*), it does not necessarily serve the political dissection
of these subjects. It may be argued that the strategy seems best suited for
properly individual, autobiographical subjects such as intrafamily relationships (*Best Boy* or *Coming Home*) or for the feminist genre that connects
individual socialization to broader political forces (*Daughter Rite, Joyce at
34*, and *Home Movie*).

While the problems of authorial voice are addressed in part by the
strategy of authorial performance, more often than not the improvised
authorial performances, representational in such films as *Not a Love Story*,

presentational and self-reflexive in such films as *Far from Poland*, raise more other issues than they solve. A whole range of other issues are raised by autobiographical performance in documentary—from ethics to narcissism to demographic representativity of the mediaworker caste—but these are beyond the scope of this paper and are receiving due critical attention (Katz 1978; Gross et al. 1988; Lane 2002).

▶

Conclusion: The Right to Play Oneself

I have offered a historical overview of the presence of performance in documentary. I have discerned alternating and simultaneous impulses toward presentational and representational performances throughout the documentary tradition, then briefly engaged the current debate about voice in political documentary, and finally only touched on the distinct subcategory of autobiographical performance. All of this has led to a global assertion of the special aptness of the presentational mode in the present context, alongside both an insistence on the continuing relevance of the interview format of oral history popularized in the seventies and an enthusiastic welcoming of the current experimentation with hybrid performance modes including dramatization. Subject performance, affirmed and enriched as a presentational element of documentary film, remains a means by which the most committed of documentary filmmakers can aspire to the realization of their democratic ideals. Collaboration between artist and subject, as elaborated by Joris Ivens at the end of the thirties, remains a meaningful political ideal as well as an artistic strategy, but the terms he set out have been somewhat transformed. "Acting to play oneself" is still the key, but "Don't look at the camera" is replaced by "Look at the camera" as a "basic necessity" of documentary collaboration. In the same decade, Walter Benjamin spoke of "modern man's legitimate claim to be reproduced"; might we not add that the individual has now established the claim also to construct that reproduction, the right to play oneself?

[5]   *Beyond Vérité*

Emile de Antonio (1977; 2008)

This much-reworked article on the pioneer of American documen-tary, Emile de Antonio, was my first publication, thanks to Jump Cut's *gracious commitment to long, long, too long term papers. I remember getting the first page back well marked up, but it seemed by the lack of red ink thereafter the three editors began actually to like the piece (despite Chuck Kleinhans's reservations about de Antonio's wild-card leftism). Bill Nichols grabbed it shortly after its initial appearance in print for the "genre section" in his legend-ary University of California Press textbook anthology* Movies and Methods, Vol. II *(1985), and goddess knows how many luckless undergraduates were forced to read all twenty-five pages. Nich-ols's introduction to the piece chided me gently for my overstated denigration of American cinéma vérité: "his criticism of cinéma vérité may be heavy handed." Nichols had progressed from being an authority on Newsreel collective's low-budget hybridity to Freder-ick Wiseman's big-budget vérité purism (he was about to publish a still-unsurpassed section on Wiseman in* Ideology and the Image *in 1981), but whatever stake he might have had in his critique of my high school-debater setup of de Antonio versus vérité it was justi-fied and I knew it. One thing Nichols did not call me on was my intransigent animosity to modernism and the New York art world in particular, an attitude that had been fomented by the networks of Columbia and New York University grad students with whom I was wrangling as I was writing this essay and whose attitude to the avant-garde I found unsufferably arrogant, elitist, imperialist, and politically off the mark—epitomized by Annette Michelson's "we had Eisenstein so we could have Brakhage" piece that had appeared in* Artforum *in 1973.*[1]

*This chapter's second section, a review of de Antonio's film
about the Weather Underground called* Underground *when it finally
appeared in May 1976, just as the first part of my essay was about
to hit the stands, also saw the light of day in* Jump Cut *at the end
of 1976 and suffers from being a bit too exhaustive. This was the
year I was hired by Concordia as an "all-but-dissertation" doctoral
candidate with the assets of Canadian citizenship, bilingualism, an
Ivy League pedigree, and one publication in* Jump Cut. *Those were
the days. This chapter's third section has been written specially for
this book in an effort to make the chapter comprehensive by including textual appreciations of de Antonio's final two films. Delivered
more than thirty years later, this final section contains its own
scene-setting introduction and obviously differs in tone from the
earnest self-seriousness of the pre-PhD job market go-getter of the
mid-seventies.*

*For one thing, the original de Antonio piece appeared before I'd
officially "come out" in* Jump Cut *a couple of years later, well after
I was hired. I was sure at the time that my hetero credentials were
impeccable for the Concordia hiring committee, but I now see that
there's a reference to Ethel Merman that should have caused some
suspicion. In any case I will leave it to the reader to develop a preference for the sober but gung-ho Parts I and II or the introspective,
retrospective, and even sentimental part III.*

Part I: Mid-Career Appraisal (1974–76)

The appearance of a whole series of impressive new documentaries over the
last few years—*Painters Painting, I. F. Stone's Weekly, Attica, Antonia,* and
Hearts and Minds are the best known—is a reminder that, with mid-decade
suddenly upon us, the U.S. documentary not only is showing remarkable
signs of vitality but also is moving purposefully forward through the seventies in its own unique direction. And it is a direction that, for all its diversity,
is markedly distinct from the cinéma vérité impulse that dominated the sixties. Despite the continuing voices of Wiseman, the Maysles, and others still
using the idiom of a decade ago, there is no doubt that the seventies have
already added a new chapter to the history of the U.S. documentary. *Gimme
Shelter*, now five years old, and even *An American Family*, almost three,
already seem curiously dated in the shadow of this imposing new chapter.

A general overview of the new films is already long past due; even radical journals, let alone *The New York Times*, have shown a tendency toward a helter-skelter, ad hoc reception of each new film as it appears, rather than a more historical estimation of the new documentaries as parts of a totality. The Museum of Modern Art's recent retrospective of the films of Emile de Antonio, most recently the director of *Painters Painting* (1972) and a film-in-progress on the Weather Underground, is an occasion to answer this need. De Antonio, long a dissenter from the cinéma vérité mainstream of the sixties—his first film, *Point of Order* dates from 1963—is confirmed in his seven-film retrospective as the pioneer and the foremost practitioner of the new documentary sensibility that has at long last reached the fore. The increasing publicity that surrounds de Antonio's work, such as his elevation by *Rolling Stone* to the status of radical saint (Biskind and Weiss 1975), reinforces the need for a comprehensive evaluation of this filmmaker's career in the cultural, political, and theoretical context that formed it.

The original impetus for cinéma vérité, as is well known, had been a technological revolution, an upheaval as radical in its own way as the introduction of the talkies had been thirty years earlier. With the first introduction of the handheld cameras and portable recorders in the late fifties, there was a sudden burst on both sides of the Atlantic of nonfiction films celebrating the new accessibility of "truth"—truth in the surface textures of audiovisual reality, in the immediacy of present time, and in the nuance of spontaneous behavior. Close on the heels of their French and Canadian contemporaries, Richard Leacock and others grouped around Drew Associates rushed into the streets with their "caméra-stylos" and discovered, as if for the first time, the vitality of "unmediated" existence. They talked of honesty, intimacy, and above all objectivity as if these old brickbats of aesthetics had been invented along with the Nagra.

This claim to a new privileged grasp of reality, which supplanted the old "subjective" documentary modes of discourse, now appears in retrospect to have been somewhat naive. Leacock and the others were of course right to hate the old newsreel voice-overs that had hammered away at U.S. audiences for generations, each inflection delivering its prepackaged interpretation of the "facts." (Later de Antonio was to derive a brilliant ironic effect from newsreel clips of Nixon's red-baiting days in *Millhouse* [1971], his analysis of the Nixon phenomenon.) Yet the U.S. voice-over with its abuses had not been the only alternative for the classical documentarist. The French had developed a distinguished tradition of the narrated documentary in which sober and unobtrusive Gallic voice-overs were personal and suggestive rather than pontifical. Alain Resnais, and later

Chris Marker, were the most celebrated arbiters of this genre of documentary. Accordingly, the French cinéma vérité movement (or "cinéma direct" as the Gallic manifestation of it is properly called) led by Jean Rouch used the spoken word as an essential material and structural principle. In fact, direct cinema's most radical achievement was as a cinema of sounds.

In contrast, the U.S. filmmakers reacted to their heritage of the authoritarian voice-over with an affirmation of the supposed objectivity of the unmediated image, creating a predominantly visual documentary form. Their aesthetic of the image, spontaneous, random, and true, was in effect a gospel of subjectivity and too often, as it turned out, of inarticulateness as well. The movement's most serious liability was not this subjectivity per se but its persistent pretense of impartiality.

Most of the films of the era bore highly charged emotional statements beneath their posture of objectivity—uncritical adulation in *Stravinsky* (1965), euphoria in *Woodstock* (1970), condescension in *Happy Mothers' Day* (1963), contempt in *Sixteen in Webster Groves* (1966), contempt in *Titicut Follies* (1967). In fact, contempt was probably the predominant tone of the entire cinéma vérité movement (probably since contempt is the stance that comes most easily to East Coast liberalism when it interacts with middle America). And contempt is the most visible residue of cinéma vérité in a film such as *Hearts and Minds* (1974) in its weakest moments.

If the artifacts of cinéma vérité now seem in retrospect to have captured so much of the spirit of their age, it is their embrace of inarticulateness, spontaneity, and entrenched emotionalism—not their aspiration to objectivity—that above all seemed linked to the decade of campus disturbances, ghetto riots, assassinations, and a counterculture based on uncritical iconoclasm. Cinéma vérité bore the imprint of all the ambiguous romanticism of the Greening of America, its adventurism as well as its fervor.[2]

The challenge to base the new consciousness in concrete change— and the Vietnam War—gave the counterculture its fatal test and provided cinéma vérité with a challenge that proved equally fatal. It was a challenge as insurmountable as the Depression had been for twenties avant-gardism two generations earlier. Cinéma vérité per se had nothing to contribute to the real job that faced the counterculture; it merely reflected and reinforced a mood that in itself was not enough. As the war escalated and escalated, cinéma vérité people were preoccupied with rock concerts and easy targets like police chief conventions and boot camps, some moving gracelessly into the commercial arena. To be sure, they often provided undeniably profound and touching works of art, but their films failed to meet the increasing need for explicit sociopolitical analysis to support the momentum of the alternative politics. This failure of Leacock, Wiseman, and others was a particularly bitter one because of their widespread reputation as social critics and because of the broad-based, potentially activist, liberal audience they addressed. Documentary has a special mystique in the English-speaking world, an aura of social responsibility not shared by the fiction film, which is perhaps its legacy from Grierson. The filmmakers were far more involved in the mystique than in the social issues they dealt with.

Nevertheless, Leacock and his contemporaries had developed an expressive and flexible language that was available for radical social criticism even if they themselves declined to use it in that direction. And three distinct currents of dissident filmmaking did emerge in the Vietnam era, all more or less adapting this language to their own particular goals. The current with the most immediate and diffuse (and no doubt the least radical) impact was based on a series of controversial television documentaries that appeared sporadically during those years, both on PBS and the commercial networks. Here, as might be expected, analytic rigor and conscience were the necessary sacrifice to the medium's huge audience potential. Nevertheless, a number of creditable documentary examinations of domestic social problems appeared from time to time. These effectively continued the intermittent but impressive tradition of conscientious broadcasting initiated by Edward Murrow in his early fifties anti-McCarthy broadcasts. Morton Silverstein's 1967 exposé of conditions for southern black migrants on Long Island farms, *What Harvest for the Reaper?* (1969), was widely praised as a sequel to Murrow's classic denunciation of the same social evil in his 1960 *Harvest of Shame. What Harvest for the Reaper?* relied almost exclusively on cinéma vérité techniques, although it was structured by voice-over narration (like most television documentaries).

A later film by Silverstein, *Banks and the Poor* (1970), which was also shown on PBS, is perhaps the most praiseworthy of this category of films during the Nixon era. It is a searing and moving indictment of the victimization of the urban poor by neighborhood banks and lending institutions. Its highlights include a hidden-camera scene in a ghetto loan office in which an unsuspecting loan shark does his pitch for a prospective client and, most memorably, an interview with a tearful black woman whose house has just been dispossessed because of a liability of only a few dollars. The canned rebuttals and denials by bank officials, including David Rockefeller, offer sharp contrast with the authenticity of the vérité language as Silverstein uses it. Here a compelling Brechtian collage effect, the clash of document and actuality, is achieved, and collage is, as we shall see, one of Emile de Antonio's trademarks. A 1968 CBS documentary, *Hunger in America* by Martin Carr and Peter Davis, was less successful, clumsy with its interviewing, and more interested in snags in welfare distribution than in the roots of the problem under scrutiny.

Only a few critical assessments of the ongoing war made it to television, understandably. Only rarely did the networks' coverage of the war yield any insight as powerful as Silverstein's domestic analysis had been. The first breakthrough here was a controversial PBS broadcast of a long segment of Felix Greene's *Inside North Vietnam* (1968), a film CBS had originally planned to show before losing its nerve. This capsule tour of enemy territory also had a limited art house distribution despite federal harassment. More important was Peter Davis's critical look at the Department of Defense in 1971, only obliquely aimed at the war, *The Selling of the Pentagon*. This denunciation of the Pentagon's promotional activities was a masterful blend of cinéma vérité language (watching children play on display bombers, for example) and traditional TV documentary structures (a voice-over commentary by Roger Mudd, official statements from the Pentagon denying all, etc.). Of course, these few successes do not substantially alter the overwhelmingly dismal record of the network news departments during those years. But what else is new?

A second current of dissident documentary during these years was based on efforts by a number of Movement[3] filmmakers, both individual and collective, to compensate for this media void. Few of these had any delusions about their potential for reaching a constituency anywhere as broad as a television audience, or even, for that matter, much broader than the already converted radical community. Impeccable in their directness and uncompromising in their anger, such filmmakers initiated a whole tradition of alternate radical documentary that is still going strong. This tradition's base was the network of radical communities scattered across the urban and campus centers of the country, its continuity often broken and its internal liaison often exceedingly fragile. This tradition tended to emphasize depth of impact rather than breadth. And for a while screenings with discussions were the pattern, until coordination problems proved too much.

In the early days, this movement's chief impetus came from the New York and San Francisco chapters of Newsreel, an organization whose pre-credits machine gun logo is still the most recognizable symbol of this whole tradition. Newsreel's strategy of polarization and confrontation differed sharply from both the networks' stance of socially conscious journalism and de Antonio's emphasis on analysis. Such spokespeople as New York's Robert Kramer (before he turned to fiction) rejected analysis as a goal entirely, championing instead the notion of film as a weapon ("Newsreel" 1968, 45). The commitment toward analysis was an "illusion," as was the

possibility of real dissent or of real understanding of the issues. The early
Newsreel film-weapons were often criticized by radicals for an "ultra-left
disdain for quality (the larger the grain, the better the politics)" (*Cineaste*
1973, 15). In other words, the potential weaknesses of the cinéma vérité
language used indiscriminately infected many of the films, and not only
in terms of production values: thematic confusion, egotism, and ideological contradictions were rampant. Nevertheless, a number of competent,
articulate films did come to be produced on both coasts and enjoyed a
surprisingly large distribution on what was in the late sixties a burgeoning
radical circuit. Such titles as *Garbage, Chicago, Boston Draft Resistance
Group*, and *Meat Cooperative* stood out above the early glut of films during the first Nixon years. As the output of films slackened somewhat, they
seemingly improved, and it is from this middle period that the movement's
best films emerged. *People's War* (1969) was another Vietnam behind-
the-lines film; this was an important documentary subgenre until quite
recently, with its own special problems arising from varying degrees of
official Vietnamese "coauthorship." *Black Panther* and *The Woman's Film*,
two of the San Francisco products, respectively dealt with the radical black
problematic and the organization of working-class women; both films
relied heavily on cinéma vérité and interview techniques and represented
the peak of Newsreel achievement both in terms of artistic impact and
distribution range. *Richmond Oil Strike*, a 1970 chronicle of a California
strike by white workers, has a special place in the Newsreel oeuvre for its
stunning revelation of incipient revolutionary consciousness among white
union members and their wives. With these latter two films, the Newsreel
crews for once started to listen, and they tapped what has become the
alternative cinema's richest resource, the voices and consciousness of its
working class constituency. Such recent films as Julia Reichert's and Jim
Klein's *Methadone: An American Way of Dealing* (1974) brilliantly demonstrate the flexibility and power of this resource.

Other Movement filmmakers, unaffiliated with Newsreel, were
also notable. From Chicago, for example, came Howard Alk and Mike
Gray's *The Murder of Fred Hampton* (1971) and Alk's *American Revolution Two* (1969), both widely distributed, powerful documents heavily
dependent on cinéma vérité language. The former, in particular, had a
large audience and was highly praised despite its susceptibility to vérité's
rhetorical excesses. Much of its impact was due no doubt to the drama of
the event it described (a frequent tendency of Newsreel films as well); in
this case Hampton's assassination occurred halfway through the shooting of a proposed film on the Chicago Black Panthers. The result is a
film on his death, half eulogistic, half journalistic. Its most interesting

feature is a de Antonio–style interplay of Chicago police Newspeak and
its own vérité investigation of the evidence. Its ultimate effect, however, is
undercut by the artists' overly sentimental approach to the subject (long
indulgent close-ups of bereaved Panther women). This seems to be a frequent liability of white filmmakers when dealing with minority agitation,
or "other people's struggles" as one Movement veteran puts it (*Cineaste*
1973). In recent years this liability has been increasingly overcome by
radical documentarists by either concentrating on struggles closer to
home or creating films about minority struggles that have genuine roots
in their subjects' consciousness.

Despite the continuing prolific output of this alternative tradition, as
evidenced by such strong films as *Finally Got the News* (1970), *Winter
Soldiers* (1972), the methadone film, and the work of the Pacific Street Collective (*Frame Up: The Imprisonment of Martin Sostre*, 1973), this current
has always been plagued by serious distribution problems, both theoretical
and actual. Most radical filmmakers of this orientation have always relied
on existing Movement structures to exhibit and distribute their work, and
the overall result has been neither efficient, systematic, nor continuous.
Inevitably the old problem of preaching to the converted has reasserted
itself. The films by and large never reached a public beyond the radical
subculture circuit despite such attempts as Newsreel's experiments with
street projections in ghetto neighborhoods and so on. Later, the weakening
of that circuit in the seventies was disastrous, though far from fatal, for
alternative filmmaking. Nevertheless, the role of this current in stimulating
and strengthening the Movement that has persisted over the years has been
immeasurable and a worthy achievement in itself.

The third current of dissident documentary, what I have already
referred to as the new documentary of the seventies, richly heterogeneous
but epitomized by Emile de Antonio, avoids the pitfalls both of TV network compromise and the isolation of the radical circuit. Admittedly, its
audience is not composed of workers, rightly a priority for radical filmmakers, or the minority communities that Newsreel tried to reach. Its
constituency includes the radical subculture but extends far beyond that to
a wider base that often assures it a commercial viability (insofar as documentaries can ever be commercial) and a certain degree of independence
as well. Speaking directly to the urban, liberal, or intellectual middle class,
it is able to retain much of its integrity as hard-nosed social enquiry. It is
based on both the recognition of where the power really lies and on the
premise of the importance of struggling on the theoretical front as well
as on the barricades, in the realm of the liberal consciousness as well as
in ghetto neighborhoods, and of the macrocosmic perspective as well as

the microcosmic. Filmmakers with this inspiration, occasionally casual or vague about their target audience and usually middle-class intellectuals themselves, find a constituency of their peers and address themselves to the task of challenging the ideological foundation of that group. Most often such films rely on financing by wealthy liberals and on theatrical distribution in the urban and campus centers; some occasionally make it to the airwaves as well. Such filmmakers are hesitant to offer solutions—their contribution is often based on their ability to pose the correct questions, to penetrate and unsettle the liberal equilibrium. Contradictions are many—but ultimately radical discourse is extended to a broader base and significantly enriched.

Emile de Antonio has set the pattern for the new documentary and embodies its inspiration and its contradictions more than any other. As one encounters him presiding over his New York office studio, one is struck by the incongruity of a battle taken up against the whole U.S. establishment by this congenial man with enormous energy, roving conversation, and a robust sense of outrage. A laureate of the enemies list? As he looks out over Union Square he points to both the pinkness of the late afternoon sky and the spot where the huge Communist marches gathered during the thirties. He wryly recalls his participation in those marches, a leader of a contingent from Harvard (the beginning of decades of FBI surveillance of his career, as he discovered recently, thanks to the Freedom of Information Act). As he braces himself for his forthcoming lawsuit against the FBI and the CIA (invasion of privacy), an outcome of the much publicized grand jury challenge to the new Weather Underground film, one senses the exhausting emotional investment of the man in his art and in his struggle to continue asking his own unique kind of questions.

Yet for all his dedication to social change and his continuously professed allegiance to Marxism, there seems a curious isolation on his part from the mainstream of both the Left and contemporary radical film culture. There is the suggestion that his now famous fascination with the Weatherpeople stems partly from an affinity with them—an embattled obstinacy, a romantic bravado, a fierce self-dependence. As he lists the stages in his career—his years at prep school and Harvard; his service in World War II; his short-lived teaching stint (English and Philosophy at William and Mary); his aimless drift through the fifties engaging in short-term business operations and hovering on the periphery of the New York avant-garde (he points out Andy Warhol's headquarters across the street and recalls his support for Warhol at the beginning of the artist's career); his sudden, almost accidental emergence as a filmmaker—he constantly alludes to the irony that he should have made his first film when already "middle aged," as he puts it, and that his political development should have most recently taken the course of support for a famous group of underground revolutionaries while already advancing through his fifties. The overall impression is one of deadly seriousness and moral fervor, and in this, his role in the perpetuation of past traditions of documentary conscience, his place in the continuum of causes, ideals, and outcries that is his legacy as a documentarist, is a clear one.

The documentary of the seventies, then, finds its roots in this man's response to the political climate of the sixties. Like the filmmakers of the dissident television tradition and of the radical underground, de Antonio assimilated where necessary the strategies and aesthetics of the vérité mainstream that dominated the decade but adapted them to the serious and modest form suitable to his moral, didactic purposes. This form, refusing the resources of both declamatory rhetoric and self-indulgent aestheticism, expanded the documentary's potential as a medium of genuine political interrogation. The pseudo-objective cinéma vérité of the sixties was ultimately bypassed by this cinema of open commitment, research, and analysis. The new U.S. documentary recognized the camera's unavoidable subjectivity and harnessed it in the service of a conscious political orientation from the start. This seriousness, this modesty, and this commitment enabled this current to withstand the traps of commercial cooptation and political desublimation that *Woodstock* and its progeny so vividly epitomized.

Emile de Antonio, then, was hardly an eager young camera wizard like the cinéma vérité people when he made his first film, *Point of Order*, in 1963. It is significant that this first gesture of resistance to the formal and ideological orthodoxy of vérité was made by a middle-aged, ex-academic culture hobo who had never touched a camera; for the new documentary was not set off by a technological revolution as cinéma vérité had been. Its roots were more in a modulation of sensibility.

This shift from cinéma vérité to the new committed documentary echoed a similar transition forty years earlier in which the first euphoric documentaries of the twenties were replaced by those strikingly subdued products of the thirties and forties. Despite the intervening introduction of sound technology, which of course had some thematic ramifications, it was not primarily technical refinement that distinguished the typical documentaries of the twenties—the avant-garde manifestos of Ivens, Ruttman, Cavalcanti, and Vertov, not to mention the Flahertian travelogues—from the restrained, earnest films of the next two decades—the sober products of the U.S. New Deal and war effort, of the Grierson bodies in Britain and Canada, and of the Soviet First Five-Year Plan and after. Both transitions

(1930 and 1970 being only schematic approximations of their dates)
were characterized by a reassessment of the previous era's technical
revolution, by a movement from "formlessness" to "form," from poesis
to thesis, from the celebration of surfaces to the probing of meanings,
from the ecstatic experimentation with new resources to their consolidation in the services of specific analysis, questions, and statements. Both
the thirties and the seventies represent a period of technological stasis
in the field of the documentary, a pause for the arsenal of the nonfiction
filmmaker to be tested, expanded, and applied to new aesthetic and political problems, not remodeled.

Point of Order, de Antonio's first film, appeared in 1963, the same
year as the release of Leacock's *Happy Mothers' Day*, well before the
zenith of the cinéma vérité movement, and yet it deserves to be seen as
an early reaction to that movement. In fact, side-by-side, *Point of Order*
and *Happy Mothers' Day* offer a strikingly clear paradigm of the twofold
direction open to documentarists in the decade or so to follow. Leacock's
film, an often snide exploration of a South Dakota town's materialis-
tic response to the local birth of quintuplets, represents the path almost
unanimously taken during the sixties. De Antonio's film, rejected by the
New York Film Festival because it was not a film, is an examination of
the phenomenon of McCarthyism through a compilation of original video
footage of the Army-McCarthy hearings of ten years earlier. It sketches the
contours of a less crowded route.

The contrast between these two directions is fundamental. The Leacock film is pure poesis, a cinema of great intimacy yet of almost baroque
stylization, at once a celebration of the present and an implied elegy for a
mythological past. The de Antonio work is pure analysis, a cinema that is
both public and visually austere, the documents of the past explored for
their lessons for the present. Leacock's *Happy Mothers' Day* expresses its
eloquent despair in the lyrical populist Flahertian tradition. It sees the ultimate betrayal of the American ideal in ordinary townspeople but rejoices
in the equanimity and grace of the babies' mother. De Antonio localizes
the object of his despair at the very seat of power, in the Eisensteinian
manner. He presents McCarthy, his cronies, and the ineffectual politicians
McCarthy confronts (not to mention the clever lawyers on both sides) as
the personifications of a corrupt and oppressive system, just as his Soviet
predecessor saw the tsarist officers, the ineffectual Kerensky, and the fat
kulaks and priests as embodiments of reaction.

The divergence between these two directions is essentially one that is
already well explored in the twentieth century's art forms: collage versus improvisation. De Antonio's basic technique is "the use of a collage

of people, voices, images, ideas to develop a story line or a didactic line, uninterrupted by external narration" (Weiner 1971, 3). He compresses and analyzes an event, assembling and juxtaposing fragments of it. *Point of Order* represents this technique in its purest, most rudimentary form, since the act of assemblage and editing is the artist's only original contribution to the raw material. In contrast, Leacock extends and elaborates an event by intuitively circling about it, accumulating a wealth of random detail into a decoratively mythologized whole. The opposition suggested by these two approaches implies among other things the irreconcilability of mythological thought and analytic thought, of the Costa-Gavrases and the Godards, of neomythologizing and demythologizing. For the radical film-maker the implications are important. It is, of course, not surprising that it should have been the neomythologists who dominated the mainstream political cinema in the early and mid-sixties. It is a tragedy archetyp-ally American that the Newspeak newsreel voice-over should have been replaced by a mythologizing all the more insidious, the fetishizing of the image by a sensibility of alienated, individualist Romanticism.

Television has naturally had a crucial influence on the work of both Leacock and de Antonio. The opposition between the 1963 works of the two men demonstrates the distinctly different mode of this influ-ence on each. Leacock was, as we have seen, one of the first to develop an integrated aesthetics from the new hardware of the late fifties, but the importance of television both in providing the economic stimulus for its development and the forum for the public assimilation of the new idiom it entailed cannot be overemphasized. *Happy Mothers' Day* was in fact originally commissioned by ABC (and then drastically reedited for the ver-sion that was finally broadcast); and the film is notable for its reliance on a filmic syntax made accessible by television, its assumption of its audience's televisual literacy. Although the Leacock version of the film is undeniably more piquant than the reedited ABC one, it is nevertheless disturbingly guilty of the increasing tendency of television to "massage" its audience under the innocent guise of objectivity.

In contrast, though *Point of Order* is composed entirely of period television footage of the Army-McCarthy hearings, compressed in a ratio of 100:1, the result is an incisive critique of the video medium itself, a documentary parallel of Elia Kazan's *A Face in the Crowd*, the 1957 Hol-lywood denunciation of the power of the tube. *Point of Order*'s impact as self-critique is stronger because of its documentary authenticity. The alien-ating effect of seeing video on the cinema screen, and the further effect of the ten-year lapse between shooting and compilation, give the film all the more analytic power. The object of analysis becomes not only the web of

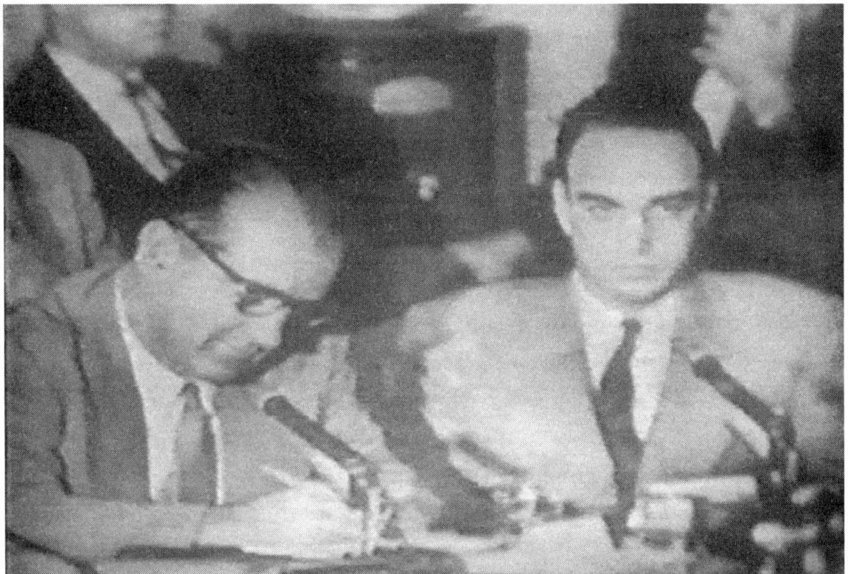

Point of Order (Emile de Antonio, 1963). Senator McCarthy (left) and flaring henchman Roy Cohn in period video footage now recycled in the service of historiographical analysis.

personality and issue involved in the historic Alice-in-Wonderland debate but also the medium itself and its power to lend dignity and legitimacy to scoundrels and demagogues, and authority and inertia to the status quo.

As de Antonio has often said, the two video cameras are the heroes of *Point of Order.* Visual rhetoric wields more weight than logic, and videogenic physiognomy and witty rejoinder have more force than conviction. Of course, the televised Senate hearings were not the first manifestation of the video politics to come. With *Millhouse,* and the later separate release of the Nixon 1952 Checkers speech segment of it, de Antonio was to trace its birth back even further. If cinema has long had a clearly articulated tradition of auto-critique, of metacinema, ranging from *Man with a Movie Camera* (1929) to *Le Gai savoir* (1969), *Point of Order* signified the coming of age of television with the now richly demonstrated possibility of the mode of metatelevision.

At the same time, *Point of Order* was also an early revelation of video's crucial potential as a tool of primary historical investigation. Period video footage now becomes an audiovisual historical record with the unassailable authority formerly held only by vintage newsreels (with the same inherent dangers of course, given video's even greater need for editing; de Antonio himself once commented that he could have made McCarthy come out looking good!). This authority is partly due to the naive, functional, purely denotative orientation of the original recording. Video's low density would seem also to minimize film's emphasis of random nuances, while it captures all the rich fabric of audiovisual inflection and detail that written history omits. Ironically, the transfer of video from the television screen to the movie screen somehow serves to absolve it of whatever lack of credibility infects it in its original, functional context. It attains purity as a document.

In this light, de Antonio appears the descendant of the first generation of Soviet cine-historians such as Esfir Shub and others, who had a comparable sense of the primary role of the film document as a raw material of historical research. Dziga Vertov's use of the cine-document was also highly skilled and all too rarely exercised, only in *Stride, Soviet!* (1926) and *Three Songs of Lenin* (1934) among his mature works. Vertov's use of newsreel footage in these films has a somewhat different orientation than Shub's or de Antonio's, more toward the modes of rhetoric and mythography than historiography proper. Nevertheless the basic maieutic rhythm arising from the conjunction of document and actuality in these films certainly anticipates de Antonio's essential strategy more than Shub's basically archival interest.

In any case, de Antonio's use of video documents, with their own freshness and impact, is his own unique contribution. Since video is a major component of the present cultural and ideological fabric of U.S. society, it becomes, with *Point of Order*, an indispensable resource for radical documentarists of both sociopolitical and historiographical intent.

Thus, while the cinéma vérité movement and *Happy Mothers' Day* celebrated the present, *Point of Order* legitimized the past as an equally rich field of documentary exploration for Americans. History ceased to mean for the filmmaker either a visual illustration of conventional historiography, such as CBS's *Twentieth Century* (1957–1970) and a host of other voice-overed, popularized historical films had been, or a pretext for heroic mythologizing, as in the Spanish Civil War subgenre represented by *To Die in Madrid* (Frédéric Rossif,1963)—a worthy exercise in itself as a prod to civilization's fading conscience but hardly a tool of new historical investigation. Instead, the documentary became a genuine instrument of historiography, a medium for diachronic social analysis with its own validity and authority, relying on visual documents in the same way that the traditional writing of history relied on written documents. (Of course, an irony is to be savored in the use of a medium, based technically on the ephemerality of the instant, as an instrument for grasping the meaning of the past.) The discovery of this potential of film and video is no doubt parallel to the changing conception of the task of history, the new emphasis, for example, on the use of oral history and, oddly enough, of statistical analysis as well.

As might be expected, U.S. film and video makers followed other groups as diverse as the Parisian Left Bank and the National Film Board of Canada in their discovery of cinema as a medium of historical analysis, though it is to their credit that they discovered video as an indispensable resource in this pursuit and have used it most successfully since. And it is no doubt video's integral auditory component, incidentally, that makes it such a valuable resource—the new documentary's revolt against the tyranny of the image was implicit in de Antonio's turn to video as the material of his first film.

As it stands, *Point of Order* is still de Antonio's only film to have been televised nationally in the United States, although there is now talk of broadcasting one or two of the others, and virtually all of them have appeared on TV in most other Western countries. When it appeared, *Point of Order* was the most controversial and critically acclaimed documentary in years (it also provoked the most hate mail) and remains today one of the most commercially successful and widely distributed of his films. Financed, as was to be the pattern, with "liberal money" and produced by New Yorker Films' Daniel Talbot, it reached a theatrical audience—unheard of for postwar documentaries (thanks in no small way to a $100,000 distribution campaign financed by Walter Reade, another unheard-of feature of the film). It is no mean feat for a documentarist to reach such a constituency, to introduce the possibility of radical discourse to the deeply prejudiced and powerful, middle-class liberal audience with its entrenched fear of Stalinist propaganda, as de Antonio can be said to have done with that first film. It is a goal on which de Antonio staked his subsequent career and one that Newsreel never even entertained.

The simple factor that most ensures de Antonio's accessibility to the "unconverted" middlebrow or intellectual audience is his respect for the integrity of the document. He retains his audience's trust by refusing to superimpose an external explanation or commentary upon his evidence. The documents speak for themselves. His didacticism in *Point of Order* as well as in his other films is democratic in a real sense. The viewer must actively meet the challenge posed by a document rather than submit to an exegesis dictated in the authoritarian manner of Louis de Rochemont, Roman Karmen, or Walter Cronkite. As de Antonio himself explained:

> I'm usually attacked for not jumping on McCarthy hard enough, or not explaining certain events with a voice-over narration. I've always thought that it's wrong to explain things to audiences. The material is there, and interpretations can be made. I mean I could have stopped the film and

inserted outside explanations, but I'm really not terribly interested in that. I disagree with that approach from every point of view aesthetically and even politically. I think it's a mistake to show everything. And I think this is what is most wrong with so-called didactic films, that they become so utterly didactic that they forget that a film is also a film. (Weiner 1971, 9)

Nevertheless, in a later interview about his Vietnam film, he expanded on a notion of "democratic didacticism" that is crucial to his work, for all its anachronistic Griersonian ring:

I have been a teacher. My work is didactic . . . I only want to think that this film on Vietnam is more complicated, has more levels of meaning than there are in a slogan or in a purely didactic message. I don't believe that such a message has any more sense than to shout in the street, "Down with war!" If you do so, that doesn't mean anything. The goal of a truly didactic work is to go beyond that and to suggest the "why." I like to describe my own feelings as democratic with a small "d," which means that if you don't want to teach things to people but to reveal things to them, you will permit them then to arrive at the same conclusion as yourself. That's a democratic didacticism, without having to say "firstly, secondly, thirdly." And that's why I insist on the word "reveal." A young American sees the film, and he doesn't hear de Antonio addressing him, but he can himself come to a conclusion about the war. (Ciment and Cohn 1970, 28)

Grierson is thus not the only ghost conjured up by this fervent ideal. The echoes of Eisenstein as well, in particular his famous invocation of Marx in *Film Sense*, are too striking to pass over and too obvious to elaborate:

The spectator is compelled to proceed along that selfsame path that the author traveled in creating the image. The spectator not only sees the represented elements of the finished work, but also experiences the dynamic process of the emergence and assembly of the image just as it was experienced by the author. And this is, obviously, the highest possible degree of approximation to transmitting visually the author's perceptions and intention in all their fullness, to transmitting them with "that strength of physical palpability" with which they arose before the author in his creative work and his creative vision.

Relevant to this part of the discussion is Marx's definition of the course of genuine investigation: "Not only the results, but the road to it also is a part of truth. The investigation of truth must itself be true, true investigation is unfolded truth, the disjuncted members of which unite in the result." The strength of the method resides also in the circumstance that the spectator is drawn into a creative act in which his individuality is not subordinated to the author's individuality, but is opened up throughout the process of fusion with the author's intention. (Eisenstein 1942, 32–33)

Of course, the question can arise whether de Antonio's appeal to a broad-based, liberal audience is consistent with the Marxist principles he professes. It is a question not easily resolved. Is his divergence from the reformist ideology of the sixties more a theoretical one than an actual one, his analytic methodology merely a style based on a theoretically constructed model of an ideal spectator who doesn't actually exist? Does de Antonio's interest in the Weatherpeople mean that his earlier faith in "democratic didacticism" has been revised? He claims not, yet the contradictions persist.

They present themselves sharply indeed in de Antonio's next film after *Point of Order, That's Where the Action Is* (1965), a fifty-minute BBC television assignment dealing with the 1965 New York mayoral race between John Lindsay, Abraham Beame, and William Buckley. The artist's first experience with a camera crew and his first encounter with an ongoing event, the result is his most journalistic film. It is also most remote from the acerbic tone of the "radical scavenging" for which he was to become famous and the least inclined to escape from the confines of the bourgeois problematic within which it is posed. Compared to the other films, it has, predictably, the impersonal air of an assignment about it, but it is executed with skill and verve nonetheless.

The film interpolates a British perspective of an U.S. election with a running discussion of the urban problems that were the issues of the campaign (a BBC voice-over introducing parties, candidates, and issues was probably unavoidable). A vivid mélange is flawlessly assembled of vérité footage of campaign activity and interviews with both voters and candidates, with lay and professional commentators. The most impressive aspect of the film is its continuation of a theme of media critique begun with *Point of Order*. De Antonio wittily undercuts the electoral system by including television spots by both major candidates, complete with unabashedly empty rhetoric and tasteless campaign songs (by Ethel Merman in the Lindsay spot). There is also prolonged scrutiny of the candidates' platform demagoguery and a caustic critique of the Lindsay style by also-ran conservative Buckley.

On the whole, *That's Where the Action Is* (it's the BBC's title, not his own) is a modest and promising second film. However, it fails to heighten the satirical bemusement in its view of electoral politics to any serious level of interrogation. Furthermore, it seems content with the classical sixties liberal problematic of urban decay in its treatment of big city problems (relying heavily on Daniel Moynihan for its commentary in this area). And ultimately the film's analysis of video politics is itself weakened by its own susceptibility to the charismatic attraction of candidate Lindsay. The photogenic, aristocratic liberal emerges relatively unscathed from the film, seeming to get the better share of the camera's attention (at one point he offers it a gigantic hot dog in close-up). And in the long run he succeeds in charming the film's audience, despite the director's attempts to undercut his appeal, as much as he charmed most U.S. liberals that year (as well as most voters).

However, if the film is unquestioningly a minor work, it constitutes an important step in the artist's career. If *Point of Order* served as a manifesto of general aesthetic principle (democratic didacticism) and strategy (collage), expressed in their most basic form, *That's Where the Action Is* and de Antonio's subsequent film, *Rush to Judgment* (1967) point clearly to the complex form of cinema, the "document-dossier," which the four following "mature" works were to imitate and refine: *In the Year of the Pig* (1968) provides a discussion of U.S. involvement in Vietnam; *America Is Hard to See* (1970) analyzes the Eugene McCarthy presidential campaign of 1968; *Millhouse: A White Comedy* offers a satirical portrait of Richard Nixon; and *Painters Painting* presents a historical survey of contemporary U.S. (New York) painting.

In *Rush to Judgment*, de Antonio confirms the interview as an integral element of his characteristic form of collage; it is a basic artifact of television culture and the basic ingredient of the television film that he had just completed. The interview had been totally suppressed by Leacock and his colleagues but had always been a standard component of the European and Canadian direct cinema (not to mention the films of Godard). Despite the interview experiments in such early sound documentaries as Esfir Shub's *Komsomol: Leaders of Electrification* (1932), Vertov's *Three Songs of Lenin*, and Grierson's *Housing Problems* (1936) and occasional reliance on it in the theatrical newsreel medium, it was only with the coming of television that this technique had been perfected as a staple of audiovisual language. By the time de Antonio took it up, it had already been totally absorbed by his video generation audience. Low key and not emphatic, the interview is essential to the functional orientation of his work. His art is an art of revelation, not astonishment, and "content," not style. His emphasis on "content" is the basis for his nostalgic admiration for the pretelevision documentaries of the thirties (particularly those of Paul Strand) and his scorn for his cinéma vérité contemporaries:

> Why did I make *Point of Order*? I wanted to make documentaries: the only documentaries I like had been made before World War II. Television and the Cold War had taken the content out of documentary . . .
>
> The audiovisual history of our time is the television outtake. Each hour, cameras, as impersonal as astronauts, grind away film and tape which the content-free networks will never transmit. Our television is content-free not because it is regulated but because it is a commodity—not news or art or entertainment but a product . . .

Dependence on the technical is also an aspect of no content. Cinéma
vérité? Whose vérité? No one can fault the development of fast, light, mobile
equipment. What is wrong is the space the best-known practitioners of cinéma
vérité occupy today: publicity films for rock groups. (Weiner 1971, 8–10)

De Antonio relies on the interview not only as a means of personal
revelation (as with direct cinema) but also, more importantly, as a medium of
"content," defying television's relegation of the interview to its most pedes-
trian, digestible, reliably content-free ingredient. The use of this traditionally
innocuous device for historical analysis, personal reminiscence, or professional (or lay) opinion made such content fresh and accessible for an audience
unaccustomed to finding such weighty matter therein. It becomes emphatic by
virtue of its flatness. The long, static interview shots in *Rush to Judgment* and
the later films force their content upon the spectator because of their visual
austerity. De Antonio's film language is more sedate, more prosaic, as it were,
and much cheaper—ultimately much more relevant to the double ideals of
democracy and didacticism than the flamboyant, poetic language of cinéma
vérité. And this visual language is by no accident an affirmation of the vital
role of speech, of dialogue, of logic in radical discourse.

The interview is also integral to de Antonio's historical perspective.
The fundamental rhythm of his mature films is a systole-diastole between
the document, a fragment from a past event, and the interview, a living
segment of a present reflecting upon and analyzing that fragment. It is the
basic Brechtian (and Sophoclean) structure of action in alternation with
analysis. *Rush to Judgment*, de Antonio was proud to claim, was the first
U.S. film that "went into really big interviewing," and his retrospective
defensiveness about its "boringness" is not at all warranted. Just as *That's
Where the Action Is* had juxtaposed documents (visual and auditory)
from an event, with commentary from observers of and participants in
that event, *Rush to Judgment* assembled film and video material from the
Dallas assassination and the investigation that followed it, with interviews
with spectators of the events. The ultimate effect is a denunciation of the
Warren Commission's (perhaps deliberate) shortsightedness.

De Antonio's collaboration with Mark Lane on the project, the author
of the investigative book by the same title (1966), is perhaps responsible
for the only major flaw in this otherwise compelling film: there is an overall
tendency to sensationalize rather than analyze the evidence that the film
gradually accumulates in the defense of the scapegoat Oswald and in addition a rather explicit, almost homiletic tone due to the awkward appearances
of Lane himself who tends to belabor the points that have already been
driven home by the documentary evidence and testimonies of witnesses.

Rush to Judgment's most interesting feature is its continuation of the previous film's excursion into the populist arena, which is more normally considered the domain of Leacock and company. Seen in the context of de Antonio's oeuvre, these two films and the later treatment of Eugene McCarthy's presidential campaign, *America Is Hard to See*, reveal a grassroots sensibility that is ultimately secondary within his vision of U.S. society; these three films contain what might be called a digression from the more central preoccupation of the artist's career, that is, the U.S. tragedy as seen in the roles of its chief protagonists not its chorus (or its victims).

Rush to Judgment, filmed only on the brink of the age of fashionable dissent, and far from the Eastern enclaves of radical chic, was also de Antonio's most dangerous film to produce until the Weather Underground film. For one thing, his customary rich liberal investors were nervous about such a touchy subject, and *Rush to Judgment* had to be financed by British sympathizers such as Tony Richardson and John Osborne. Realized with an amateur crew, terrorized while in production by local and federal police, and hampered by official hostility, the film provoked de Antonio's first real taste of the harassment that was to dog him for the rest of his career. Distribution was also a problem: theater owners were threatened with vandalism and the release date coincided with the outbreak of the Six-Day War, which provided serious competition on the small screen. As a result, it was de Antonio's least widely distributed film.

Remarkable then for its very existence, *Rush to Judgment* is all the more impressive as an exploration of a popular response to bewildering political events:

> What I wanted to show, at great length, was that one guy could take on the FBI—or two of us really, Mark Lane and I, and the Warren Report, and prove that they had lied, by filming people at great length describing events that had happened in Texas in November of 1963. I felt that the Warren Commission's investigations, or really lack of them, was outrageous, so I went down and filmed these witnesses. I like the idea of their slow Texas speech while telling a story just ordinary working people, not Marxists or anything, just guys who worked for the railroad or whatever and I didn't give a damn if people were bored by it or not. I liked it. (Weiner 1971, 8)

De Antonio thus hits upon a basic principle of the French and Canadian direct cinema: Not only can nonparticipant, nonexpert subjects offer profound, illuminating discussions of the social forces that affect their lives, but their testimonies alone, by virtue of their very existence, can also themselves, in the specific sociopolitical context of their lives, constitute the basis of a moving and provocative aesthetic/political experience. This insight was later the basis for Newsreel's most solid achievements, as we have already

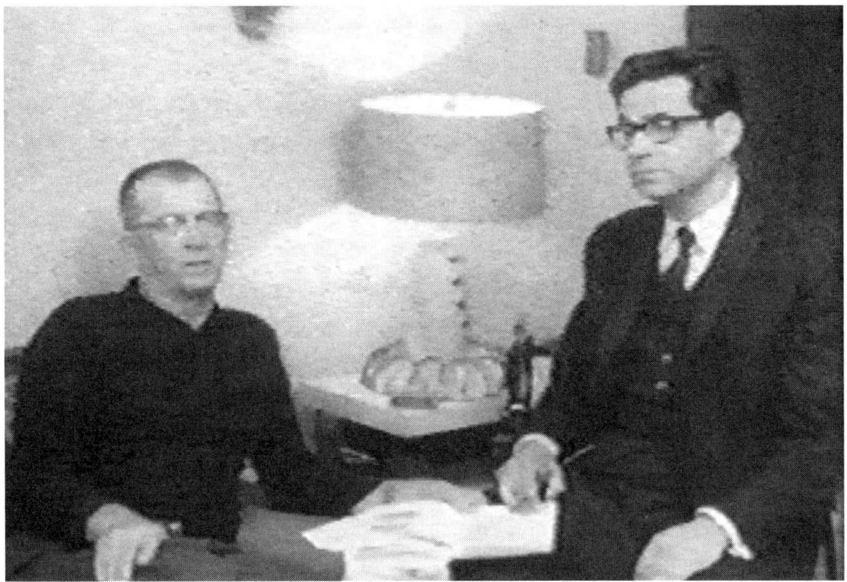

Rush to Judgment (Emile de Antonio, 1967). Collaborator Mark Lane (right) and the interview subject in his unassuming Dallas living room, a nonexpert subject providing an illuminating discussion of social forces affecting his life.

seen, in such films as *The Woman's Film* and *Richmond Oil Strike.* It is certainly telling to compare the dignity of the witnesses in *Rush to Judgment*, pictured in their unassuming living rooms (doilies in place) or in the open spaces of the assassination site with the shallow, condescending portraits of ordinary Americans one encounters in the films of Leacock, Wiseman, or Arthur Barron. Unhappily, de Antonio seldom returns to build on this talent he shows in *Rush to Judgment* or to confirm the populist sensibility that is too often lacking in the consciousness of the New Left.

De Antonio's art is always highly evocative visually; he can extract as much visual power from a static close up interview as exists in a Godard monologue or in a Pasolini close-up of a wrinkled extra. Nevertheless, the ultimate impact of his art is fundamentally aural. If the U.S. vérité filmmakers banished the soundtrack to a minor role (despite their delight in noise), the reverse is true of de Antonio. His films are essentially sound films, or more specifically, films of verbal language and dialogue. As with television journalism, the dominant logic of the de Antonio film is verbal and the image often functions simply as a contrapuntal accompaniment to the primary current of the film, its voices arising out of the documents from the past, with voices from the present echoing, interpreting, mocking, judging, analyzing, and exorcising them. The voices of the interviewees regularly leave the image of the present and accompany the documents

as they unfold, so that the past–present, document–actuality oppositions
become not only sequential but simultaneous. With *That's Where the
Action Is* and *Rush to Judgment*, the voice-over, banished by cinéma vérité
as a vestige of a tyrannical past, is reclaimed and liberated. No longer the
voice-over of *Twentieth Century* and *The March of Time*, it is the voice of
a witness participating in a discourse extracting the meaning hidden by the
image, bringing the reflection and the perhaps greater wisdom of the present to bear on the inscrutability of time past as it unrolls once again.

The word becomes the basic structural and organizational principle of
the film:

> Words are very important in my film (*The Year of the Pig*) and in all of
> my work, and that's how I do the editing: I start with the transcription of
> the soundtrack and put all of these pages up on the walls of the big editing
> rooms where I work and begin to assemble the papers before the film: that's
> how the structure begins; then I take the film, and I go endlessly from the
> text to the film and from the film to the text, and I change them around,
> switching the sheets of paper with each other. I have a good visual memory.
> When you have so much filmed material, you think of a shot you want and
> the list of shots is no use because no list of shots can describe everything
> with precision (you know, the list of shots says: buffaloes, peasants, air-
> planes, medium shot of buffaloes and peasants). Even if it's well drawn up,
> it's not as exact as your own memory. (Ciment and Cohn 1970, 30)

It is no accident that this methodology is extremely similar to that followed by many direct cinema filmmakers. A related structural principle is
implied by the ratios of document to actuality, both aural and visual, in this
particular film: On the soundtrack, the interviews overwhelm the documentary sound in a ratio of eight to one, but the image track presents four times
as much vintage document as it does de Antonio's own shots. Visual memory
is restructured vocally, and only then is it useful to the present. Proust's voice
extracted redemption from the unorganized mass of visual fragments in his
memory, and the voice is no less the instrument for de Antonio's characters
(and the other personae of the new documentary, such as I. F. Stone, Antonia
Brico, Tom Wicker, Dan Ellsberg, etc.) to confront the visual fragments from
the past and to shore these fragments against ruin. When the enemy has
learned to hide its face behind a screen, only the faculty of speech exercised
in naming it, denouncing it, can begin the confrontation with it.

In the Year of the Pig, de Antonio's Vietnam epic, separated by an
interval of three years from the Dallas film, is the artist's only film to have
reaped the dubious honor of an Oscar nomination; fortunately it did not
win (according to de Antonio because of a closed-shop town's hostility to a
nonunion film). And the monolith's infinite capacity to absorb even its most

ardent opposition was temporarily forestalled (although this oversight can be said to have been amply rectified by the Academy's later gestures toward Joseph Strick's *Interviews with My Lai Veterans* [1971] and then *Hearts and Minds* [1974], in the true Hollywood tradition of hindsight, surrogate recognition). *In the Year of the Pig* was also one of de Antonio's three biggest commercial successes (along with *Point of Order* and *Painters Painting*, but none of his films has ever lost money), focusing as it did on the decade's most divisive national issue. Financed readily by various peace movement millionaires and such prominent liberals as Paul Newman, Leonard Bernstein, and Steve Allen, the film was one of the first documentaries about the Indochina struggle, and it still remains the best.

Yet despite its place at the center of the antiwar movement in the late sixties, the film's mood seems in marked contrast to the predominant spirit of the movement as it now appears in retrospect. Instead of the passionate moralistic tone of the marches, de Antonio's rhetoric is cool, scholarly, and articulate. Its aim was to convince, not to inflame, and to do the homework that the marchers had no time for. In contrast to the two famous French antiwar films of the period, *In the Year of the Pig* is notable for its shrewd, deliberate, cerebral tone: a far cry from *The Seventeenth Parallel* (1968), Joris Ivens's epic tribute to the heroism of the North Vietnamese peasant defense, or the emotional, subjective *Far from Vietnam* (1967), the collective statement of the Leftish fringes of the New Wave.

In a cultural climate already charged with the divisive rhetoric of the war and distrustful of radical polemic, de Antonio's strategy was probably the right one. U.S. liberals were ready for this cold chronological collage of documents arranged with the artist's customary matter-of-factness and unmediated by any external narration. The documents outlined with precision and clarity almost forty years of the history of the Vietnamese struggle; a counterpoint of long authoritative interviews with experts as diverse as a French scholar of Buddhist thought and U.S. congressional leaders provided analysis and background at each stage of the chronology. The faces of the interlocutors repeatedly surface from the past, become familiar guides, and then vanish again as their voices continue on, disembodied, over the stream of visual artifacts. Motifs and refrains, both visual and aural, appear and disappear: early in the film a specially commissioned concerto of helicopter noises drones out of the silence in a deafening crescendo (when the projectionist resists the urge to turn down the volume, as occasionally happens), thereby introducing a major aural motif of the film and the war.

Much of the film's documentary footage came, predictably, from sympathetic sources, the National Liberation Front and North Vietnam. However, considerable amounts also originated with ABC, the BBC, and the French Army, and the film often achieves a dramatic emphasis because of this, with the editor's reversing the original intention of a clip through judicious cutting or juxtaposition. Again it is a question of the removal of newsreel and video material from its original context and exploiting the profound distanciation that results. Particularly the U.S. television footage of the war displays its startling contradictions when shown on a cinema screen, suddenly having lost the lulling effect that its continuous low-definition saturation in U.S. living rooms is said to have had. Media critique is thus once more de Antonio's stance:

> There is nothing as bad that's happened concerning the war as the network's coverage of it, because it seems as if they're covering the war whereas in fact they're not. The networks have made the U.S. people comfortable with the war because it appears between commercials. There's never the question asked, "Why are we doing this? What is this war about?" It's never suggested by anything that occurs on television that we should even be interested in that type of question. Television is a way of avoiding coming to terms with the fact that we're in this war. (Weiner 1971, 7)

In contrast to the previous film's populist flavor, a vivid record of ordinary people caught up in a political turmoil, *In the Year of the Pig* has little sense of public perspective of the war. The interviewer's encounters with the French scholar and Ho Chi Minh are no doubt highlights of the

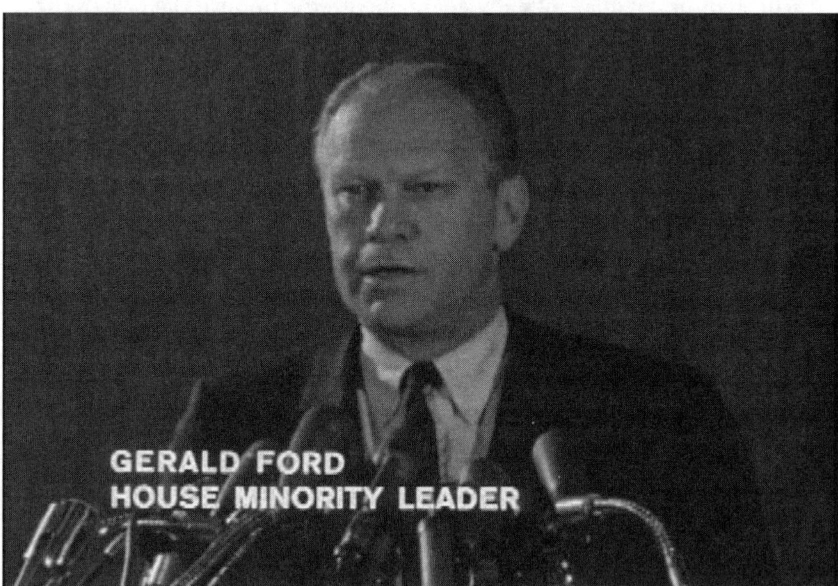

In the Year of the Pig (Emile de Antonio, 1968). A cold chronological collage of television documents analyzing the folly and evil of U.S. political leadership over thirty years.

film; but however indispensable the artist's attention to the experts and the protagonists to his analytical goals and his exposure of the folly and evil of the U.S. leadership, there is a sense that this irrepressible Jeremiah might have profited from the cinéma vérité model of interest in ordinary people. The concluding credits of his film about U.S. painting, *Painters Painting*, unroll over footage of expressionless crowds wandering around the Museum of Modern Art, and at this point one is suddenly struck by how much this film, as well as others of his oeuvre, would have been enriched by the reflection of the consciousness of such crowds. In *Year of the Pig*, de Antonio's short encounters with a deserter and with GIs on active duty are high points of the film, but this exploration of the human, everyday dimension of the war is tantalizingly brief. In *Painters Painting*, as in the art world in general, the absence of lay perspective is total.

With *Hearts and Minds*, Peter Davis makes some progress toward correcting this deficit, aiming for a populist perspective of the war that is not present in de Antonio. Davis's involvement with individual Americans who obediently waged the war is often sensitive and profound and almost compensates for occasional lapses into clumsiness and offense (the Saigon bordello cinéma vérité sequence) or facile crowd scenes that rival Leacock and Wiseman in their arrogance and undercut the sensitivity displayed elsewhere in the film. If de Antonio saw the war as a debacle of international imperialism and domestic intrigue, Davis sees it as a national tragedy, not primarily for the Vietnamese people (though he doesn't understate their suffering), but for the U.S. people. Employing a characteristic de Antonio collage, though in a less rigorous, nonchronological manner, Davis confronts participants and witnesses both in the present and the past, from the Oklahoma ex-flier who weeps as he remembers his bombing raids, to the infamous Colonel Patton who, in a video tape from the late sixties, praises his men for being "good killers" (de Antonio used the same tape but not in Davis's living color). A sense of national failure of spirit emerges from this application of the collage approach despite the ideological confusion of the overall effect, the blurring of class lines in Davis's conception of the U.S. people and a tendency toward a muddled sentimentality. Like de Antonio, Davis also presents the chief protagonists in the conflict (Ellsberg, Rostow, Westmoreland, etc.), but what finally remains with the spectator is the impression of a community divided, defensive, penitent, and fearful.

Davis's early television documentary, *The Selling of the Pentagon* (1971) is on the whole a much better film, ironically because network requirements apparently demanded more coherence (the topic, the public relations activities of the Defense Department, was also much more compact and assailable). However, the topic was less amenable to the kind of populist sensibility that Davis later reveals in the best moments of *Hearts and Minds*. Morton Silverstein's TV films, as we have seen, represent the potential of television journalism to reflect the lives and viewpoints of ordinary people at its best.

Cinda Firestone's *Attica* (1974) is another contemporary documentary that builds upon de Antonio's formula in *Year of the Pig* (she is a former editor of his) and in addition shares in the populist sensibility that is the most important achievement of the radical underground current of films. She relies much more than her mentor does on long interviews with her subjects, the participants and witnesses in the prison revolt. And unlike Davis, she does not lose sight of the political basis of the tragedy and resists the easy resources of sentimentality.

De Antonio's fifth film was *America Is Hard to See*, a title taken from Robert Frost. It dealt with a single event from the recent past rather than an ongoing historical process of several decades like the Vietnam War. By restricting his focus to Eugene McCarthy's campaign for the presidency in 1968, de Antonio created a more concentrated, more specific kind of political analysis than the unwieldy subject of the war permitted. In addition, the McCarthy film was closer to its subject chronologically than any of the others, with a time lapse of only two years separating document and event from recollection and analysis. This is a very short historical perspective indeed, but a dramatic one nevertheless. The abrupt changes in even the sartorial aspect of the campaigners as they emerge from the 1968 documents into the 1970 interviews, the pronounced oscillation between the 1968 campaign euphoria and the 1970 sober realism tinged with nostalgia, the hagiographical atmosphere with which only two years' hindsight surrounds the documentary appearances of Robert Kennedy and the references to Martin Luther King—all contribute to a sense of the uncontrollable acceleration of the historical process, two years having seen such a radical transformation of cast and ambience in the U.S. political arena.

The film is at times a critique of the naive enthusiasm of the McCarthy supporters, from the gloomy perspective of Nixonian 1970, and is at other times a meditation on the very real possibility of a reformist alternative politics within the system. *America Is Hard to See* is at once a (relatively) bright film and a highly ambiguous one. The victories in New Hampshire and Oregon are miracles captured on video, Johnson's resignation speech a tentative defeat of the enemy, and the charm and affable rationality of the chief protagonist of the film himself a refreshing glimpse of an apparently real, attractive alternative. Yet the awareness is always present that the film is, after all, a postmortem, and the campaign so euphorically pursued and relived was indeed a failure.

Again, a low-key chronological approach follows the event from its beginning, slowly and conscientiously to its end. As a historian de Antonio is fastidious: he is careful to balance whatever mythologizing is inevitable in his subject matter—the heroics, the flag waving, the paranoia, the despair—with a down-to-earth examination of the mechanics of electoral politics on the smallest level. He seeks out documents that show the moments of groundwork and individual effort that cumulatively make up the historical process. The potential of alternative politics is discovered in the images and voices of ordinary people with specific goals and in those of top strategists planning and then evaluating the maneuvers.

De Antonio's focus on specific topical issues—a senate hearing, a war, a political campaign, and so forth—does not mean that his interest is restricted to these events, as we have seen. The challenge of addressing abstract theoretical problems through immediate, topical subjects is a traditional one for the radical filmmaker: he or she must always satisfy the demands for the concrete and topical, by box office and audience and perhaps even by the photographic, representative nature of the medium, despite whatever interest he or she may have in more abstract or theoretical issues. It is to de Antonio's credit that he habitually succeeds in extending the microcosm to the macrocosm yet never makes this extension in a way that is "undemocratic" or facile. The step from the specific to the general is never transparent and often difficult, yet it is always there implicitly, engaging his spectators to complete the connections themselves. It is perhaps this aspect of de Antonio's films that is most responsible for their extraordinary durability, a feature that is by no means a common one in the radical cinema.

The Army-McCarthy hearing, as we have seen, for example, becomes a pretext for an analysis of what de Antonio saw as a symptomatic emphasis on "technique" in U.S. life (Weiner 1971, 8). In the same way, *Rush to Judgment* becomes an attempt "not to prove the innocence of Oswald, but to show how the U.S. machine works" (Weiner 1971, 7), and *Year of the Pig* is an analysis of the media's role in legitimizing the politics of imperialism and monopoly capitalism. Similarly, *America Is Hard to See* contains a consciousness, beneath its surface optimism, of the grim inevitability that the system must ultimately defuse even this hope, using even dissent to entrench itself in its own inertia. From this viewpoint, de Antonio's entire oeuvre becomes a continuing Marcuse-style essay on the modern state and its manner of making its tyranny palatable. Yet the films continue, one by one, with no end in sight, and their presence themselves contradicts de Antonio's apparent recognition of this fatality.

America Is Hard to See treated a personality as the symbol of the system's potential to renew itself from within. *Millhouse*, a different kind of

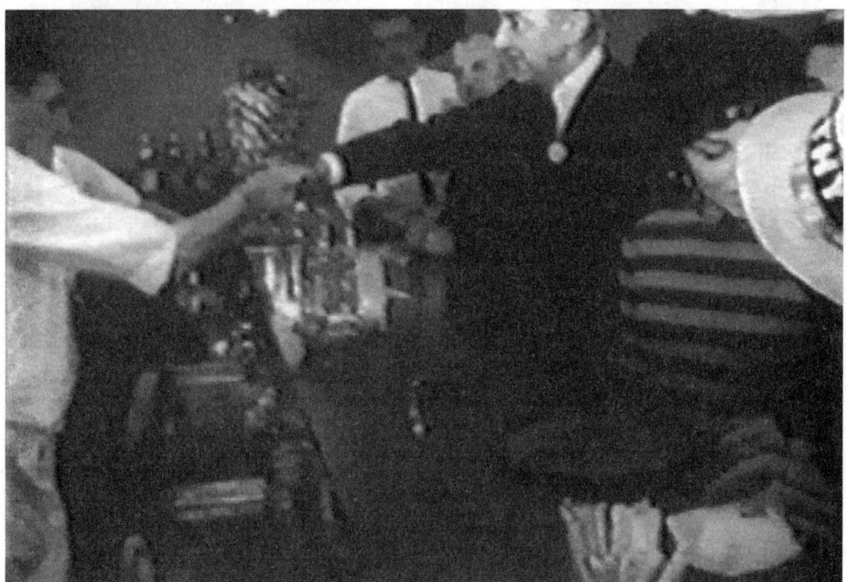

America Is Hard to See (Emile de Antonio, 1970). Senator Eugene McCarthy (right), a personality scrutinized two years after the fact as a symbol of the system's potential to renew itself from within.

portrait, appeared a year later and treated another personality, Nixon at the height of his power, as emblematic of the corruption of the System and its tenacious opposition to that self-renewal: "The film attacks the System, the credibility of the System, by focusing on the obvious and perfect symbol for that System" (Weiner 1971, 6). De Antonio's blackest, most sardonic, and most despairing film, *Millhouse* is also his funniest, as he himself terms it, "the first real attempt at a real documentary comedy" (Weiner 1971, 15). But immediately Marcuse's problematic again imposes itself: is the ability of the radical subculture to laugh at the enemy merely the reverse side of that enemy's power to absorb its dissent with just as much glee?

Though the filmmaker was to claim that *Millhouse* is not a personal attack, whatever else it may be, it is indeed an attack, par excellence, merciless and brilliant, worthy of Swift and Pope, delivered ad hominem and below the belt. De Antonio certainly deserved the honor of inclusion on Nixon's celebrated enemies list as much as anyone. *Millhouse* (its full title is *Millhouse: A White Comedy*) is predictably conducted as a chronological record of Nixon's career, in fact as a parody of the famous crisis-to-crisis chronology that Nixon himself set forth in his prepresidential memoirs. The system that Nixon had manipulated continuously to his own advantage for over a quarter century is closely scrutinized.

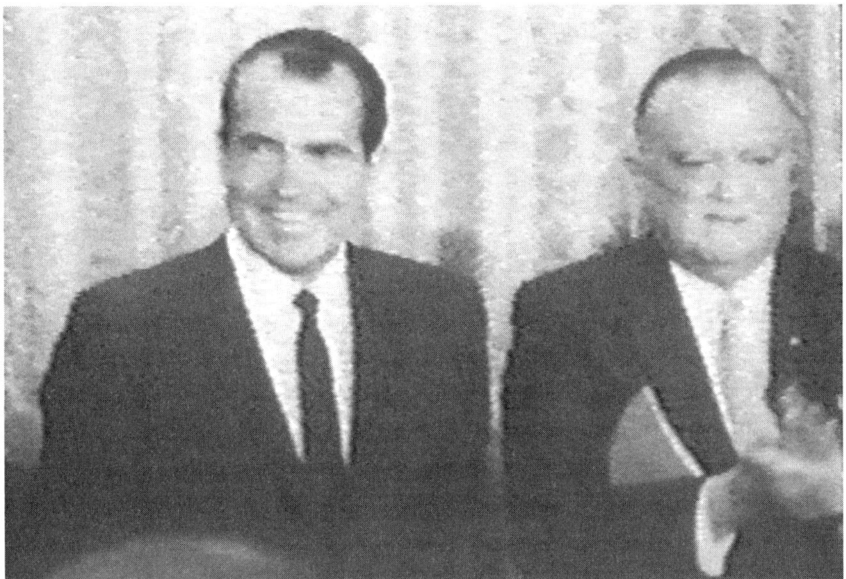

Millhouse, A White Comedy (Emile de Antonio, 1971). The Nixonian face (seen with J. Edgar Hoover, right) as the perfect symbol for the system of media duplicity. A scene used again in *Mr. Hoover and I* (1989).

As with the previous films, the basic strategy is to remove documents from their original context and reexamine them in a context of (here, satiric) juxtaposition with actuality. The most memorable example is the infamous Checkers speech, where the nervous young candidate gravely tries out the ropes of the medium to which he would habitually resort when under attack over the next twenty years. Once removed from its intended context it becomes a monument of hilarity. An additional twist in *Millhouse* is the humor derived from the art of the outtake. This means of confronting the public man with the private man is developed here to perfection, often without cutting. The changes the Nixonian face undergoes as it confronts the video cameras constitute a sublime image of the duplicity fostered by the system of media politics. And Nixon's unwitting contributions to de Antonio's art of collage are more expressive of the man than any other moments in the film.

Although ad hominem mockery hardly seems a legitimate tool of "democratic didacticism," there is a stratum to the film of utmost gravity, developed by serious commentators in the traditional de Antonio style. The homework is done no less efficiently for the fun: the facts and the documents are presented with equal authoritativeness. De Antonio's scrutiny of the political personality— from the earliest red-baiting and smear campaign days to the smoothest White House piety—is as methodical and thorough as it is irreverent.

It is ironic that *Millhouse*, that arch-example of an antiexemplary biography, should provide the model for an important subgenre of the new documentary, the exemplary biography, or the documentary homage. Jerry Bruck's *I. F. Stone's Weekly* (1973) and Jill Godmilow's *Antonia: A Portrait of the Woman* (1974) are two of the best known of these biographical films, all built more or less faithfully on the model provided by *Millhouse*, that is, the collage of vintage document and commentary and the extensive use of interviews and monologues to penetrate the personality under examination. (The National Film Board of Canada's film biographies of Dr. Norman Bethune [1967] and John Grierson [1971] are two other admirable prototypes for this subgenre.)

Such films, given the advantage of the posture of tribute rather than attack, have often been able to enlist the cooperation of their subjects, thereby making the invaluable addition of the subject's own voice to the commentary and varying amounts of cinéma vérité footage to the collage as well. The latter brings to the portrait cinéma vérité's undeniable talent for capturing behavioral authenticity. In contrast to the cumulative effect of the seventies film portrait, those of the sixties relying solely on vérité language seem superficial indeed, for examples, Stravinsky, Fonda, Dylan, Cash, and so on. De Antonio has demonstrated that the addition of historical background, contemporary and external commentary, and the direct on-camera confrontation with the subject are essential to the genre. Instead of the suggestive cinéma vérité cameo, limited by the counterculture and the "system's" shared, synchronic conception of the personality, we have in this way a more penetrating diachronic exploration of individuals, one elaborating their growth in relation to the social forces around them. Cinéma vérité reinforced individualist, behaviorist ideology; the de Antonio collage makes possible a different collective, materialist view of the human reality.

If *Millhouse* is de Antonio's most exaggerated rejection of the network and vérité ideal of "objectivity," *Painters Painting* (1973) hovers disturbingly close to that dubious standard that the filmmaker's previous career had so convincingly repudiated. Outside of the film, de Antonio made no secret of the definite reservations about contemporary painting that we might have expected from him:

> If you consider American art since the war, it's a cold art for a cold war. It's an art "non-engagé." The best American painters have no point of view on the world. They have become part of the world of business. The rich families collect their works. McLuhan admires technology, as John Cage does in music, who has passed from music to technology. This is political, because

you are upholding in this way American values; when you are neutral you
defend the existing order: and that's the danger of McLuhan. (Ciment and
Cohn 1970, 36)

And criticism of postwar U.S. (official) art might well be the duty of
an artist who has spent a decade of his life in films denouncing the triumph
of technique over content in politics, in communications, in film, and in
every phase of U.S. life (including the film aesthetics of that group of New
American independent filmmakers, most akin to the postwar movements
in painting, and whom de Antonio once termed "Jonas Mekas and his
troupe of trend-sniffing mercenary cavalry" [Weiner 1971, 10]). However,
the viewer is hard pressed to read such an attitude into *Painters Painting*. In fact, it is a film that even CBS might be proud to broadcast it is so
wary of evaluating the phenomenon under study. As a film, then, by an
avowed Marxist about an artistic avant-garde, *Painters Painting* encapsu-
lates all the contradictions in the murky relationships of the Left to such
avant-gardes.

Predictably, de Antonio readily admits to such contradictions in the film:

it's presented me with several problems personally, which anyone who has
seen my work would guess, since I regard myself as a Marxist social critic of
the existing social system in this country and yet the painters and the way in
which they work are essentially manifestations of a very conservative aspect

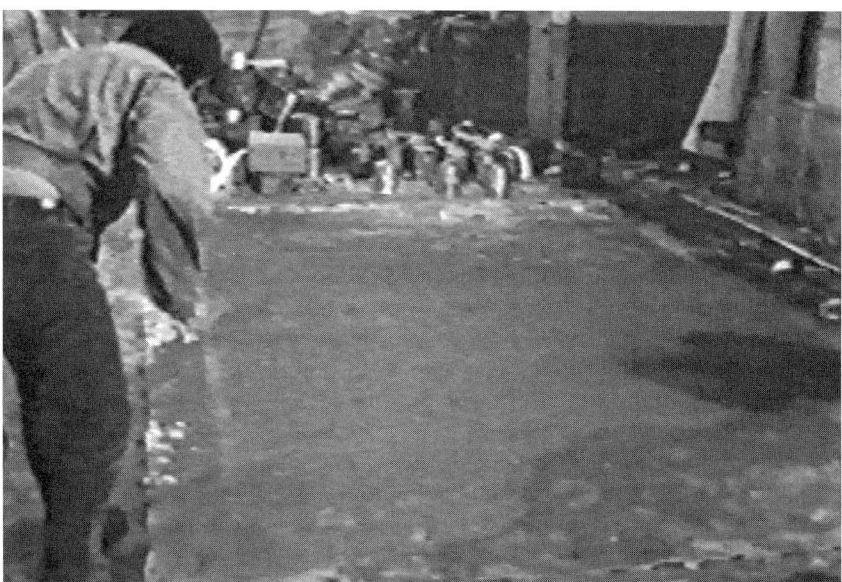

Abstractionist pouring in *Painters Painting* (Emile de Antonio, 1973). "The
painting itself is not conservative (though it is apolitical) but it's part of a machine
which runs this country."

of America. The painting itself is not conservative (though it is apolitical) but it's part of a machine which runs this country. And so, if I have to make a choice between American painting and the attempt to turn men's [sic] minds and the search for a collective soul, then I'm more interested in what Mao is doing than in the art of my friends. And yet I'm making the film: perhaps it's something I have to do to get it out of my system. (Weiner 1971, 14)

The film's virtually sole critical perception comes from the half-satirical encounter with Robert Scull, the self-styled Maecenas of the New York art world, and his since-jettisoned wife. The interview brings out only a momentary flash of the de Antonio that created *Millhouse*, as the realization half emerges that virtually all contemporary painting depends on the whims of these dubiously motivated, superficially endowed nouveaux-riches and on the personal tastes of the establishment art critics whose pontifical pronouncements on surfaces and textures are also part of the collage.

Still, as an uncritical chronicle of postwar painting (with an evaluation of its elitist audience; marketplace orientation; and incestuous, conspiratorial inspiration hardly implied), *Painters Painting* represents an additional refinement of the essay-collage form that de Antonio had been developing for a decade. Now the past and present, document and analysis oscillation is sharpened by the 35mm definition and brilliant acrylic color of the footage from the present. The documents recording the masters in the act, Pollack pouring paint and de Kooning and the others doing whatever we are told they were doing, presented in reverent fifties black and white, form an evocative counterpoint with the color images of their completed work and of their successors working and talking a generation later. The tendency of the present generation of painters and sculptors to talk and conceptualize at least as much (and as well) as they create makes the interviews all the more penetrating. The only exception to the respectful bourgeois Romantic perspective of art adopted by the film as a whole arises from the interview with Andy Warhol. This artist is easily as fascinating on the screen as the haunting menagerie that he himself has led across it over the last ten years. In the film, he is unique among the artists interviewed for his refusal to play the self-important, oracular role that attracts the others.

Painters Painting also continues the tendency of the historical films of the seventies to incorporate some elements of cinéma vérité into the structure of the collage. De Antonio balances the interviews, ranging from manifesto-like monologues to *Chelsea Girls* chitchat (1966), with revealing though somewhat stiff footage of the personalities outside of the interview format. The flexibility of such eclecticism is richly demonstrated.

However rewarding this film might be for those observers of Rock-efeller art who would not be disturbed by such a noncommittal attitude, it is to be hoped that with this film (partly financed by the sale of paintings de Antonio himself had collected during the fifties from his artist friends), the artist has indeed "got it out of his system."

A far more rewarding film on avant-garde culture is Jean-Marie Straub and Danielle Huillet's excellent short work, *Introduction to Arnold Schoenberg's Accompaniment to a Cinematic Scene* (1973), also a film based on the structural principle of collage. In it Straub no doubt shares de Antonio's reverential attitude to his subject but balances it not only with a clear elaboration of the historical context for Schoenberg's work but also, importantly, with a statement by Brecht reflecting on the very problem the earlier biographical material had dealt with (anti-Semitism). The insight provoked by this disruption of the biographical moment with a (literally) Brechtian intervention is an achievement that de Antonio might profitably have imitated in *Painters Painting*, to redeem what otherwise is a disturb-ingly ambiguous homage to an avant-garde movement that could use more analysis than accolades.

Now that *Hearts and Minds* has finally succeeded in reaching its public, and public anticipation of the Weather Underground film is high, there seems no reason to doubt that the new documentary is in reason-ably good health, with every possibility of expanding its audience even more. Despite the enormous debt that Davis clearly owes de Antonio, there are important differences between them. Davis belongs more to the tradition of liberal, humanitarian journalism than to that of incisive, political analysis and thus bears less resemblance to de Antonio than to Marcel Ophuls, with whom he has already been compared in the popular press several times. Though both Davis and Ophuls use modified ver-sions of the basic de Antonio "document-dossier" format, they share the explicit moralistic, bourgeois humanist perspectives of history that de Antonio has always been careful to avoid.

For de Antonio, history is neither therapeutic, nor cathartic, nor, worse still, a paradigm of the moral relativity of human acts—it is instructive. Weeping over Vietnam with Davis and meaculpa-ing over the Occupation with Ophuls only serve to becloud the social forces in play. De Antonio's review of *Hearts and Minds* in a 1974 *University Review* con-demns the Davis film for "political emptiness," "an inability to understand either the United States or Vietnam," a "(sneering), japing, middle-class liberal superiority," and "patronizing attitudes,"—in short it is "heartless" and "mindless" (de Antonio 1974, 21).

De Antonio's objections are by and large valid; nevertheless, Davis's film deserved the wide audience it reached even if it only serves to prevent people in the United States from forgetting Indochina as quickly as they seem to be doing. And it is to be praised for speaking to its audiences with moral and emotional force. It can't be denied that Davis's broad appeal is a tactical virtue that other more rigorous and uncompromising Vietnam films lack, for example *Year of the Tiger* by Deirdre English, Dave Davis, and Steve Talbot (1974; a casualty of the "official tour behind the lines" syndrome), or the Jane Fonda and Haskell Wexler work, *Introduction to the Enemy* (1974; a far superior film because it is more personal, but one apparently still restricted to the committed circuit). Of course the definitive film of the Vietnam war—and the Cold War—has still to be made. And de Antonio has provided the surest models with which to begin.

In the meantime, as the Weather film nears completion, the filmmaker has two projects in the conception phase. Both ideas are for fiction films, a shift in gears of no small consequence for a documentarist of his standing. Which project will materialize first, if either, is anybody's guess: a fictional treatment of Philip Agee's book, *Inside the Company: CIA Diary*, or a story of a famous radical filmmaker seen through the eyes of government agencies who keep him under surveillance! What is certain is that de Antonio, in leaving behind him (temporarily, it is to be hoped) the documentary mode of discourse, will not abandon the rich creative energy, the obstinate commitment to rationality and to change, and the clear sighted historical consciousness that have made him one of the major U.S. filmmakers of our time. It is perhaps this last dimension of his art, its investment in the importance of historical analysis, which has constituted his most significant contribution to U.S. radical culture and will no doubt continue to do so with his new turn toward the mode of fiction.

▶──

Part II: Weatherpeople at Home (1976)

Underground has surfaced at last. When the much-heralded film on the Weather Underground by Emile de Antonio, Mary Lampson, and Haskell Wexler finally opened early in May 1976, it was a relief to see that it had all been worth it.

It was almost a year since the federal subpoenas on the film-in-progress had blown the cover of the most delicate film operation this side of Uruguay. The subpoenas had led to a brouhaha of no small dimensions, with a whole array of liberal editorialists and Hollywood luminaries rushing to the defense of the First Amendment. Now the result of all of this commotion has quietly appeared. Although the ripples it has set off are nothing compared to those of *Hearts and Minds* a few seasons back, *Underground* is still a major film, by no means an anticlimax to the cloak-and-dagger, cat-and-mouse maneuvers and the civil liberties outcry that preceded it. By any standard, *Underground* is an important intervention into the debate about the course of the Left in post-Vietnam United States.

The word on the grapevine for weeks before the opening had been that the film was excruciatingly boring, admittedly a potential liability for any featurelength interview with five faceless militants in a closed-in space. But people feared that worse than boring, the film would be a serious embarrassment to the radical community as well. A widely publicized film endorsing such questionable politics as those of the Weatherpeople could only be a weapon in the hands of the status quo, just as the media circus around the Symbionese Liberation Army had proven to be.[4]

There has also been considerable impatience among some radicals with de Antonio himself. Since his 1963 denunciation of Joseph McCarthy with *Point of Order*, he has been the most widely distributed and probably the most accomplished of U.S. filmmakers on the left. However, there has been some uneasiness about the occasional ideological ambivalence of his work, especially that of *Painters Painting*, his last film before *Underground*, an examination of New York avant-garde painting since the war. There have also been complaints about his undeniably individualist presence and his allegedly divisive behavior within the radical community. It was uncertain whether the veteran documentarist's fascination with the Weatherpeople stemmed from a legitimate political interest or from either radical chic or encroaching senility.

The other possibility was that the contradictions that had been latent in his films since the very beginning had finally come to the fore. Basically, some criticized the futility of his reliance on the commercial circuit of the liberal, "prestige" documentary as a forum for addressing the issue of social change in the United States. However justifiable such reservations about de Antonio might have been in the past, they must now be tabled indefinitely in the face of this solid new work.

Underground has confronted the project's detractors by being both decidedly watchable in filmic terms, indeed compelling, and in political terms, a document of unassailable relevance. Only those radicals can afford to dismiss the film who reject out of hand the importance of continuing dialogue within that urban liberal and campus audience that the film will certainly reach. Such a dialogue, to be sure, must be a complement to more concrete agitation and organization among working people and minorities. But in itself, this dialogue has an undeniable role within the context of a heterogeneous and nonsectarian Left. In the U.S. situation, such a left presence must surely be nourished by the consciences of intellectual and liberal groups as well as by the revolutionary consciousness of the oppressed.

It is perhaps the film's very emergence as an underground film that is at first most compelling. It is an underground film in the real sense, a kind of U.S. *samizdat* if you will, subversive as the innocuous Soho stuff they used to call underground never was. As viewers see the film, they confront the backs of the fugitives' heads or the gauze scrim that occasionally shields their faces from us (four or five different such setups are alternated, for visual variety, I assume). The audience hears a Weatherman interrupt the discussion to ask Wexler, the cameraperson, with almost panic insistence if the camera had not just accidentally caught his face. We may marvel at the bravado of the street interviews by two Weatherpeople at the film's end or catch ourselves trying to make out the details of a profile or a hairstyle. All of these moments constantly remind us of the other similar underground documents of film history, those stirring but rare representatives of perhaps the most select genre of them all.

One is reminded, for example, of Joris Ivens's *Borinage* (1933) or his *Indonesia Calling* (1946), the former a record of a Belgian miners' strike. That strike was filmed literally one step ahead of the police with the filmmakers often saving the camera with its precious contents by throwing it from hand to hand or by hiding equipment from police informers. One thinks as well of the virtually forgotten tradition of U.S. labor newsreels of the interwar years that stayed alive despite red scares and goon squads. Or one thinks of the rare documents of racial oppression that have been smuggled out of South Africa over the years. There is also *On est au coton* (1970), the legendary treatment of the Quebec textile industry that the National Film Board commissioned from Denys Arcand in 1970 but hastily suppressed as soon as they caught onto its subversive content. In this case, a pirated video edition began its permanent circulation through the Montreal radical subcultures immediately thereafter.

No doubt *Underground* is most reminiscent of those countless underground films from Latin America in the last decade. The most notable is, of course, Fernando Solanas's *Hour of the Furnaces* (1968), the four-and-a-half hour epic of the Argentine struggle, filmed clandestinely over a period of years and later distributed underground in Super 8—to this day, I hope. The most exact parallel is with the Uruguayan short *Tupamaros* (1974), like *Underground* based on interviews with fugitive revolutionaries, masked like the Weatherpeople from public identification because of the very real danger that doesn't take Costa-Gavras to help us imagine.[5]

It is the aura of danger and the presence of courage that give such films their dramatic intensity, quite apart from any purely aesthetic qualities they may have. Indeed, the unavoidable roughness of the truly underground film adds to its impact; our response to it as film per se is always tempered by a special dispensation. In this light, it is curious that technically *Underground* suffers none of the shortcomings one expects from an underground film. It had a healthy budget of $55,000, of which de Antonio and Wexler each put up $5,000. The rest was raised from apparently well-heeled radicals. It also had a professional crew and a leisurely postshooting schedule, all of which have guaranteed a film of considerable polish. Surely it is only in a civilization based on repressive desublimation that an underground film could look so good, not to mention have a gala benefit premiere a block from Lincoln Center. Nevertheless, the aura of risk and sacrifice is still present, and my admiration for these courageous artists cannot be withheld. It is not every U.S. filmmaker who risks imprisonment for refusing to cooperate with a grand jury.

The history of the film is already well known, thanks to articles and editorials in *Rolling Stone* (1975) and a good many newspapers at the time of the subpoenas last summer. No doubt, the initial publicity had something to do with the embarrassed withdrawal of the subpoenas a short time later. The feds saw that they had more face to lose in the outcry than faces to gain in the footage, presumably long since well sanitized. The harassment is not over apparently. Mysterious circumstances surrounding the last minute elimination of the film from the running at Cannes seem to be another link in the chain.

In any case, the film is based on several days of interviews by the three filmmakers in a "safe" California house with the five best-known members of the Weather Underground Organization—Bill Ayers, Kathy Boudin, Bernadine Dohrn, Jeff Jones, Cathy Wilkerson. That organization was the offspring of the early sixties Students for a Democratic Society. They had gone underground in 1970 after an explosion killed three of their members in their Greenwich Village basement bomb factory that year.

The organization had electrified the U.S. Left by the clandestine publication in July 1974 of *Prairie Fire*, a manifesto of their political principles. Ever since, the group has been putting out a quarterly paper called *Osawatomie*, named after an 1856 battle of John Brown and his abolitionist followers against slave owners. The press on which the organization personally prints their publications is shown in the film, together with stills of their gloved hands compiling *Prairie Fire*.

The group also claims responsibility for what they call "armed propaganda," to date a series of twenty-four symbolic bombings of political targets that, as de Antonio repeatedly points out, are always executed with professional polish and no casualties. *Underground* can in one way be seen merely as a filmic extension of *Prairie Fire*. But the film is ultimately much more than a podium for the group's views. The filmmakers have used the interview format as a departure point for a historical analysis of the past fifteen years of radical action and an assessment of current and future strategies for the Left.

Actually, the burst of harassment, and the subsequent spotlight that surprised the filmmakers last summer, have in the long run had a salutary effect on the film, and not only in providing priceless free media exposure and the ad copy: "The FBI doesn't want you to see *Underground*." The surveillance began just after the crew had completed filming the astonishing person-on-the-street interviews that climax the film, so there was no interference with the actual shooting. It was in the editing stage that the film really evolved, under the publicity and paranoia, with the interview material serving as the base for the complex collage that slowly developed. Once the enterprise was out in the open, the filmmakers were free to search aggressively for the stock footage they needed to illustrate and complete the oral history that had emerged from their conversations. And their search paid off in one of the most vivid collections of filmic documentation from that period that has been compiled.

Although the original conception included the extensive use of stock material, as might be expected in a de Antonio project, it is difficult to imagine how it could have been achieved without letting the cat out of the bag. As it stands, the film's contributors now include many of the most prominent radical filmmakers of the last decade. In addition, the film includes the usual efficient contributions from network camerapersons who are customary but rarely acknowledged in such projects. The film benefits greatly from consequent expansion of its range of focus: it becomes not only a study of the origins and development of the Weather movement but also a history of the entire U.S. Left over the past fifteen years.

Underground's achievement as a work of historical investigation is of course part of the continuity of de Antonio's career. He has consistently confirmed history as a crucial concern of U.S. radicals. And he has inevitably relied on collage as the most expressive and rigorous means of pursuing this concern on the screen. Topical issues have repeatedly served de Antonio throughout his career as pretexts for such projects. With *Underground*, the growth of the New Left is traced from its roots in the civil rights struggles of the early sixties right through the South Boston antibusing riots of 1975. Hence, *Underground* is not only a perspective of

one particular group of survivors of that period, although, as such it is a
valuable companion piece to *Milestones* (1975)—which, however much we
might object to Robert Kramer's and John Douglas's object and angle of
focus, is also a suggestive evocation of a specific group of castaways from
the New Left. More importantly, *Underground* offers a contemplation
of the history of an entire generation. The answer to de Antonio's blunt
question put to the group early in the film—"What the hell is essentially
a white, middle-class, revolutionary group doing in America in the year
1975?"—is an exploration of what it meant for all radicals to grow up in
the sixties and come of age in the seventies.

A viewer no doubt feels considerable interest in the details of underground living, in the drama of narrow escapes and constant fear, and in
the schizophrenic ambience of normality and paranoia that radiates from
the screen. But the filmmakers and their subjects wisely downplay this
automatic element of fascination, providing only a few cloak-and-dagger
anecdotes to appease the Hollywood-whetted palate. Happily, the job is
seen to be more serious than the production of a documentary thriller.

Among the autobiographies that are more or less sketched in during
the course of the discussion, only those of Dohrn and Boudin go into personal detail at length. This is regrettable insofar as the distinct outlines of
the five personae and their backgrounds are blurred. A heightened personalization of the five might have made the film more palatable for a general
audience without compromising the film's analytic task. I personally
couldn't keep the three women and two men apart, although my friend,
the ex-SDSer, had no trouble whatsoever.

In any case, the group's collective reminiscences link virtually all the
causes that have enlisted the Left in a meaningful continuity since 1960. It
is striking to see a medium more often attracted to topicality than history
and more often employed for synchronic analysis rather than diachronic
used in such a way. An entire succession of struggles over the years are
described as reactions to facets of a single system. These include the
struggle for rights for blacks and other third world groups, antiwar mobilization, Native Peoples' and Puerto Rican nationalist movements, protests
against the current crises of unemployment and urban decay, and, perhaps
most important in terms of the Weatherpeople's internal functioning, the
feminist movement. (There is no reference to the related agitation for the
liberation of sexual minorities, an unfortunate lacuna, I think, in view of
various alternate modes of sexual community the Weatherpeople are said
to have experimented with.)

The film's sense of the monolithic coherence of the System is articulated with often startling perceptiveness. For example, lavish camera

movements of gleaming hotel complexes in Puerto Rico are abruptly transformed into tracking shots along the devastated street fronts of the South Bronx, while a Puerto Rican poet, Miguel Algarin, recites a stunning indictment of the U.S. presence in his hometown. Such a juxtaposition is a brilliantly succinct statement of the contradictions of our society. At one point there is even a reference to the McCarthyite problem of the fifties and the implication of this particular root of the New Left: Dohrn's first memory of politics is of watching the televised Army-McCarthy hearings of the mid-fifties, an event that ironically provided de Antonio with the raw material for his debut as a radical filmmaker in the following decade.

Excerpts from vintage news footage purchased by de Antonio and Lampson document much of the history described. Their budget for stock acquisitions was only $10,000, almost a fifth of their budget, and such material is prohibitively expensive. This factor alone explains why radical film historiography of this scope is seldom attempted. However, in this case, the bulk of the stock material in the film, especially from the later years of the period in question, was donated by various filmmaker friends of the three filmmakers. As a result, passages from many of the major radical documentaries of the last decade have found their way into the film, including a number of the original Newsreel productions and such obvious choices as Gray and Alk's *The Murder of Fred Hampton* (1971), Chris Marker's *Le sixième face du Pentagone* (1968, on the 1967 *Armies of the Night* Pentagon demonstrations), Cinda Firestone's *Attica*, Wexler-Fonda-Hayden's *Introduction to the Enemy*, Peter Biskind's *Don't Bank on Amerika*, and, of course, de Antonio's own *In the Year of the Pig*.

As the collage unfolds, we see one by one the various strategies of opposition over that time period being tested and analyzed. The actions go from nonviolent resistance at Maryland lunch counters and demonstrations in Selma to Martin Luther King's confrontation marches through white Chicago neighborhoods not long before his death, to the armed resistance at Wounded Knee a few years back. They move from the peaceful antiwar rallies and draft card burnings of the early Vietnam years to the guerilla theater of the Vietnam Veterans against the War and the outbursts of spontaneous anger of the famous 1969 Days of Rage in Chicago, or the Santa Barbara burning of the Bank of America. Ultimately the Weatherpeople's 1970 decision to take the struggle underground and the tragic explosion that instigated that decision are presented and analyzed. Then the succession of symbolic political bombings that followed are enumerated and discussed.

One can also trace the development of revolutionary practice on the microcosmic personal level in terms of the group's internal dynamics.

Here again it is regrettable that the group resisted the filmmakers' urge to go even more deeply into this particular area. The evidence of personal and collective growth since the late sixties—as shown by some striking period footage of Dohrn, Ayers, and Jones—is one of the important revelations of the film. Highly suggestive is the contrast between the glaring, haughty radicals of those years, confronting cameras and reporters and haranguing their followers, and the subdued patient manner of conversing in the present interview.

One unfortunate gap in the film's history of the Weather Organization seems partly the result of the conditions of the production—that is, an explicit analysis of the group's current tactics. No doubt, security considerations forestalled any serious exploration of the group's present interaction with any particular constituency other than their propaganda efforts. There are no real answers provided to the crucial questions of whether the group is working in romantic isolation, or whether their revolutionary practice is rooted in relations with working class or radical communities. One senses that the group attempted to address this absence by their decision to take the camera out onto the streets and into an L.A. unemployment center (not to mention the visit to the hospital strike at which the FBI finally discovered that something was cooking). The two Weatherpeople's chats with a number of working people are impressive on their own terms—a middle-aged white woman talks of lack of opportunities, a welfare mother complains of how little her check will buy, a Chicano speaks in Spanish of the economic crisis. However, such brief interviews do not provide any sense of the Weather Underground's contact with such people other than through their media-oriented theatrics and their publication.

One of the major insights of the group during their years underground has apparently been the importance of self-criticism. The five have clearly had a lot of time over the last five years to evaluate their own past strategies. And as such, self-criticism becomes a major current of the film, a continuation of a similar vein in *Prairie Fire*. Not only are the radical tactics of the entire period of the New Left evaluated, but the group members' involvement in such tactics also comes up for analysis. "We were arrogant," they admit, and then talk about the importance of challenging their audience without condescending to it, of real dialogue.

No doubt they do not go far enough in this direction. They can probably be faulted for occasionally slipping dexterously by a few obvious pretexts for self-criticism, in the course of the interview. For example, when Mary Lampson forthrightly asks whether the charges of adventurism

and terrorism against the group had ever been warranted, Dohrn neatly
sidesteps the question:

> We believe in self-criticism. We believe it's a major way in which the revo-
> lution moves forward. We have a responsibility to have a strategy that
> takes into account the ups and downs that it's going to go through, and
> doesn't see only in the down an endless down, or only in the up an endless
> up. It's going to be a struggle that peaks, and then rests, and gathers back
> its strength, and learns from violence that's embedded in the system.
> So the mistake was not taking into account the long road—the whole
> thing—and understanding how much work was going to have to go into
> organizing the people through every form of struggle, and every form of
> resistance, and every form of fighting back—and focusing in on the one
> means of the struggle . . .

Unfortunately, the filmmakers themselves occasionally indulge such
reticence. For example, a discussion of the group's single most glaring
error, the Timothy Leary prison break fiasco, mentioned in Peter Biskind
and Marc Weiss's article in *Rolling Stone*, has been edited out of the
finished film. Nonetheless, this tendency toward evasion is more the exception than the rule: the overall spirit of the group's self-analysis is sincere
and hardheaded.

This self-critical tone of the discourse infects the entire filmic project as well. Hence, we are spared the embarrassment of an unmediated
endorsement of Weather politics by a constant reference to and analysis of
the meaning and purpose of the filmmaking enterprise itself. (De Antonio's
public pronouncements on the Weather Organization usually lack this self-
reflective posture.) "What is the best way for us to make a film that moves
other people, that moves many people to feel that they can make a revolution in this country?" This question, posed by Boudin at one point, is a
recurring preoccupation of the conversation. Self-interrogation is the basic
posture of the filmic discourse.

At one point, the Weatherpeople initiate a tense exchange about the
goals and the conditions of the filming by complaining of the discomfort
and artificiality of the setup. The position of a fugitive from the FBI complaining of his leg falling asleep does more than set off nervous laughter
among the crew. It is a vivid reminder of the artifice of the filmic situation
and of the conditions of its address. At another point, a similar discussion
includes recognition of the ambivalent political meaning of the project and
the film medium itself. Here is an admission that the overwhelming array
of equipment surrounding the five could possibly be used by either the
ruling class or the revolutionary class. Such frank self-questioning subverts
any tendency toward mystification. And it stops short of romanticizing

the figure of the revolutionary that less restrained filmmakers might have
catered to.

Perhaps it is Lampson's influence that has been responsible for
mediating de Antonio's enthusiasm for the Weatherpeople. Both she and
Wexler had serious reservations about the Underground's politics and
about the project itself. It is uncertain what effect her collaboration with
de Antonio has had on the film or will have in the future. (Lampson was
de Antonio's editor on three of his previous films and worked on *Attica*
as well. Whether she will continue to express her undeniable talent in
collaboration or independently will be interesting to see. It is not the first
time that a silent and efficient woman assistant of the sixties is claiming
an equitable share of the top billing in the seventies, and the process is
not yet complete.)

The *Village Voice* effected a particularly vicious use of that form of
prior restraint that the Constitution permits New York film critics (and
that the FBI would do well to emulate, although on second thought the
critics do the feds' job better and more subtly than they themselves could).[6]
Its notice declared, with a flash of typically devastating wit, that *Underground* was a "bomb" before it even opened and "of very limited interest
to cinema." Whether there is any connection between this *ex cathedra* pronouncement and the fact that the film had to be yanked from its New York
showplace after two weeks is hardly a taxing question (in those cities in
which it has been doing well, *Underground* was well received by the liberal
press). In any case, contrary to the *Voice*'s assessment, the Weatherpeople's
discussion is neither "boring," nor is Wexler's photography "static" (*Voice*).
Instead, the filmed interview material is austerely absorbing, contemplative, and demanding. Perhaps the visual style of the interview, with its
tendency to emphasize random details and surface textures, teapots, and
wristwatches, is Bressonian (as the *Rolling Stone* article suggested in a turn
of phrase that must have made many readers switch channels). However,
the directness of its address and the relentlessness of its scrutiny are surely
evocative of late Godard or of Straub.

The details of the curious minimalism of the mise-en-scène are
fascinating on their own terms. When we see the head-on faces of the
filmmakers, Wexler is poised and cool, but the other two are anxiously
and self-consciously engrossed in their subjects' words. Silhouetted in the
frame's foreground are rear views of the Weatherpeople's heads (seen in
a mirrored reverse-shot arrangement that the filmmakers rely on most).
A fascinating detail among the spare, bright furnishings of the room is
a huge, quilted wall hanging behind the crew whose inscription is only
gradually revealed in the course of the film, "The future will be what the

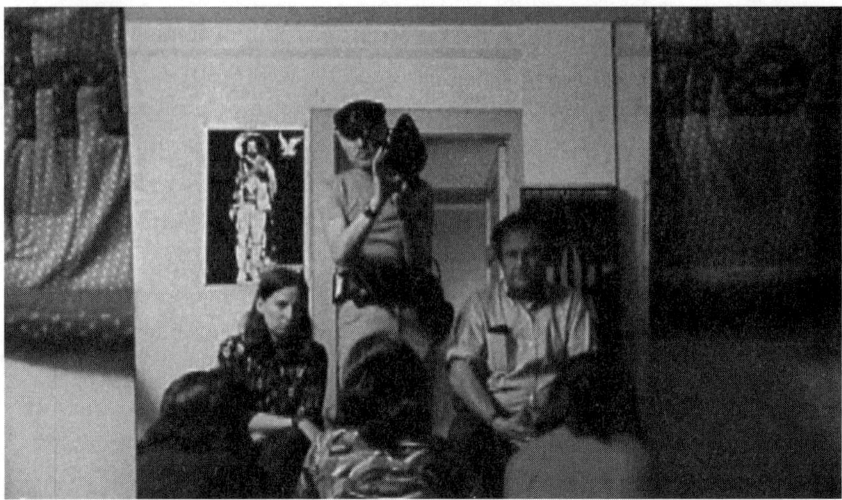

Underground (Emile de Antonio, 1976). Weatherpeople (rear view foreground) facing the crew, right to left, Emile de Antonio, Haskell Wexler, and Mary Lampson: the fascinating minimalism of the interview setup.

people struggle to make it." (The quilt was the Underground's present to the filmmakers at the end of the shooting.)

The filmmakers seem to have discovered, like Godard and Straub in their distinct ways, how to employ visual bareness as a means of underlying the auditory component of a scene. For, above all, *Underground* is a film to be listened to. The film derives much of its pace from the slow, deliberate style of dialogue that the Weatherpeople have evolved in their five years of underground communal living. As such, the work relies less than any other de Antonio film on the dynamics of visual momentum or editorial collision for its impact. At several points, the film even pauses while members of the group recite poems they have written—on the 1970 explosion, on the hatred aroused by the events in South Boston.

Near the end, the screen is even blacked out while a Weatherwoman recites her poem dedicated to Assata Shakur (the Black Liberation Army heroine on trial beginning in 1973), a poem about the loneliness and sacrifice involved in being underground. It is a digression of unusual power (if the concept of digression is permissible within that of collage). In any case, there is no question but that the spectator must listen attentively to the deliberate but leisurely unfolding of the conversation. In fact, spectators must listen even more attentively than has been demanded by de Antonio's films in the past, films always notable for their discursive composition in the first place. Such films as *Hearts and Minds* rely on a node of address distinctly different from this, their structural affinities to *Underground* notwithstanding, propelled solely through their visual energy. With *Underground*, voices and ideas are integrated with the images in a dialectical momentum that is forceful and articulate.

In one sense, the austere visual style of the interviews provides a perfect setting for the interpolated stock material. The structural opposition of the interview passages with the archival passages can be well imagined by those familiar with the work of de Antonio and his imitators. The interviews, with their slow, deliberate, analytic rhythm and their contemplative tone, have the effect of sharply setting off the inserts. And the visual inserts have a black and white dramatic intensity with their connotations of the turbulence and passion of that already thoroughly mythologized period.

There seem to be a few deficiencies the three filmmakers betray as filmmakers. That is, there might have been more dynamic interplay between the groups on either side of the camera and less feeling of intimidation on the part of the filmmakers. However, such deficiencies are abundantly compensated for by de Antonio and Lampson's brilliance as editors. Again and again, a point is made or a feeling explored by a masterful juxtaposition or superimposition of contrasting filmic materials, visual and auditory, present and past. One outstanding example is centered on the group's discussion of their coming to grips with the problem of sexism, both in terms of their interior collective functioning and their outward political stance. It is conducted as a voice-over carried above late-sixties footage showing Jones and Ayers addressing a demonstration. Their masculinist posturing and strutting behind the podium provide vivid flashback evidence here for the voice-over critique, with its affirmation of the necessity of strength and gentleness at the same time.

Elsewhere, a savagely brilliant montage evokes the ending of the Vietnam War. It does so by using excerpts from films such as *Year of the Pig* and *Introduction to the Enemy*, as well as other footage from network and official sources assembled by the editors. The sequence is introduced to the tune of Phil Ochs's "The War Is Over." We see splendid Navy footage showing a disabled U.S. helicopter plummeting from the deck of an aircraft carrier and floundering in the water. The progression of images that follows includes rare, almost hagiographic footage of Ho Chi Minh, a confident interview with Provisional Revolutionary Government spokesperson Madame Binh, a glimpse of smiling women militia, and then a *Millhouse*-style montage of Agnew and Kissinger giving identical good-bye waves from airliner ramps, as Ochs resurges on the soundtrack. The topical and structural center of the sequence then appears. We hear a presidential announcement by Ford that the war is over and a sharp contradiction by a Weatherwoman's voice-over: "We are not going to let the war be over."

The discussion that ensues, an affirmation of the priority of people over technology, of people as the subject of history, continues over long eerie slow-motion movements from a U.S. bomber showing jungle landscapes bursting into flames, their colors distilled with surreal brittleness. More *Millhouse* rhetoric is next. A collage follows of the Saigon branches of U.S. multinationals and some footage of the Nixons deplaning, all smiles and waves, at a Saigon airbase. At the same time, the Dylan song that gave the Weather Organization its name provides the musical coda to the sequence. De Antonio has lost none of his passionate anger, his caustic wit, nor his acute political insight in the years since *The Year of the Pig*.

The film's appeal, then, as will be clear from this passage, is by no means solely intellectual. Its predominantly analytic approach is often balanced by a rhetoric that is as gut-level as the declamatory and emotional Vietnam sequence. The Dylan and Ochs songs, for instance, are not the only use of music in this direction. Elsewhere, snatches of the same music, as well as of Nina Simone's "There's a New World Coming," capture the flavor of the era the film is trying to evoke. The Simone song, for example, is played climactically over the concluding shots of Native People activists at Wounded Knee, contemplated in stoic, silhouetted close up, rifle at the ready. As a kind of theme music for the film, these songs impart a tone of stirring optimism to the project as a whole. This tone, stemming in no small way from the confident pragmatism of the Weatherpeople themselves, is reinforced, it is true, by a sense of nostalgia for the days when a revolution did seem to be going on in the streets. And such nostalgia will no doubt be inferred from much of the film's stock footage—in the almost beatific aura of the clips of black martyrs, Malcolm X, King, and Fred Hampton, for example. But this enthralling, almost innocent optimism is also a product of a hard-headed materialist analysis. It is inspired by the Vietnamese victory against all odds, and by the growing base of the movement for change in the United States, not by any deluded estimation of the impact of underground resistance within the fortress of monopoly capitalism itself. As Dohrn puts it in the film:

> The lessons of the war are subversive . . . If you understand what happened in the Vietnamese war and why the Vietnamese defeated the U.S., it makes the possibility and the inevitability of revolution in the United States very clear. The United States government is not invincible. It didn't exist for all time, and it's not going to exist for all time.

It is a lesson Peter Davis had neither the courage nor the insight to induce in *Hearts and Minds*, nor Emile de Antonio in any previous films in an unequivocal way, for that matter. But here it is repeated with contagious confidence.

If de Antonio, Lampson, and Wexler now succeed in bringing this message to a substantial audience along with the crucial questions that are part of that message, it will be of utmost importance for the U.S. Left. At this point plans for a TV sales pitch are being formed but are still provisional upon the theatrical showing. But even within the liberal and campus constituency for such a film, if the stereotype of the committed revolutionary as a lunatic terrorist has been demystified by the image of these earnest, dedicated, tea-drinking people; if the media theme of the failure of the New Left has been subverted; if the possibility of negative discourse has been extended; then *Underground* is a film for which we cannot but be grateful.

▶

Part III: De Antonio's Final Two Films (2006–2008)

I come back to Emile de Antonio's last two films, *In the King of Prussia* (1982) and *Mr. Hoover and I* (1989), after three decades of fascination with his work, and sixteen years after the year that saw both the completion of his last film and his sudden, premature death at the age of seventy. My last publication on de Antonio—the preceding section on *Underground*—appeared in 1976, and find myself troubled by mixed feelings. I feel pride in the vindication of my youthful admiration for his work so many years later, vindication by both the enduring power and canonical status of most of his nine films (availability on video and DVD being one measure of such status), and by the two handsome scholarly books that appeared in 2000, one an anthology of writings on de Antonio's films, edited by Douglas Kellner and Dan Streible, and the other a monograph of contextual and artistic biography by historian Randolph Lewis.

I also feel awkward about this return to finish off the job I started so long ago. I had sidestepped the two eighties works of De (as I shall henceforth call him) as I moved on with other interests. The world of queer representations was coming to the foreground of my scholarship and seemed light years away from the world of this Marxist political artist-prophet and heterosexual serial monogamist for whom sexuality seemed simply not political. When sexual identity finally caught up to him, when in his parting shot *Mr. Hoover and I*, this friend of Andy Warhol, John Cage, and many other gay Manhattanites tackled head-on the notorious closet case who headed the FBI and had stalked De most of his life, the filmmaker stammered a bit and fumbled the ball, unsure how to factor

in sexual perversity with constitutional villainy. This was more than two
decades after the pre-Stonewall *Point of Order*, where he could perhaps
be forgiven for the glee with which he had demolished another odious
closet case, Senator McCarthy's first lieutenant Roy Cohn, who had got
caught trying to secure privileges for an inamorato and faced congressional scrutiny as a result. In that film, De's rhetoric and editing flowed with
the homophobic innuendo of McCarthy's opponent, lawyer Joseph Welch,
who used McCarthyite tactics himself to bring down the ogre and his
acolyte. (Welch had said that the Senator's fabricated evidence must have
been planted by "pixies," the Senator had taunted him to define "pixie,"
and Welch famously hit back "It is my understanding that a pixie is a close
relative of a fairy," bringing down the hearing room with a knowing mockery of the targeted, flaring Cohn.) I simply didn't have the language or
the critical tools to bring this up in my first article on De, written in 1975
(although in rereading Part II of this chapter, written in 1976, I see that I
was straining at the closet door).

Even earlier in the seventies, I don't remember whether my discomfort
about *Painters Painting* had to do even in part with De's hesitation to mess
up his ideological line on American pop art with personal sexual identities,
even with gay stars Warhol, Jasper Johns, Robert Rauschenberg, Henry
Geldzahler, and Philip Johnson dominating the screen (all now part of queer
art history). Hell, I was in the closet myself. All the same, this perhaps anachronistic negotiation of this intersection of art history and subcultural identity
politics in Part III in 2006–2008 does not placate the feelings of regret that
also well up. I taught *In the Year of the Pig* faithfully every single year during the eighties (and *Millhouse* almost as frequently, until students eventually
emerged who did not know who Richard Nixon had been), and every showing of *Year* deepened my reverent attachment to its indisputable greatness.
Yet I never had time for the aging artist during that decade, despite a few of
his overtures and encounters. Been there, done that—I had already heard all
the stories, had little tolerance for high-octane substance issues, and so let a
younger generation of Canadian documentarists, Peter Wintonick and Ron
Mann in particular, take over the shrine.

Now there is the inevitable regret I experience at the recognition that it
is a much older—and not necessarily wiser—person now looking at De, now
a historical figure with a guaranteed place in a canon of artistic and political
tradition rather than the foibled and contradictory living artist I had once
championed and then tactfully, tactically abandoned and betrayed. This
regret, however, only slightly taints the inestimable pleasure in this task of
this return and rediscovery. For *In the King of Prussia* and *Mr. Hoover and
I*, which I had seen several times over the years and liked but never written

about, are, despite the lackluster critical consensus, jewels of documentary
art and "commitment." Positioned at the start and the end of the eighties,
respectively, and fully resonant with the finest fulfillments of the cinema's
potential for resistance in that dark decade in American history, they also
hold up miraculously well two decades later, not as the quasi-senile testamentary utterances that reviewers sometimes implicitly saw in them (though
the latter is of course testamentary in both the symbolic and the de facto
senses). They both hold up as bold, vibrant, even heroic works of art and
politics. Both extend the distinctive preoccupations of De's first seven films:
historical investigation through the collage and interrogation of archival
documents; didactic, intellectual analysis anchored within an interactive format and the interview idiom; radical critique of the American political state
and the civilization that sustains it. Both films also stake out new territories
in both the form and the discourse of that critique, an achievement that
some of De's most ardent defenders have failed to pick up on.

In the King of Prussia emerged in 1982 after a hiatus of six years
since the release of *Underground*. De's career had staggered after the
mostly mixed critical reception and uninspired box office that had greeted
the earlier film. He had then failed to find funding for his long cherished
CIA-themed project based on the book of Philip Agee, and it was only
in 1980 that a new film idea awakened. In September of that year, the
filmmaker's old allies from the antiwar movement, Daniel and Philip Berrigan carried out an act of civil disobedience in a General Electric nuclear
weapons factory, as part of a group of fellow Catholic peace activists who
collectively became known as the Ploughshares Eight. Slipping into the
manufacturing facility in King of Prussia, Pennsylvania, the group symbolically hammered the cones of the warheads, poured their own blood over
the paperwork, and prayed until the police came. As the accused prepared
for the trial that they saw as a public airing of their anti-arms race cause,
De decided to give them a cinematic forum for their actions, their critique,
and their defense. As Lewis recounts, De hoped to film the trial itself, but,
refused by the courts, he decided to shoot a reenactment of the trial by
the eight original participants and by actors playing judge, jury, and witnesses. Fundraising was difficult in the first months of the Reagan regime,
especially among De's traditional bankrollers, wealthy liberal intellectuals
who looked askance at the Berrigans' pro-life, pro-Palestine advocacy,[7] so
De unprecedentedly coughed up half of his budget out of his own sav-
ings. Though reviewers would often comment on the project's stringent
resources, purportedly visible on the screen, the total budget of $400,000,
four times larger than the bill for *Underground*, was relatively posh for an
oppositional documentary at the time, even a feature length one. However,

with De's idea to reconstruct the trial as a so-called docudrama, money soon felt extremely tight. So did time, since the Eight had only three days to participate in the dramatization of their trial on a rented New York City set before a scheduled court appearance for sentencing in July of 1982. For both reasons therefore the filmmaker decided to shoot the film on one-inch video, a practice still almost unheard of in the independent documentary sector where by and large 16mm would prevail for another decade. For this purpose he recruited leftist cinematographer Judy Irola, known for her work on late-seventies De-inspired interview-and-archive rad docs like *The Wobblies* (Deborah Shaffer and Stewart Bird, 1979). More recently and more to the point for De, Irola had shot the 1980 historical reconstruction, *Northern Lights* (John Hanson and Rob Nilsson, 1978), a narrative of grassroots resistance, albeit set sixty years in the past rather than a few months earlier like the Prussia script.

Another higher profile recruit was De's old friend and funder Martin Sheen who agreed to play the part of the unsympathetic presiding Judge Salus. With the Eight reperforming their own roles, and Sheen alongside a half dozen other actors recruited to play GE employees and other witnesses, De was entering new territory that was unfamiliar to him. As Lewis reminds us, De was joining a rich tradition of docudrama, or more precisely documentary works deploying various levels of dramatization, dating back almost to the beginnings of cinema (although it could be argued that the elaborate artifice of the Weatherpeople interviews had foreshadowed the later interest in docudrama). What Lewis neglects to mention was that De was in step with the younger eighties generation of documentarists who were also experimenting with dramatization, in part in reaction against the entrenchment of the De formula as virtually hegemonic by the end of the seventies. Other than Nilsson and Hansen's work, among those whose interest in the possibilities of hybrid documentaries had preceded or were contemporary to *Prussia* were Marin Karmitz (*Coup pour coup*, Fr. 1972), Peter Watkins (*Edvard Munch*, Nor. 1974), Martha Coolidge (*Not a Pretty Picture*, U.S., 1976), Michelle Citron (*Daughter Rite*, U.S., 1978), Tony Garnett (*Prostitute*, UK, 1979), Kay Armatage (*Striptease*, Canada, 1980), Bruce Glawson (*Michael a Gay Son*, Canada,1980), Denys Arcand (*Le confort et l'indifférence*, Canada, 1981), Marilú Mallet (*Journal inachevé [Unfinished Diary]*, Canada, 1982), Paul Cowan (*The Kid Who Couldn't Miss*, Canada, 1982), and Carolyn Strachan (*Two Laws*, Aust., 1980), strong works without exception that are in some cases undeservedly now forgotten. The fact that most of these films come from outside of the United States—and that the American examples come from what was still the feminist countertradition—suggests that a still influential vérité culture discouraged Americans from experimenting with the options of documentary dramatization. Be that as it may, an international current of filmmakers clearly anticipated and shared De's oppositional instinct and personal motivation to compensate for absent or missing histories and images with reconstruction and dramatization. And this current, with De resolutely on board, represented a prophetic collective, generational impulse to invent a new documentary idiom.

A new surge around mid-decade of what Bill Nichols would come to call the performative documentary was not long in coming.[8] The surge would include a wide range of documentaries incorporating dramatized material, from Nichols's exemplary *Sari Red* (Pratibha Parmar, UK, 1988) and other British "black" works like *Looking for Langston* (Isaac Julien, 1988) to the procession from the same period of canonical films like *Sans soleil* (Chris Marker, 1983), and several prominent American entries *Far From Poland* (Jill Godmilow, 1984), *Before Stonewall* (Robert Rosenberg, John Scagliotti, Greta Schiller, 1984), *The Thin Blue Line* (Errol Morris, 1988), and *Tongues Untied* (Marlon Riggs, 1989). This is not to mention a small avalanche of major Quebec works undeservedly neglected south of the border: *La Turlute des années dures* (Richard Boutet and Pascal Gélinas, 1983), *Quel numéro what number?* (Sophie Bissonnette, 1984), *Not Crazy Like You Think* (Jacqueline Levitin, 1984), *Le Dernier glacier* (Jacques Leduc and Roger Frappier, 1984), *Passiflora* (Fernand Bélanger and Dagmar Gueissaz-Teufel, 1985), and a bit later *Au Chic resto pop* (Tahani Rached, 1990). Although De cannot be credited with sparking this new exemplary current of the decade as he had in the sixties, his innovations with *King of Prussia* were nevertheless undeniably at the forefront of the new horizon in documentary experimentation, helping to set the stage for a current of similar hybrid work throughout the eighties.

Neither De nor Irola had ever worked in video, but De also had aesthetic reasons alongside the budgetary ones for the switch to the electronic medium, though these have been characterized as "concocted" "rationalizations" by Lewis. He felt that video was suitable for his desired "rough looking aesthetic" and had been inspired by Antonioni's experimentation with the format in a work he had just seen at the New York Film Festival of 1981 (Lewis 2000, 215). He "didn't want to make it look rich—I wanted it to be what it is. I was interested in a film of meaning and content. The dryness of its aesthetic would be more interesting than all that lace-and-teapot stuff" (Seitz [1983] 2000, 321). Even as sympathetic a critic as *The Progressive*'s Michael Seitz opined that the film "is not an especially good-looking movie," and Lewis points to "limitations of the video format" and to "not only . . . poor quality and composition of the image but also a muddied soundtrack" as well as problematical performances (Seitz [1983] 2000, 321). Meanwhile mainstream reviewers like *The New York Times'* Janet Maslin referred to the film's "plain rough-edged style," its "crudely staged courtroom scenes," and the "film's plainness border[ing] on the bland" (Maslin 1983, 57). At least Maslin had used the notion of "minimalism" to acknowledge that an aesthetic intent of "less is more" was indeed in operation, and now in retrospect, after our two decades of acclimatization to video documentary, the film looks much better than its original detractors allowed.

Although it is now seldom possible to see *King of Prussia* on the big screen, on its circulating video version, technical problems are no longer conspicuous (if such was ever the case), and De's and Irola's apprenticeship with video seems vindicated. The courtroom scenes have an austere spare elegance, with a distinctive visual texture that operates self-reflexively to capture the stress and urgency of the shoot as well as to optimize the viewer's full attention to the speeches. Like all courtroom narratives, this film and the courtroom dramatizations are talky, but this talk is dense and rich in its pulsating texture of ideas and ideals: De can be seen as part of a significant thrust of independent cinema of the early eighties that reclaimed speech and textuality as a legitimate element of the cinema. *In the King of Prussia* calls for positioning alongside works as diverse as Yvonne Rainer's *Journeys from Berlin/1971* (1980); Louis Malle's *My Dinner with André* (1981); Jean-Marie Straub and Danièle Huillet's *Trop tôt, trop tard* [*Too Soon, Too Late*] (1982); and, to cite a work without the foregoing works' avant-garde influences, that other great anti-arms race documentary of the same period, Terre Nash's Oscar-winning *If You Love This Planet* (1982), a twenty-six-minute condensation of a single lecture by an antinuke doctor, Helen Caldicott, interspersed à la De with archival shot interludes. Still the talkies went somewhat against the grain of the prevailing winds: in contrast to *Prussia*'s discursiveness, the other great anti-arms race American documentary of the early Reagan era, *Atomic Café* (Jayne Loader, Pierce Rafferty, Kevin Rafferty, 1982), though clearly building on the De formula of archival collage to subvert and excoriate history, embodied another reaction to the entrenched interactive "interviews and archives" formula enshrined in the seventies. *Atomic Café* completely eschewed interviews, narration, and all textuality not present in its very rich lode of documents. Ironically Loader and the Rafferty's, with their sexy, colorful, and wry work, acerbic where De was earnest and idealistic, completely dwarfed their mentor in terms of critical and box office success. They could not dwarf him, however, in his proffering of pragmatic avenues for dissent in the forthcoming Star Wars era.

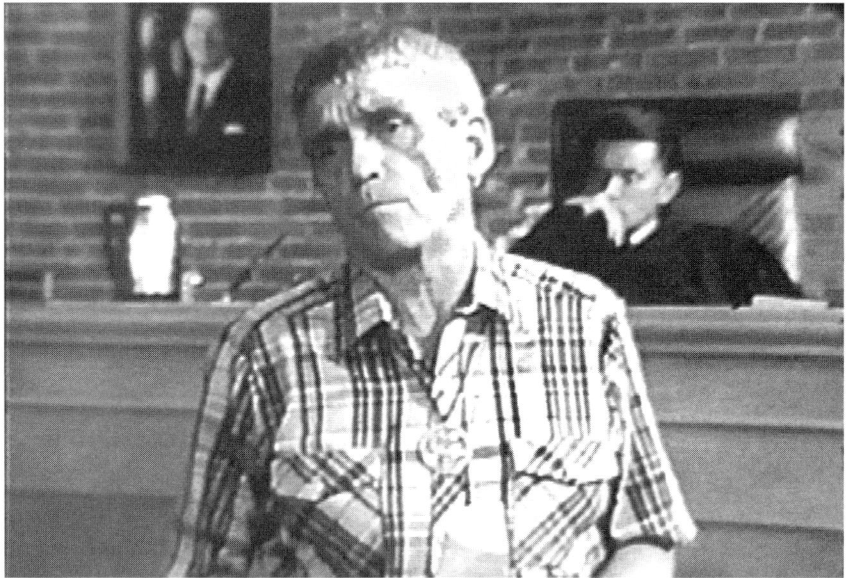

In the King of Prussia (Emile de Antonio, 1982). Left to right, Ronald Reagan, radical antiwar saint Daniel Berrigan reenacting his defense of necessity, and Martin Sheen playing the scowling Judge Salus.

My updated and retroactive response to *In the King of Prussia* may seem to benefit from hindsight in the form of the foregoing lists of documentary film titles, but this comes hopefully less out of my obsessive pedantry than out of a realization that the full history of documentary in the key moment of the eighties remains to be written, and it will crystallize first and foremost, as always, in films themselves. Meanwhile what remains most with me from De's unique 1982 filmic text is the artistic rendering of moral and political authority—some ventured "clumsily propagandistic," "maudlin quality," and "unrelenting jeremiad" (Lewis 2000, 220–21)—that arises out of the nonprofessional performances of the Ploughshares Eight. The interpolated framework of archival materials is vivid, as are the vérité inserts of testimony on the courthouse steps, the activists' prayerful pep rallies, and the public theater of disobedience. But it is the performances of the Eight, especially of Molly Rush and Daniel Berrigan, that have special affect and effect. All agreed that Berrigan's performance was at the center of the film, even those who found it sanctimonious and grating; I found it riveting, then but much more so now, even coming to it from the opposite end of the ideological spectrum like De himself. It works all the better since Berrigan, consummate performer, was well prepared, did not read a transcript as others had to do, and delivered his *apologia pro sua vita*-cum-sermon as if transported back to the moment of crisis, or to a fresh audience: "we could not *not* do what we did." It is not surprising that De at the time also personally felt its impact, giving it the weight of uninterrupted screen time. In interviews he almost sheepishly testified to his own personal growth and spiritual awakening, so much so that his experience became in Lewis's words a shortlived "conversion yarn," bringing the director back from his temporary flirtation with violence as an oppositional strategy at the time of his encounter with the Weatherpeople. Berrigan's eloquent centerpiece presentation is in answer to Sister Anne Montgomery's questions, which are themselves all the more effective because their stiffness operates as guarantor of their authenticity. Sheen had clearly never been so upstaged and his sweaty fury is as ambiguous as it is excellent. At the same time, Rush is also extremely affecting, perhaps because compared to her mentor she is clearly the amateur in public oratory: she is shown saying farewell to her children in her kitchen, narrating the events leading up to the arrests, and later offering a layperson's interpretation of international law and its application to a Pennsylvania courtroom.

The long-take integrity of the testimony is challenging to the uninitiated viewer, and on this point, De was justifiably uncompromising: "if people are too bored to look at Berrigan for ten minutes, let them get out of the theater. I'm not going to change it, speed it up, make a cut, just to make it palatable for them" (Lewis 2000, 224). This obstinacy has an alienating effect that deepens its impact all the more. Otherwise a concluding interview with one of the jurors, an unpretentious but dignified mechanic seen in his workplace, echoes some of De's finest interviewing from the sixties, respectful and humbly attentive. Lewis critiques the "substitution" of the "unbearable earnestness" of such scenes as the collective singing of the sixties campfire piety hymn "Kum ba ya" for "cold dialectical analysis of his earlier films, which set charge and countercharge in opposition for the audience to interpret"(Lewis 2000, 222). But De's 1982 rhetorical structure is in effect a new rendition of the figures of lament or mourning that punctuates much of his work: for example, the tragic coda to *Year of the Pig* is surely no less earnest in its layering of the "Battle Hymn of the Republic" over the footage of GI casualties. *In the King of Prussia* brings to the fore, and in effect rediscovers the power of affect that had been an unacknowledged feature of most of De's work.

Was this strategy appropriately tuned to the new reality of Reagan-Thatcher Star Wars hysteria and the attendant demoralization of the U.S. Left (Reagan is seen throughout the film, grinning out from his framed portrait behind Judge Salus)? Arguably yes. Nevertheless, the film more or less flopped in the United States, with New York's Film Forum ten-day run serving as the

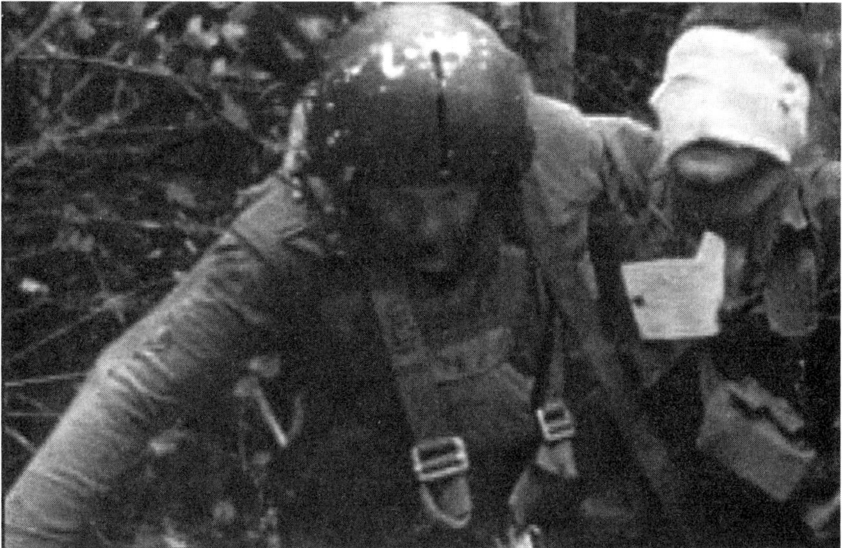

At the conclusion of *In the Year of the Pig* (1968), wounded GIs stagger under a stylized track of "Battle Hymn of the Republic," a reminder of the intense melodramatic thrust of de Antonio's oeuvre after all.

flagship venue for minimal art house exposure in several of the usual urban liberal strongholds. Domestic broadcast was out of the question, purportedly for technical reasons, but prizes in several European festivals ensured a strong critical and exhibition impact throughout much of western Europe, including raves in a U.K. then reeling from the worst of Thatcherism.

In the King of Prussia had the misfortune to come out cotemporaneously with—and to be compared unfavorably with—another major film that celebrated civil disobedience, albeit safely tucked away in its heritage epic costumes: *Gandhi* (Richard Attenborough). De's next and final work, *Mr. Hoover and I*, was to bow more than six years later in the surge of critical excitement over Michael Moore's *Roger and Me* (1989), a hip, youthful film that seemed to epitomize a new lease on life for the theatrical documentary and a new thorn in the flesh for Reaganomics and the Republican state. The revival of documentary thus heralded seemed to have little space for a reflective, minimalist memoir by an alcoholic has-been, in fact one that was to be released posthumously and largely miss the new momentum signified by Moore.

In fact, although *Mr. Hoover and I* is a one-of-a-kind film, it too demonstrates De's uncanny ability to be fully in step with the aesthetic and political issues of the moment. For western nonfiction filmmakers of the late eighties these issues crystallized in forms of first-person filmmaking.

A surge of works, mostly nonfiction, testify to the convergence of various kinds of identity politics abroad in civil society and the zeitgeist, together with the search for a new energy in documentary aesthetics, inevitably cross-pollinizing with the avant-garde. These energies led to Nichols's categorization of performative documentary in 1994, as we have already seen, but the momentum of autobiographical nonfiction was recognized as early as the seventies by John Katz's and P. Adams Sitney's rigorous research into emerging first-person modes (Katz 1978; Sitney 1977–78). According to Lewis, *Mr. Hoover and I* had gestated in autobiographical musings inscribed in the artist's journals from the mid-seventies onwards, fortified by the devastating impact in the same decade of the discovered FBI files that had dogged him for almost forty years. De's correspondence claimed erroneously and with characteristic glibness that no one had ever made an autobiographical film before (Lewis 2000, 229). De might be forgiven for having been unaware of precursors from the "periphery" as disparate as queer pioneers Jan Oxenburg, Terence Davies, Tom Joslin, and international one-off examples like Raj Kapoor, Santiago Alvarez, Derek May, and Kathleen Shannon, not to mention the feminist documentarists already invoked at the outset of this section and seventies video pioneers from Lisa Steele to Bill Viola. But De's neglect of Chaplin, Welles, and arguably Vertov, as well De's fellow downtowners Stan Brakhage, Jonas Mekas, and Leo Hurwitz, makes one relieved that this lapse was not a public pronouncement. Nevertheless it cannot be denied that when *Mr. Hoover and I* finally appeared at the Toronto International Film Festival alongside *Roger and Me* only three months before De's death, it was on the cutting edge of a whole new movement, propelled in most cases by artists a generation or two younger than him. In this respect, we can endorse Lane's positioning of *Mr. Hoover and I* in respect to the work of such late-eighties American pathfinders as Su Friedrich, Ross McElwee, and of course Moore, not to mention Marlon Riggs (cited by Lewis 2000, 230; see also Lane 2002).

De had always been interested in biography, notably in his demonic portraits of Joseph McCarthy and Nixon, and his almost hagiographic portraits of the Weatherpeople and that other Senator McCarthy: Eugene. Autobiography might be seen as an outgrowth of this interest, but a number of aesthetic experiments could also be foreseen and serve to make *Mr. Hoover and I* an original work, unique in the late-eighties flood. *Mr. Hoover and I* might begin with the requisite childhood snapshots, but the film soon veers off course from the already conventional formula. It does so through marshalling an assortment of materials that Jonathan Rosenbaum respectfully inventoried in his appreciation of De and the film:

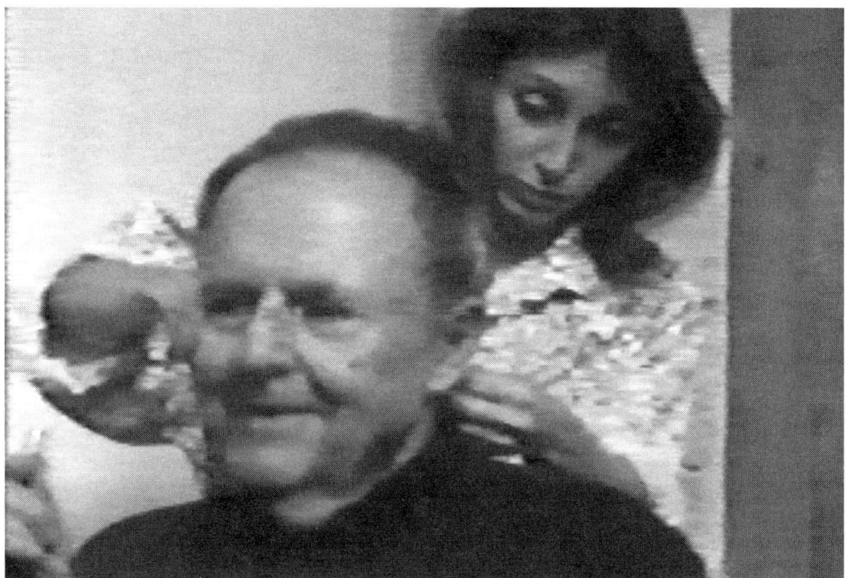

Mr. Hoover and I (Emile de Antonio, 1989). In one of several first-person threads in this testamentary film, the ad-libbing director receiving a fastidious haircut from spouse Nancy.

- Two different setups addressing the camera in his own apartment, extemporizing from notes. I would add to Rosenbaum by seeing these tropes as a vindication of the "talking head" by the film-maker who had rescued it from broadcast oblivion two decades earlier, now proffering his own talking head.
- An observational record of a lecture presented to an appreciate audience at Dartmouth College, in conjunction with a revival of *Point of Order,* in the same spontaneous standup mode as in the apartment monologues and not without some repetition.
- A vérité sequence, shot by Canadian acolyte Ron Mann in 1985 but never used, depicting De's conversation with John Cage in the composer's kitchen, in which the filmmaker is asking his friend about the aesthetic principle of indeterminacy and the composer is determined to finish the loaf of bread he is baking.
- A self-conscious observational sequence performed by De and his wife Nancy, as the latter cuts the ad libbing filmmaker's hair with excruciating fastidiousness. My own gloss is that here is an obvious homage to a film called *Haircut* by De's friend Warhol (1964), who had died only two years earlier. The earlier film's teasing homoeroticism is missing, of course, but the couple's tender November–July conjugality is arguably eroticized.

- Archival shots focusing on Hoover's relationship with Nixon, notably jovial sequences of after-dinner speechmaking and mutual fawning lifted almost intact from *Millhouse.*
- Archival still shots of Hoover himself and of the FBI documents on De (Rosenbaum [1990] 2000, 335–44).

These materials might seem cobbled together rather loosely, even to provide their own demonstration of indeterminacy. But Rosenbaum correctly discovers in the eighty-six-minute film's self-reflexively "dialectical" structure the intent and effect of art (and of art cinema): beginning with the long-take rigor developed in *Prussia* and slowly tightening the rhythm, implementing despite a circuitous sensibility its own linearity of argument whose spareness is a tribute to the aesthetic and discursive clarity of Cage and Warhol's respective minimalisms. The ultimate effect is, as Rosenbaum decides, "an autobiography that dialectically and persuasively defines itself as a sane countertext to the demented biography of De compiled by the FBI" (Rosenbaum [1990] 2000, 337).

But *Mr. Hoover and I* is also more than that, a melodramatic construction of the self through the alterego of the tormenting, pursuing nemesis, with shades of *Les Misérables* and *Crime and Punishment*, not to mention *I Am a Fugitive from a Chain Gang*! Meanwhile, the warp of the fabric is a free flowing essay that meditates on everything from the New York art world to De's relationship with Nancy. Unsurprisingly, not everyone shared Rosenbaum's empathy: *The Village Voice* is no country for old men, and rock critic Gary Giddins, having trouble distinguishing between persona and film, found both "tiresome" (Giddins, 1990). Another case of a critic reviewing a film he or she wanted (a *Millhouse* on Hoover) rather than the film seen, this misunderstanding of a favorite son's final film was especially grating coming from the progressive downtown weekly that had in many ways been the voice of de Antonio's constituency throughout his career.

I have argued that in the intervening decades De's final two films have grown in standing and freshness in the context of the other breakthrough documentary currents of the eighties. Both now command attention with their charged cross-pollination of performance, vérité, and document and with their articulations of the artist's political meanderings in the last decade of his life, his personal search for an ideological resting place as he moved through passive resistance and antiwar activism to a place as a constitutional Cassandra alongside a renewed historical decortication. At the very least, they both clearly deserve a more balanced evaluation and place in the documentary canon and de Antonio corpus than were accorded them by many critics, friends, and foes, when they came out—as opposed to the instant "thumbs-up, thumbs-down" consumer ratings of the dawning Sundance era.

Ironically, *Mr. Hoover and I* appeared almost at the same time as *Une Histoire de vent* [*A Tale of the Wind*], another major autobiographical testament by an elderly artist in whom I felt a major stake, Joris Ivens. (The two films rubbed shoulders at the 1989 Toronto International Film Festival, three months after Ivens's death at the age of ninety, three months before de Antonio's death.) What felicitous comparisons the winds of film history blow upon us! The irony is compounded when one recalls that two of the most productive Marxist filmmakers of the century marked the last year of their lives—the year the Berlin Wall fell, don't forget—with a first-person testamentary work that seemed to bracket and to reinvigorate at the same time earlier ideological fervor—as well as thereby jointly closing a chapter of documentary history. (Nichols grasped the momentous synchrony in dedicating *Representing Reality* to the two men jointly in 1991.) Both artists scrupulously avoided referring to the tectonic shifts in Eastern Europe in their final works, though one infers from Ivens's brush with incipient Chinese capitalist bureaucracy and de Antonio's despair at the erosion of the U.S. constitution in the first Bush presidency, that emerging mythologies of the so-called "end of history" were very much on their minds. The fascinating convergence is that both artists had hitherto shyly eschewed any onscreen appearance,[9] and suddenly in their last films burst in from the wings for a corporeal performance of intense cinematic palpability, the elder filmmaker frail, diminutive, and asthmatic and the younger one corpulent and sanguine, both bodies and careers ravaged by history. The two filmmakers' self-dramatizations perform a Benjaminian bidirectional retrospection, combining regret, ambivalence, and exhaustion with narcissistic self-mythologization, pride, and defiance. *Une Histoire de vent* is as rich, exotic, and over-the-top as *Mr. Hoover and I* can be called minimalist, domestic, and quotidian, but both films present the filmmaker's body as the crux of a poetic meditation on the artist's career and legacy and on the historical arena in which his works unfolded.

Both final works were greeted respectfully, though with the slight embarrassment that greeted the last works by Ford, Hitchcock, and Antonioni, and both seemed to be indulged as unnecessarily inconsequential in comparison with the world-historical weightiness of the filmmakers' oeuvres as a whole. I admitted earlier with regard to both the American and the Dutchman that I was experiencing a kind of fatigue in the eighties and hesitated about some of the artistic and discursive choices of either—a lack of loyalty that shames and puzzles me in retrospect when I remember

the exasperating deserts of cancelled projects and recalcitrant budgets
both filmmakers were traversing throughout the decade (seven years for de
Antonio between his second last film and last, eleven years for Ivens). No
doubt both final films work best with dewy-eyed young liberal audiences
in the process of discovering a major historical figure and his legacy
of committed art—such as those smiling wire-rimmed New England-
ers shown at the Dartmouth College screening of *Point of Order* in *Mr.
Hoover and I* and who had clearly never heard the stories before.

Filmmakers don't often get to choose their testamentary utterance.
Ivens may be the exception, and it is unlikely that de Antonio sensed the
tolling of the bell as clearly as Ivens, or knew how little time he had to
accompany the film on its rounds. Despite my saturation and cynicism, I
feel a strong sense of what I might call "radical pathos" in the two films, in
the two heroic revolutionary artists surveying their toil in the superstruc-
tural vineyard with such contradictory feelings. I feel this pathos especially
in the face of the two worn authorial bodies occupying the lens so unfor-
gettably for the first and last times. Jane Gaines, in her sustained effort
since the nineties to probe the encounter of radical cinema with Marxist
ideology and aesthetics has developed the concepts of "pathos of fact" and
"socialist melodrama" (1996, 64, 67); "sensuous struggle" (1999, 91); and
"realism beyond realism" (2007, 19) in order to theorize cinematic narratives of class conflict and revolutionary struggle and our engagement with
them as spectators. Though her essays do not apply to my argument in the
narrow and literal sense, these explorations of "the compatibility of intel-
lect and affect" (1996, 64) may have bearing on de Antonio's and Ivens's
two documentary mises-en-scène of geriatric disempowerment, autobiographical melancholy, and testamentary passion. It is not for nothing that I
have parenthetically invoked two of the most melodramatic of nineteenth
century novels, especially *Les Misérables*, Victor Hugo's epic tear jerker of
the righteous renegade hounded by a Parisian Hoover throughout his life,
reanimated in 1980 as the twentieth century's soapiest musical—not incidentally full of as much public socialist melodrama as the private familial
variety. With *Mr. Hoover and I* seen alongside *Une Histoire de vent*,
another melodrama, this time disguised as Shakespearean tragedy, *King
Lear*, cannot be kept out of the picture—all the more so with Ivens's flaring white locks and his clouded corneas. Neither filmmaker is willing to go
quietly, and de Antonio and Ivens construct an individual pathos in their
backward look upon a life's work of cinematic critique and solidarity, and
in their performances of verbal and gestural defiance toward an unknown
"postcommunist" future respectively. Each film vividly expresses in its
way a moving personal sensitivity to and artistic confrontation with the

betrayals of the realms of the material and of ideology, frustration at the uncooperativeness of history, flirtations with renunciation, apostasy and compromise, fascination with the unexpected detours in what Eisenstein termed the road to truth, true investigation and the creative act (invoked at the 1974 start of this essay). Both films ultimately embody rage and then a persistence that is obstinate but serene in the face of the Revolution still deferred. Neither film should be seen in isolation from the larger filmographies, of course, and de Antonio's in particular highlights the underrecognized pathos underlying of his earlier films. That de Antonio's film was posthumously misunderstood and undervalued adds of course to the revolutionary pathos it builds, and to the melodramatic arc of his three-decade, nine-film oeuvre.

[**6**]

Sufficient Virtue, Necessary Artistry

The Shifting Challenges of Revolutionary Documentary History (2006–2008)

This chapter was written the most recently of the ten essays in The Right to Play Onself, *but it in many ways embodies the anthology's title better than many others with its exploration of a crucial moment in the history of media democracy. "'Sufficient Virtue, Necessary Artistry:' The Shifting Challenges of Revolutionary Documentary History" also constitutes the book's Canadian Content with a vengeance—a sort of my coming out of the closet as a Canadianist for American readers who may have developed an appreciation for Cronenberg, Egoyan, Arcand, and perhaps even Bob and Doug MacKenzie or the Trailer Park Boys over the years but for whom the epicurean delights of Allan King or Anne Claire Poirier are still an unheard-of delicacy.*

Situated halfway through this collection by reason of the chronological place of its corpus within the heady sixties and seventies, it could also serve as an introduction to the volume as a whole. It helps set the stage for the other pieces and represents some of my current research interests in Canadian documentary—as well as a kind of mea culpa for not treating Challenge for Change/Société nouvelle (CFC/SN) somewhat more seriously in the seventies when it was still in existence (I was clearly aware of the experimental program in 1975 when I implicitly compared it to Vertov's schemes to promote the masses' right to be artists [see chapter 2] and in the early eighties when I somehow ended up squeezing it out of "Show Us Life"). As usual, it shows my great affection for documentary makers and subjects and even for my academic peers (though a little less patience for the latter): a gentler, more tolerant and generous, less dogmatic Waugh? Or the encroaching signs of senility?

▶

Challenging Archives or Canonizing "Challenge"

It is a commonplace that the DVD revolution that got under way in the
mid-nineties radically altered the way we teach, study, understand, and
remember film history. This is all the more true for those of us toiling in
the rockier, more marginal vineyards of the cinematic heritage. Somehow I
seem to have ended up working in several of them, from Canadian cinema
to queer cinema to Indian art film to documentary. Certain key films on
my syllabi I show on the precarious and fragile VHS's once coaxed from
friendly but diffident executors, now turning into dust, from the American
queer autobiography *Blackstar: Autobiography of a Close Friend*, made by
Tom Joslin in 1977 and known to most audiences only via its excerpts in
his posthumous DVD *Silverlake Life* (1993) to the 1936 Indian devotional
epic *Sant Tukaram*, a key work by the pioneer Marathi-language directors Damle and Fatehlal. If one thinks the situation couldn't possibly be
worse than that for vintage indie queer cinema and archival Indian epics in
the regional languages, look at the field of radical documentary, where it
clearly is, if not worse, certainly no better.

As an example of the dire situation for historians of Left documentary, consider that of the several dozen films discussed in detail in my 1984
anthology *"Show Us Life": Toward a History and Aesthetics of the Committed Documentary* only an erratic handful seem to be available on DVD.
Regarding my section on the pre–World War II precursors of the tradition,
the Soviet documentarists are perhaps the exceptions that prove the rule:

the key features by Esfir Shub are available, as are the three late features
by Dziga Vertov that were canonized in the West since the sixties, plus his
first feature *Kino-Glaz* (1924). (But where are Vertov's crucial early newsreels discussed in the book?) Thereafter in my chronological corpus things
quickly get worse: of the entire selection of classical sound documentaries
covered, only Joris Ivens's *The Spanish Earth* (1937) and Frontier Film's
final feature *Native Land* (1941) are represented on DVD and the latter only in a twelve-minute excerpt. The others, from the American and
European workers' newsreels to the French Communist Party campaign
feature *La Vie est à nous* (1936), are unavailable (despite the fact that the
latter docu-hybrid is by Jean Renoir). With regard to the period I referred
to as "contemporary," films that had emerged in the two decades or so
prior to 1984, readers wanting to verify on DVD my contributors' analyses
must take their pick among a couple of Newsreel classics (*Black Panther*
and *San Francisco State on Strike*, both 1969); the Oscar-winning classic
Harlan County, U.S.A. (Barbara Kopple, 1976); a late installment in the
New Left radical history cycle, *The War at Home* (Glen Silber and Barry
Alexander Brown, 1979); and finally and most surprisingly the recently
issued collection of works by Cuban collagist Santiago Alvarez. For a
whole raft of indispensable films from *Hours of the Furnaces* (1968) and
Waves of Revolution (1974) to the pioneering U.S. feminist documentaries
Self Health (Catherine Allen, Judy Irola, et al., 1974) and *Rape* (JoAnn
Elam, 1975)—all crucial to an understanding of the peripatetic twentieth-
century history of committed documentary, one simply has to rely on the
spotty and staggering VHS market, to memories of screenings decades in
the past, or worst of all, to almost always unreliable secondary reports.

   We must thank capitalism for small mercies, of course, for it occasionally allows us to be cautiously optimistic about imminent access to
important fragments of our Left documentary heritage. For example, the
Joris Ivens estate seems to have overcome its anachronistic celluloid-centric
piracy paranoia enough to push along a DVD release of a serious package
of sixteen Ivens films it first announced in 2006, then for 2007, finally out
in 2008 (with excellent quality but not without some symptomatic gaps).
Not unrelated is the late-breaking release on DVD of a selection of militant
documentaries from the fecund milieu of Paris in May 1968, namely those
produced by the legendary Groupe Médvédkine, including Chris Marker's
À bientôt j'espère (1968) and thirteen other titles produced on the frontline of workers' and students' revolts over the following few years. There
are certainly no English subtitles, but should we let this cloud the fact that
after a whole generation the epochal documentaries of the French student-
worker revolts of May 1968 will finally become available to allow us to

fine tune or toss out the legends that have grown up around them? Meanwhile further advances will doubtless be made in terms of the availability of shorter works within the canon through downloading or streaming from Internet platforms. Of course the VHS video rental and sales market, though doomed, has still not yet wound down and is still maintaining in its barely sustainable way a global living archive of committed documentary.

All this to say that the exercise of talking about a canon or archive of radical documentary is still a highly provisional and otherwise problematical exercise. In a genre that by definition fastens on to the actual causes of the present world, and thereby can doom itself to ephemerality, is canonicity a contradictory issue? Will Emile de Antonio dominate the future historiography of New Left cinema because his estate has had the marketing savvy that de Antonio had in real life and enabled the DVD release of most of his films (with some symptomatic exceptions)? Will a full de Antonio or Ivens oeuvre at our fingertips shore up an arguably inappropriate auteurist framework for the historiography of the field? One might have similarly worried that the historiography of Vietnam antiwar documentary activism in the United States was to be shaped by virtue of the presence of DVDs of de Antonio's *In the Year of the Pig* (1968) or by Peter Davis's more mainstream *Hearts and Minds* (1974) and *The War at Home*. But with the recent felicitous rerelease of *Winter Soldier* (collective, 1972), timed to support the anti-Iraq War constituency, this film that no one had seen in the intervening thirty-five years since its original release will at least permit a greater range of resources for this enterprise.

There is little that is new in this discussion: canon formation has always depended on the vicious circle of availability and distribution, exacerbated by the thorny mess of copyright, and preservation is even more precarious. In the arena of film and media studies, there is a serious risk in scholarship that is neither based on visual apprehension of the materials discussed nor validated by access to these materials on the part of readers. This is more the case with us than in our sister disciplines like art history or literary studies where the processes of canonization and historiographical analysis without the consultation of primary materials would be simply unthinkable.

The challenge of canons and accessible archival memory is especially urgent with regard to the audiovisual legacy of the New Left. By this moniker, I mean that enormous transnational corpus of nonfiction or semidocumentary works accumulated between the early sixties and the historical watershed/turning point of approximately 1990, a moment that might be defined as the convergence of the first Bush presidency, the collapse of the Soviet bloc, the first Gulf War, and the digital revolution. This quarter century was very productive of radical cinematic interventions into struggles for equity, justice, and transformation (and of analyses of past struggles). The New Left's visions continue to grow in their relevance for our desperate current situations, local as well as global, all the more so since the young generation of activists keep doggedly reinventing the wheels once honed by their parents and grandparents.

▶───

Challenge for Change/Société nouvelle

All of this is in the back of my mind as I return again and again to a particular and very special New Left corpus I've been teaching off and on since the mid-seventies, a treasure hoard of over two hundred films and videos produced between 1967 and 1980 by the National Film Board (NFB) of Canada, within its twin activist documentary programs called respectively in English and French, Challenge for Change and Société nouvelle (New Society). This state-financed initiative in film and video community intervention is unique within Canadian—and indeed world—film history. Nowhere else did such a relatively well-financed program test in such a consistent and focused way many of the tenets of the international New Left and its cinematic cohort, the idealistic armies of shaggy baby boomers wielding 16mm cameras and Sony Portapak videos throughout the industrialized democracies as well as much of what we then called the "third world," most notably Latin America and India.

I described the New Left documentary current at its climax during the first Reagan term in terms of the ideals of grassroots democracy and the practices of "letting the people speak," "giving communities media technology." (See chapter 1.) I identified a historically based tendency that, however multivarious it was, had in common a conception of filmmakers

> rooting [their films], working *within* actively ongoing political struggles; by making films . . . not only *about* people engaged in these struggles, but also *with* and *by* them as well, and through this process, and with full awareness of the contradictions in play, hammering out the shapes of an evolving new revolutionary ideology around those struggles. This third and final criterion for commitment, this "subject-centered" or "contextual" ideal expressed in my string of emphasized prepositions, is as essential an element of my notion of commitment as the first two: ideological principle and activist stance.

Of the approximately 145 films and videos produced in English and over 60 produced in French for the CFC/SN programs at the National Film Board, the majority were made in 16mm but an important minority saw the light of day on Sony Portapak video (most of which are now seen as VHS or DVD copies of 16mm prints of the original video documents—a

fascinatingly symptomatic technological peregrination to say the least).
These four corpuses are all distinct, not surprisingly, given the sharply
different cinematic cultures artists like Peter Pearson, John Kemeny, Bonnie Klein, George Stoney, Anne Claire Poirier, and Maurice Bulbulian all
brought to the project. They are distinct also in the institutional subcultures (and budgets) that characterized the anglophone and francophone
branches—of which the average running times are only the most obvious
index: twenty-four minutes on the English side and fifty-five minutes with
Société nouvelle. All four subcorpuses however are united by the common
aim of community empowerment through media and together test a wide
variety of technological and aesthetic approaches to activism. At one end
of the spectrum, some aimed at producing film or video texts in the traditional aesthetic sense ("necessary artistry!") and, at the other end, some
aimed at reflecting more the processes of empowerment and enfranchisement rather than delivering a conventionally finished object ("sufficient
virtue!"). The collection of films and videos is marked also by the regional
roots that the programs officially encouraged, as well as several fundamental divides that are intrinsic to Canadian culture of the sixties and
seventies—urban–rural, English–French, settler–aboriginal—and thus also
demonstrates the ways media activism is inflected by specific cultural environments. The period corresponds roughly to the Trudeau era of Canadian
history, the triumph of liberalism—in both the higher-case and lower-case
senses of the word. Marked by the traumas of peacetime (first the "apprehended insurrection" of October 1970 [Marchessault 1995, 159], and
somewhat later in the seventies the epochal recession of that decade), this
period is dramatically different from the same period in U.S. Left history,
dominated in many ways by the antiwar movement.

And miracle of miracles, the collection is there waiting to be seen.
About half of the approximately 145 English-language products are available for sale on the studio's Web site, while three quarters of the roughly
sixty-three French films are available.[1] Though the French studio has been
more proactive in maintaining its films on the marketplace and bringing
them to DVD format, there exists a bountiful corpus of over 130 works
in total available on either VHS or DVD—and since 2008 via online
streaming from the NFB Web site in many cases—certainly luxurious in
comparison to any other corpus of New Left material anywhere in the
world.[2] While the tapes or discs are not cheap, especially for institutional
customers (U.S. customers pay $225 for a long film, $89 for a short film,
and prices for individual "home" consumers are much less), they are still
good value in the context of the larger audiovisual marketplace. The
situation could clearly be much worse, and one suspects that the materials

have been kept in circulation mostly due to the inertia of the peculiar
genus of the Canadian civil service. (But here is not the place to burden
my international readership with a very Canadian rant about the bizarrely
unaccountable bureaucracy of the institution with which Canadian cinematic stakeholders have had a love–hate relationship for seventy years.)

Challenge for Change/Société nouvelle has been the object of modest
critical and historiographical study almost continuously since its existence,
certainly within Canada—by insiders to the program (Dansereau 1977;
Hénaut 1969; Hénaut 1991), by contemporary observers (Kurchak 1977;
Watson 1977), by outsider historians and theorists (Burnett 1995; Dick
1986; Evans 1991; Jones 1981; MacKenzie 2004; Marchessault 1995), as
well as activists (Thede and Ambrosi 1991). American and other foreign
scholars have occasionally shown a selective interest: experts in women's
cinema and video art are most aware of the program's offshoots, Studio
D and Vidéographe, respectively. U.S. scholars interested in the pioneering
feminist documentarist Bonnie Sherr Klein, best known for her controversial 1981 documentary *Not a Love Story: A Film about Pornography*,
and especially in George Stoney, the influential American documentarist
who was parachuted into the National Film Board between 1968 and
1970 to replace founder Colin Low and get the program on its feet, have
also published on the subject. American documentary textbook authors
Erik Barnouw (1974, 258–60) and Jack Ellis (together with the latter's
updater Betsy McLane [2005, 245–47]) both offer concise, sympathetic,
and well-informed two-page summaries of the English program's early
years, stressing not surprisingly the American second director of the outfit,
Stoney, alongside a lively still in both books of a scuffle between natives
and white cops in *You Are on Indian Land*. Other survey historians from
Richard Barsam to Brian Winston do not mention the program, and
British Stella Bruzzi, author of a "critical introduction" to *New Documentary* doesn't even mention the NFB! Americans who have discovered the
program and give it attention often coat it in idealizing colors. So aston-
ished at the idea of the state funding radical cultural gestures and lacking
the specific cultural and historical context, they fall short of the sense of
contradiction and complexity that underscores Canadians' accounts.
Peter K. Wiesner's "Media for the People: The Canadian Experiments with
Film and Video in Community Development" is one of the more interesting examples of this literature.[3]

Most of these existing studies, whether Canadian or foreign, have
favored institutional, auteurist, political, and contextual approaches—
everything but textual analysis, despite the availability of many of the
works. The byproduct is a literature with a skewed relationship to its

corpus, which remains virtually unknown (especially abroad and on either opposite side of the language divide): decidedly, the most overtheorized and underwatched parcel of any national cinema and in this case one that is itself pathologically underwatched. Scholars have also favored the English side rather than the French side of the bicephalous studio. Both biases have led to misapprehensions of the cultural as well as the political achievement and significance of the program as a whole. Ultimately however, for whatever reason, despite the maintenance of film and video access for both Canadians and foreign customers over the years—from 16mm to VHS to DVD to streaming—this pioneering experiment in political film and video during the era of the New Left has remained marginal within the standard histories of Leftist documentary cinema and video, Canadian or otherwise.

Why this marginality? Is it at least in part the perennial Canadian bugbear of language? Unfortunately one cannot even assume that unavailability *in English versions* of so many bold, original, and distinctive French films is the major factor in their neglect since the neglect is no less rampant within French-language film literature, whether in Quebec or France (the major Québécois documentary specialist Gilles Marsolais [1997], for example, looks almost entirely the other way). I accept some responsibility for the oversight—the program didn't make the final cut for my 1984 anthology, as I recall, because in my politically correct early eighties judgment, government-financed films, originally funded on the pretext of the need of federal ministries to hear from their clients and often caught up in the governmentality of citizens demanding services owed them by the state, just weren't "committed" enough. Also a factor is the NFB's own complacency and inertia about its historical legacy, the confused priorities of its bureaucrats over why, how, and for whom their films are to be preserved, promoted, and distributed. Finally one can assume that it is in no small part the parochial charms of a so-called minor cinema that fails to attract the imperial gatekeepers: how can Londoners or New Yorkers understand the urgency of Canadian politeness, of shy Prince Edward Islanders listening silently to their community priest urging them at their public meeting to think carefully about their government's development plans for "the island?" Is it surprising that the laconic Mohawk and Cree youths sparring with verbose and aggressive American inner-city "organizer" Saul Alinsky (invited by his disciple Bonnie Klein soon after she had landed in Canada with her draft dodger husband) have less charisma for metropolitan film historians than the iconically wailing widows of *Harlan County* or more recently the larger-than-life characters acting out in the films of Michael Moore? Yet here is not the place to agonize over the status of Canadian documentary as a "minor cinema" in the Deleuzean sense or any other but rather to wrestle with this minor corpus and suss out its undeniable muscles.

Now almost thirty years after the demise of CFC/SN there has been a renewal of interest in activist, community-based documentary, what is now called "media democracy"—even by the NFB itself. The new viability of dissident theatrical documentary and the post-9/11 ratcheting up and revival of geopolitical problematics for young activists focused not only on the war on terror but also on the entire gamut of globalization and environmental challenges requires us to reopen the epic chapter of the New Left activist documentary in general, and of Challenge for Change/Société nouvelle in particular. We must maintain and renew our perspective and understanding of this key chapter in the history of committed documentary. In the remaining sections of this chapter I will lay the groundwork for this task of integrating CFC/SN into an international history of committed leftwing documentary, a task I'd left on the back burner since the shrinking of *"Show Us Life."* First summarizing the basic contextual history of the experiment as it has been already fairly well established in the literature, I will then demonstrate the indispensable role of textual study in this process, of actually looking at films and videos.

Discovery

In 2000 I was asked by the NFB to program a public tribute to the founding director of Challenge for Change Colin Low on the occasion of the release of his autobiographical documentary *Moving Pictures*. We all assumed that this farewell film had a kind of testamentary stature as retirement loomed for the grand old seventy-four-year-old pioneer. Wearer of many hats, Low excelled in everything from animation to Studio B masterpieces like *Universe* (1960 Oscar nominee) and *City of Gold* (1957 Oscar nominee), from Expo 67 showcase work and IMAX to ethnographic cinema. Regardless of how the latter-day IMAX guy could be heard downplaying the artistic achievement of Challenge for Change, I was determined not to let the more glamorous achievements outshine his contribution as its founding director and innovator of the legendary Fogo Island project that dominated the first two years of CFC. All the same I found myself stuck with a tiny programming slot for CFC, so opted for a less known piece in the Fogo Island series, only eleven minutes long, that would carry the whole weight of the project for the brassy audience in expectant attendance.

Thus transpired my accidental discovery of *McGraths at Home and Fishing* (Low 1967). The audience and I were amazed at the beauty of this film, one of several dozen in this series shot in the Newfoundland outport of Fogo Island at the outset of the program. The makers used the simple, elegant device of cutting back and forth between conversation among family members in their homey kitchen and then action footage of their livelihood on their small vessel bobbing up and down in the swell of the richly dark and luminous ocean. This confident 16mm black-and-white masterpiece is a modest celebration of a way of life and a discussion of how to confront threats thereto, with the retroactively added aesthetic layer of its bold synthesis of discourse and movement. Imagine my annoyance when I discovered the film was not available in any way other than special command performances for retirement tributes, not even at the studio's downtown storefront and cinema, the Ciné-robothèque! I therefore decided it was time to act myself and dedicated my 2002 master's seminar in documentary cinema to CFC/SN.

I was thus responsible for introducing my fifteen grad students to the contradictions and passions of Challenge for Change/Société nouvelle. It was I who forced them to watch such gems as *Prince Edward Island Development Plan* (1969) and Michel Régnier's not-at-all-pedestrian *City Centre and Pedestrians* (1974). Just as pleasurably, they were also required to go and meet a network of surprised veteran filmmakers in their sixties, seventies, and eighties—even nineties—who no doubt thought themselves forgotten. We ended up collectively discovering a whole circle of charming and provocative prophet-artists, some very grouchy—justifiably—as well as a historical moment rich in implications for the troubled present we live in. Both of which have much to teach us.

There is a received wisdom that has accumulated over the years both in our discipline and in the corridors of the NFB itself (Goldsmith 2003),[4] that yes, Challenge/Société was indeed an interesting experiment, vindicated by its offshoots Studio D and Vidéographe, but practically flawed as well as ideologically and theoretically naive and moreover no great shakes cinematically speaking (Burnett, 1995; Marchessault, 1995; MacKenzie, 2004). This is perhaps the reason that the recent anthology on images of the working class in Canadian cinema, Malek Khouri and Darrell Varga's *Working on Screen: Representations of the Working Class in Canadian Cinema* (2006), astonishingly skips over this most pertinent corpus in its entirety. My students and I would not dispute that many of the films are documents of the "process" of community intervention and empowerment, its discreet euphorias and pitfalls, works that admittedly are an acquired taste as art (albeit vivid documents). But to our collective surprise, my seminar group and I found that at least half of the films stand alone as films, no less than *McGraths at Home and Fishing*, and reward even the most jaded cinephile viewer with their unpretentious yet assured artistry. Both the English and the French corpuses are full of exemplary works of committed art, resonating of their Canadian/Québécois cultural roots, their documentary genres and their turbulent, momentous epochs. One gap in the literature, namely the acknowledgment of the exemplary artistic quality of so much of this unwatched cinema, was rectified in 2006 by Jerry White (2006) and Farbod Honarpisheh (2006) (the latter a survivor of my 2002/2003 seminar)—as least as far as two such films go, *The Winds of Fogo* (1969) and *You Are on Indian Land* (1970). Similarly the process of reclaiming the creative and political energies of the sixties and seventies, the history of the Left in Canada, as Varga and Khouri are doing along with several others (Khouri and Varga 2006), also involves reclaiming dozens of these works that have been banished to the sidelines because of the unfair stigma that Challenge/Société has accumulated, both inside the NFB and outside. Moreover, it is a question of not only reclaiming them—looking at them and testing our Gramscian theorizing in their earnest grain and flickering luminosity—but also recycling and disseminating them. This is not just a cinephile indulgence, as White has argued, not just filling in the corners of the museum, but also restoring to life "beautiful films" (as Hénaut puts it), whose historical setting has faded, but, like *Kino Pravda*; *Spanish Earth*; *Hour of the Furnaces*; *In the Year of the Pig*; *Harlan County, U.S.A.*; *When the Mountains Tremble*; and *War and Peace* are still alive in the way they speak to us—artistically, affectively, culturally, and politically.

▶ ──

Five Films

> *I was a bit distanced from the philosophy of "since we're shooting people's problems, we don't need an artistic approach, we only need a factual approach." This is TV news ultimately, and I didn't agree. I believe the role of the filmmaker is to try to bring together two things: his or her art and his or her capacity to become aware of the truthfulness of what one films. We can look for artistic expression in the smallest things.*
>
> *. . . even if we're making films with poor people it's not necessary to use poor means: you can't take away the aesthetics of a film by saying no more aesthetics.*

These two citations of course echo debates that have been familiar within politicized cinematic cultures for almost a hundred years. But this time they were uttered by two of the most unfairly unrecognized filmmakers within the Canadian corpus, both Société nouvelle stalwarts, Maurice Bulbulian (b. 1938) and Léonard Forest (b. 1928), respectively, in interviews gathered by my master's students.

Let's have a look at a couple of films by these two exemplary artists, both all but unknown to non-Canadian documentary specialists because of the National Film Board's (symptomatic?) negligence in not "versioning" their films in English. Let's look as well at a few other "interesting" films in English as well as in French, for a total of five exemplary film analyses. Along the way we shall arrive at a summarization of the generic features of the corpus as a whole, which the selected films exemplify. It is impossible in a chapter of this length to do justice to the rich mosaic of genres, formats, themes, and sociocultural contexts and to the spectrum of political gestures represented by our four corpuses (English or French, 16mm or video). Fortunately in terms of textual appreciation of individual works, not only has the founding film in the whole project *The Things I Cannot Change* been extensively covered in the literature but so also has the English-language feminist corpus that led to the founding of the famous women's Studio D in 1975 (Evans 1991; Anderson 1999). Moreover White's book has cast the spotlight on the two already mentioned exemplary films from the Newfoundland project and the aboriginal network productions, respectively, so the responsibility for me to be encyclopedic is alleviated somewhat—all the more so with 2010's publication of my comprehensive anthology on the program (Waugh, Baker, and Winton). A faithful introduction to this corpus, the following five textual analyses must for the moment bear the weight of suggesting directions for future research, read in complementarity with the literature just mentioned. I say "introduction," for the book this episode in the history of political documentary clearly deserves still remains on the horizon.

La P'tite Bourgogne

A much-loved film on the contemporary city, *La P'tite Bourgogne* (Maurice Bulbulian, 1968, 44 min.) might be considered one of the half-dozen flagship films of the program, one of the most evocative imprints of sixties New Left idealism and collective resistance—as well as of strategic compromise. It is all the more emblematic as virtually the only one of the CFC/SN films to straddle Canada's linguistic barrier since it focuses on the bilingual Montreal neighborhood of Petite Bourgogne (PB, or Little Burgundy)—a depressed, multiracial working-class community in the historic industrial core. The district was one of the most conspicuous targets of "urban renewal" during the development frenzy fueled by Montreal's Universal Exposition of 1967 and other projects of "world-class" aspiration. In fact the opening shot of the film refers directly to this context, showing the much vaunted "Habitat" complex, Expo's architectural showcase originally touted as social housing but that epitomized for the narrator the dehumanizing silence and sterility of urban development.[5] This ominous prologue finished, the bulk of the film encounters PB residents and follows them as they struggle for solutions to the problematic of humane urban design.

Director Bulbulian, a trained teacher turned filmmaker who first cut his teeth on scientific audiovisual works, has only recently slowed down his prodigious output as a pillar of Québécois documentary. But he is known to English-language audiences only for a couple of epics on Canadian constitutional quagmires and West Coast native issues in the eighties and nineties, respectively. In his three later seventies films for Société nouvelle, none available in English, he would later present rural settings, enlisting the dispossessed and disenfranchised of Quebec's economically challenged outlying regions, specifically of the resource-based and agricultural sectors. However, *P'tite Bourgogne*, his first work for the fledgling program (1968), is resolutely inner-city in its setting and sensibility. The previous year, the program's inaugural epic of urban poverty, *The Things I Cannot Change*, also set in Canada's then-largest city the year it hosted the world at Expo, had been controversial for its perceived ethical shortcuts, its victim aesthetics, and the spectacularization of the poverty of its spotlighted family. Bulbulian fell into none of these traps with *P'tite Bourgogne*. In fact, rather than the voyeuristic liabilities of cinéma vérité, Bulbulian had been inspired by the social science–inspired methods developed by the French-language Groupe de recherches sociales, which had anticipated Société nouvelle with its grassroots community accountability and empowerment activities in such precursor documentaries as *Saint-Jérôme* (1968). Cinematographer Michel Régnier (b. 1934) and producer Robert Forget (b. 1938) had both also been GRS stalwarts: the former (a French immigrant) went on to become one of the most prolific of SN directors, specializing in scholarly but imaginative, high-budget essays on urbanization, and the latter, once the Sony Portapak fever seized the francophone networks, went on to found Vidéographe, the legendary Montreal video cooperative that is still in operation to this day as an independent cooperative.

Originally planning to develop a project on the depressed "rust belt" along Montreal's Lachine Canal, Bulbulian discovered by accident the turmoil in Petite Bourgogne, the nearby working-class residential district that had just received its death sentence from the urban renewal–frenzied municipal administration. Citizens' committees had sprung up when the first wave of demolition notices were delivered to the tenants of a quadrilateral called Les Îlots St-Martin. Bulbulian hooked up with one of the community animators and the citizens' committee, especially the avuncular Noël Daudelin, a portly grandfather, and the determined, soft-spoken Jeanne Leblanc, a single mother. The filmmakers offered not only to record the citizens' push to participate in the political decisions that affected their future but also to get them involved in the conception and development of the film. The names of Daudelin and Leblanc and the other committee members, and those of many other citizen participants, would be named and thanked in the credits, an unusual procedure for the NFB up to this time but one that became an eloquent custom throughout the CFC period. The filmmakers' catalytic efforts specifically brought about an encounter between the committee and the leaders of the Montreal administrative council and the provincial ministry of housing, the NFB letterhead turning out to be very effective where the citizens' groups' pleas had always fallen on deaf ears. A key six-minute sequence thus shows a long, in-studio consultation between the citizens' committee and the provincial and municipal authorities. Among the latter is the notorious Lucien Saulnier, the authoritarian "modernizing" technocrat who spearheaded the city's development mania[6] and who rebuffs the citizens' request for a formal consultative role all the while performing the congenial, responsive politician for the federal cameras. This trope of citizens encountering the state was already becoming another formulaic fixture of the program's output, its original mandate having to no small extent having focused on the job of bringing together citizens to voice their needs to their representatives. The dozens of bureaucrats and politicians preserved for eternity in these films generally put on their best behavior in the same way as Saulnier in this film, and Wiseman's institutional guardians in so many of his, for the most part discreetly protected by their neckties and desks. Such tropes in CFC/SN, one suspects, are sometimes tokenistic efforts to placate ministerial funders and the original program mandate, but local issues were also sometimes resolved in this way. Of course the larger political and ideological issues were skirted through the desublimatory dynamic of the confronting-the-bureaucrat trope (whether meeting with politicians provides more cathartic release than political empowerment depends on the context). Aside from Leblanc's ironic smile at Saulnier's condescending comment on citizens' committees, Bulbulian's stiff scene scarcely provides the most riveting "cinema" in his forty-four-minute film.

Other sequences better exemplify the balance of aesthetics and ethics vaunted by Hénaut and Bulbulian in the epigraphs I have chosen. In contrast to the "silence" of the emerging concrete landscapes of "renewal," Bulbulian juxtaposes the ebullient noisiness of family and community life in Petite Bourgogne's shabby but comfortable streets, stoops, yards, and kitchens. Here the archive of memory and cultural heritage and what one of the inhabitants calls "a whole way of living" is boisterously captured as it is transmitted by an eighty-five-year-old folksong-singing grandmother to her grandchildren on a creaking backyard swing. Régnier's landscape tropes are especially haunting and poetic: his camera glides up and down the evocative streetfronts, running into bulldozers, then imaging first the modest but comfortable brick row houses, and then the vacant lots where dispossessed children play among the rubble of their former homes. Bulbulian's gift for encountering and animating stressed social actors is also evident, especially with Daudelin and Leblanc and their families and with an anglophone black family, the Croxens. Intradiegetic music continues to be used to very stirring effect throughout the film, especially a solo performance of the sixties folk hymn "Five Hundred Miles" sung by Croxen's daughter, a young female evictee whose fragile but true voice and guitar strums soar out over the entire neighborhood and its soon-to-be-destroyed streets with their affect of loss and exile "away from home." These poetics of lament over abandoned dwellings and livelihoods, are deployed not only with nostalgia but also with a lucid anger at the willful, impersonal destruction of homes and violation of democratic process. The song is a processing of collective and individual trauma. This potent mix would become another hallmark of not only Bulbulian's films but across the board at CFC/SN in film after film, which retroactively come together as a mosaic of ghost towns, ruins and abandoned homes, farms and factories.

One strong sequence brings an especially acute analysis to the work: the filmmakers accompany the citizens' committee to inspect a previously built "social housing" project, Les Habitations Jeanne-Mance, in the south central part of the city, where they get a discomforting view of their future as prisoners of impersonal high-rises, of lives marked by economic pressure and surveillance. In like vein, the contradictions and ambiguities of citizen protest, participation, and cooptation are gently probed in the bittersweet ending to the film: a glitzy parade complete with marching bands, drum majorettes, and clergy marks the ceremony of breaking the sod for the new Îlots St-Martin. The committee leaders are seen sheepishly on stage, Leblanc with Saulnier, and Daudelin with smug Mayor Jean Drapeau. The triumphalism is qualified by a typically open and ambiguous ending: Leblanc's oratory about rights to housing and the "human side of development" is eloquent, but the filmmakers return to melancholy traveling shots of the rubble-strewn landscape of the once vibrant neighborhood.

As for the thirty-year-old Bulbulian, his later three films for Société nouvelle would all elaborate this tone of lament and loss, of trauma transformed by critique and defiance. Misunderstood by the studio as too personal and less pragmatic than the program mandate dictated, Bulbulian may have been an awkward fit, but it is from this tension that the enduring quality of these works arises. *La Revanche* (*Revenge*, 1974) may be his most perfected enactment of the mandate, a poetic call for the collective ownership of forest wealth by resource industry workers, an innovative merger of filmic practice and social catalysis that is also prophetic of more recent models of ecoactivist art. Bonnie Sherr Klein (b. 1941), also an activist in the same corner of Montreal as Petite Bourgogne, was responsible for the English version of *P'tite Bourgogne*. Called, not surprisingly, *Little Burgundy* and shortened by fifteen minutes thereby shortchanging the film's discursive undergirding in politics, poetics, and process, the English version manages to retain most of the inspiration of the original.

Up against the System

Up against the System (Terence Macartney-Filgate, 1969, 20 min.) is another CFC/SN landmark film, this time of the program's second phase. After the initial momentum of the Fogo Island project had died out, John Kemeny, initial program director, moved on to Hollywood. American documentarist George Stoney had been recruited to head CFC for a two-year stint beginning in the fall of 1968, and *Up against the System* was the flagship of his mandate as director. His baptism by fire, *Up against the System* is as much of a Toronto film as *P'tite Bourgogne* belongs to its sister metropolis. As Gary Evans (1991) and Deirdre Boyle (1999) tell the story, *Up against the System* was based on an inherited commission about welfare recipients' attitudes, arising out of the program's original anti-poverty vocation. Stoney no doubt brought with him some of the sparks from the parallel American "War on Poverty" campaign, which had been initiated by President Johnson and in fact had been part of the original inspiration for CFC. Disgruntled anglophone directors were not interested in this proposed project about welfare recipients, according to Evans, because the topic had come from an unpopular Department of Agriculture official. Stoney then used his own outside-NFB networks to recruit Terence Macartney-Filgate (b. 1924) to direct the project. A brilliant pioneer of direct cinema camerawork, Macartney-Filgate had made his mark on Canadian documentary beginning in the late fifties with the Candid Eye series, helming such epochal films as *The Days before Christmas* and *The*

Backbreaking Leaf in 1958 and 1959, respectively, before wandering off
to the United States in the sixties. Macartney-Filgate pursued the project
not in the Montreal backyard of the NFB headquarters but in the Ontario
capital, where he somehow knew the Minister of Welfare and welfare
rights activists, according to Doyle. Clearly inspired, his footage includes
classically anomic social observation of outcasts in decrepit alleyways
and lineups in welfare offices. But his vision is most remarkable for its
anchor in a wide range of outspoken subjects, most speaking passionately
and insightfully to the camera, welfare clients ranging from single mothers to pensioners to an ex-convict, and welfare "administrators" including
ministry bureaucrats, a Salvation Army official, and a dissident social
worker named Joanna Stern whose impassioned critique of the inhumanity and inefficiency of the "system" would come close to stealing the
film. Other striking material is an interview with some boys playing on a
street, explaining to an offscreen interviewer that they shoplift because it's
cheaper than buying.

After trying out Stoney's unprecedented idea to test screen the thirty-
two-minute fine cut with ten audiences around Montreal, the producers
decided that spectators were discussing characters rather than issues.
Macartney-Filgate agreed to trim twelve minutes off the work for a
final running time of twenty minutes, more suitable for the Board's traditional "trigger" screening format. However uneven the film's shifts

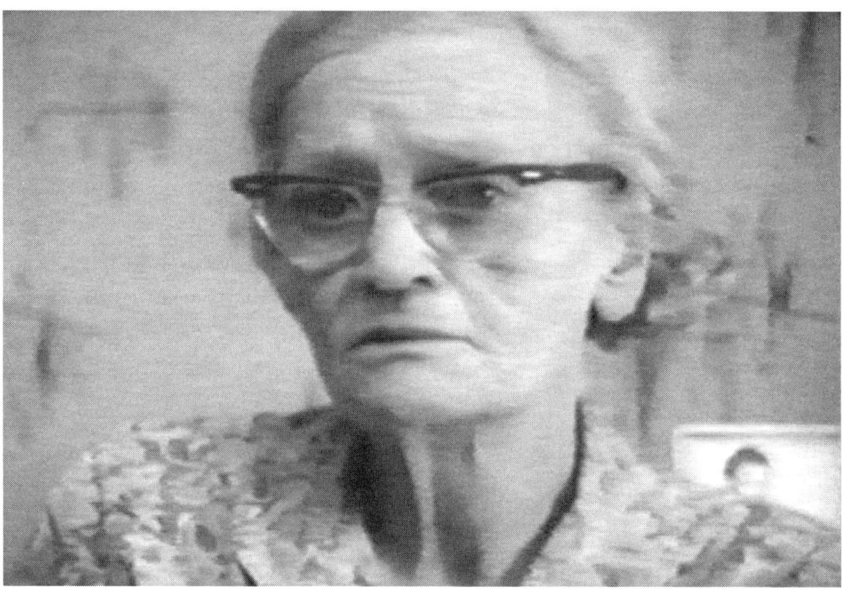

Up against the System (Terence Macartney-Filgate, 1969). Elderly welfare recipient
delivers the CFC flagship film's peroration "What we need here is a revolution!"

from miserabilism to defiance and back, it is easy to understand how
Macartney-Filgate's final mosaic reportedly made spectators angry, since
it effectively dissects editorially the urban environment that commingles
deprivation and overconsumption. However in retrospect the articulate
and charismatic subjects put their stamp on the film, and a charming angry
granny gives the final moment a lingering punch with the defiant slogan
about revolution cited in my epigraph. Regretting the enforced compres-
sions, Macartney-Filgate recycled the Stern footage into an entire separate
film, *A Young Social Worker Speaks Her Mind*, an unrecognized twenty-
four-minute tour de force (naturally unavailable to twenty-first-century
viewers). With its single setup of the angry young woman across her desk,
this short film vindicates the much-maligned talking head as a potential
strategy of untapped and enduring power to raise issues and invoke affect.
The footage of ministry civil servants was left on the cutting room floor for
once, and Evans extracts an archetypally Canadian story of "government-
sponsored subversion" from the production.

Macartney-Filgate's bold cinematic denunciation of the welfare
"system" served reportedly to whip up public discussion of the issues
of welfare reform in the media and elsewhere and even to inflect policy
reform. Both Boyle and Evans set up the film also, based on Stoney's own
viewpoint, to epitomize different Canadian and American attitudes to social
change and the involvement of state agencies therein, different national
philosophies focused on consensus and confrontation respectively—however
much tongue we Canadians might want to apply to these cheeky national
stereotypes. In contrast to *P'tite Bourgogne*, *Up against the System* can be
seen as a mosaic of lament, resignation, and anger, lacking in the exemplary action or processing of trauma undertaken by Bulbulian's patient
and communitarian protagonists (aside from the boys' strategy of shoplift-
ing and the subjects speaking their minds). Perhaps this liability reflects
Stoney's and Macartney-Filgate's parachute approach to poor Toronto, as
opposed to Bulbulian's grassroots research-oriented production method,
though the outsider–insider tension is a recurrent specter of the entire
CFC/SN corpus. Nevertheless as part of a cluster of CFC/SN films on poverty, public housing, and the right to shelter (including Kathleen Shannon's
I Don't Think It's Meant for Us, shot in Toronto's same housing project
ghetto two years later), this film stands up well as a resonant visual and
oral manifesto.

La Noce est pas finie

A Brechtian docu-fiction feature, *La Noce est pas finie* (*The Wedding's Not Over*, Léonard Forest, 1971, 86 min.) is a cross of Pasolini's *Teorema* and Wiseman's *High School*. As such, one can understand how Léonard Forest's ambitious, risk-taking project about rural cultures and change encountered some trouble passing muster with the Société nouvelle brass. But led by its committee of filmmakers, the program finally gave the green light to this most anomalous of the films made in the program's fifteen years. This feature-length, semimusical, semifictional narrative was based on script ideas developed by citizens's consultation in Gloucester County in the Acadian heartland of northeastern New Brunswick. Société nouvelle was much more open to feature length filmmaking and experimental, semi-documentary narrative formats than their anglophone counterparts, who were caught up in the direct cinema orthodoxy and trigger-film utilitarian-ism and considered their francophone counterparts a bit "happy-go-lucky" (Bulbulian [2003] 2006).

Léonard Forest was a robust and prolific seventeen-year veteran producer-director of the Board and one would have been surprised if he had been turned down for anything at the institution of which he had been a stalwart for so long. Forest had entered the Board as a hotshot twenty-five-year-old researcher-director under the wing of producer Guy Glover and by 1957 had himself become a busy producer who would accumulate over fifty titles on his scorecard. His return to directing toward the end of the sixties and to his native region of Acadia, then undergoing a cultural and political renaissance in the spirit of the decade of worldwide "national liberation" movements, had provided the spark that led to what is called his Acadian trilogy. The trilogy's first entry, *Les Acadiens de la disper-sion* (1968), is a two-hour epic survey of the Acadian diaspora, searching for a common identity with an orientation that the catalog description describes with odd understatement as "even political." Future star singer Édith Butler is the spokesperson just as Noce would have a singer as its narrative hook a few years later. The emergence of Société nouvelle gave Forest the framework for the subsequent two films, *Noce* (1971) and the more conventionally essayistic *Un Soleil pas comme ailleurs* (*A Sun Like Nowhere Else*, 1972, 47 min.), the only one of the three parts deemed worthy of an English version. Notwithstanding the fact that the first two installments exist only in French versions, the trilogy is the best known of Forest's works and led to his unofficial status of filmmaker laureate for the tenacious Acadian "nation" that was suddenly facing new threats of assimilation in the age of television and secularization.

Noce's self-reflexive narrative structure is shared with an international sprinkling of feature films of the late sixties and early seventies, all inspired by the political dramaturgy of Bertolt Brecht and the self-conscious experimentation of the politically motivated art cineastes of Europe and the third world from Anderson, Pasolini, and Oshima to Ghatak and Littín. (Anne Claire Poirier was the other SN director most influenced by the Brechtian aesthetics of the decade, while Gilles Groulx, Denys Arcand, Derek May, and Mort Ransen working outside SN at the Board, showed similar "political modernist" tendencies.) Thus Forest's classically simple narrative of an outsider coming into a conservative rural community and stirring up trouble is interrupted periodically as the script committee assesses the action, the characters' options, and the directions of the narrative. Intradiegetic musical interludes provide further analytic distance.

A charismatic and mysterious blond male folksinger arrives from big-city Montreal in an Acadian fishing town in Gloucester County, perhaps modeled on Tracadie, and takes up the post of biology teacher at the local high school. The character, named Georges Martin, was played by folksinger Georges Langford, a glamorous songster originating in Îles-de-la-Madeleine but who at the time briefly rivaled Édith Butler as the musical epitome of the Acadian renaissance. Martin pitches his tent on the

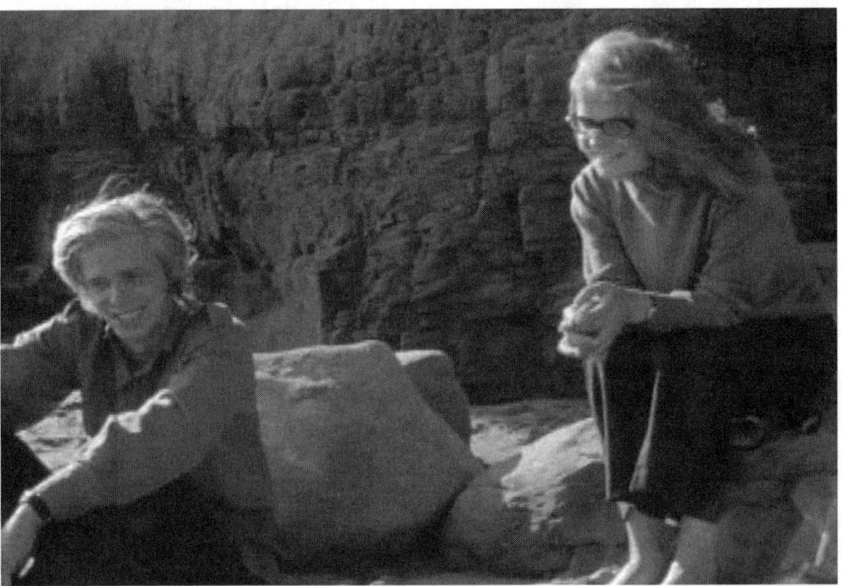

La Noce est pas finie (Léonard Forest, 1971). Outsider teacher Georges (left) camping out on the beach with his student girlfriend, in a citizen-scripted self-reflexive docudrama about conservative rural values in Acadia.

local beach because of a shortage of accommodation in the town. Flirtations with the Baudelaire-reading principal's wife, risqué lessons with his students about sexual mores and stereotypes rather than biology, and eventually a liaison with one of the female students, all cause scandal in the community. A wedding erupts in guitar smashing and fisticuffs after a song disrespectful of Acadian heritage, the teacher's tent is set on fire, and an open ending leaves lessons still to be learned. Along the way, ethnographic glimpses of local livelihoods and landscapes and long conversations about poverty and social assistance all unfold (one within a CFC-esque encounter with a welfare/unemployment insurance bureaucrat behind his desk), along with five or six already mentioned insertions of analytic performances of intradiegetic songs by the teacher and lively organ-based rock interludes by a local band. *Noce* is couched in less conventionally political terms than Forest's next film *Soleil*, which is built on a canvas of demonstrations, debates about rural economies, and unionization drives. Instead *Noce* proposes a political language of rural community cultural values and their resistance to freedom of expression and social change and prophetically mixes in political discourses of sexuality, desire, and youth revolt, another rare issue for CFC/SN. Indeed *Noce* is one of the few CFC/SN films to acknowledge the sexual revolution and to link it however ambiguously to the overall platform of community empowerment.

Scott MacKenzie sees the film as a document of a failed and contradictory process wherein "the need to produce images [was] the fulcrum upon which community action becomes based. Local groups continued to need an external, and highly public catalyst that they believed validated the process of social transformation" (MacKenzie 2004, 152). This may well be, but the English programming committee must have had its pragmatic considerations in not taking up *Noce* for English versioning. They were wrong: this slow-moving docu-fiction holds up both as a film and as a document of an unprecedented social and cultural experiment in artist-community collaboration, reflecting the greater risk-taking and aestheticism endemic to the French side of the program and bearing its historical weight as a masterpiece of Acadian cinema in its own luminously uncompromising way.

Chez nous c'est chez nous

Another film unknown outside its narrow constituency, *Chez nous c'est chez nous* (Marcel Carrière, 1972, 81 min.) is an epic of the transformation of the Canadian countryside during the postwar period—the industrialization of agriculture combined with the urbanization of

Canadian society—a conscientious probing of the human price paid for modernity. Unlike Bulbulian and Forest, Marcel Carrière (b. 1935) was already well known even in English Canada as one of the pioneers of direct cinema in Quebec and may have been one of the big name directors who saw the program as a site for opportunity "slumming" when a project couldn't pass the hurdles elsewhere in the studio.[7] A specialist above all in sound recording, Carrière had been immortalized as the sound recorder of Pierre Perrault's *Pour la suite du monde* (1963) and director/soundperson of dozens of other classic shorts from the NFB's *équipe française* during the Quiet Revolution. Carrière's genius and technological knack for empathetic listening enabled a wealth of compelling oral histories throughout *Chez nous*, and there is no reason to doubt his sincerity as an artist based on the resonance of this 1972 Société nouvelle contribution alone.[8]

Chez nous was a study of "territoires marginales," that is "unproductive" farmlands of the Gaspé and other outlying regions that had been colonized by successive Quebec governments throughout the first half of the twentieth century and were formally closed by the same governments in the late sixties and early seventies. The declining village that is the focus of *Chez nous c'est chez nous* is symptomatically called St. Octave de l'Avenir (St. Octavius of the Future), and had declined in population from 1,100 to 150 in the 30 years before its forced closure in 1971. Carrière's recording achievement with elderly trappers, farmers, and lumberjacks fits his film well into what I call the "old-timer testimony" trope that was one of the staples of CFC/SN. He's also good at eliciting the stuttering confidences of the day's youth as they face the challenge of moving out in order to survive and grow. The film's title, translated as "Where we live is where we live" or "Our home is our home," comes from the testimony of Jocelyn Fraser, a teenage musician whose family was forced off their land by the closings and whose anxieties over moving out of his rock star–postered attic bedroom into the world away from where he was born are also at the center of the film. Perhaps reflecting Perrault's influence, Carrière maintains the compellingly deliberate rhythm and focus of the feature-length film through returning repeatedly to the youth's family, the sad but articulate Fraser parents who finally capitulate and accept inadequate compensation from the state bureaucracy for their bucolic but unprofitable farm. Meanwhile work must go on, and *Chez nous* is remarkable for capturing the texture of the everyday toil that is sustained despite the crisis. World documentaries of the last half of the twentieth century were full of images and testimonies of traumatic rural displacements and catastrophic urban migrations, but Carrière provides some of the most eloquent and unrecognized oral records thereof.

The film also stands out for its unexpected and no less felicitous use of archival montage, which contrasts the broken pastoral dreams of today with the expectations of the past. The latter is evoked in moving period footage of the ill-considered "colonization" of the New Lands in the interwar and postwar period (namely footage taken by Quebec's legendary priest-cinematographer Abbé Proulx). *Chez nous* is thus one of the small group of films from the program to undertake both a political historiography of change and a contemporary critique—perhaps the best one. Carrière is far from the only Quebec documentarist of the Quiet Revolution to mine the riches of the footage of the colonization period (Perrault, Bulbulian, Lamothe, Arcand, and Groulx all did so), but Carrière's marshalling of present and past in a bitter dialectic relationship, structured with tragic rhythm of deliberateness, compares memorably with the better known directors. One recurrent trope has a woman narrator reading in voice-over various clergy's declamations from 1919 and 1946 of high hopes for the new lands, extolling the Christian and patriotic mission of the agricultural vocation, only to be challenged in the present day by alternative reminiscences by the film's grizzled interlocutors. These voices are all counterpointed visually by a mosaic of pastoral period footage intercut with in-color appraisals of current realities, picturesque ruins, and idle farms. Smug black-and-white celebrations of the churches, masses, and prosperous priests that were fixtures of the colonization period, when churches were vaunted as community centers (certified by shots of wagonloads of parishioners in their Sunday best arriving at mass), segue into shots of the current church where a solitary altar boy services the gleamingly hollow sanctuary and a dwindled (but tenacious) congregation persist in their worship as their community puts out the lights.

The CFC "process" is not explicit in this film, as with *Up against the System*, unlike my five other examples, and no solution is even envisaged. The oral histories and reflections, however rich they are in their processing of historical trauma, and the critique of state bureaucracy that comes out of the interviews and a few lively community meetings, the attentive—almost ethnographic—recording of hard work that is sustained even in the face of shutdown, all stop short of the gospel of collective empowerment that otherwise underpins the CFC/SN corpus. Though it might seem that the repeated but futile claims to adequate compensation constitute a microcosmic political discourse of the relationship of the citizen and the state, they otherwise might hardly seem to constitute a symptomatic political problematic that can be easily abstracted beyond the there and then. The film's participants say as much themselves. Mme Fraser acknowledges at the end of the film, after the final sticks of the household have been

loaded on the moving van along with her frantic poultry, the resigned
sensibility of Gaspé people, their tendency to always accept and their inca-
pacity to revolt. An elderly grizzled solitary trapper Hilaire Minville who
periodically tends to his traplines throughout the film, gathering frozen
hares and offering jocular reminiscences of times when all we had to eat
were potatoes, has the last word, constructed not as a solution or a symbol
of revolt but as a living archive, an anachronistic, romantic holdout.

The presence of this big-budget work by a big-name director, a work
whose political mission seems limited to resignation and elegy, is no
doubt a reflection of the greater range of practice that the Société nouvelle encouraged than on the English side (and of the greater presence
of big-name auteurs on the French side of the studio divide—not only
Carrière but also "auteurs" like Poirier, etc.), rather than the application
of the intervention principle. This may be why *Chez nous* was yet another
film the English programming committee never saw the point of providing in English, however rich its Perrault-esque folkloric iconographies of
waning ways of life, from communal jigging in soon-to-be-demolished
living rooms with rolled up carpets to pillows of rising bread dough being
punched down in a sunny farmhouse window. It may be ironic that the
rich salvage self-ethnographic tapestry offered by most of the works in
CFC/SN constitutes an important part of the legacy of this radical documentary experiment, but it is not the only one. Unlike the salvage nostalgia

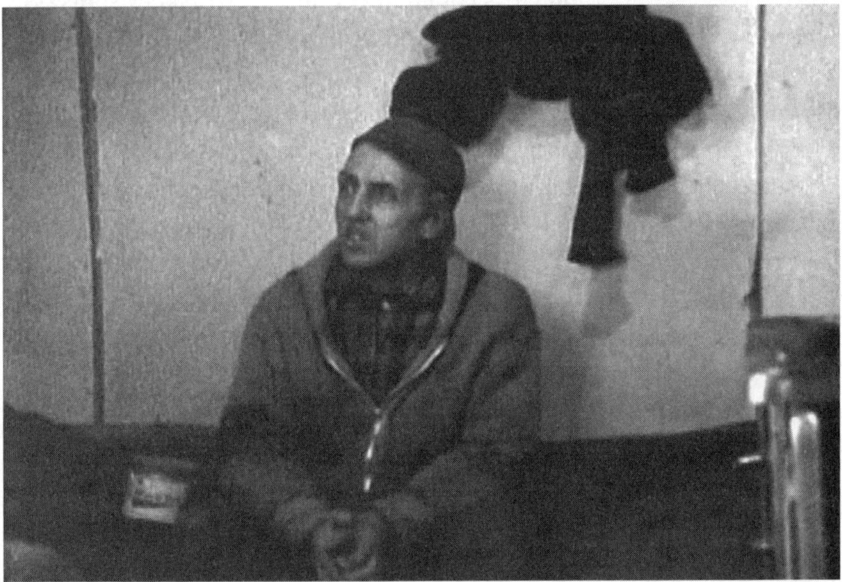

Chez nous c'est chez nous (Marcel Carrière, 1972). Old-timer trapper Hilaire
Minville, a living archive and a romantic holdout, reminisces about the history of
his doomed rural community.

documentary genre, *Chez nous* confronts change face to face, confronts
its own impotence, and looks not only to the past but also to the future,
poeticizes uncertainty and frustration, contradiction and denial, injustice
and resignation, trauma and scar tissue. We might find evidence of the
pertinence of such films in the fact that several of the CFC/SN films—*Chez
nous* most explicitly—had their fictional analog within the fledgling feature
film industry of the late sixties and early seventies. Jean-Claude Labrecque,
the distinguished cinematographer, who was otherwise not interested in
SN, produced, directed, and photographed a feature film depicting revolt
against the closures in the same period. *Les Smattes* (*The Wise Guys*,
1972) was part of the day's generic series of populist rural violence at the
commercial box office, a film no less resigned than *Chez nous* for all its
apocalyptic violence.[9]

VTR Rosedale

For its example of Portapak documentary, existing literature on CFC/SN
usually focuses on *VTR St-Jacques*, a 1969 document of the CFC process
in another urban core district of Montreal, credited to Klein and available
in both English and French versions (VTR means "video tape recorder").
This tape shows vividly the process of an urban citizens' group—and
several of the original CFC-ers, including a sprightly Dorothy Hénaut (b.
1935) just one step ahead of her "clients" learning both the ropes of the
new technology and the political peripeteias of community action. However, in order to suggest a representative sampling for the purpose of this
introduction to the corpus of both English- and French-language works,
of works released after Stoney left in 1970, and those developed within
rural contexts, I am looking at a similar tape, produced almost four
thousand kilometers to the west of Montreal in Rosedale, a small village
on the Red Deer River in the declining erstwhile mine-rich hinterland of
central Alberta. The credits for *VTR Rosedale* (31 min., 1974) are telling:
the NFB catalog credits it to Len Chatwin (1913–2000) a veteran NFB
photographer (and mountaineer) who had become the low-profile execu-
tive producer of the CFC program after Stoney's departure in 1971 (until
1976, when he was replaced by social worker Peter Katadotis, who was to
oversee the final dismantling of the program). Chatwin is thus credited on
more than a dozen CFC productions of the seventies produced in various
regions of Canada but may well have never left Montreal. Hénaut and
two other easterners were also involved in the Alberta project as "resource
personnel," but most significant are the editing credits to Peter Ludwig.

This charismatic fiftysomething citizen of the village set in motion, along with four others, a group they called "The Rosedale Citizens' Action Committee." The leap into collective image production was facilitated by Tony Karch, a community development worker affiliated with the then-fledgling University of Calgary ("I hear these problems, and something should be done by someone, but it must be the community's initiative . . . It's in your hands").

In contrast with the saga of St. Octave de l'Avenir in *Chez nous*, *Rosedale* is a narrative of rural decline transmogrified into an upbeat success story: the village once called the "rear end of Alberta" (by Ludwig himself) is transformed into an active community aggressively solving its problems. Ludwig shoots much of the half-inch video material, which his group edited at various points along the project's trajectory, and showed it to community meetings captured in turn on mise en abyme video (video screens within the video screen). The package was finally released as a thirty-one-minute black-and-white 16mm film in 1974. More than three decades later, this exemplary case study in the CFC method is now notable also for the ghostly luminosity of the video–film–DVD transfer, the color-ful geezers who testify on camera often with Eastern European–accented English, and a strong upbeat narrative that perhaps protests too much. We see local citizens gripe about underdevelopment on camera, come together to discuss problems, watch video, and come up with solutions

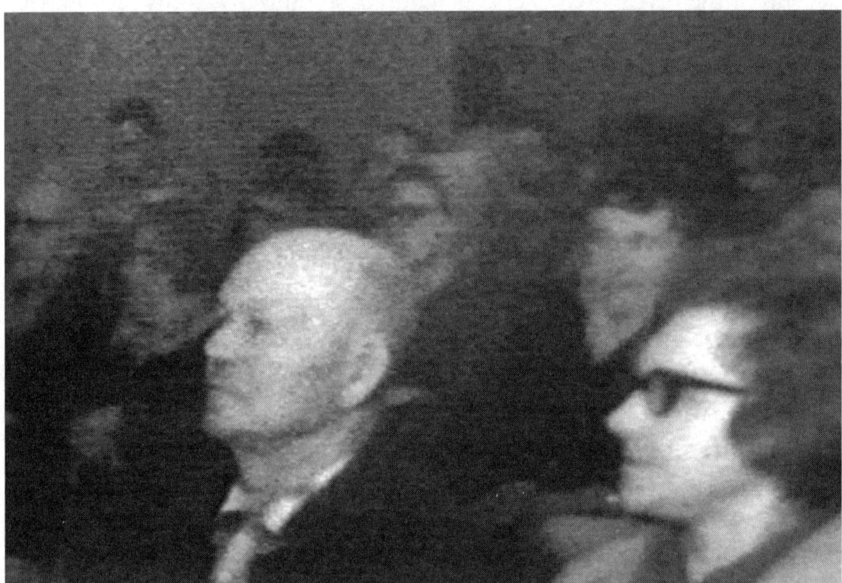

VTR Rosedale (Len Chatwin, 1974). The ghostly video-16mm-DVD transfer shows citizens of the "rear end of Alberta" being constituted as a problem-solving community through watching themselves on video.

again on camera. They finally bring about their modest objectives: new water and gas lines along with the unexpected pluses of a general town cleanup, a public park, a new fire truck, finally the ear of the provincial government (as the prim voice-over layered in 1974 tells us), and "even a beer garden." If the tape comes across as something of a panacea, the simple message is not undermined by its ebullience—warranted or not—and now acquires like the other films a rich ethnographic flavor, an oral and dim visual history of a now vanished worldview and culture—its high spirits in sharp contrast to the mournful sense of tragedy that arises out of *Chez nous*. If the footnotes of history now cast Rosedale 40 years later as a quaint suburb of Drumheller, complete with a few tourist attractions and a posted population of 135, this does not necessarily mean that the Board's dream of rural development was futile or betrayed in the march of urbanization. If the struggle over gas and water lines seems oddly beside the point alongside heroic conflicts over First Nations rights and the plight of the urban poor, this is precisely the point of the rural CFC films, the struggle for legitimacy of voices and experiences disowned by urban political elites. The sequence of elderly villagers coming together to clean up vacant lots is all about the everyday meaning of both change and democracy.

Conclusion

> *The medium itself may not have the importance that is so often attributed to it by social and cultural commentators, analysts and practitioners.*
> :: Ron Burnett

> *Facts became engraved in feelings.*
> :: Joris Ivens

For all their diversity the foregoing five films do not reflect anywhere near the full range of the CFC/SN corpus in terms of cinematic styles and social themes. Still, in concluding I would like to accent certain elements of commonality—around spaces and around storytelling—that extend throughout these films and the whole eclectic program and argue for the relevance of maintaining the films as a living archive of artworks—and the actions, processes, analyses, visions, and feelings they registered—rather than an archeological curiosity of failed transformative dreams.

One of the most important aesthetic characteristics of the CFC/SN corpus as a whole was brought out to me a few years back when I showed the engaging 1969 First Nations classic, *You Are on Indian Land*, at a conference in Kerala to a different genus of Indians, South Asian academics specializing in Canadian studies. For them one of the most visible features of the film was indeed "the land." No doubt for the Canadian Mohawks shown in the film, the politics of occupied territory and their improvised blockade of traffic through their land were more on their minds that blustery winter day in Akwesasne than pastoral aesthetics, as they confronted the police, cooled down tempers, and tried to stay warm at the same time (several having forgotten their gloves). But the South Asian Canada buffs more than three decades later were enthralled by the snowy sense of place and the almost spiritual sense of belonging to it "performed" visually and aurally by the film. They did not separate the demonstrators' corporeal occupation of the access to the blocked "international" bridge from the filmmakers' imaginary or artistic occupation of it.[10] This inseparability of the intradiegetic politics of space from the extradiegetic aesthetics of space, discerned by outsiders, is clearly a central feature of the CFC/SN poetics, one might even say a deep structure of the corpus: the artistic investment in the survey, stewardship, cultivation, and fortification of space, inhabited or husbanded but contested. We witness the performance of political agitation within space in this case or in other cases the corporeal or discursive movement through landscapes, urban or rural, individual or collective, exterior or interior. This structure transforms the neutral or constative filmic apperception of background into a performative of a dynamic environment that is the stake in livelihood, struggle, and transformation. This is as true of private living spaces as of public spaces, the domestic interiors with their worn kitchen tables and personalized wall hangings, whether of rented dwellings or cherished homesteads; of workspaces, occupied or transformed with matter of fact familiarity and pride, whether traplines, wharfs, fields, mines, factory floors, classrooms, or kitchens; and of community and play space, the space of sustenance, sociality and play, of shared food, music, storytelling, games, and dance.

This vivid cinematic inventory of spaces in the CFC/SN corpus, inhabited or worked, contributes in no small way to its operation as a rich register of the regional variation so beloved of Canadian national mythologies. It was also the essence, according to most historians, of the institutional shifts toward regionalization under way historically at the NFB at that time (Jones 1981; Dick 1986). (It also registers profoundly and intransigently the fundamental linguistic dichotomy that as we have seen so persistently befuddles and enriches our "country" as well as our political and cinematic research around that country.) But more importantly for us, the CFC/SN cameras penetrate specific and concrete local geographies, terrains of struggle in the here and now.

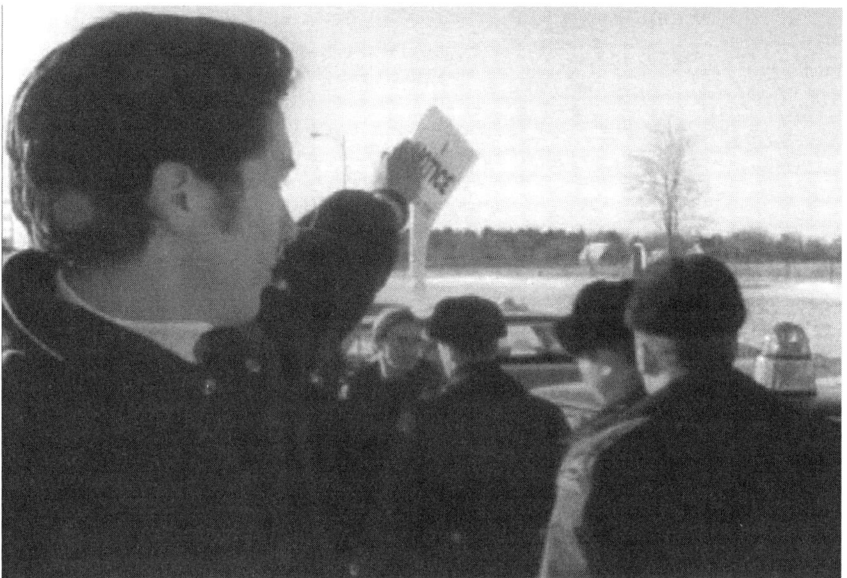

You Are on Indian Land (Mort Ransen, 1969). Mohawk leader Mike Mitchell (foreground) gesturing with his expulsion order toward white police, his fellow demonstrators, and the politicized snowy landscape.

There are many aesthetic devices that embody this penetration of space, but here are four especially interesting and characteristic tropes that encapsulate the films' political performance of space:

1. Tropes of politicized gatherings, most predictably, are among the most visible in the corpus. In many cases catalyzed by the camera or the filmmakers, these are often direct-cinema records of tense public demonstrations, that is, occupations of public space with all the ideological implications I have elaborated elsewhere (see chapter 10), and of which the vibrant material of *You Are on Indian Land* is most often remembered. Or else, perhaps even more common, there are the public meetings that begin characteristically polite or listless in those generic church basements and sometimes escalate into passion or acrimony, sometimes peter out in compliance, denial, or resignation. In chapter 10, I have emphasized the central significance of the trope of the public demonstration within the radical documentary corpus, exploring the valences of both filmic and profilmic street theater in contested public space. However, CFC/SN reminds us of how the informal citizens' gatherings in kitchens, living rooms, and backyards are constituted as politically as those in public space; the exploratory language of

gesture and speech in those private settings functions differently
but no less politically than those of collective slogans and orchestrated group demands.

2. The trope of the citizen exploring space with either his or her body
   or his off-screen voice is another generic standard. Most often this
   seems to be a senior citizen, a cinematically charismatic old-timer
   revisiting old spaces, the moment usually set up by the filmmakers
   as the collaborative mise-en-scène of "lived cinema," or *cinéma
   vécu,* as we say in Quebec. This trope sparks the active encounter
   of space and remembered trauma, the clash of ideal and reality,
   promise and betrayal, the motor of political consciousness. Noël
   Daudelin's ambulatory stroll down the street of soon to be demolished row houses in *La P'tite Bourgogne,* his running commentary
   on each tenant and their lives, is a typical example. (Among other
   things, this recurrent trope's affirmation of generational continuity and discovery of local histories dispatch any lingering myths
   about the alleged gerontophobia of those oedipal amnesiacs, the
   baby-boomer New Left.)

3. Another trope often accompanies or is corollary to the foregoing
   one, but is of a purely landscape orientation and distinct from the
   old-timer mise-en-scène per se. Landscape tropes are insufficiently

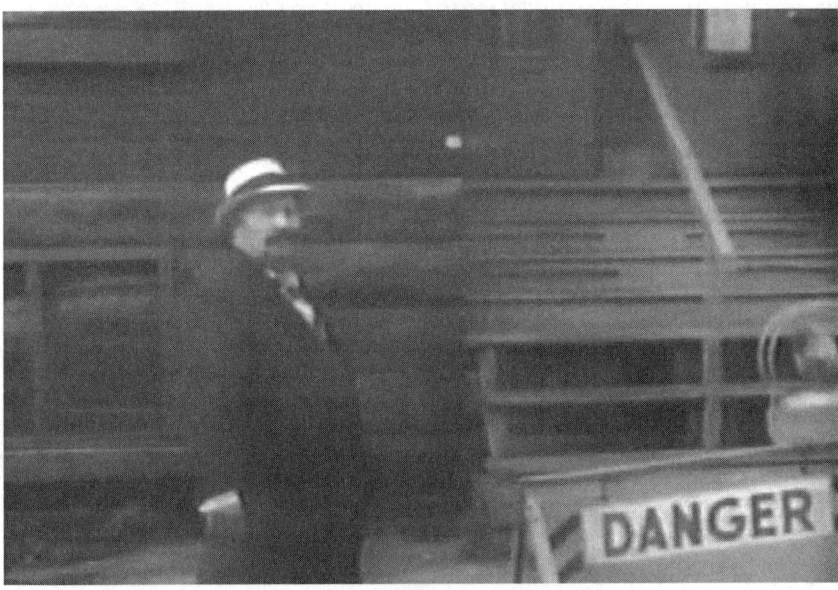

La P'tite Bourgogne (Maurice Bulbulian, 1968). Grandfatherly Noël Daudelin
leads the Nouvelle société camera on an insider narrative tour of the row houses
slated to be demolished.

theorized in documentary studies, and deserving of much more attention. Frequently in the CFC/SN corpus, places of human abundance or natural fertility, or of idleness or devastation, are encountered with intense affect and solely through the eye of the lens—thus coming closer to restoring the point of view of the filmmaker as artist rather than as social facilitator. Most characteristically within the mode of radical critique, these landscape moments are aesthetic denunciations of uncontrolled "development," the spaces of lived trauma, inhuman man-made ecodeserts, demolitions, ghost towns, and clear-cut forests. With or without onscreen human guides, whether a dramatic discourse or a dystopian lyricism, these tropes cement the overall tragic sensibility of the corpus at large.

4. Perhaps most dramatically innovative in CFC/SN's repertory is the trope of intertextual space: either a structural play with the onscreen presence of the mediated, relayed space of the "live" closed-circuit video image or its replayed record. Both appear as video screens within the screen. Of course, we cannot say that this is the first instance of intertextual self-reflexivity in radical documentary history. Vertov, Resnais, de Antonio, and other Western leftists from the thirties to the sixties frequently used newsreels and archival footage in a way that anticipates Carrière's use of archival footage in *Chez nous*. But what the Challengers innovated was the practice, thanks to the Portapaks (notorious or legendary, depending on your point of view), of setting up live local transmissions or replays as a personal or ideological screen-mirror, a reflex or catalyst for their protagonists. Most common was the *VTR Rosedale* model wherein the community is constituted by the collective watching of locally produced video material with an eye toward identifying local concerns, sparking further discussion and the imagining of solutions. But other practices can be found, for example using closed-circuit TV to follow a campus occupation by sequestered student protesters in the seldom-mentioned *Occupation* (Bill Reid, 1970); the replay of video materials for bureaucrats with the goal of improving or bringing new services to constituencies; or the native network's use of video footage to virtually bring together far-flung constituencies. This aspect of the CFC/SN mandate was one that fascinated contemporaries around the planet because of its novelty and one that has disproportionately preoccupied historians and theorists, but in fact it was but one element of their practice among several. Druick says correctly that this

trope is in fact an extension of the Board's push toward realism in the three decades of its existence (Druick 2007, 127–32, 144–50), while theorists of the nineties saw in it the whole program's ultimate hubris, as Ron Burnett's epigraph above makes clear.

These four cinematic spatial articulations of the local and the global, in both the French and English corpuses, recapitulate the sensibility of loss fostered by late capitalism and modernity, our pervasive trauma of displacement. But these articulations do not simply echo conventional urban anomies, or nostalgias for bucolic heartlands or erstwhile communities. Far from succumbing to the lure of salvage ethnography or the reactionary ethnocentrism of Québécois poet documentarist Pierre Perrault (and I would be the first to admit that not all the CFC/SN films rise above this liability), these and the other CFC spatial tropes enact a precarious but progressive politics of spatial transformation. This politics comes alive in the ethical tenterhooks of collaboration and in the indeterminacy of the outcome, as well as by insertions of intertextual space. In general, these spatial tropes are answers to the question so hauntingly posed by one of Bulbulian's old-timers in his forestry manifesto *La revanche* (1974), when confronting the devastation of an overharvested woodland, "Will we have the courage to recover what we have lost?" The films' and videotapes' enactments of political space utter the answer everywhere, whether tentative or bravado, and the answer is yes. It is a yes not only to the will to recover what we have lost but also to discursively identify and visually imagine what and how we want to gain, and to timidly, imperfectly, courageously, collectively embark on that process.

Interestingly, the films most focused on recovering what is lost in the literal sense, such as *La Revanche, P'tite Bourgogne,* and *Chez nous,* acquire retroactively a resonant pertinence to the ecopolitics of our own era. This pertinence arises not only in the iconography of devastated natural resources but also in cinematic articulations of the right to housing and to the sustainability of rural and urban economic, social, human, and natural space. CFC/SN films show that we had the courage to confront the traumas of modernization and "development," even when we did not win, and these films share this courage with our inherited, international corpus of radical documentary over a century, their active political aesthetics of fraught, occupied, and contested spaces.

I will address more briefly the element of storytelling that constitutes a second essential commonality of these films. The filmmakers, in addition to joining their bodies and their technologies in their subject's aesthetic and political occupation of space, joined their voices also with their subjects' voices in the telling of their stories, of their lives, and of their struggles. The practice of self-narration, of not only *performing* one's relations to space but also *telling* them, was not limited to the scriptwriting committees of Gloucester County nor to old-timers' narrations of how it used to be. It spans over the entire corpus—in voices telling stories of how things once were, stories of then and now and the imagined future, open-ended narratives of actions undertaken and results still not measured. What would now be called "focus groups" were one of the favorite devices of the project, anticipating the "consciousness-raising" circles of feminist filmmaking of the seventies with their "deep structure" of collective learning and strategizing through speaking, listening, and exchanging (Lesage 1984). Editorially, many of the films matched the long-take rhythm of real-world conversation and exchange, and mostly eschewed the Perrault formula of constructing chronologically and spatially disjunctive thematic threads. As I mentioned in regard to *Chez nous*, the corpus is a bountiful repository of oral histories with rich ethnographic value, but it is also more than that. I am borrowing obviously from Kenneth Plummer's *Telling Sexual Stories* in my sense of storytelling as a essential ritual of modernity in which CFC/SN's citizens are caught up (Plummer 1995), but go further than a sense of the therapeutic value of storytelling in its processing of individual trauma toward its collective political application as problem solving and community building. Collaborative local histories, self-portraits, and storytelling, rendered choral through the devices of editing, enact the confrontation with, and the processing of, the traumas of the postwar world: loss, betrayal, governmentality, cultural genocide, attack, disempowerment, deprivation, and isolation.

For an archive of radical political documentary to maintain its currency four decades later and to speak to us in a relevant and engaging way about the traumas of poverty and powerlessness, about empowerment through the collective enactment of politicized space and the collective telling of stories, is not only to speak of recovery or gain but also to speak of democracy. In my introduction I referred to the lessons an archive of New Left documentary activism can inject into our present era of renewed documentary culture. One of CFC/SN's lessons is clearly that the democratic aspiration need not deal with world-historic events like the Vietnam War or the Iraq War. Everyday space and narrative transformations are also a crucible of struggle and everyday courage, the mundane, tentative, public, and private performance of democracy. This aesthetic pursuit of democracy set the tone for much subsequent activist documentary in Canada and elsewhere, eschewing the inherited aesthetics of victimization, silencing, and unacknowledged trauma. CFC/SN consolidated as an artistic practice the strategic pursuit of collaborative process, of not only encountering the other but also working alongside, thereby enabling community empowerment and the resolution of trauma. Where change turned out to be ephemeral or superficial, the challenge (with its felicitous etymological link to "calumny," "insult," and "trauma") remained.

As the fourteen-year experiment wore on, the initial fervor for process, for the artists' embrace of the facilitator role, ceded on many fronts to a revived directorial practice suggested by my opening salvos about aesthetics (Marchessault 1995). Throughout these shifts, embodied by the broad trajectory from the Fogo "process" films (1967–68) to the more "authorial" Mistassini films (1974–76), the overall democratic aspiration of artist-community collaboration, of bodies and groups enacting the occupation or transformation of space or performing the narration of self-empowering lives and communities—with credits proudly listing citizens' committees— was maintained as an aesthetic and discursive ideal in dynamic tension with the reassertion of the auteur. This aspiration lasted until the end.

In the early and mid-nineties, Ron Burnett, Janine Marchessault, and Scott MacKenzie—then all at McGill University, the site of the student protest featured in *Occupation* a quarter century earlier (one of the few explicit reflections of campus politics in the corpus)—provided a sustained theoretical reflection on the CFC/SN program. These analysts, whom I shall call the "McGill Three," thinking behind the screen for the most part rather than looking at it head-on, diagnosed with eloquent and perceptive skepticism the liabilities and fallacies in the CFC/SN process and its aspiration to arbiter and trigger social change. They critiqued the program's democracy of delusion, focusing almost entirely on the Portapak corpus and the experiments with video. Burnett argued that the use of electronic images as a "fulcrum"—"for public forms of discourse" and "for political change"—was a misguided process based on presuppositions of a "transparent relationship between human activity and motivation . . . between the electronic image and presumptions about truth," between knowledge and action. Video was an "attractive" technology and documentary an "attractive" form, but they played "a far less important role" in political process than was presumed. Burnett's insight into our "overinvestment in the power of the image to transform culture, and not the audiences around it, to bring about social and political transformation" is echoed more recently in the different context of trauma evidence by Guerin and Hallas who likewise point to "the history of aesthetics which expects too much from the image" (Burnett 1995, 158; Guerin and Hallas 2007, 8).

Marchessault, for her part, had related worries about exaggerated confidence in the entire CFC/SN program's political agency as well, about its invisible complicity in the apparatus of state liberalism and the Liberal state:

> The interactivity and participation that video delivered instituted access without agency. It instituted a particular form of self-surveillance rather than transforming the actual institutional relations of production and knowledge . . . And most of the community experiments with video never went beyond this initial positivism, beyond this social reproduction. (Marchessault 1995, 19)

She furthermore argued that the CFC/SN's

> "authentic" expression of community was made to replicate the instrumental discourses of the state. More often than not, community video was synonymous with the transparency and certainty of public service information . . .
>
> To what degree were established structures of authority recognized and challenged?
>
> This process . . . could not challenge an authority that it worked to obscure. Instead, the Fogo process consolidated a version of community identity largely determined by the directives of Liberal reform. (Marchessault 1995, 19–20)

One of the main criticisms of Challenge for Change has been that it worked to diffuse direct action, to contain and stabilize, as television can do, the potentially explosive effects of difference. It is easy to see how Challenge for Change is entangled in that web of coercion and consent, technologies of domination and technologies of the self, that define the functioning of power in the liberal democratic state. As Chantal Mouffe has remarked, liberalism must continuously deny its own limits in order to maintain political legitimacy and its foundation in civil society. Discourses of access and participation often work to conceal the institutional conditions of access and the political limits of coming to voice (Marchessault 1995, 21).

Marchessault's Foucauldian pessimism is corroborated unfortunately by the NFB's own recent document of CFC/SN veterans celebrating, with justifiable pride but through surprisingly simplistic lenses, their own success stories, minimizing the contradictions and glossing over the imperfections of the process.[11]

MacKenzie agrees with his two mentors and argues that the Société nouvelle process, especially that of its Vidéographe wing, "abstracted community action further and further away from concrete reality and more and more toward the world of images":

> While the advent of easily available video technology offered the possibility of representing oneself through culture's dominant modes of representation, it did not offer the kind of power that typically goes hand in hand with

it . . . The new and rediscovered communities that were founded around
video images in the late 1960s failed to take on a life of their own; instead of
images being a starting point for community development, they became the
raison d'être of many of these communities. (MacKenzie 2004, 157)

Burnett, preferring canonical conceptual-minimalist American video
art to the earnest stumblings of Canadian idealists and activists laboring
under all those presumptions, presuppositions, assumptions, and hypo-
theses, asks questions that are undeniably apt but that inevitably tend
toward an immobilization of the impulse to change. In fact the practitioners, frustrated and uncertain, asked themselves the same questions, even
I am sure those collaborators within existing community and political
groups, from the Comité de citoyens des Îlots Saint-Martin to the Rosedale
Citizens' Action Committee to the Company of Young Canadians (the
state's short-lived activist youth corps that was connected to several of the
CFC/SN projects and is most visible in *Encounter with Saul Alinsky—Part
I: CYC Toronto* [1967]). No one in the original movement claimed that
films alone could or would change the world. In the present moment, it is
undoubtedly easier to dissect excessive idealism than to encounter texts
on their own terms as works of political art caught up in all the contradictions, imperfections, and potentialities of the real historical world.

No doubt the disciplinary consensus about a discreet historical corpus
within a national cinema—like CFC/SN's 230-odd films—goes through
dialectical cycles just like any other consensus. No doubt either that the
New Left generation's enthusiasm about the potential of the image needed
the corrective of the stern reality check provided by the McGill Three in
the nineties. Now it is time to come back, all the wiser thanks to their
astute analysis, and recognize the exemplary courage, strength, democratic
vision, and beauty of the original experiments, for all their flawed idealism and aesthetic imperfections, for all their premature truncation in the
forge of history (as with Vertov's and Ivens's experiments before them). Let
us also reexamine them as a model for the ethical, affective, and political
challenges of our own day and our own consensus about the potential of
nonfiction culture to transform the world and the scope of these ancestors
to show us how—and how not to. This reexamination must of course be
carried out in the context of a historiographical reappraisal of the New
Left as a whole, as well as of the heritage of radical documentary, of which
CFC/SN is one of the most complete available corpuses.

This chapter began with hand-wringing over the availability of the
canon of a century of radical documentary film and video and urged its
resuscitation as a living archive. In wrapping up this preliminary exploration of Challenge for Change/Société nouvelle and in arguing for the

renewal of its activist legacy, I am inspired by Ann Cvetkovich's linking of trauma and activism and the essential political role to be played by an archive that sustains the history and effects of activism (2003).

While the CFC/SN saga is fundamentally different in its scope and narrative than the more recent archives of lesbian public cultures and AIDS activisms that Cvetkovich explores, and while the status of the two hundred odd CFC/SN films and videos made between 1967 and 1980 is fundamentally different from the more recent multidisciplinary archive of texts and oral histories that Cvetkovich scrutinizes, I think we can benefit from her discovery of the broad import of archives of activism for recharging the public spheres of today. However limited the effect of the CFC/SN archive's pragmatic political aspirations may have been historically, as the McGill Three have demonstrated, we must broaden the import of these films to include affect as well as effect. We can rework Cvetkovich's objective "to create political history as affective history, a history that captures activism's felt and even traumatic dimensions. In forging a collective knowledge built on memory . . . , [we can] produce not only a version of history but also an archive of the emotions, which is one of trauma's most important, but most difficult to preserve, legacies" (Cvetkovich 2003, 167). If we position the CFC/SN archive as an archive of communal and individual creative responses to the collective traumas of postwar modernization in Canada, those both everyday and historical-catastrophic—from bureaucracy to cultural genocide—this archive can reenergize twenty-first-century public spheres not only in Canada but everywhere where twenty-first-century social traumas are being felt. To maintain this archive "in order to find what remains does not have to be a nostalgic holding on to the past but can instead be a productive resource for the present and future" (Cvetkovich 2003, 165).

In short, the films of CFC/SN, the five I have briefly highlighted and many of the other two hundred, have an enduring and exemplary aesthetic quality and a political effect that surpasses the value as historical documentation of the political and artistic processes, achievements, and shortcomings of the programs. Almost all of CFC/SN's even most ephemeral films provide this archival function (I use the word "films" advisedly to remind us that 16mm films form the larger part of the accessible archive, in contrast to the inference that it is all too easy to take from the CFC/SN cohort and their McGill nineties successors that it was the Portapak activity that constituted the major thrust of the programs). The five works that I have selected for this scrutiny, and many more, retain a quality to stir future audiences still caught up with the heritage of sixties utopias or even more insidious ones—whether of urban planners or community activists. Among such audiences, to whom the New Left visions of democracy have not been transmitted or imperfectly transmitted, the vivid traces of this contained experiment can stir up aesthetically and affectively, pedagogically and politically, art and evidence and can both imitate and reinvent. This, I am sure, is what Hénaut meant by "longer life" in the epigraph I set at the start of this chapter.

What she meant by "virtue" and "artistry," the two terms I have appropriated for the title of this chapter, I am sure that she would be happy to keep dynamically vague. Grierson's Calvinist ghost would prefer "virtue" to "artistry" but it is the dynamic tension between these two concepts and ideals—the utilitarian and the imaginary, the political and the poetic, truth and utopia, effect and affect—that is essential to the historical achievement of the program and to its legacy as a living archive. It is this tension that keeps alive the works of Bulbulian, Carrière, Forest, Hénaut, Klein, Low, Macartney-Filgate, Mitchell, Poirier, Stoney, and all the others as much as it has done the cinematic legacy of Vertov, Ivens, Solanas, de Antonio, Kopple, Sigel and Yates, Patwardhan, and all the others.

Many of the key CFC/SN films are unfortunately not available on DVD or in English as I have complained at the outset. The vicious circle of technology and marketplace is compounded by the historiographical negligence of the institutional steward of this legacy. (Or, as Jerry White puts it, "the NFB is often its own worst enemy" [2006, 75].) With the amnesia or ahistoricity and culture-centrism of both the Left and the mainstream, it is very optimistic to hope that this unprepossessing corpus can break into the international canons of documentary history, as I hoped in my introduction, especially the inclusion therein of so-called "minor" cinemas, whether Canadian or Left. Nevertheless optimism defined CFC/SN, and I offer a parting call to the NFB to restore to circulation, with subtitles aplenty, the seventy-three missing works (sixty-one in English and twelve in French). Perhaps the Internet and its acceleration of streaming platforms will solve this problem before the institution does, an irony that is all the more delicious in the sense that CFC/SN was in many ways as prophetic an anticipation of virtual community as Vertov's kinoks, forty years earlier.

[**7**] Lesbian and Gay Documentary

Minority Self-Imaging, Oppositional Film Practice, and the Question of Image Ethics (1984)

Chapters 7 and 8 are two articles on somewhat overlapping corpuses written over a decade apart but for vastly different audiences, and it shows. The dogmatic, prescriptive me of the eighties reflects a readership I envisaged as primarily straight and anchored in the neighboring disciplines of communications and journalism, and who needed to be told a thing or two about queer politics and independent documentary filmmaking and video making in the present-day of Reaganite America. In contrast to this tense polemicist, in chapter 8 the more relaxed and confident queer me of the nineties will show my age by reminiscing volubly about the seventies and pontificating to a younger generation of LBGT readers and film fans. Speaking of younger generations, the exclusionary shortfall of my 1984 nomenclature "lesbian and gay" will sound rather grating to postqueer ears, and this despite the ample gender diversity in this 1984 corpus: I was apparently not ready to expand my alphabet soup for another fifteen years.

Invited by my friend Larry Gross to a couple of conferences on image ethics at the Annenberg School of Communications at the University of Pennsylvania, I ambitiously tried to destabilize the sets of assumptions underlying what I took to be the prevailing discourses of mainstream media and media studies: basically, "we're not playing by your rules." It was meant as a challenge to the top-down notion of media ethics from the point of view of on-the-street sexual minorities. And by this unproblematical "we" I meant what we then called "lesbian and gay" media and community activists (although this nomenclature was clearly already in flux, auguring the advent of "queer" several years later). The bizarre inclusion of Taxi zum Klo, *a feature-length fiction film, in this compendium of documentaries, came about when a friend in communications (whose daughter later came out as a lesbian) persuaded me that it was probably the only queer film that some of my readership might have seen.*

The developed article was included in the anthology that came out of the conferences, thanks to Oxford University Press (incidentally a publisher I otherwise must reprimand for their jelly-spined approach to censorship), edited by Larry along with Jay Ruby and John Katz. As far as I can make out, though queer scholars have occasionally cited it, this piece was politely ignored by its intended audience until a Norwegian colleague constructed a fine updating of the very heterocentric "Challenge for Change" legacy on it (Corneil 2010). No doubt much the same for Larry's critique of mainstream televisual representations of sexuality minorities in the same volume. So much for synthesizing queer media critique with mainstream liberal communications discourses of the mid-eighties. Still "Lesbian and Gay Documentary" serves as a useful stock taking of international queer documentary as "we" moved through the second post-Stonewall decade—especially for U.S. academics who are so often oblivious to what is going on offshore.

A decade later the tide would have turned within communications studies, thanks in part to Larry's influence, and along with film studies it's now one of the queerest disciplines in the academic marketplace.

▶

To Whom Are Lesbian and Gay Documentary Filmmakers Accountable?

Ever since Stonewall, the Greenwich Village uprising of street gay people against the police that symbolically inaugurated the era of gay liberation, documentary film has been a primary means by which lesbians and gay men have carried out their liberation struggle. Most of the Western industrial democracies have seen a lively proliferation of documentaries by lesbians and gay men, gaining momentum in particular in the late seventies. This proliferation has occurred both within the mainstream media and within the alternative circuits and has aimed at both general and specialized audiences, gay and nongay.

Lesbian and gay documentaries have addressed both general issues—identity and consciousness, civil rights and political transformation—and the stakes of specific and/or localized struggles, for example, child custody or local mobilizations in Toronto or Sydney. Coming from different cultural, political, and personal backgrounds, the films, as might be expected, range across a broad spectrum of ideological, technical, and aesthetic choices. At the same time, seen together as a single corpus, they reflect the shared evolution of the international lesbian and gay movements over the years, their shift of focus from pride to power, from crisis reaction to strategy building and community consolidation. This paper addresses ethical issues that arise from these endeavors by lesbians and gay men to use documentary film to represent themselves, to mobilize their communities, and to achieve goals of social and political change.

To date, most discussion has centered on mainstream media and state legal apparatus. Even lesbian and gay critics raising questions of image ethics tend to do so in terms of how we are represented by straight image makers, that is, *their* ethical accountability to *us*, rather than in terms of the ethics of our own self-representation. Such criticism seldom achieves concrete results; the dominant media, on those rare occasions when they in fact do listen to us, invoke a code of ethical principles and procedures that from our point of view is nothing more than rationalization for silencing, scapegoating, trivialization, tokenism, contempt, sensationalism, and ridicule. How many times, for example, has the media blackout been lifted briefly only to have us debate our right to live and love with, at best, apologists for discrimination and, at worst, proponents of concentration camps and even capital punishment?[1] It's called the ethics of balance. Lesbians and gays have this in common with other disenfranchised groups: that media access is systematically blocked, not *despite* codes of journalistic ethics but *because* of them. For lesbians and gays, this impasse is especially frustrating because of our status as a largely invisible minority, for whom the already complex issues of representation are compounded by our straddling of boundaries of race, gender, class, and culture.

Rather than playing by the rules of the dominant media, lesbian and gay documentarists must develop an independent set of ethical principles suitable to an oppositional or radical film practice. Such principles apply regardless of whether the documentaries aim simply at filling the representation vacuum left by the dominant media, whether they aim at political reform or integration or whether they aim at fundamental societal transformation. In fact, such a code has already evolved in practice for lesbian and gay documentarists, just as similar codes have evolved in parallel areas of cultural practice committed to social change and/or minority empowerment (though these oppositional and minority ethical codes have seldom been formulated in systematic ethical terms).

What are the ethical principles that we have developed in this work
of counterinformation, community mobilization, and the undermining
of the system? And which of these principles are specific to us, which do
we share with other minority cultural workers, and which are common
to all cultural workers committed to change? How are these principles
derived from our experience as oppressed sexual minorities living under
patriarchal capitalism? If, as recently argued, the three fundamental ethical
principles of the gay movement may be summarized as a basic truthful-
ness engendered by respect for the self, the freedom of individual (sexual)
choice, and—believe it or not—love, how are these translated into the nuts
and bolts of documentary film technique? (Millard 1983, 32–33).

This chapter attempts to locate a number of areas within which the
ethical principles of lesbian and gay self-representation may be hammered
out. But since an ethics of minority culture is surely a code of moral and political relativity, I will try not to offer a list of prescriptions but rather a series
of foci around which lesbian and gay documentary filmmakers must make—
and have been making—informed and relative ethical choices. My emphasis
on oppositional self-representation is not meant to denigrate the work of
those trying to assert our right to control our images in Hollywood or CBS
or the publishing industry or wherever. Rather it is intended to underline our
crucial stake in radical cultural practice in a conjuncture that, for the fore-
seeable future, will continue to impede the aspirations of lesbians and gays,
of women, of the working class, and of all disenfranchised people.

I am basing these reflections on twenty-four lesbian and/or gay documentaries for which I provide the credits and a brief summary of content
and method in the following table. The works originate in the United
States, Canada, Australia, England, West Germany, and France and within
the national groupings reflect many more different political, economic, and
cultural contexts. They are arranged chronologically within the national
groups. Although my primary focus is film I include two of the more
prominent videotapes to have emerged recently: as the current funding crisis deepens, more and more work by lesbian and gay documentarists will
be appearing in this medium.

▶──

The United States

- *In the Best Interests of the Children* (Frances Reid and Elizabeth
  Stevens [Iris Films], independent, 1977, 53 min.). Portraits of
  eight lesbian mothers and their children, based principally on
  first-person participant testimony.

- *Word Is Out* (Mariposa Film Group, independent with PBS hookup, 1977, 135 min.). Subtitled "Stories of Some of Our Lives," portraits and first-person case histories of twenty-six men and women.
- *Double Strength* (Barbara Hammer, independent, 1978, 16 min.). Wry autobiographical and diaristic reflection on artist's past relationship with a trapezist—infatuation and rupture.
- *Loads* (Curt McDowell, independent, 1980, 20 min.). Diaristic, participatory account of author's casual sexual encounters with straight men, erotic and ironic.
- *Greetings from Washington* (Lucy Winer, independent, 1981, 30 min.). Vérité images of the 1979 march on Washington by 125,000 American lesbians and gays.
- *We All Have Our Reasons* (Frances Reid and Elizabeth Stevens [Iris Films], independent, 1981, 30 min.). Study of alcoholism as a women's issue via a portrait of a Los Angeles center for lesbian alcoholics.
- *Pink Triangles* (Cambridge Documentary Films, independent, 1982, 35 min.). Essay on homophobia, historical and contemporary, including some archival material on Nazi gay holocaust, establishing analogies with current New Right.
- *Choosing Children* (Debra Chasnoff and Kim Klausner, independent, 1984, 45 min.). Essay on lesbians having and rearing children via portraits of five different representative "families."
- *Silent Pioneers* (Lucy Winer, independent with PBS hookup, 1984, 45 min.). Portraits of gay and lesbian senior citizens based primarily on interviews.
- *The Times of Harvey Milk* (Robert Epstein and Richard Schmiechen, independent, 1984, 87 min.). Narrative of career of gay politician and its context, ending in his assassination and its aftermath, constructed from TV archives and first-person participant interviews.
- *Before Stonewall* (Greta Schiller and Robert Rosenberg, independent with PBS hookup, 1984, 87 min.). Archival compilation of U.S. gay and lesbian history, supplemented by interview and vérité reminiscences by first-person participants.

- *Some American Feminists* (Nicole Brossard, Margaret Wescott, and Luce Guilbeault [National Film Board of Canada], 1977, 55 min.). Interviews with six U.S. feminist leaders and theoreticians, including lesbians Rita Mae Brown, Kate Millett, and "political lesbian" Ti-Grace Atkinson with a concluding account of the Susan Saxe case.[2]
- *Michael, A Gay Son* (Bruce Glawson, independent with NFB distribution, 1980, 27 min.). A young man comes out; discussion with a peer support group followed by role-playing of family confrontation improvised also by peers.
- *Track Two* (Harry Sutherland, Gordon Keith, and Jack Lemmon, independent, 1982, 90 min.). Study of community resistance to police oppression, focused on 1981 bathhouse raids and unsuccessful municipal electoral campaign; many interviews plus vérité coverage of rallies and demonstrations.
- *Heroes* (Sara Halprin [formerly Barbara Martineau], independent, 1983, 23 min.). Collaborative self-portraits of an elderly handicapped woman, an elderly immigrant black woman, and a middle-aged lesbian carpenter developing the concept of everyday heroism.
- *Orientations* (Richard Fung, independent, 1985, video, 56 min.). First-person discussions by a dozen lesbians and gays of different Asian backgrounds looking at the interface of gay and lesbian identity with their cultural heritage.

Australia

- *Witches, Faggots, Dykes and Poofters (One in Seven Collective,* independent, 1979, 45 min.). Sydney gay and lesbian resistance to police oppression in 1978–79; first-person participant testimony with vérité coverage of police attacks, counterdemonstrations and political meetings, and archival prologue.

West Germany

- *It Is Not the Homosexual Who Is Perverse, But the Situation in Which He Lives* (Rosa von Praunheim and Martin Dannecker, state TV, 1971, feature length). Self-oppression in gay culture conveyed through fictional didactic sketches and analysis of the sketches.
- *Army of Lovers (Revolt of the Perverts)* (Rosa von Praunheim, state TV, 1978, 93 min.). Journalistic survey of American gay community, including recent history, based on participant interviews and some sketch material.
- *Taxi Zum Klo* (Frank Ripploh, independent, 1981, 93 min.). Autobiographical episodic narrative of personal and professional adventures of Berlin gay school teacher against backdrop of sexually active ghetto; includes humor, eroticism, domestic melodrama, and some media collage.

France

- *Race d'ep: Un Siècle d'homosexualité* (*The Homosexual Century*, Lionel Soukaz and Guy Hocquenghem, independent, 1979, 105 min.). Four "moments" from twentieth-century gay history conveyed through some archival material but primarily through interpretative sketch reconstructions; includes von Gloeden, turn-of-the-century photographer of male nudes; Hirschfeld, scientist victim of Nazi terror; the late sixties sexual revolution; and a late seventies stock taking in the Paris ghetto.
- *L'Aspect rose de la chose* (Chi Yan Wong [a.k.a. Jean-Luc Wong], independent with some public funding, 1980, 74 min.). Current lesbian and gay problematic explored through eleven collaborators' statements on various subjects, plus vérité group discussion; Brechtian in tone.

England

- *Framed Youth* (Lesbian and Gay Youth Project, independent, London, 1983, 45 min., video). The problematic of lesbian and gay youth through participant interviews, vérité group discussions, and media collage.

- *Breaking the Silence* (Melanie Chait, Channel 4 TV, 1984, 60 min.). Lesbian mothers and their struggle to retain custody under patriarchal law, explored through group discussions and individual statements.

Our Constituency and Ourselves

These twenty-four documentaries crystallize ethical discussions that are all relative to their specific conjunctures but all revolve around a notion of accountability. Conventional assumptions about a documentary filmmaker's ethical accountability point to the subject (the subject must consent to the use of his or her image, must not be exploited, etc.) and secondarily to the audience (the audience must not be misled, etc.). This paper maintains of course these two ethical foci but adds two others: that of the constituency and that of the self. Gay and lesbian cultural workers share their accountability to their constituency with all minority and oppositional activists. In fact mainstream media workers and journalists are also accountable to a constituency—white middle-class heterosexual man—though of course this accountability is unacknowledged and masked by the media's claims to be speaking for society as a whole. My notion of accountability to the self is more distinctive, in fact unique to lesbians' and gays' identity as an invisible sexual minority.

In the scheme of things that I propose, accountability to the constituency and to the self cannot be secondary to either the subject or the audience and in some cases may even have priority over these two traditional ethical foci. With regard to the subject, for example, I could not easily refute a justification of the easy superficial caricatures of homophobic subjects in *Pink Triangles* (an ex-Marine, a Catholic housewife) established through person-on-the-street interviews (a device that is ethically delicate in any circumstance, though the authors of *Framed Youth* and *Silent Pioneers* include similar material with seemingly much less of the caricatural bent). My reasoning is that the filmmakers' decision to dramatize the universality of homophobic discourse threatening their constituency takes precedence over the filmmakers' responsibility to homophobes (whose views are fully represented in the media anyway). Or, to take a more distant example, would anyone argue with the well-known use of false credentials by progressive Chilean and East German film crews in Chile in 1973 to gain access to reactionary interview subjects?

As far as lesbian and gay filmmakers' audience goes, this is not always identical to their constituency, that is, the lesbian and gay community or its parts. The films under review have a wide variety of audience goals from the broad general public broadcasting audience (*Word Is Out, Before Stonewall,* and *Breaking The Silence*) to the alternative lesbian feminist network (*Heroes* and *Double Strength*) to the specialized public of professional decision makers in child custody litigations (*In the Best Interests of the Children*). It is therefore not difficult to conceive of many other instances where a filmmaker's accountability to his or her constituency might be seen as having priority over a broad general audience. Certainly the several filmmakers represented here who have suppressed easily misinterpreted and controversial aspects of gay lifestyles, say promiscuity, have weighted their responsibility not to disseminate harmful stereotypes or AIDS panic or whatever over the general public's "right to know."

As for accountability to the self, I cannot conceive of any circumstances in any of the six countries in question where a filmmaker's masking of his or her sexual orientation, and the toll of self-oppression this entails, would be warranted by accountability to subjects or audience. Admittedly some situations are ambiguous: for example, I could not easily criticize a lesbian filmmaker of my acquaintance who stayed in the closet during the shooting of a film about strikers' wives so as to not alienate her sexually conservative working-class subjects. Yet for any project related to sexuality or to sexual politics, a filmmaker's choice of the closet, either on the set or in the text, seems categorically unacceptable. The closet is an institution to which I will return (in this chapter). One final corollary to the foregoing discussion of accountability is that gay or lesbian filmmakers' accountability to the mainstream media and other institutions of heterosexist patriarchal capitalism (such as the law) is negligible. Beyond their responsibility to stay solvent and out of jail wherever possible, they must as a general principle avoid all collaboration with the dominant media (except where concrete short-term goals are clearly achievable) and above all with the police (except, for example, to help in the apprehension of queerbashers, etc.).

Moreover, lesbian and gay media activists must not hesitate to engage in extralegal activity wherever this is in the interest of lesbian and gay self-representation, resistance, and liberation. By this I mean civil disobedience, ranging from smuggling and copyright commandeering to the reappropriation of equipment and resources and to the active sabotage of homophobic image makers and censors inciting violence against us. Cultural work is not all arts and leisure.

To what degree and under what circumstances can an ethically accountable documentarist representing an oppositional minority be justified in telling less than the full truth? Self-censorship is perhaps the thorniest ethical issue raised by the twenty-four films under review. However, it must first be recognized that self-censorship is often if not always motivated by the realistic apprehension of potential external censorship. Many of the filmmakers under consideration here have faced and experienced that danger whether it took the form of bureaucratic obstacles to broadcast access (*It Is Not the Homosexual*), police harassment and threatened confiscation (*Track Two*), actual confiscation by official censors (*Loads* and *Framed Youth*), threatened funding cutoff (*L'Aspect rose de la chose*), mutilation by official censors (*Race d'ep*), and so forth. The ensuing discussion must be balanced by an awareness of this harsh reality. Each decision about "controversial" content must reflect a careful weighing of the ethical and political risks of each individual context. A reckless taunting of the censor, inviting suppression and vengeance upon the constituency at large, is as ethically problematical on the part of the filmmaker as an unjustified withholding of the full truth of a situation. At the same time, a minority's self-appointed image representatives have the ethical duty to run reasonable risks, and most of those discussed here have by and large fulfilled this duty courageously.

Very few minority or other political documentarists accountable to a specific constituency manage to avoid being taxed with sins of omission. Gay and lesbian documentarists in particular continually face criticism for leaving out this or soft pedaling that. This is not only because of the context of media inaccessibility, causing even single-issue films to assume the encyclopedic mission of documenting the entire condition of homosexuality. It stems also from our long collective and individual histories of invisibility and silence in the closet, of the hiding and self-censorship necessary to avoid daily violence and rejection. The reflex of self-censorship still comes automatically, every day, to all of us, and so innocent omissions take on the character of self-censorship no matter how well motivated. *Word Is Out*, for example, is charged by Ray Olson with having suppressed, despite its 135-minute length, the following list of subjects: work, politics, systematic oppression, legal persecution, street violence against gays, the lack of gay access to public media, benighted attitudes of church and psychiatric institutions, and most important, the gay liberation movement (Olson 1979, 9–12). While we may wonder whether some of these might not be legitimate omissions in a film showing twenty-six individuals' personal evolutions, the final item—the omission of the mention of the gay liberation movement—seemed a valid complaint when it was revealed that at least nine of the twenty-six subjects are political activists in that movement and that this aspect of their personal evolution had been downplayed by the editors. This omission was apparently not motivated by any expectation of censorship (though it is obviously no accident that the film that systematically understates collective activism achieved the broadest distribution of all the films under consideration, whereas *Track Two*, unforgettable for its strong images of angry unified crowds in Toronto's wintry streets, has run into obstacles at every turn).

The same issue is raised by the debate around the "positive image" question and by the confusion of audience goals that frequently permeates this debate. Reacting to generations of mainstream images depicting our loneliness and depravity, lesbian and gay documentaries quite naturally seek to provide self-valorizing yet self-critical, exemplary yet realistic models to their lesbian and gay audiences and antistereotype, positive images to the general public. These two options seldom coincide and attempts to combine them sometimes result in films that are stilted, schizophrenic, or bizarrely discontinuous. This double bind, I think, is behind the distinctly rosy tint of *Michael, A Gay Son*; *Greetings from Washington*; and the two Iris Films productions (*In the Best Interests of the Children* and *We All Have Our Reasons*) to mention only four (though none of these is any less cathartic for lesbian and gay audiences for all their glow). However valid and real the injunction against washing dirty linen in public may be, we have much to gain by washing it in private. Now, in what might be called a third generation of lesbian and gay documentary, past the stages of self-recognition and of self-valorization (of which *Word Is Out* marked perhaps the end), we are now engaged in a stage of gay power and politics and of collective memory: an essential component of that stage, in fact an ethical imperative, is the kind of self-analysis, self-criticism, self-evaluation necessary to any healthy community. Confusion over audience goals on the part of filmmakers, or the appeal to multiple or overlapping audiences, has tended to remove the element of self-criticism from our films.

Track Two is symptomatic of this problem. Originally intended for general, theatrical audiences (unrealistically, it may be argued), designed to build alliances with the straight liberal public and only secondarily aimed at gay spectators, the film glows with self-righteous sanctity: no acknowledgment of "street people" despite the title's reference to the police habit of grouping gays with prostitutes; no trace of "effeminacy" in its roster of witnesses, in contrast to very useful appearances by "queens" and "butch" lesbians in *Word Is Out*, *L'Aspect rose de la chose*, *Before Stonewall*, and *Taxi Zum Klo*; no analysis of the pedophile issue despite its prominence in Toronto's local hate literature and New Right mobilization, and the police exploitation of the issue as a pretext for their first attack; no analysis of the institution of the commercial ghetto, which was after all the target of the police raids that set off the chronology of the film and that is perhaps a key to a historical understanding of the gay male movement (as Rosa von Praunheim hints suggestively in his two films without further development of the idea). In short, a conceptual and strategic miscalculation snowballed into an ethical and political blunder when the film reached its real (gay) public, primarily on the alternative circuit.

Ray Olson complains of the tendency toward sexual self-censorship in a group of similar films he labels as "accommodationist":

> Their collective motto might be "We are normal, and we want our piece of the action." This is disingenuous. Gays are not "normal." They are homosexual, something these films are very chary of acknowledging, betraying deep-rooted insecurity vis-à-vis the straight norms . . . To avoid even frank discussion, let alone full and frank information, on homosexuality as much as these films do, is to risk being crucially beside the point . . .
>
> The only way to address the homophobe and homophobic society in a liberatory gay film is to unflinchingly present the reality and pervasive presence of homosexuality in our society. There must be frank and totally unapologetic discussion and illustration of how homosexuals make love and how they respond sexually to their environments. And this explicitly homosexual contact must be personally presented. (Olson 1979)

Along these lines, one may wonder the rationale for apparent gaps in the sexual thematics of the two most recent U.S. features: the omission from *The Times of Harvey Milk* of the hero's personal sexual identity and relationships with lovers; the omission from *Before Stonewall* of the most plentiful cinematic documentation of the gay male past, namely, erotic materials.

In contrast mainstream depictions of homosexuality seldom flinch from dealing with sexuality but from a sensationalist, voyeuristic, heterosexist point of view. In fact, Canadian Broadcasting Corporation cameras had followed a documentary character down the same sauna corridors as in *Track Two*, tailing him even into a cubicle for a sexual encounter, taking exactly the same route as the police would take a few weeks later with their clubs.[3] We do not need to worry about providing our enemies with evidence and negative stereotypes when they so easily manufacture their own. I would even argue that no independent lesbian and gay documentary in the present context will reach a broad or a susceptible enough

audience in the alternative circuits to do any serious social damage no matter how frank and self-critical the film is, and this includes films frankly
depicting sexuality. We do ourselves a grave disservice in suppressing our
sexuality, that factor of our identity that distinguishes us as a group. We
will never win over straight liberals and civil libertarians by masking the
issue of our sexual rights by a respectable discourse of civil rights. And in
speaking of our sexuality, we must be sure to search for alternative formats
to both the heterosexist sensationalism of the mainstream media and the
macho fantasies of current commercial gay male pornography.

Oppositional documentary is clearly an ideal medium for this search.
Of the twenty-four films under review, five films deal explicitly with sexuality: *Double Strength*, *Loads*, *Army of Lovers*, *Taxi zum Klo*, and *Race
d'Ep*. Interestingly, these are the films that have the least connection with
the lesbian or gay movements, and they all overlap more or less with the
experimental and art cinema constituencies. *Double Strength* is at the same
time a joyous, athletic celebration of sexuality that manages to completely
shun *Penthouse* pseudolesbian clichés and a seminarrative analysis of the
evolution of the author's relationship with another woman, including
vividly symbolic reflections on romance, passion, and separation that never
lose the grain and wrinkle of documentary despite the abstract and stylized
"artistic" vocabulary.[4] Of the male films, *Loads* and *Taxi zum Klo*, like
Double Strength, are personal, confessional, and autobiographical; for that
reason, they are vastly superior as sexual discourse to the sensationalistic
Army of Lovers or the voyeuristic *Race d'Ep*. Irony, humor, collage, sound-
image opposition, and collaborative performance (to which I will return)
are some of McDowell's techniques that may be useful models for our
future documentary explorations of sexuality, and to this Ripploh adds the
intimacy and lyricism of improvised reenactment and the bite of archival
compilation. Whether or not *Loads* and *Taxi* are, as has been argued, com-
promised, like *Army* and *Race*, by their ethical and ideological complicity
in the masculinist imaging of sexuality, both are at least partially successful
in representing and discussing male sexual behavior—the authors' own
and that of their partners—in a manner that raises critical questions about
gay sexuality and in fact about all male sexuality.

In conclusion, the representation and discussion of *sexuality* are ethical tactical minefields, but gay and lesbian documentarists must not claim
audience considerations as a pretext for avoiding them any longer.

From Consent to Collaboration

Traditional consent contracts signed by documentary subjects during filming have usually formalized more than consent. In fact they formalize the
subjects' surrender of their images: the agreement that filmmakers may
impose their own voices over the images of their subjects. In the lesbian
and gay movements, the ethical lessons we have learned about individual
freedom, the respect we have developed for the variety of human sexual
and cultural expression, have encouraged our filmmakers, perhaps more
than those of any other constituency, to seek alternatives to the traditional
consent ripoff. As we continue to emerge from our invisibility and silence,
lesbian and gay filmmakers are often reluctant to reimpose that invisibility
and silence on their subjects and seek means by which they may let their
subjects speak rather than speak for them, let their subjects control their
images rather than control them for them.

The present twenty-four films show many different techniques and
procedures whereby the traditional consent/surrender of the subject is
replaced by strategies that heighten collaboration between filmmaker
and subject and that maximize the subject's control over his or her
image. Needless to say, this is often in direct contradiction of the spirit of
orthodox American vérité à la Wiseman, in which observational, noninterventionist discourse imprisons the individual subject's soul in the black
box. Significantly, not a single one of the twenty-four films rely to any
major extent on observational vérité: whether or not budgetary factors are
the determining factor here, our souls have been imprisoned too often for
us to be easily led to oppress each other in the same way.

To begin with, lesbian and gay documentary is most often collective
filmmaking. Of the twenty-four titles, only four can be considered products of individual authorship—*Loads, Taxi zum Klo, Double Strength,*
and *Army of Lovers*—and all four of these films employ important collaborative techniques. It is by no means a coincidence that all four of these
filmmakers come from an "art film" milieu, a constituency whose mystique
of individual creativity has gained very few footholds in lesbian and gay
documentary. Other individually signed films are based on such close collaboration with producers (*Harvey Milk* and *Silent Pioneers*) or subjects
(*Orientations* and *Michael, A Gay Son*), that they are to all intents and
purposes joint films, films of shared creative responsibility rather than of
personal expression. Rob Epstein, a member of the Mariposa Film Group
and author of *Word Is Out*, describes how that film's collective authorship
ensured the film's political and ethical accountability to its constituency:

Individually we saw different needs for the expanded film (as did the
audiences). It became evident that a group, working as a unit with several
different points of view, would be more likely to produce a "broader look
at gay life" than several people working together under a more hierarchical
setup functioning to bring the director's "singular vision" to life. And the
thrust, so necessary in forming such an alliance, was forming as a result of
our work. (Epstein 1981, 9–10)

Of the many collectively authored films in this survey, a further important distinction may be noticed in passing. At least nine are joint lesbian-gay
projects. This proportion may seem remarkable in view of the autonomous
and relatively separate constituencies represented by the two gender groups,
each one with its own press and cultural institutions and only partly overlapping political agendas. This encouraging pattern obviously indicates
a crucial need for resource sharing and coalition in the present political
conjuncture. Beyond the fundamental character of collective authorship, the
films under review show many techniques facilitating collaboration between
author(s) and subject, of which the most important is more than familiar:
the interview. The interview has long been shunned by the purist inheri-
tors of the noninterventionist American school of vérité, macho fetishists
of untampered visual surfaces; it has been denounced by critics muttering
about "talking heads" as if they had never seen *The Sorrow and the Pity* or
Portrait of Jason. The interview, however, has been reinvented by lesbian and
gay filmmakers. Or rather, reinvented by the "consciousness-raising" feminist
films of the early seventies, it has been refined and shaped in new directions
by the present filmmakers. A flexible and sensitive format for subject–artist
interaction, the interview is at the most basic level a more faithful reflection of the actual circumstances of filmmaking than the pretense of pure
observation affected by the Wiseman school. The variety of approaches to
the interview visible in almost all of these films, each variation with aesthetic
and ethical overtones of its own, suggests that the filmmakers are aware of
the special ethical traps inherent in the interview technique: after all, the
networks rely on the interview as a basic means of manipulation and distor-
tion, primarily through careful selection of the subjects, through selective
editing of the responses by means of abridgement and contextualization, and
if necessary through aggressive interrogation.

By conventional standards, all the present films tend to be too long
(though lesbian and gay audiences I've been part of have never been bored)
because subjects are usually heard out. The interviewer encourages them to
develop arguments, explain in personal terms, even to prepare statements (as
we shall see). As for the editing, as often as not it endeavors to preserve the
full scope and rhythm of the interview. The editor in fact becomes a key to

the filmmaker's ethical accountability to subject, constituency, and audience: the longer the take, the more control the subject tends to have over his or her speech. One extension of this principle is the reluctance to edit out the role of the interviewer, a rejection of the ethically dubious tactic of stringing together a series of answers as a continuous spontaneous statement. In these films, the presence of the interviewer varies from a sporadic acknowledged visibility in much of *Word Is Out* and *Heroes*, to a much greater presence in parts of *Some American Feminists* (equal visual weight for speaker and questioner/listener at several points). Of course the strategy of keeping the interviewer in the frame, a refusal to hide the subjective presence that has catalyzed the subject's contribution, requires at the same time a refusal to grandstand, a personal humility. Interestingly enough, both Hammer and McDowell, whose avant-garde formation perhaps discouraged them from the shared control of the interview format, have experimented with interviewing in their more recent films, *Audience* and *Taboo*, respectively.

Another format, one step beyond the interview proper, present most notably in *Heroes* and *L'Aspect rose*, can allow even more input from the subject: the "statement." Here the subject prepares and delivers his or her own intervention in an on-camera direct-address statement to the camera. The director of the latter film, Chi Yan Wong, describes how this strategy was effected, replying to the question of how he worked with "actors":

> I would say "interveners" rather than actors. Their commitment goes beyond the notion of a role, they do not play a fictive part. Their participation goes further: they assert themselves [*s'assumer*, also sometimes used in French for "come out"—TW] in front of the camera, both body and words. The members of the GLH [Groupe de Libération Homosexuelle, of which the sponsoring "cell" is a part] at least those who agreed with the principle of the film, were enthusiastic. I had explained to them the different parts of the film as well as my aesthetic choices. A series of determined themes (ghettoes, "queen-dom," pedophilia, sisterhood, activism, aging, etc.) had been divided up according to each person's desire to work on some aspect of our experience. Each one wrote a text, worked on it at great length, sometimes individually, sometimes collectively. I gave them some guidelines such as "I want a text that is analytic but also sufficiently personal, with anecdotes, a text that could not be said by anyone but its author." Then each person chose their set, their place where they felt comfortable, their clothes, in order to be filmed. Everyone rehearsed. We lived together during four months before the shoot. This tenderness that exists among us is visible on the screen and that's good. (Wong 1981, 97–98, my translation)

This is the film that the apostles of vérité must really hate, all of their bugbears together at one: "talking heads" compounded by staging, rehearsing, and scripting. The effect is refreshing, fascinating, and in my opinion an ethical as well as an aesthetic breakthrough. Halprin uses a similar technique in *Heroes*: the three subjects prepared in advance their answers to three questions about their lives and then their formal direct-address statements were included in the film without editing. One final variation of the "statement" is of course the nonverbal statement, or direct-address "performance." In *Silent Pioneers* and *Before Stonewall*, it is a question of musical performances by subjects. *Loads* makes use of erotic performances. Here, the sexual interaction between camera operator and subject is foregrounded, and the subject looks into the lens with honesty, vulnerability, submission . . . pride? In short, *Loads* is one of the most startling and probing films on male sexuality I have seen, though it might have gone even further if McDowell had added to the nonverbal performances the verbal dimension of conventional interview or monologue techniques.

Other techniques go beyond the two-way structure of the above films to show multiple interactions and collaborations. In several films, a group discussion is set up with the same interventionist premeditation as the interview and then catalyzes within this artificial framework a spontaneous collective reflection on a given issue. This is the format that reflects most the genius of consciousness-raising as a format of politicization. The filmmaker may or may not be present: she is present in memorable scenes from *In the Best Interests*, where Liz Stevens talks with a group of lesbians' children, and from *Word Is Out*, where the women collective members chat around a table with elderly poet Elsa Gidlow, facilitating a stirring exchange of points of view among different generations of lesbians. In *Pink Triangles*, *Framed Youth*, *Before Stonewall*, and *We All Have Our Reasons*, several group discussions among subjects, both expert and lay, succeed admirably in getting intellectual and emotional juices flowing, with only a rare overtone of dogmatism.

Still another variation is closer to traditional vérité and may be called "collaborative vérité." A semicontrolled event, usually within a defined space and one that might have taken place without the filmmakers' intervention, proceeds with all participants aware of and consenting to the camera's presence and with an unspoken but visible collaboration shaping the event. In *Before Stonewall*, for example, the filmmakers arranged a reunion of former habitués of a historic San Francisco bar, and in *Breaking the Silence* lesbian mothers assemble within the ominous architecture of the courthouse that symbolically menaces their families. Here, as in others of the present films, both group interactions and individual self-perceptions remain lively and things actually get said; this mise-en-présence occasioned by the camera provides just enough artifice to break up the naturalistic surface of the event and reveal its true political insight. This artifice, like

Brechtian stylization in fiction, falsifies neither the event nor the subjects but heightens the filmmaker's accountability to them.

Thus far in discussing collaborative techniques, I have emphasized the stage of cinematography, but collaboration is a feature of lesbian and gay filmmakers' methods at other stages as well. The Mariposa Film Collective's extensive consultation with national lesbian and gay communities over a period of years prior to the final shooting of *Word Is Out* is a well-known model for politically and ethically accountable procedures during the preproduction stage. Rob Epstein provides a glimpse of how midshooting consultation shaped the direction the film was taking:

> Peter cut a three-hour assembly which he screened to predominantly gay audiences for feedback and financing, not necessarily in that order. We realized then that people were somehow seeing the film as a definitive statement on gay life, so we felt it needed to be broadened beyond the scope of the eight people we had already filmed. (Epstein 1981)

Epstein's candid reference to the role of fundraising in this process is not irrelevant. For his most recent film, *The Times of Harvey Milk*, the financing was based on the same consultative process around a sixteen-minute sampler reel that made the rounds for years. Of course, the danger exists in such a process that filmmakers' accountability will be directed toward investors rather than toward their constituency, but this is a danger that grassroots financing tends to minimize. It is no accident that the two films for which the financing seems to have been least difficult, the West German television films, *It Is Not the Homosexual* and *Army of Lovers*, would seem to be those that, in view of their sometimes eccentric subjectivism, might have profited most from prior consultation with their constituency.

Another cautionary note in regard to community consultation has been founded by the dispute that arose between the *Before Stonewall* authors and gay and lesbian historians whose research preceded and inspired the production of the film. Collaboration, consultation, and resource sharing by media workers must be extended throughout the still fragile cultural networks of gay and lesbian constituencies and must be based on the utmost consideration of those individual and collective moral and political rights not enshrined in the legal apparatus invoked and enjoyed by mainstream media.[5]

Postshooting consultation is another matter. Ever since Flaherty's legendary screening for *Nanook*, this process has been a common ideal and a less common practice of documentarists. The normal procedure of testing a rough cut on a fresh mind has often been expanded in the films under review to incorporate a larger dynamic of community accountability. By this means, subjects and constituencies may heighten their control over their image—not only the way it is photographed but also the way it is contextualized. Community dialogue during or after the shoot is now less the exception than the rule in lesbian and gay documentary in North America.

The final stage of exhibition also becomes for most of the filmmakers under discussion a context for consultation. Postscreening discussion is a regular feature of exhibition for most of the filmmakers in this sample, an interest they have inherited from other alternative and especially feminist filmmakers, even where, as with Sara Halprin, this means a deliberate abandonment of the ideal of a large audience.[6] Von Praunheim is another interesting case in point, despite his roots in an art-cinema background where community consultation is virtually unknown: the American version of *It Is Not the Homosexual* incorporated footage of angry American gay audiences reacting to the film. Whether or not this kind of postscreening consultation that in fact becomes part of the text is as useful and accountable as ongoing consultation before and during the creative process is another question.

Coming Out

The single ethical problematic that is most characteristic of and is in fact unique to the lesbian and gay movements and our cultural work is summed up in the two words that are both our collective battle cry and the key challenge of our individual lives: "Come Out!" Our variation of the "The Personal is Political," the concept of "coming out" connotes not only a personal self-affirmation—to self, family, friends, coworkers, media—but also an affirmation of collective political empowerment.

The earliest gay documentaries often achieved their most striking impact by simply concentrating on one or more subjects "coming out" to the camera. *Word Is Out* was a kind of milestone in that respect, a "talking heads" epic of twenty-six individual comings-out that still had devastating impact even ten years after Stonewall but that symbolized in a way the end of that period of gay pride. All the same, this basic political ritual continues today as a basic aesthetic device and ethical problem of our culture. The consent to declare oneself before the camera still has for every potential subject of a lesbian and gay documentary all the dimensions of an irreversible life-changing political commitment, whatever may be the other normal implications of the decision. It is for this reason that the autobiographical subgenre well represented in my selection has such a centrality in our culture, far beyond the boundaries of the cinema.

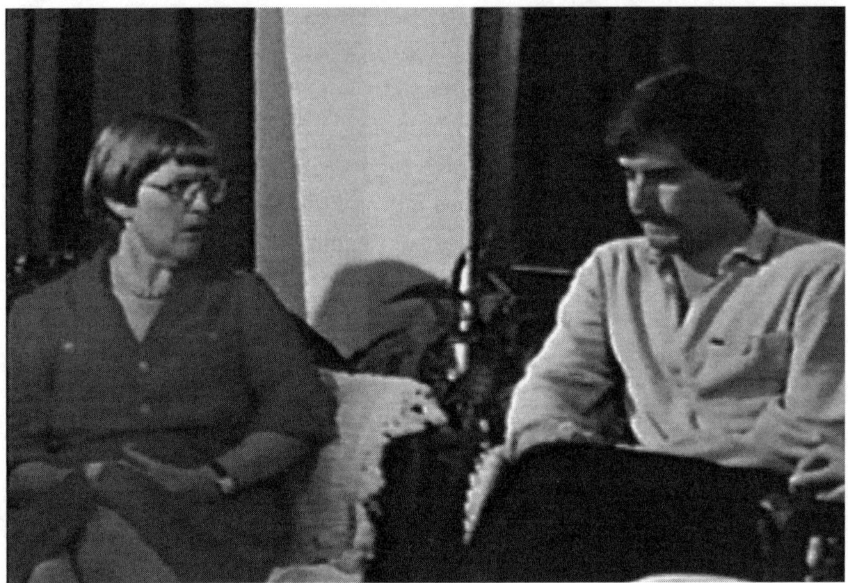

Michael, A Gay Son (Bruce Glawson, 1980). Coming out as a fraught political ritual and distinctive ethical problematic: Michael (right) role-plays with his fictive family of queer peers, his "mother" on the left.

Michael, A Gay Son is not an autobiographical work but presents at very close range an exemplary case study of one individual's realization of the act of coming out. It is an act so fraught with psychological, social, and ethical delicacy as well as technical problems and excruciating dramatic tension that the filmmakers render it only at a distant remove, through the mechanism of improvisational semifictional role-playing by members of Michael's support community. This mechanism nonetheless does not fail to document in very authentic terms the place of coming out in our collective and individual aspirations—a very real Michael interacts through the mediation of a very real social worker with his fictive family. More recent works have sustained and enriched the iconic power of the coming out ritual within our culture by dealing with coming out in ways that challenge the media's seventies gay-lib stereotype of the rootless young white middle-class male, for example, coming out within nonwhite cultures in *Orientations*, *Framed Youth*, and *Pink Triangles* or coming out as middle-aged lesbian mothers in *Heroes*, *Breaking the Silence*, *Choosing Children*, and *Best Interests*.

A whole set of consent procedures has evolved for ensuring that each individual has the right to come out on his or her own terms at the chosen moment, to the chosen degree. The authors of *Track Two*, for example, decided not to film some indoor political rallies that were part of the mobilization campaign covered by the film, at the request of the organizers, in deference to the rights of participants not ready to come out in the media. Our filmmakers can never forget that the single act of filming a gay person can expose them to eviction, firing, family rejection, violence, loss of child custody, and even criminal charges. The authors of *Pink Triangles* allude to the delicacy of this matter in their credits acknowledgment of "the many people we cannot name publicly because of family pressure, child custody battles, immigration laws and job discrimination." In *We All Have Our Reasons*, interviews with "drinkers" in a lesbian bar setting are reenacted rather than caught in spontaneous vérité for at least partly the same reason; one wonders whether the frequent recourse to dramatized formats by European documentarists in this sampling has something of the same rationale.

A scene from *Before Stonewall* capsulizes the entire problematic of coming out. To film a subject remembering her victimization by McCarthy-era armed forces purges, the filmmakers agreed to preserve her anonymity by use of a silhouette setup. Unprecedented in gay and lesbian liberation cinema, the silhouette device originated generations ago in mainstream depictions of homosexuals—it evokes all the shame and fear that society has wanted us to feel and that we have had to struggle against. One hopes that there were good reasons for seemingly thoughtless repudiation of every principle of our movement. Surely if an anonymous witness was indispensable, this exigency could have been foregrounded in such a way as to contribute to the political discourse of the film rather than undermining it: *Breaking the Silence* includes the audio-only voice of one participant, protecting her identity for fear of custody battles, but somehow presenting the anonymity in a way that breaks through the closet rather than shores it up.

As for lesbian and gay documentarists themselves, in the face of society's heterosexist assumptions about everyone being "straight" (especially people strong enough to hold a camera), the ethical obligation to come out is clear. The self-declaration of the filmmaker has a crucial pragmatic relation not only to the lesbian or gay spectator's extension of trust and belief but also to the film's political and ethical integrity. Filmmakers who are unwilling to "make an issue of it," who "don't believe in labels," cannot be delegated the responsibility of representing us, of making our self-images. This is particularly important in the light of the oppressive and fraudulent representations handed down to us by Hollywood and the networks by straight and some gay liberals who solicit our identification only to pull the rug out from under us. Nongays usually understand this principle instinctively in reverse, witness the never-fail formula of actors and directors who, being interviewed about their gay or lesbian roles or films, trot out their heterosexual spouses, children, and grandchildren in response to every question and claim the film is about universal human relations. The authors of *Pink Triangles* make it very clear in their promotional material that they are a "group of nine women and men, both gay and straight."

The declaration of an even greater personal stake is evident in *Heroes*, where it is revealed in a pleasurably incidental manner that the lesbian character is the filmmaker's lover. The effect in this modest film about a range of feminist issues beyond sexual orientation in itself is significant. It is essential for our political empowerment that lesbians and gays establish our right to speak out on all issues, as in *We All Have Our Reasons*, which speaks out with great clarity on alcoholism as a general women's issue but from a lesbian viewpoint. *Some American Feminists*, although lesbian authored in part, unfortunately doesn't go that far: though there is perhaps an implicitly lesbian point of view in the film's central focus on lesbianism within a survey of American feminism, the ultimate avoidance of the explicit lesbian voice is an unfortunate reminder of the need for discretion within a homophobic state apparatus like the National Film Board of Canada.

Feminist umbrella films, lesbian authored or not, have a crucial responsibility to contradict the invisibility of lesbians within the women's community. This is especially true in an atmosphere where right-wing pressure groups are coopting feminist mobilization around such issues as pornography, "family rights," and abortion: a documentary about such an issue that does not at the same time make explicit connections to less cooptable issues such as lesbian rights or sex education is a backward step, a serious political and ethical compromise as well as a tactical error. (By the same token, at a time when the dominant order survives by dividing oppositional constituencies, a lesbian or gay "single-issue" film that does not include coalitionist discourse and that does not link sexual orientation to other issues of race, class, and gender inequity is no less retrograde. *Track Two*, *Framed Youth*, *Orientations*, and *Harvey* are all exemplary in this regard in their linking of discourses on labor unions and racial minorities to the gay and lesbian struggle.)

The ethical imperative of coming out on the part of the filmmaker, or more generally the filmmaker's revelation of his or her interest in the film, may be extended further to include the revelation of sexual and financial interest. This takes the rather particular form of a confessional self-critical gloss with three of the male filmmakers in this survey who deal most directly with sexuality itself: McDowell, Ripploh, and von Praunheim (*Army of Lovers*). For one thing, all take the act of coming out to

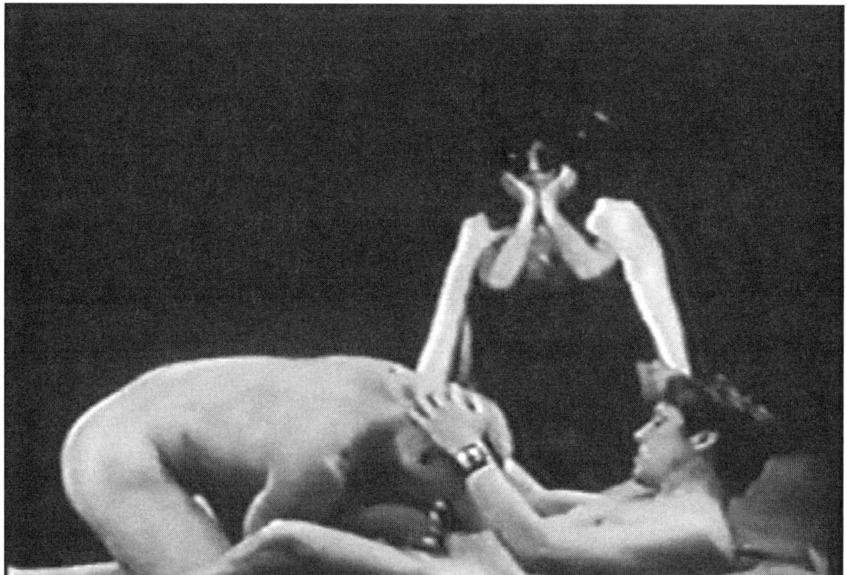

Army of Lovers (Revolt of the Perverts) (Rosa von Praunheim, 1978). The filmmaker (right) taking coming out to an ultimate degree, offering first-person sexual performance in defiance of privatized, patriarchal, reproductive sexuality.

an ultimate degree, all engaging in on-camera sexual acts: Not only am I gay, but here I am sucking cock (with McDowell and von Praunheim both incidentally incriminating themselves in relation to American state sodomy statutes). While courageously offering images of personal performance as a challenge to patriarchal notions of privatized, reproductive sexuality, all three directors also acknowledge and analyze in a very revealing way their complicity in self-oppressive and oppressive behaviors and attitudes. As for financial and other equally figurative levels of coming out, a full financial accounting and declaration of political affiliation, and so forth, is in my opinion a bottom-line requirement of all political filmmakers, not only of lesbians and gays. One of the most endearing aspects of *Greetings from Washington* is that the credits with its list of contributors, participants, and institutional sponsors is almost longer than the film itself! It is to be hoped, for example, that the new cycle of gay health films already undertaken in response to the AIDS crisis will be as frank in their disclosure of pharmaceutical company investments, for example.

I recognize that the ethical dimensions of the issue of coming out are not always clear-cut because of certain strategic options around a given film. The authors of *In the Best Interests* for example obviously sensed that a too fervent declaration of interest on the part of the three lesbian filmmakers would compromise their effectiveness with their primary audience,

mostly straight social workers and legal officials who make the life-
effecting decisions in child custody cases. For the secondary lesbian and
gay audience however (numerically the larger audience as it turns out—the
film went on to become the most respected and popular lesbian documentary in the United States), the price must be paid. Though the stake of the
filmmakers could never be doubted by an alert lesbian and gay audience
thanks to a nebulous but unerring sixth sense, few spectators would not
notice at the same time that the issue is carefully avoided.

A related problem is familiar in most political documentaries, but it
is feminists who have focused on it most sharply: the invocation of expert
authorities as witnesses to pronounce upon the subject at hand. Whereas
the appearance of an openly gay or lesbian expert can have a refreshing
counterstereotype effect as in *Pink Triangles* or *Silent Pioneers*, the effect
is as often a mystification of science and professional knowledge and the
dismissal of ordinary people's knowledge of or their right to control their
own lives. With films about lesbians and gays, the expert witness usually
belongs to the professional institutions that have had the most direct hand
in our oppression: medicine, psychiatry, law, academia, legal enforcement,
the social sciences, the church.[7]

Track Two reveals its own unique entanglement with this problem.
The filmmakers present ten or so straight expert witnesses, all community or political leaders or media stars (like author Margaret Atwood, or
ex-mayor John Sewell, who incredibly gets the last word in the film), who
are clearly intended to be seen as vital allies of the gay struggle against the
police (as indeed they were, bringing a huge morale boost to the belea-
guered lesbian and gay communities and adding to their credibility in
the public eye). All the same, there is an uncertain boundary between the
invocation of alliances and coalitions, and the deference to heterosexual
authority to legitimize our struggle. *Track Two* hovers dangerously close.
Somehow, the heterosexual witnesses (one in fact is a famous closeted jour-
nalist whose presence in the film is ethically scandalous and intolerable:
the ethical imperative of coming out becomes proportionally clearer as one
ascends the hierarchy of power, wealth, security, and celebrity) are coded
both within the profilmic event (speaking at a rally on a platform with a
microphone, gratefully applauded by the gay masses down below) and in
the editing, so as to appear to justify our struggle by their support rather
than to consolidate it. One final qualification of the foregoing discussion
of coming out is that this personal and political ritual has admittedly a
slightly different significance for lesbians than for gay men (just as it is
different for me, an associate professor with tenure in a liberal faculty
of fine arts, than it is for friends who are unemployed, underemployed,

or insecurely employed). It also arouses different questions for lesbian filmmakers who want to stress the importance of the lesbian perspective within a spectrum of feminist causes. All the same, closet lesbians and gays must confront this question with full realism and ethical accountability in this era of rising threats and heterosexual backlash.

Conclusion

A number of tentative conclusions may be drawn from this discussion of four basic ethical foci for lesbian and gay documentarists. Two fundamental overlapping axioms of image ethics, demonstrated I hope by my references to these twenty-four sample documentaries, are that, while there are inherent connections between specific aesthetic or technical forms and specific ethical liabilities, the ultimate determination of these connections is relative to the individual historical conjuncture of each film. Lesbian and gay filmmakers must continue to pursue a double tack. They must continue their exploration of alternatives to forms that have evolved within heterosexist (patriarchal capitalist) culture—a random listing of such forms would include those that mystify "expert" knowledge or the authorial voice; that use lives and bodies as intellectual abstractions or sexual objects; that foster a cult of "personal" expression; that profess such ideals as "objectivity" and "balance"; and that effect such results as disenfranchisement, sensationalism, and voyeurism. At the same time they must base these explorations on close analysis of the global and historical context of their work, weighing in each circumstance their ethical accountability to subject and audience together with their accountability to constituency and self.

The concept of a collective ethical accountability implied by the notion of constituency provides no easy challenge to our documentary filmmakers. Many different notions of what our constituency is or should be are of course in constant collision within our communities; gay chambers of commerce could naturally never agree with gay radical organizations as to what that constituency is, and lesbian separatists and artists working within traditional frameworks would likely provide two more completely opposing conceptions. Gay and lesbian documentarists must reflect and be accountable to this pluralism, even when they ally themselves with a single one of the tendencies or factions within our communities.

The problematic of the collective and the constituency contradicts, as I stated at the outset, the traditional individual focus of (image) ethics. This is why the term "ethics" in this chapter has frequently tended to overlap with, or to be interchangeable with, the term "politics." This overlapping is intentional. The twenty-four documentaries discussed in this chapter demonstrate, as do the issues they raise, that there is no ethics for lesbian and gay cultural activism, of our oppositional self-representation, separate from its politics. For us, as for all oppositional cultural workers, the ethical, like the personal, is ultimately the political.

 Walking on Tippy Toes

*Lesbian and Gay Liberation Documentary
of the Post-Stonewall Period (1997)*

*In contrast with the preceding article on queer documentary
written more than a decade earlier, "Walking on Tippy Toes"
was like, well, walking on tippy toes—a pure, joyful labor of
love, and the wisecracks and sexual double entendres gushed. A
complementary take on some of the same corpus as discussed in
the previous article, it is in many ways more insightful about the
creative process.*

*There was some tension in the production process however.
Based on a paper I gave at the Visible Evidence III Conference
held at Harvard in 1995, the article was solicited by my Tennes-
see friend Chris Holmlund and her collaborator Cindy Fuchs for
their anthology on queer documentary,* Between the Sheets, in the
Streets. *Chris and Cindy were eager to include the cutting-edge
debate animated by the queer diversity agenda that had emerged
from young scholars within the post-queer-theory surge of the
nineties, and they were not, I felt, giving me the space that my
little-studied historical topic of the post-Stonewall doc deserved.
Furthermore I developed an allergy to my no doubt exaggerated
feelings of being treated for the first time by queer colleagues as
an antediluvian white tenured male patriarch—which was probably a healthy growing experience. My generational vantagepoint
is used effectively I think. But I had trouble not being permitted
to use the first person plural pronoun "we"—as my irritable end-
note attests. Also I believe I was also the only guy in the volume
writing about women's work, but stress around this issue was
unspoken. These joys of coalition are all water under the bridge*

*now, and Chris's and Cindy's diligent editorial therapy resulted
as usual in a much stronger piece than otherwise might have been
the case.*

MOTHER. *It started actually in high school. You were in the plays in high
school and did a beautiful job. And that's why I think that speech and
drama was a very good start for you . . .*

FATHER. *Well, all I can say is I think that you get mixed up in the drama,
the music and the arts of that type, I think it's a . . . Most people who
are in arts and drama are walking on tippy toes, a little fluttery, you
understand what I mean. When I was a kid, the guys that played the
violin, with the long hair, that kind of stuff, they were a little more
effeminate than most people, so when you get mixed up with the arty
people, that's it. You just join the gang, I guess.*

        ::   From *Blackstar: Autobiography of a Close Friend* (Tom Joslin,
1977)

▶

Years of Famine

"The famine is over." Uttering these portentous words in 1980 from my
podium as a gay movement film critic, I declared the start of a new era
of visibility and productivity in lesbian and gay film (Waugh 1980, 32).
I recently sifted through my once-urgent dissections of the state of gay
cinema (ca. 1976–1985), denunciations of various capitalist-homophobe
conspiracies and celebrations of each new "breakthrough," and was
reminded of how desperate it felt in those days before queer film and
video festivals and twenty-year-old video queers in every city. "Famine," "drought," "silence," and "invisibility" were indeed the words that
self-styled cine-pinko-fags like myself used to describe the audiovisual
environment in the first decade after Stonewall.

Perhaps my own frustration was exacerbated because the post-
Stonewall famine had coincided, paradoxically, with an age of feasting
for the 16mm social-issue documentary film. From *Harlan County,
U.S.A.* (Kopple, 1976) to *The Battle of Chile* (Guzman, 1977), what
a thrilling trajectory it was for artists and audiences who wanted to
change the world with images of reality! So why, as I started assembling an anthology on "committed documentary" in 1980, could I not
include a single gay male documentary in my "radical" corpus and only

a single, discreet lesbian-authored short that addressed sexual orientation as part of a spectrum of feminist issues (Waugh 1984)?[1] For my next two attempts to assemble a more inclusive body of lesbian and gay documentary, a 1982 lesbian and gay film and video festival and a 1983 curriculum package, the pickings were still very slim. By then I could draw on a growing but eclectic crop of 16mm documentary shorts, some uneven work in Super 8 and community video and ambiguous films by feminists who were not yet willing or ready to claim publicly the L-word label. Why had there been no queer *Harlan County*?

My international working filmography for this article, approximately twenty-five pre-1984 documentaries, may now seem too ample to justify the word "famine." Famine is of course relative (African American documentarists were then even scarcer than lesbians and gays), but the lesbian and gay corpus of the seventies is indeed tiny, dispersed, and erratic compared say to the sustained wealth of women's movement image making at the same time. A 1978 review of *Gay U.S.A.* and *Word Is Out* by Lee Atwell blamed lingering closets and difficulties in financing for the six-year gap between the promising *Some of Your Best Friends* (Robinson, 1971) and *Word Is Out* (Mariposa, 1977), but other obvious factors were in play. In the United States, it took some time for Carter-era liberalism to penetrate the blackout in public broadcasting and in the funding bodies. Lesbians and gays remained invisible within the still largely homophobic Left and New Social Movements networks, and it was only in the eighties that the alternative distribution outfits would take on gay and lesbian titles. Future troupers of eighties lesbian and gay documentary were tactfully present within Leftist and feminist organizations: Richard Schmiechen and Margaret Wescott, for example, were quietly at work at Chicago's Kartemquin Collective and Montreal's Studio D, respectively. It was only on the tenth anniversary of Stonewall at the 1979 Bard College Alternative Cinema Conference that North American lesbian and gay media activists actually came together for the first time and surprised straight Leftists with their unified demands (Waugh 1979, 39). The rightwing backlash of the late seventies fanned the new militancy all the more: Atwell thought that the 1977 Dade County catastrophe (Anita Bryant) got socially conscious filmmakers like artsy porn-maker Artie Bressan on the bandwagon, and California's 1978 Briggs Initiative was the catalyst for what would eventually be *The Times of Harvey Milk* (Epstein and Schmiechen, 1985). Suddenly at the turn of the decade, there did seem to be a few more documentary projects in sight, especially in the United States and Canada, films that would not be able to get away with being underfunded, mediocre, local, or single issue because they were no longer solitary voices in the wilderness. In 1984 when I wrote an overview article on post-Stonewall documentary (published in 1988; see chapter 7), my sampling had swelled to twenty-four documentaries from six countries. Most were titles from the first half of the eighties, and seven were dated 1977, 1978, or 1979. The only earlier film was the 1970 German anomaly *It Is Not the Homosexual Who Is Perverse but the Situation in which He Lives* (Rosa von Praunheim, 1971). In addition to discussing particular problems around community accountability and (self-) censorship, I argued that distinctive aesthetic strategies had evolved in response to the identity politics and volatile audience dynamics of a minority steeped in what Jack Babuscio called "the passing experience" (Babuscio 1977, 40–57). Most importantly, I noticed performance-based techniques for incorporating the input of subjects and for filling in gaps left by conventional documentary methods. Parents of gay filmmakers of the seventies thought that performance had something to do with homosexuality, as we have seen, and indeed their sons and daughters seemed to bear this out. Their performance-based techniques included inflections of standard interviewing, editing, and expert testimony styles; "coming out" variations of consciousness-raising formats borrowed from women's movement documentaries; and expressive elements that were more theatrical than the standard documentary idiom of the day allowed, such as dramatization; improvisatory role-playing and reconstruction; statements and monologues based on preparation and rehearsal; and nonverbal performances of music, dance, gesture, and corporal movement, including those of an erotic and diaristic nature.

What I didn't realize in 1984 was that I was summing up the first generation of lesbian and gay documentary. Nor did I realize that by squeezing in the first works of 1984 and 1985 by lesbians and gays of color,[2] the first few references to AIDS, and *The Times of Harvey Milk* (whose 1985 Oscar symbolized once and for all the real end of famine), I was heralding the next period of what Richard Dyer calls "postaffirmation" cinema, marked not only by the AIDS epidemic and postcolonial voices but also by a discursive flux around issues of identity (Dyer 1990, 274ff.). Looking back now in 1995, I am struck by the diversity of this corpus that once seemed so sparse, and by the sense that performance-based aesthetics was both its distinctive contribution and its link with the queer nonfiction film and video of the late eighties and nineties. I would therefore like to devote the rest of this space to extending my reflection on performance as the crucial idiom of the years of famine.

Performance and Performativity

First I need to define more precisely what performance means as a documentary ingredient. The commonsense layperson's notion of documentary is as a window on an unscripted, undirected, unrehearsed, and unperformed reality. Nevertheless, as I have argued elsewhere, performance and mise-en-scène have been a basic syntax of realist discourse throughout the entire hundred-year documentary tradition: "Performance—the self-expression of documentary subjects for the camera in collaboration with filmmaker/director—was the basic ingredient of the classical documentary" (see chapter 4). And not only of the classical documentary: throughout the modern phases of documentary as well—if we use Nichols's neat but useful categories, the *observational* impetus of the sixties (Leacock, Wiseman), the *interactive* impetus of the seventies (de Antonio, New Day Films), and the *self-reflexive* impetus of the eighties (Trinh, Marker)—collaborative performance has maintained its centrality in the lexicon of documentary realism (Nichols 1991, 32–75). This has been consistently true of that vast majority of documentary productions where subjects have been aware, actively or passively, of the camera and by extension of the spectator.[3]

"Perform" words are very popular in both gender/queer theory and documentary theory these days, and a few overlaps must be sorted out before I proceed. Slippages between the two principal relevant dictionary senses of the word "performance"—"the execution of an action" and "a public presentation or exhibition"—can be as confusing as they are stimulating. The term "performative," deriving from the first sense and borrowed from speech act linguistics, defines a category of utterance that executes, enacts or performs the action that is uttered, for example, *I apologize, I sentence, I welcome,* or the *I do* of the marriage ceremony. Hence Judith Butler theorizes that "gender reality is created through sustained social performances," that maleness or femaleness are "performative in the sense that the essence or identity that they otherwise purport to express are fabrications manufactured and sustained through corporeal signs and other discursive means" (Butler 1990, 136, 141).

Similarly, Bill Nichols posits performative documentary as a dominant of nineties documentary, reflected in such works as Sari Red (Parmar, 1988) and *Tongues Untied* (Riggs, 1989) that are not only referential (or *constative* to continue the speech act terminology) but primarily performative. Like an utterance that not only describes but also executes a transformation in the relationship of speaker and listener,

> [performative documentaries] address us . . . with a sense of emphatic
> engagement that overshadows their reference to the historical world . . .
> mak[ing] their target an ethics of viewer response more than a politics of
> group action or an analysis of the ideology of the subject . . . Performative
> documentary attempts to reorient us—affectively, subjectively—toward the
> historical, poetic world it brings into being. (Nichols 1994, 92–106)

However, as Eve Kosofsky Sedgwick explains with regard to Butler's gender theory, the term "performative" seldom loses the connotation of performance as exhibition and presentation—in short, theater—primarily because Butler maintains the "apparently unique centrality of drag performance practice as—not just the shaping metaphor—but the very idiom of a tautologically heterosexist gender/sexuality system, and the idiom also of the possibility for its subversion"[4] (Sedgwick 1993, 1).

Nichols as well maintains the connection of performativity to *theater* in the sense that most of his prototype performative films are those documentaries relying on dramatization and self-conscious theatricality (including several by Pratibha Parmar, Isaac Julien, and Marlon Riggs that have become canonical paving stones of the new international queer documentary). Nichols also names as an ancestor "the avant-garde tradition of autobiography that coincides in many aspects with the confessional quality of a number of performative documentaries" and mentions as an example Kenneth Anger (one could add two other performer precursors of queer documentary, Jack Smith and Andy Warhol).

For me as well the etymological and homonymic overlap of *performative* and *performance* is significant. Thus, although I would like what follows to focus primarily on performance in the sense of collaborative self-expressivity of a theatrical order—which to avoid confusion I will henceforth call "performance," between theatrical quotation marks—I fear that I too shall ultimately end up discovering "performativity" as well.

Realism and "Performance": From Public to Private

> *"Ain't nothing like the real thing, baby."*
> :: Song overlaid on climactic montage of anal penetration shots in
> *Erotikus* (de Simone, 1972)

> *This film is about who lesbian mothers and their children
> really are.*
> :: Prefatory credit, *In the Best Interests of the Children* (Reid,
> Stevens, Zheutlin, 1977, my emphasis)

> *In the field of documentary or cinéma vérité . . . the index of
> reality is somewhat more reliable, and . . . we at least have
> the advantage of experiencing not actors impersonating gay
> types, but the real thing.*
> :: Lee Atwell (1978–79, 50–57)

Songwriters, filmmakers, and critics notwithstanding, what I would now
like to show is how, during the post-Stonewall famine years, many lesbian
and gay documentarists did *not* rely on the real thing. To a remarkable
extent they eschewed the standard documentary realism of the day, the
available repertory of documentary idiom that Nichols calls "interactive."
Like cinematic realisms of any period, interactive realism, a formulaic mix
of interviews and archival footage joined by a mortar of observational
vérité and musical interludes, was basically invisible to the audience of the
seventies. Bent documentarists bent this realism out of shape, evolving a
wide spectrum of distinctive "performance" strategies, idioms of subject
self-expression—verbal, dramatic, cinematic, and sexual—that were both
an answer to, and an explanation of, the invisibility that we felt.[5] Seventies documentary realism may have seemed adequate to visualize other
fixable identities it would construct and cement, mix and match, in the
seventies—"worker," "visible minority," "third world subaltern," and above
all "(straight) woman"—but it wasn't up to the job for a new political constituency characterized by both invisibility of social existence and fluidity
and hybridity of identities.

Instead, lesbian and gay documentarists seemed intuitively to prefer
artificial and hyperbolic "performance" discourses that pushed through
and beyond the observational and interactive realist codes, performance
discourses that put "the referential aspect of the message in brackets,
under suspension," as Nichols would put it (Nichols 1991, 96). The extent
to which they did so and the particular "performance" formats they
chose depended on whether their films treated public spaces of political

mobilization; semipublic territories of traditional social networks and
sexual undergrounds; or private spaces of domesticity, relationships, sexuality, and fantasy. Many films would treat two or more of these domains in
the same film, hence the tutti-frutti compendium of performance styles that
characterizes so many of them.

Public Space

The everyday performance discourses of lesbian and gay public life as it
emerged after Stonewall (marches, parades, demonstrations, press conferences, zaps,[6] electoral campaigns, concerts, raids, trials) were handily
recorded intradiegetically through realist codes. Hence the parade/march
genre of which two pioneering 1971–72 films offer prototype glimpses,
Kenneth Robinson's *Some of Your Best Friends* and Jan Oxenberg's
Home Movie. Bressan's jubilant, sunlit *Gay U.S.A.* (1977) is the most fully
developed example, and the angry nighttime demonstrations of Toronto
(*Track Two*); Sydney (*Witches, Faggots, Dykes and Poofters*); and San
Francisco (*The Times of Harvey Milk*) amount to a contrapuntal negative
image. Most of the films of this genre couldn't get over the novelty of visible queer public life, which after all had been unthinkable as recently as
the sixties.

Before Stonewall (Schiller and Rosenberg, 1984), our attempt through
the interactive compilation-interview format to retrieve an earlier social
history (in the United States), came up with only one or two cinematic
images documenting public life—most memorably a dignified procession
of New York drag queens into a paddy wagon and the lonely shots of the
1965 Mattachine demonstration in front of the White House. Around
the same time as *Before Stonewall*, *The Times of Harvey Milk* is such a
breakthrough in the homo history genre because of the wealth of audiovisual documentation of newly visible gay public life in the late seventies
and early eighties, especially with respect to mainstream electoral politics.
These shifts from public invisibility to visibility also account for the staggering difference between von Praunheim's two films of this period: *It Is
Not the Homosexual* was shot entirely in "performance" modes in 1970
(scripting, sets, dramatization, even makeup!), while his American *Army
of Lovers, Revolt of the Perverts* (1978), was able in the last half of the
decade to mix a "performance" shell (agitprop street theater) with strong
realist inscriptions of the gay public life that had surged into U.S. streets
(observational vérité, stock shots, interviews, etc.).

For *radical* politics in the same period, interactive realism was less reliable. Political *theater* was sometimes captured intradiegetically through observational vérité (zoomy and swishy), as in an early zap of a convention of aversion therapists immortalized in *Some of Your Best Friends*. Otherwise, von Praunheim's *Army* is probably typical in that movement radicals are self-consciously static and anemic, leaving the real vigor of radical gay liberation for agitprop skits by the Gay Sweatshop troupe, who camp it up in front of the Meat Rack and undercut the mainstream political agenda of "seven hundred leather bars and the right to serve in the army." In *Blackstar*, Joslin likewise turned to "performance" not only for vigor and camp but also for the utopian rhetoric of alternative politics, letting his lover Mark Massi declaim a gay lib manifesto, literally from the rooftops, alone in a wintry landscape, a long-take long shot at once parodic and straight. In one of Barbara Hammer's few films that deal with public space, *Superdyke*, the artist orchestrates a "performance" of excess, parody, and artifice: Amazon warriors assault urban space and repossess its institutional and commercial fortresses (e.g., Macy's), on a rampage of street-theater repossession. In short, realism was adequate for mustering ourselves as an electoral minority, but for *real* change (as we used to say) "performance" strategies were preferred.

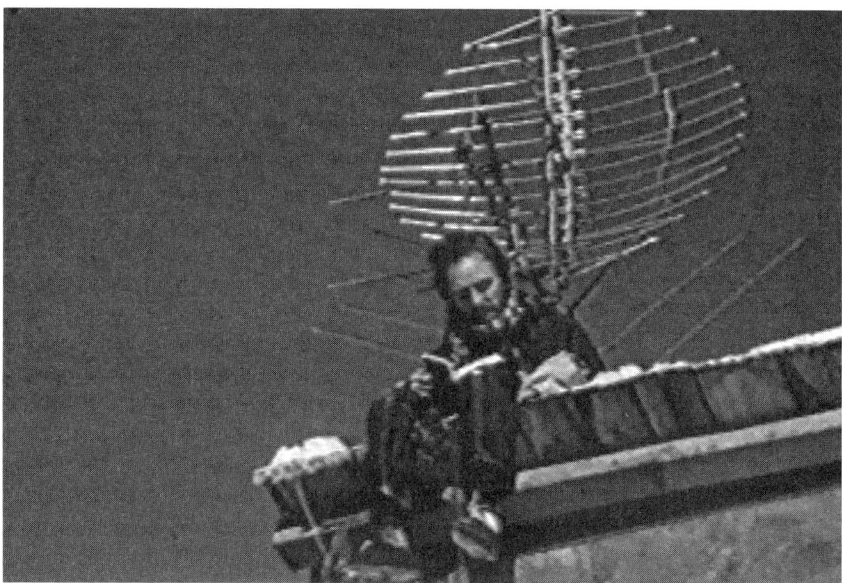

Blackstar: Autobiography of a Close Friend (Tom Joslin, 1977). For "radical" identity politics, realism was not enough: Joslin's lover Mark performs a gay liberation manifesto literally from the rooftops.

For depicting the traditional semivisible social networks of bars and parties and the coded male sexual underground of toilets, baths, parks, and street cruising, "performance" techniques were de rigueur—even though observational vérité might well have been deployed with the day's portable equipment and sensitive color stocks. Though the semipublic sites of community building, socialization and political resistance are at the center of same-sex histories (as recalled by the nineties genre of lesbian herstory bar films), they are zones fraught with ethical, logistical, and technical tensions. I can't think of a single bar scene developed through observational or interactive realism in the entire corpus, although *We All Have Our Reasons* (Reid, Stevens, 1981) does construct a bar scene in well-rehearsed simulated vérité, and *Before Stonewall* stages a bar reunion of original participants who intradiegetically "perform" old songs and rituals.

In *It Is Not the Homosexual*, von Praunheim sets up flamboyantly stylized "performance" scenes of parties and bars, only to denounce with his shrill voice-over their undercurrents of self-hatred. The most appealing bar scene in the film, in a neighborhood hangout populated by drag queens, mixed-race couples, leathermen, and other salt of the earth who "don't feel comfortable in piss-elegant bars," is bursting with transvestite yodelling and other "performance" excess. Here the "desperate and lonely" allegorical hero meets his ideological prince, who leads him back home to his anarchist *Wohngemeinschaft*. In this urban commune the hero discovers anarchism, and von Praunheim accidentally pastiches women's movement documentary style: thirty-something, longhaired, nude chain-smokers lounge on pastel comforters and consciousness-raise about the self-hatred of ghetto and underground. But this "realist" vision of community is ultimately as "performed" as garish scenes of alienation.

The underground of parks, toilets, and bathhouses was even more of a challenge to documentarists. Sites of state terrorism and social violence as well as sexual community, they obviously required highly contrived dramatization: *Some of Your Best Friends* reenacted police entrapment in a park in which the victim's resistance became the interactive denouement of the film; a decade later *Track Two* reconstructed the infamous police raids on Toronto bathhouses that triggered the community mobilization recorded for the rest of the film in standard interactive realism. But a much shorter film is the real gem of the underground subgenre, abjuring realist imagery *in toto*: Michael McGarry's *In Black and White* (1979) encapsulated the private space of the public toilet with stylized visual closeups of

carnality, terror, and resistance, laid under a "documentary" montage of
conflicting public social voices.

Von Praunheim's stunning toilet queerbashing scene in *It Is Not the
Homosexual* is in typically theatrical long shot. Toilets, parks, and streets
are here the on-location settings for Brechtian agitprop and what the narrator calls "the tense choreography of men," all anchored in historical space
through his run-on voice-over denunciation. In *Army*, von Praunheim is now
a nonjudgmental libertine, acting as on-camera guide to the underworld
as the camera follows him cruising Central Park, the Piers, and the Trucks;
inspecting a Manhattan bathhouse (where not surprisingly the underground
has been appropriated and commercialized in the Glory Hole Room); or
accompanying John Rechy on a nostalgic, leather-decked vérité prowl
through some nighttime city, lamenting the subversive undergrounds of yore.
To me, the ideological evasions of voice and the complicitous voyeurism
of this observational realist format make *Army* seem more dated than von
Praunheim's earlier high artifice.

Jan Oxenberg's *Comedy in Six Unnatural Acts* (1975) matches *It Is
Not the Homosexual* and *In Black and White* in its full deployment of
"performance" (not a flicker of documentary realism). But Oxenberg was
"performing" another kind of border zone between public and private:

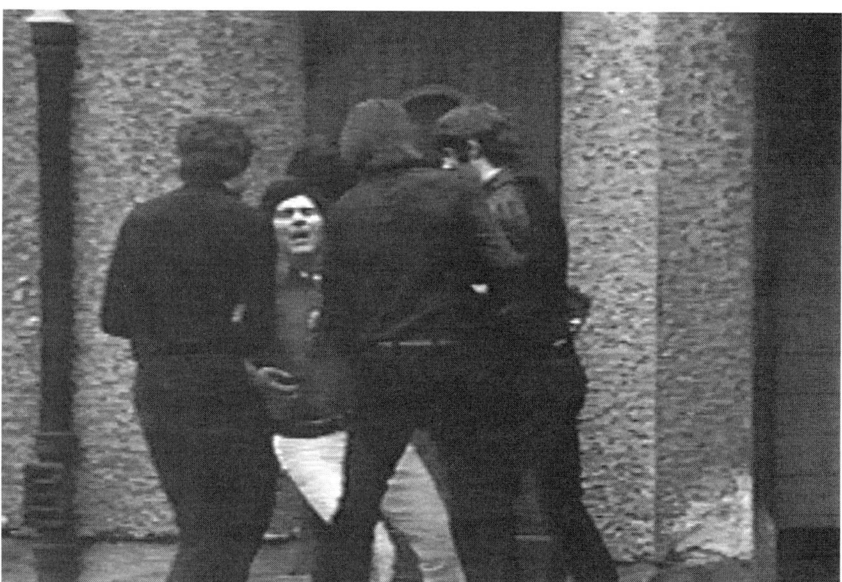

It Is Not the Homosexual Who Is Perverse, but the Situation in Which He Lives
(Rosa von Praunheim, 1971). A dramatized queerbashing in front of a public
toilet: for depicting the semipublic network of bars and the sexual underground,
"performance" techniques were indispensable.

lesbians' subcultural myths and fantasies and appropriations of mainstream cultural baggage (from child molester stereotypes to romance). Oxenberg's indulgent and affectionate skits are just as self-consciously theatrical as von Praunheim's, but they effectively engaged community approval rather than the almost unanimous outrage sparked by *It Is Not the Homosexual*'s distancing effects. PBS, however, balked at the intimacy of *Comedy*'s "performance"-based subcultural circuitry, pretexting amateurism (Becker 1980, 39–40). In short, "performance" aesthetics may not have been an always reliable resource for exploring semipublic space—especially as regards audiences and broadcasters—but lesbian and gay filmmakers had few other choices in such uncharted waters.

Private Spaces

Consciousness-raising documentaries from the women's movement provided a language to some post-Stonewall lesbian and gay documentarists for dealing with private life and the domestic sphere. But not all were as successful as *In the Best Interests of the Children*, which became the best received and most circulated realist lesbian documentary of the period through its instrumentalist focus on on the heartstring single issue of custody. Otherwise, trying to express "the personal is political" through realist codes was often a frustrating experience, especially on a low budget. *Word Is Out* scored thanks to its epic vision of cultural and class diversity, the comprehensiveness of its interviews and its feature-length confessional "coming out" narratives (which I will discuss later in this chapter). But by 1980, films of this nature were being disparaged, and not only against ideological checklists that constituted so much movement film criticism of the day. Pioneering lesbian film theorist Caroline Sheldon had already challenged "the assumption of film as 'pure' objective recording device" in 1977 (when as an afterthought she listed five documentaries that constituted a "start" for lesbian political cinema) (Sheldon 1977, 5–26), and Jacquelyn Zita took up the thread in 1981, lambasting the "pretended truth of objective documentaries," the "operatic confessionals of personal life," and the "'talking heads' of political documentary" (Zita 1981, 27). Quite simply, the antistereotype rhetoric of positive images, role models, and community enfranchisement didn't always fit realist documentary idioms, whether observational or interactive, that had evolved in order to communicate the texture of individual experience and yet were weighted with a liberal heritage of voyeurism and victim aesthetics. Films deploying collaborative and expressive "performance" seemed to surmount this problem, especially those dealing with the past or present private space of personal identities and relationships, with sons, daughters, and lovers. (The alternative families of *friends* are mostly missing from the period's documentary iconography, especially on the gay male side—perhaps they didn't match preexisting cinematic iconography as readily as parents and lovers.)

Barbara Hammer's films, known at first only within the women's constituencies to which they were restricted, were exemplary for conveying the give and take of sexual passion and exchange, relationships and rupture. They did so not only through the highly stylized editing and image processing she shared with her avant-garde mentors and peers but also through corporeal and facial acrobatics. *Double Strength* (1978) and *Sync Touch* (1981), for example, enact erotic vocabularies that are respectively balletic and gestural, based on a collaborative interaction by Hammer and her lover of the moment, "performed" intimately to the camera.

Joslin's *Blackstar* bravely tackles not only connubial intimacy but also familial stress. In contrast to the evasive father and controlling mother of my opening epigraph, the filmmaker's complicitous elder brother offers a jovial vérité monologue, but its phony spontaneity is unmasked when the editor includes all three takes. There are more stiff theatricality and more open wounds in Susana Blaustein's approach to similar territory, *Susana* (1980). The film lines up frontal declarations "performed" by the

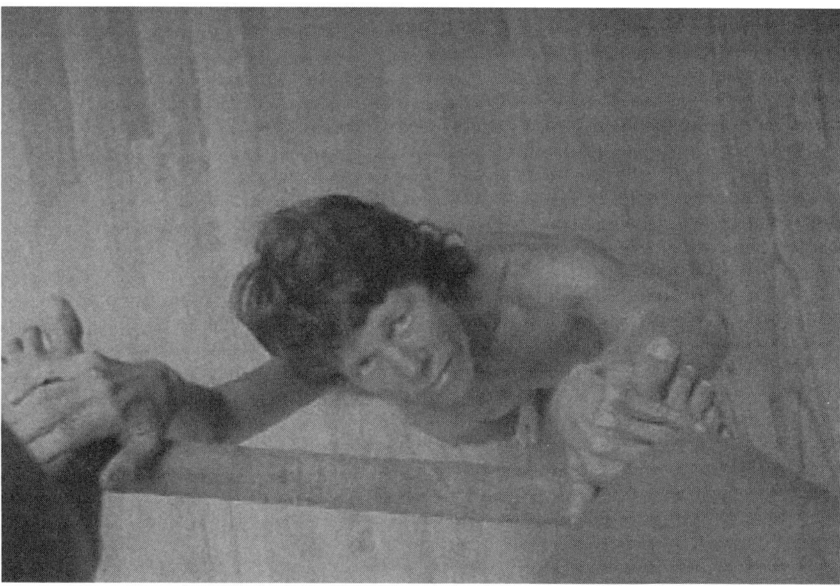

Double Strength (Barbara Hammer, 1978). A first-person vocabulary, erotic and balletic, performs the give and take of a relationship; the filmmaker films her girlfriend grasping her feet on the bar of a flying trapeze.

author-protagonist's sister, ex-lover, and parents; only the tearful pleading sister, the sardonic lover, and brutal Susana ("No, Father . . . You kept
telling me to imitate my sister.") are actually visualized, while the parents
are mercifully provided only in voice-over sound. If "performance" opens
wounds in *Susana*, it heals them in *Michael, A Gay Son*, which rechan-
nels familial trauma by casting the protagonist's peers as his parents and
siblings in role-playing improvisations of rejections and reconciliations.

As Hammer's and Blaustein's films demonstrated fully, lovers can be
more cooperative than parents. *Word Is Out*'s realist lovers perform indulgent smiles beside the narrator at the mike. In contrast, Joslin's Mark is
bristlingly aware of the inadequacies of cinematic realism for capturing his
relationship with the filmmaker and fills the film with self-reflexive chatter
about its uselessness:

> MARK. What about us? I mean this isn't us, and I'm kind of . . . I feel
> bad that I'm afraid that we're not going to get us in the film.
> TOM. Why is that?
> MARK. It's those seven years we shared together, the love that held us
> together—you know the life and things we share.
> TOM. What's missing?
> MARK. This is a construction for a film . . .
> TOM. Yes, no, you keep saying, we keep saying it has to come out in
> dialogue because there's no way to do it visually . . . And you keep
> saying maybe there's nothing between us because we can't find a
> way of doing it visually and I think that's worth pursuing.
> MARK. OK. Pursue. I'll follow.
> TOM. Tell me Mark, do you think there's nothing between us?
> MARK. There doesn't seem anything that we can do visually, that's
> for sure, right?
> TOM. There's nothing visible between us?
> MARK. Maybe.
> TOM. So there's something invisible between us?
> MARK. Christ. Stop it . . . I wanted just to show what we're like, and
> that's where we ran into vacancy.

The crisis within the realist effort to render a private partnership—
"running into vacancy"—is crystallized in this mattress dialogue. The partners
improvise with a prop, a spaghetti-like mass of outtake trims that have
literally come "between" them. And when the couple finally agrees on "performance" ("planning something out") as a means of expressing the invisible
element of their relationship, what to do? Sex is too highly charged to perform

for the camera, except a little discreet cuddling under the sheets, and realist dialogue also went nowhere fast. Thus vaudeville banter and a two-minute disco pas de deux to a Laura Nyro song, climaxing in a presentational pose and kiss for the camera, were chosen to conclude this film. This "performance" scene would be recycled in a similar place fifteen years later in Joslin's posthumous *Silverlake Life: The View from Here* (with Peter Friedman, 1993), summing up the relationship once and for all but now in the before-and-after iconographical context of AIDS memorialization—the flashback of an artist who has just performed that most private and visual act of all, his own death. In the nineties, it seemed natural for Joslin to choose a hybrid interactive-observational video style to tell his last story, but in the seventies, when private gay space was still contested, "performance" got the nod.

Coming Out, Cumming Out

> *I'm coming out now, right? Here I am on television. Big white face on the screen saying "Yeah, you know, I'm gay!"*
> ::   Pat Bond, *Word Is Out* (1977)

The Stonewall generation's political ritual of coming out mixed private and public, "outed" the personal, and thereby transgressed the social silence

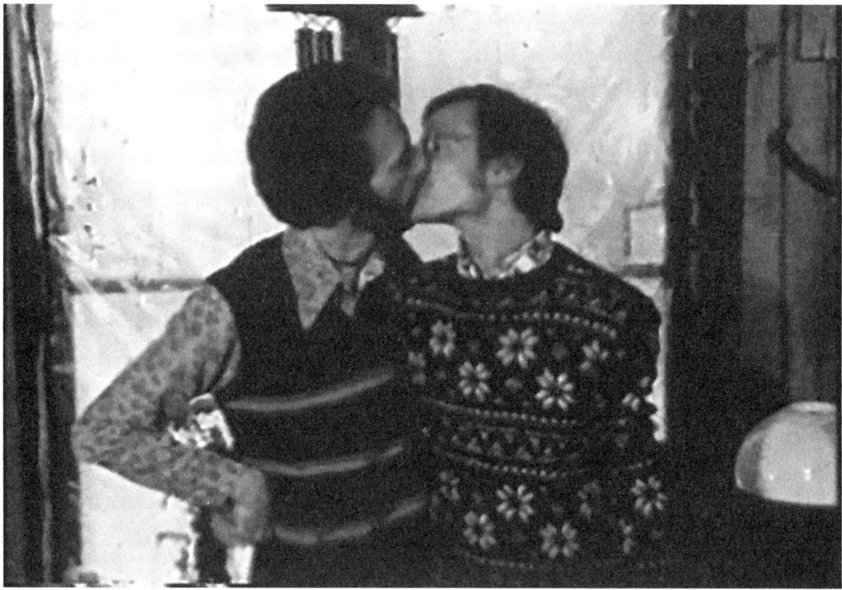

Blackstar (Joslin, 1977). How to render private life? Instead of observational realism, the couple opts to perform a disco pas de deux climaxing in a presentational kiss.

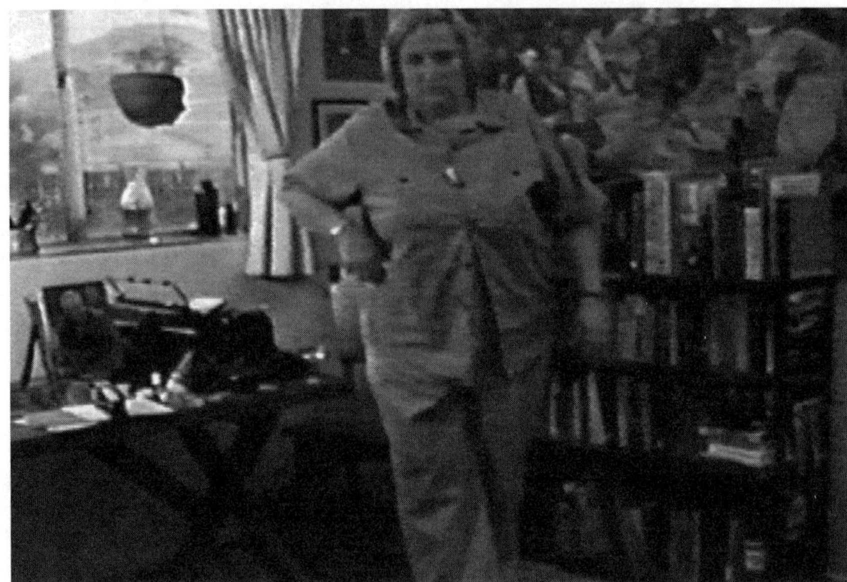

Word Is Out (Mariposa Film Group, 1977). Pat Bond's laughing confession performs a public coming out: "Yeah, you know, I'm gay!"

around sexuality and difference. The queen and the butch had played this transgressive role in pre-Stonewall public life as well as in representation (the sixties had been the great decade of queens on documentary, from Warhol to *Portrait of Jason* [Clarke, 1967]). However in the seventies, the transgressive role was to be played not by the queen, who was quickly shuffled offstage by the positive-image agenda of liberation politics (reappearing only in the eighties), but by the assimilationist lesbian or gay who was by definition invisible and therefore required to *speak* his or her transgression.

One might expect that realist modes were more appropriate than theatrical "performance" for capturing this confessional moment because of its premise of spontaneity and inner authenticity, and indeed interactive realism was often the aesthetic strategy of choice. Yet this ritual is invariably performed and often "performed." I am referring not only to some of the most expressive moments of the coming out repertory, where interviewees intradiegetically perform gestural amplifications of their narratives, for example the butch Dorothy Hillaire in *Before Stonewall* showing the camera how she literally booted harassers across a bar thirty years earlier. I am referring also to the ritualized, premeditated quality of the coming out performances, invariably delivered by a preselected (and *prevideotaped* in the case of *Word Is Out*) subject in close collaborative relationship with the filmmakers.

Coming out requires the interactive mode of interview and monologue by its very nature, and its confessional operation also requires the presence of the spectator, mediated through camera and crew. This operation thus posits performance but also performativity in the linguistic sense, *executing* one's identity of outness as well as *describing* it. It is performative also in Nichols's sense, making the viewer who is engaged by the on-camera confession a documentary referent, along with the speaker. This was assumed by Pat Bond's laughing confession in *Word Is Out* (epigraphed earlier) and by Bruce White, whose voice on a sixties radio broadcast replayed in *Before Stonewall* says, not laughingly, that not only will his family find out but also "I'm quite certain that I will probably lose my job as a result of the program too . . . I hope that through this means I can be some use to someone else other than myself." These two speakers of different periods know that they are enacting as well as signifying a relationship—cultural, affective, and political—with the viewer.

Coming out involved transgression of the public–private divide, as I said, but even its transgressive power became formulaic. Films such as the staid *The Advocate*'s production *Who Happen to Be Gay* (Beldin, Krenzien, 1979), for all their instrumentality in the political context of the seventies, were also the ones most complicit in social invisibility and in the rote recapitulation of the interactive recipe (interview/snapshots/observational rock-climbing interlude/interview/workplace interlude/interview). The more these films began to pile up after 1980, the more they deserved Dyer's complaints about "hidden agendas," the erasure of "conflict, contradiction, and difficulty" and "the quest for sameness" (Dyer 1990, 245ff.).

Was it to express the essential theatricality of the "gay sensibility" or to escape these complicities of realism that there evolved highly theatricalized "performance" variants of the coming out formula, from Oxenberg's own cryptic juggling act in the "nonmonogamy" sketch in *Comedy* to the explicit self-scripted and self-costumed monologues in *L'Aspect rose de la chose* (Wong 1980), in which each character controlled his own identity "performance"? In any case, the memorable queen who stole this latter film from her fellow collective members with flounces and fabrics was prophetic. For, as the effect of seventies positive images and realism wore off, coming out "performances" would become all the more prevalent in our nonfiction and would increasingly deploy, not rock climbing, but more and more of what Sedgwick calls "flaming" lesbian and gay "performative identity vernaculars": "butch abjection, femmitude, leather, pride, SM, drag, musicality, fisting, attitude, zines, histrionicism, asceticism, Snap! culture, diva worship, florid religiosity . . . activism" (Sedgwick 1993, 13).

Evolving from the very beginning of the seventies was a particular subgenre of "cumming out" films, autobiographical sex "performances" that enhanced the power of coming out both as "performance" and as

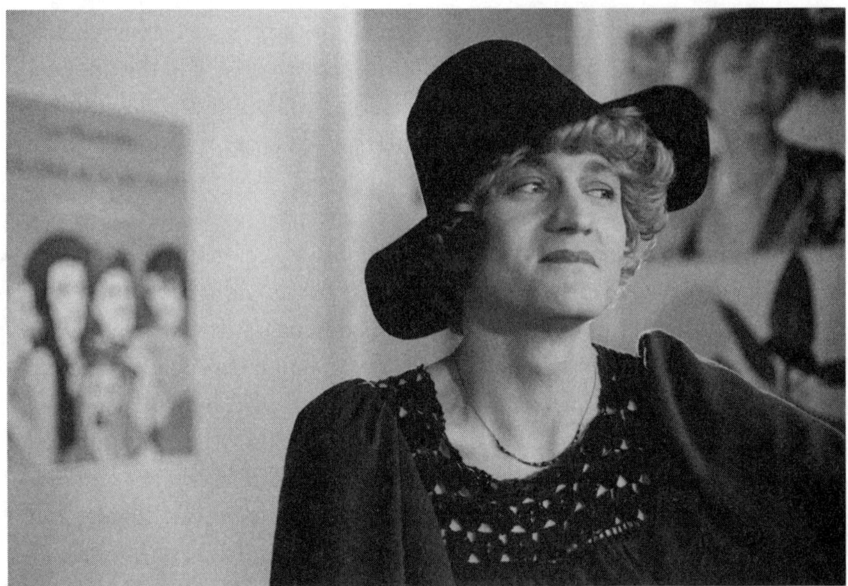

L'Aspect rose de la chose (Chi Yan Wong, 1980). Denis, the memorable queen whose explicit self-scripted monologue, enhanced with flounces and fabrics, constructs his own identity "performance" (production still).

"performativity." In view of criticism already current during the seventies about the censorship of sexuality in lesbian and gay documentaries (Olson 1979, 9–12), it is surprising to rediscover how frequent and brazen the self-erotic imagery of the decade really was. I have written elsewhere of the extraordinary achievement of Curt McDowell's diaristic *Loads* (1980), with its multipartner performance of erotic exchange and fantasy (Waugh 1985, 30–36). In fact in *Women I Love* (1976), Hammer had already matched McDowell's on-camera authorial orality and one-upped him with a seventies-style lesbian reciprocality ("you-do-me-I-do-you") that McDowell's trade partners wouldn't dream of. McDowell and Hammer were far from unique, rivaled in their bravado by von Praunheim's sex acts in *Army of Lovers* (he performs a graphic blow job for film production students and has midinterview sex with Fred Halsted, their telephoto encounter framed with flowers and liberation dialogue).

Halsted, author and star in another genre of seventies "documentary," hard-core porn, is sex "performer" in the porn milieu's own attempt at the docu-history genre, *Erotikus* (1972), where as on-camera narrator lazily masturbating for the camera he steers us through the porn industry's selective autobiography. At the same time, soft-core moments seemed equally transgressive. Andrea Weiss complained in *Jump Cut* that the protagonists of *Lavender* (Monahan, Jacobs, 1972) "embraced constantly" (Weiss 1981a,

22). *Home Movie* and *Susana* went further, the former with Oxenberg's touch-football pileup borrowed from sixties surrogate eroticism and the latter with its sexy chiaroscuro stills and its dramatized shots of topless cuddling, faces obscured and breasts caressed by long, straight seventies hair.

Like all "body" genres, the sex "performance" extrapolations of the coming out ritual executed a complex, even troubled, performativity. On-camera erotic behavior both described and enacted the utopian confrontational track of identity politics, an in-your-face alternative to the assimilationist politics of invisibility. At the same time, the viewer's arousal was qualified by genre clash; documentary tact was scrambled by erotic exhibition, and vice versa. The spectator was engaged, linguistically, politically, and affectively but also physiologically. Minority politics was not only asserted but also "performed" as sexual exchange.

▶

Shots from a Queer Canon

My conception of seventies documentary is not a monolithic or unitary one. Far from it: famine or no famine, a rich diversity of cultural roots, aesthetic strategies, and ideological negotiations resists efforts to generalize about this important moment in the history of "new social movements" in the West and its intersection with *the* medium of social change par excellence. One can risk the following generalization however: those documentaries closest in organizational links or sensibility to gay and/or lesbian movement agendas are those that remain most anchored to the prescribed realist discourses of seventies documentary and were most visible in community media at the time. In contrast, most of the prophetic "performance" films that stand up well in this retroactive view—autobiographical, experimental, and erotic—had uneven relationships with the lesbian and gay masses who allegedly preferred positive images and realist convention. Self-indulgent or self-reflexive mannerisms were liabilities in the post-Stonewall political context of simultaneous mobilization and backlash, and much important nonfiction was undervalued or at the very least controversial, never reaching its full potential audience.

Even without these cultural biases, as Nichols explains, performative documentary by definition runs the risk of misunderstanding (Nichols 1994, 97). Audiences are often disturbed by shifting borders between fiction and nonfiction, and indeed the "performance" films I have privileged in this analysis necessitate a retroactive expansion in the definition of documentary. At the time who would have called *It Is Not the Homosexual* or *Comedy* "documentaries?" But now the post-Stonewall generation's documentary image of itself cannot be separated from films that were then marginalized as dramatized, experimental, weird, personal, short, fictional, politically incorrect, amateurish, divisive, pornographic, and inaccessible. In fact if Nichols is right in identifying performative/"performance" documentary as the key mode of the nineties, the lesbian and gay "performance" documentaries of the seventies—and earlier (perhaps Warhol or Jack Smith?)—must be reclaimed as not only the key to our past but the key to the present.

Who says reclamation and redefinition says canon. My post-post-Stonewall queer students of the nineties who watched the seventies documentaries I showed them in stony silence were not only generational chauvinists (and admittedly the captive audience of a perhaps nostalgic and unimaginative teacher). They also saw themselves, I think, as canon busters, queer iconoclasts criticizing the complacent legacy of lesbian and gay baby boomers. They may have been right, but busting a nonexistent canon—fragmented and fragile if it exists at all—may well be misdirected energy. Only a few documentaries from the seventies are available on video, and the texts that are constituting our cultural history, such as *The Celluloid Closet*, *Queer Looks*, and *Vampires and Violets*, jump over much of this generation's artistic and political practice (Russo 1981; Gever, Greyson, and Parmar 1993; Weiss 1992). A canon of post-Stonewall documentaries may be exactly what we need. Challenging queer amnesia is not only a question of restoring our cultural history, our performances, and our "performances" of the post-Stonewall years. Nor is it only a question of preventing young video queers from reinventing the wheel. With the funding crises and political backlash of the nineties, the threat of famine is back, and glimpses of the resourcefulness, courage, energy, and erotic pleasure of our performances during earlier famines may help us tiptoe through the next one.

9

"Words of Command"

Cultural and Political Inflections of Direct Cinema in Indian Independent Documentary (1990)

This was the first major piece I published on Indian cinema and reflects a shift in my two-decade-old personal love affair with South Asian culture and society, a search for its professional research applications as film studies. It's the fruit of a couple of small grants I received in 1988 to research independent Indian documentary, having been transfixed since the late seventies by the work of Mumbai-based activist Anand Patwardhan (whose first-person reflection on his underground work during the "Emergency" of 1975–1977 I had published in "Show Us Life"). Indian cinema would never become a major research area for me, mostly because of my linguistic backwardness, but I have maintained the field as a teaching focus and subject of occasional publication ever since, all the while deepening my personal fascination with and roots in the soil.

The passion palpably shows through, I know, but once again there is tension in the air. The concept of "third world cinema" was already on its way out when I wrote this essay in 1989, and nomenclature was typically in crisis. This explains the many parentheses in my starting concept of "Third (World) Cinema(s)," which as my note makes clear was intended as a rejoinder to Paul Willemen's prescriptive and idealizing broadside on "third cinema" that had just appeared that year. Willemen apparently aimed to delegitimize the transcultural comparative work that had animated "third world" cinema studies in the North in the seventies and eighties (culminating for example in two 1987 U.S.-published books, Roy Armes's Third World Film Making and the West *and John Downing's* Film & Politics in the Third World, *both of which lined up South Asian cinema alongside African, East Asian, Middle Eastern, and Latin American work). However, so little research had been done on*

*documentary from Asia and Africa (this is slightly less true of Latin
America) that I felt I had permission and an open playing field
for this effort to grapple with the cultural specificity of independent Indian documentary. If my passing comparisons to Bolivian
and Senegalese work seemed reductive, I was confident enough in
my observations about how documentary vernaculars were being
inflected by the encounters of documentary technology with modernizing agrarian and urban working-class cultures to try it out.*

*If the reader has sensed a tone of defensiveness in this preface,
it has arisen no doubt from a critique of my piece (which had been
inconveniently hidden in the Canadian journal* Cineaction!*) by
Chon Noriega, American authority on Chicano cinema (Noriega
1996, 211). Noriega was as annoyed at the frequent essentialism of
Euro-American postcolonial cinema studies as I was, and situated
nonfiction audiovisual discourse in relation to the generic tradition of the* testimonio *as it had been identified in Latin American
documentary. He expressed worry about the "danger in equating
the representational strategy of the* testimonio *with geopolitical,
cultural, and racial formations, thereby producing a rigid taxonomy
in which form determines ideology"—a danger allegedly symp-
tomatized in my essay. Part of me wants to argue: "Racial?—of
course not; geopolitical?—perhaps only in a complex way related
to technological, institutional, and economic infrastructure; but
cultural?—does anyone seriously believe that representational
strategies are not determined in a substantial way by cultural
formations?" Nevertheless, I understand how Noriega's essentialism alarm bells went off, how such a misreading could arise out of
the excessively neat and symmetrical "binarisms" that shaped my
drive to understand why the Indian documentaries I was examin-
ing looked so different from the films that were being produced
in North America; how "individualism" and "collectivism" were
indeed diffuse political energies that translated into what we see
on the screen; and why* Roger and Me *could not have been made in
India, at least not in 1989 (things have changed!). Ultimately I was
reassured that Noriega agreed with my emphasis on "subject–
camera relations" and that he and I agreed fully that "mise-en-scène
nonetheless remains a site in which we can read social relations . . .
that the 'talking head' must always belong—at some level—to a
body politic." That said, although my cited generalizations from
Tshome Gabriel about "third world chronotypes" have their own
essentialism that has held up in the intervening decades about as*

well as Frederic Jameson's arguments about all third world literature being allegory (Jameson 1986), there is much in them—including an alertness to social space and time and the constitution of the subject—that can be fine tuned, localized, and built upon in their application to culturally specific texts.

Otherwise, rereading my piece two decades after my Indian research project was launched, I am struck by the personal even confessional tone that reflects my love for these films as well as for their filmmakers, most of whom are still my friends. Of course that does not rule out a kind of northern sentimentality in my arguments, a phantasmatic nostalgia for premodern forms of community that I have obviously never known personally. I am not exactly a collectivist person by nature or history, so my hyperindividualism must compute oddly with this wandering panegyric to the group. Fortunately it ends up in my own backyard—where perhaps it should have also begun.

———————————

The lament first makes the indictment; and then it makes an appeal. In the period that follows, the words of command are heard.
:: Frantz Fanon, *The Wretched of the Earth*

The discussion around "Third (World) Cinema(s)"[1] as it has been proliferating in the film studies milieu gives short shrift to documentary work despite the fact that many of the prototypes of this cinema, from *Hour of the Furnaces* to *The Battle of Chile*, are within the documentary tradition. At the same time, we still pay considerable attention to nonfiction images by Euro-American image makers of Third World societies. All but swamped under the media flood of earthquakes, violence, deprivation, and indebtedness, "Northern" independents making images of the "South" tend to fall into three main camps: (1) the left solidarity advocates, following in the tradition of Ivens and Marker and showing no signs of slowing down in the nineties; (2) the "ethnographers," descendants of Flaherty from the mystic Robert Gardner (*Forests of Bliss*) to the antiethnographic ethnographer Trinh T. Minh-ha; and (3) the occidental tourists, "personal visions" of "auteurs on tour" from Roberto Rossellini and Pier Paolo Pasolini in the fifties and sixties, to Michael Rubbo, Louis Malle, and Werner Herzog more recently. However progressive and useful these three groups of independents may sometimes be, they can't help being part of the unequal flow of images from North to South. Somehow Euro-American mediators still seem to be the required filter for images of our third world Other.

The situation with India is a case in point. Despite the current Northern boom of interest in the Indian cinema—in particular a long overdue scrutiny of Indian popular cinema in such periodicals as *Screen*, *Framework*, *Continuum*, and *Quarterly Review of Film Studies*—independent documentary film and video from that country are unjustly neglected. This dynamic countercinema is in effect a domestic third world cinema, a small but effective irritant in the flank of the elephantine first cinema, the crisis-prone Bombay-Madras industry, and the anemic second cinema, the prestigious state-subsidized art cinema that still monopolizes our attention in Western festivals and even in progressive periodicals like *Framework*.

This neglect is not only the result of careful orchestration on the part of the Indian state cultural bureaucracy but also unfortunately a reflection of Northern taste. Somehow Indian documentary seems less translatable than the exotic mysteries of Indian auteur fiction for first world audiences—at least for influential festival programmers, especially North American. With its frequent availability in domestically circulated English versions and despite its use of a largely familiar documentary vocabulary, this impermeability of taste is paradoxical to say the least. The cultural untranslatability of Indian documentary is perhaps because of (not despite) its familiar vocabulary. By this I mean that Indian documentary inherits the same dread Griersonian legacy as our own. Its insistently "realist" mode, increasingly discredited in the North (even without the authoritative voice-overs that Indian practitioners are maintaining, for reasons I will elaborate later), rings just a little too close for comfort and is not quite either inscrutable or glitzy enough for our jaded postmodern and orientalist tastes.

The Grierson legacy in India is heavy indeed: the Films Division of the Ministry of Information and Broadcasting was modeled after a colonial institution developed during the War—at the same time and with the same mission as our own National Film Board of Canada. The Films Division held a virtual monopoly on the documentary film in India during the first four decades of independence, fattened by a regimen of omnipresent and compulsory (but little heeded) theatrical screenings.[2] Only in the eighties was its paralyzing grip—aesthetic, political, and economic—eroded by upstart independents and television documentarists (once again the analogies with the Canadian situation are chilling!). The Films Division has ensured at least one consensus among its independent successors, and this in terms of audience practice: Films Division fare has been so universally hated that commercial theaters are the last place anyone will ever want to show a documentary! Instead richly diverse and resourceful distribution strategies are being built up, based on settings as different as rural educational networks, improvised urban slum screenings, hand-to-hand videotape circulation, and specialized or elite networks within the labor or civil liberties movements. Some films have even made it onto Doordarshan, the state-owned national TV network—not without occasional litigation to pry open the airwaves.[3]

Otherwise, after scarcely a decade of work, it is too soon for a distinct Indian national school or style of documentary to have emerged—even if a homogeneous school were likely or desirable in the face of proud regional autonomies. Still, for all the variation in technique and cultural positioning among the young independents, there are certain commonalities beyond the inherited baggage of Films Divisions formats that they all have simultaneously clung to and cast off. Something is to be learned from looking at certain corners of this work as a corpus and thinking about how the idiom of direct cinema is being inflected by the cultural, political, and economic imperatives of a postcolonial society.

One major inflection of direct cinema is apparent as soon as a generic inventory of the films in question is undertaken, namely the conspicuous absence of important Euro-American documentary genres. Both the compilation-interview genre (de Antonio) and pure observational documentary (Wiseman) are very minor traditions indeed (the limited development of the 16mm infrastructure is an obvious material factor here). At most, observational and compilation work are occasional components of a hybrid vocabulary (significantly, two women's films that use observational strategies, Mira Nair's *India Cabaret* and Nilita Bachani's *Eyes of Stone*, were directed by individuals trained or residing abroad and shot by Northern cinematographers). As for autobiographical, experimental, or otherwise self-reflexive strands, these are almost nonexistent in India. Virtually the only exception is Mani Kaul, state-funded author of *Siddheshwari*, Indian cinema's most visible presence on the major international art cinema festival circuit this year (a first for documentary); however, Kaul's astonishing oeuvre can be explained in part by the fact that its ethnomusicological orientation falls within the Films Division's cultural vocation.

A far cry from Kaul's formally challenging exploration of traditional cultural forms, the didactic social documentary, the most-favored genre of the Indian independents, is in some ways a look-alike of its institutionalized Northern counterpart and no less questioning of its "realist" stance. Anchored in the interventionist mode of direct cinema consolidated in the North in the early seventies by the New Left and the women's movement, it deploys a similar mode of collaborative low-ratio mise-en-scène and relies heavily on interviewing. This formula is nurtured by an oppositional political context and marginal economic basis not dissimilar to that in the North. However, what is specific and distinctive to the Indians within this general model are certain variations in direct cinema vocabulary and structure on a microcosmic level. These variations, related no doubt to the generic pattern observed above, are largely cultural, one suspects, but have distinct political ramifications.

"Talking Groups"

The ensemble of these Indian variations in the direct cinema lexicon crystallize, I would argue, in the trope that might be called the "collective interview" or the "talking group." Though this trope is not statistically overwhelming, it is specific to and symbolically representative of the independent documentary current, as I will attempt to demonstrate through referring to three representative films made in the eighties by different directors in various regions of India: *Voices from Baliapal*, *The Sacrifice of Babulal Bhuiya*, and *Bombay Our City* (see text boxes).

In the key scenes described in this chapter, as in several more like them in each film, everyone is often talking at once. The speakers' address is

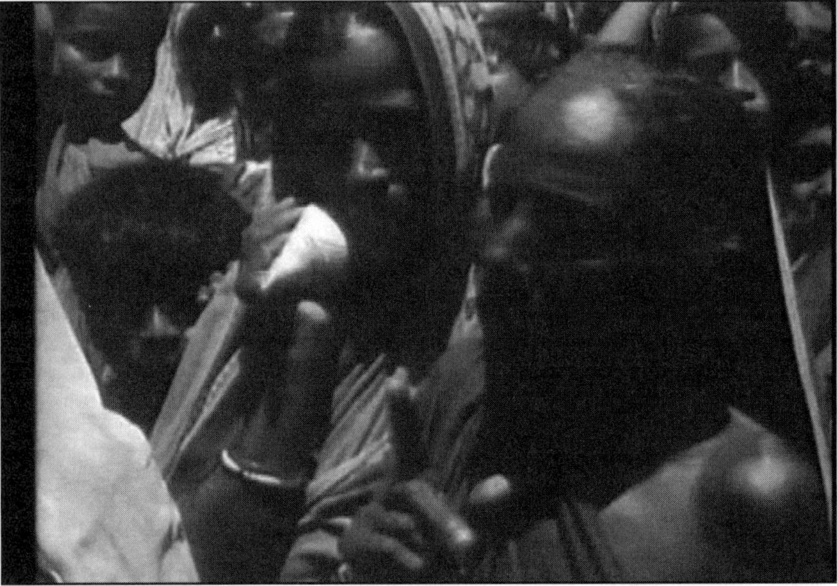

Voices from Baliapal (Ranjan Palit and Vasudha Joshi, 1989). Women demonstrators collectively speak to the camera of their defiance of the government order to vacate their land for a missile base.

Voices from Baliapal **(Ranjan Palit and Vasudha Joshi, 1989)**

Peasants and fishing people in a fertile region of Orissa State on the
Bay of Bengal resist expropriation of their lands by the government
for a missile base. In the two-minute scene evoked by this still, women
demonstrators talk together to the camera about their refusal to leave
their ancestral land. In the five shots that make up this scene, a handheld camera keeps the tight frame full of the faces of the women as they
speak one by one, following the wandering, back-and-forth thread of
the conversation:

> Our committee has instructed us to raise an alarm with conches and
> thalis [metal food trays]. Then we go and block the road. If the men are
> out, women lie down in front of vehicles.
>   Who has brought the women forward today? The Government.
> Their land is also ours. How will we leave our Mother? How will we
> leave? They have everything, let them kill us. Why should we wander
> from place to place? They will turn us into beggars. Let them see who is
> more powerful.
>   We'll lie down in front of their vehicles. We'll die. That's all we can do.
>   What knowledge do we have? They have everything. They have
> weapons—We have thalis which we bang, to call people out, to find
> courage together.
>   With our kids in our arms, we'll stand and die. If we die alone the
> kids will suffer. They'll have to kill us and the kids.

Elsewhere in the film groups of fishermen are set within a
similar construction, expressing to a hovering camera their protest
and defiance.

direct, aimed at the filmmaker who is standing or seated beside the camera
(in fact the director is operating it in the case of *Voices*). The voices are fast
and emotional, in unison, overlapping, yielding to each other and taking
turns, or interrupting, seconding or disagreeing with each other. There are
also natural pauses and moments of silence. The camera is mobile without
being flamboyant, moving from medium to close range and back, either
fluidly mounted or tightly handheld. Together with the microphone, the
apparatus has a finely tuned sensitivity to the shifting organic equilibrium of
individual and collective voice. The profilmic event is set up in collaboration
between subjects and filmmaker at either their advance suggestion or his or
hers or else, if more spontaneously, still based on a prior relationship and an
instinctively agreed-upon format of the group interview/declaration. Trigger
questions are sometimes retained by the editor but seem hardly necessary.

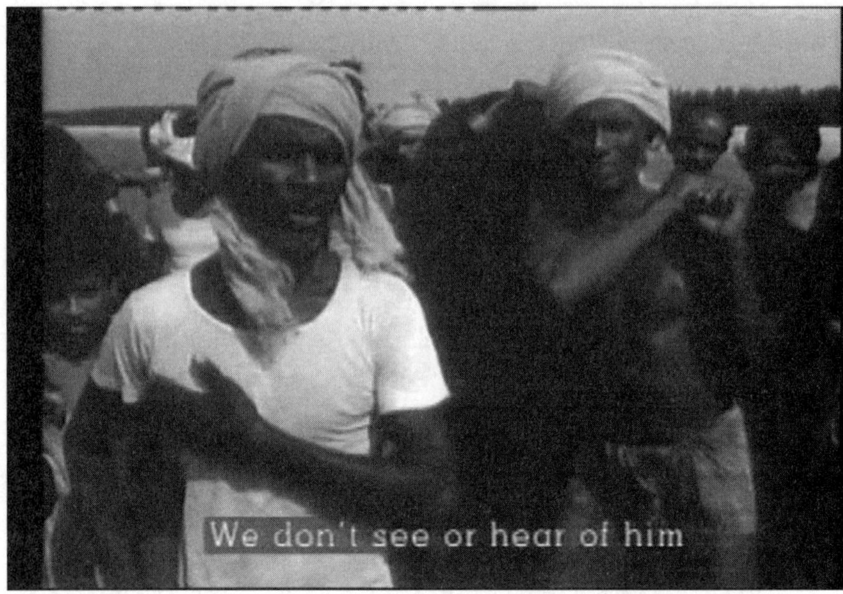

Voices from Baliapal (Ranjan Palit and Vasudha Joshi, 1989). Village fisherman constitute a talking group, their shared pride in their work bolstering their rhetoric.

One of the fascinating revelations of the "talking group" is the social functioning and constitution of the group. Roles within a group are usually understood and prescribed through an unspoken consensus (or, sometimes, a *spoken* consensus signaled by a "You tell it!" from off screen or else triggered by the filmmaker's "Let Mother speak!"). This process in which a spokesperson is designated to express a collective will, whether spontaneously or through deliberation, is of course dependent on which preconstituted group entity is present. In *Bombay* the scene I have described involves a large extended family who are introduced one by one by the materfamilias and who provide the paternal grandmother with honorary space for her commentary. In other examples the group is an occupational or economic community whose shared but unspoken pride in their catch and their tools bolsters their rhetoric of solidarity and defiance. Or else the group is composed of victims of a shared calamity, as in two Indian documentaries about the Bhopal industrial catastrophe in which case panic and grief are closer to the surface, making consensus both easier and more difficult than with a preconstituted occupational or gender group.

The "talking group" trope arises from a society where the group rather than the individual is the primary site of political discourse and of cultural expression. Or, as in Raymond Williams's classic formulation in a somewhat different context, a society that is

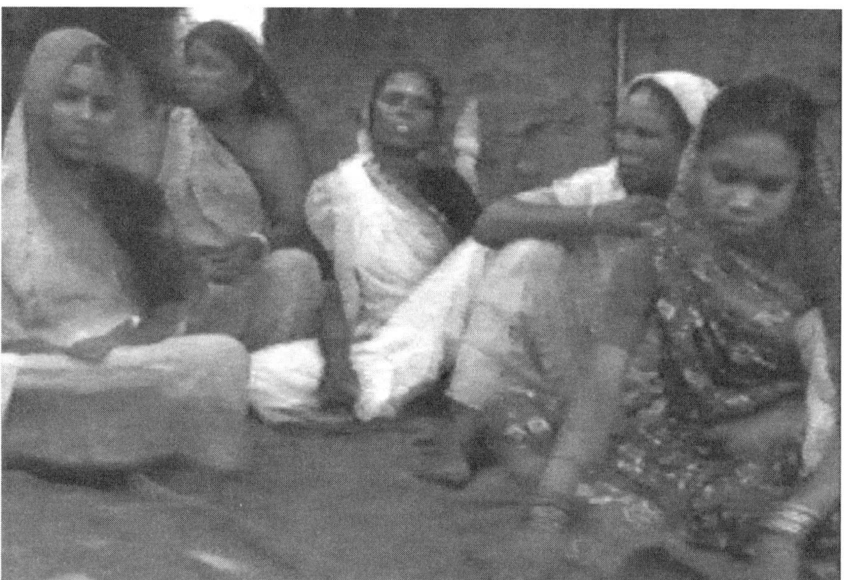

The Sacrifice of Babulal Bhuiya (Manjira Datta, 1989). A single long-take record of a group of women remembering and interpreting the titular sacrifice.

the positive means for all kinds of development, including individual development. Development and advantage are not individually but commonly interpreted. The provision of the means of life will, alike in production and distribution, be collective and mutual. Improvement is sought, not in the opportunity to escape from one's class, or to make a career, but in the general and controlled advance of all. The human fund is regarded as in all respects common, and freedom of access to it as a right constituted by one's humanity; yet such access, in whatever kind, is common or it is nothing. Not the individual, but the whole society, will move. (Williams 1958, 326)

The Sacrifice of Babulal Bhuiya (Manjira Datta, 1989)

A community of poor coal-dust (slurry) salvagers at the bottom end of an industrial economy in Bihar state resist harassment by police and local bosses, and offer sometimes conflicting reminiscences of a fellow salvager who has been enshrined as a martyr to the Cause. In the one-take, two-minute scene evoked by this still, a half-dozen women are seated in a communal village space under a tree, captured by a close panning camera mounted on a low tripod inside a group of houses, and discuss their memory of the titular hero's death with the filmmaker.

FILMMAKER. Does the CSIF (Central Industrial Security Force)
     intimidate women here?
They still do.
FILMMAKER. Poonamji, you tell us.
Yes even now the sepoys pester women.
They're covering up.
In Damadar colliery we heard that Babulal's sister was being pes-
     tered. He couldn't bear that so the fight developed. If not why
     did the fight start? Just tell us that. Why did it start? Why did
     the murder happen?
Only a witness can say what happened. They wouldn't let us take
     out slurry or light a kiln. They wanted protection money. So they
     picked a fight. All we know is work. The boss and the accountant
     will give the money (to the racketeers), not us? Why should we?
FILMMAKER. Let Basenti tell us what happened that day.
Why was it that Babulal was killed that day? It was reported in
     the colliery that the CISF had abused Babulal's sister. Probably
     he was working, digging at the time—but he saw what was
     happening to his sister. The CISF men used dirty language to
     her. A fight developed.

A social actor's identity is defined by his or her relation to a group, rather
than through a distinctive individual psychology. His or her first alliance
is not to the self or the state, but to the immediate community, on whom
rests the responsibility for responding collectively to an outside threat and
for working out a solution.

A number of theorists of Third (World) Cinema(s) have elaborated
on a cinematic articulation of group society in fiction. Teshome Gabriel
locates it in the integration of the individual and the social manifest in

1. the constitution of the subject, which is radically different from a
   Western conception of the individual;
2. the nonhierarchical order, which is differential rather than
   autonomous;
3. the emphasis on collective social space rather than on transcenden-
   tal individual space (Gabriel 1989, 59).

Burton refers to "more integrative interactional concept of being-
in-the-world" proper to Third World societies (1985, 17). She goes on to
describe Jorge Sanjinés's encounter with Andean villagers who refused to

let a communal spokesperson appear alone in the filmmaker's frame during the 1969 shooting of *Blood of the Condor*; thus emerged the concept of the collective hero in Sanjinés's subsequent work, where he eschewed *Condor*'s one-shot web of shot–countershot and reaction close-ups, as well as its climactic rhythm of suspense and dénouement. Burton also mentions the work of Ousmane Sembene, but interestingly both the Bolivian and the Senegalese directors work in dramatic fiction (in the usual sense), rather than in documentary. Furthermore films such as *Emitai* and *Blood of the Condor* rely extensively on nonverbal communication rather than verbal dialogue within their narrative structures, with the imperatives of working with nonprofessional actors on location apparently prevailing over the potential benefits of oral culture. Sanjinés's more recent work, such as *¡Fuera de aquí!* (1977), based for the first time on extensive use of direct lip-sync dialogue by nonprofessional performers reenacting collective struggles, offers a fascinating approximation of documentary group speech all the while maintaining the syntax of "don't-look-at-the-camera" narrative. Here fluid sequence shots facilitate a privileged audiovisual inscription of communal process that is quite unique in cinematic fiction, unforgettable for its vivid mosaic of excited voices and babies' cries from a culture too often represented by impassive silent faces and aestheticized flute scores. With documentary it is a very different story: The group image recurs transculturally throughout the Third World wherever traditional societies resisting the dehumanization of "modernization" and "development" address the direct-sound documentary camera—not Sanjinés's or Ousmane's silent groups, but groups that talk.

In Indian documentary, articulations of the "talking group" often revolve around the private/public spatial dimensions of the individual/collective dichotomy to which Gabriel points. For one thing, there are few interiors in Indian documentary. This is partly due to climate and technology—the small, dark, but cool living spaces of the poor are often unwired, though Datta managed a few inside shots, using available light through the door of the hut in question. (A more famous poet of doorways and available light, Trinh T. Minh-ha enters the West African dwellings of *Naked Spaces: Living Is Round* to construct a sense of dwellings as dim and mysterious social corridors; Datta does so to get away from the police!)

In the talking group convention, allowing oneself to be filmed is not a private affair but a participation in collective speech, in group identification and affirmation. As such, being filmed takes place in public space. Talking groups are often shot in community meeting places, in *Sacrifice* almost ritualistically under a beneficent community shade tree. Or, very commonly, the setup is in semipublic courtyard space in front of dwellings, that space where food is prepared and where sleeping cots are moved in the hot weather. In *Bombay*, interestingly even when the dwelling is demolished by municipal bulldozers, the semipublic courtyard spaces continue to exist, and the talking group is filmed there, the matriarch fully in control of her continuing domain. Otherwise communal working space is featured, as on the beach at Baliapal: here the busy backdrop of sea, equipment, and catch constitutes a cinematic arena for the subjects' proud declarations. Thus this film about the defense of space integrates the talking group into a cinematic articulation of subject-controlled space.

One of the most common mis-(pre-)conceptions about documentary filming in India is that you can't shoot in public spaces because of the camera being jostled by the crowds, the crew threatened by mobs, the lens invaded by grandstanding street urchins. Many of the independents have shown this to be utter nonsense. Several films in my corpus take to the streets or factories, even where filming is forbidden and must be through subterfuge, whereupon the lack of control of social space becomes the filmic and the profilmic issue. The taboo on street shooting is a culture-centric conception that denies the genius of group culture and of collective social life, assuming Northern and bourgeois standards of individualized speech and the fetishized one-shot subject.

▶ ──

Oral Culture

The concept of oral culture may be all too often the idealized focus of alienated political nostalgia, but it still provides the necessary and concrete framework for looking at the Indian documentaries. Cultural articulations of space and time that are specific to preindustrial or "modernizing" societies come inexorably to the surface in collective speech; this may well be the material of the elusive third world chronotype that has been the target of theorists such as Gabriel (though he oddly doesn't pursue it with regard to documentary, a rather obvious place to begin because of documentary's aspiration to record "real" time and space). All the sample Indian films I have selected are structured by these dynamics of oral culture crystalliz-ing in the trope of the "talking group" rather than, say, in the isolated and sentimentalized storyteller of a film like *Sugar Cane Alley*. In particular, *Sacrifice* can be said to be specifically *about* oral culture as well. Different memories of the eponymous martyr and absent hero come out of different segments of the community (women and men, the union and Communist Party officials), each with its own agenda for a mythographic oral con-struction of the remembered sacrifice and fused through group speech. The

film is a spectacular demonstration of how the processes of oral culture
create a catalytic dialectical tension among different groups and enter into
community consolidation and problem solving. Group speech operates on
a collective scale with a transformative power that is analogous to that of
the individual subject's access to language in the psychoanalytic process.
In the "talking group" scenes of *Sacrifice* and the other Indian films, the
camerawork, movement, and composition, as well as the cutting, match
the slow give and take of group speech. The camera pans back and forth
over the group, following the dynamic of individual speakers chiming in to
reinforce each other, pausing to give someone else the authority to speak,
or whatever. The process involves the choruses and refrains, repetition
and cadences of group discussion (and incidentally of other time-based art
forms from music to theater). The overall pattern of shot length, sequence
structure, and editing meter often replicates the slow but inexorable group
process: the first confrontation with the crisis is followed by repeated inter-
rogative rhetoric in the first person plural ("How can we leave [the Earth]
our Mother?"); the slowly cemented communal resolution; and an affirmation still in the first-person plural ("If we stood together and fought, we
could get something").

In the sentences at the head of this chapter, Frantz Fanon detailed
a similar evolution of rhetorical modes—from lament to indictment and
then from appeal to command—undergone by the Third World subject
as he or she moves from isolation from the people to alignment with the
people (though of course Fanon's specific concern is the intellectual and
artist, rather than the slum dwellers or fishermen who appear in these films)
(Fanon 1968, 239). The process is not easy, and the "talking group" tropes
reveal the needs for continual repetition and confirmation at each stage. One
wonders to what extent culture-centric criteria entered into the rejection of
Voices from Baliapal, an Indian National Prizewinner, by an efficient Ober-
hausen Festival selection committee on the grounds of its "repetitiveness."[4]

For the historian of the documentary, there is much that is recognizable in the Indian independent films of the eighties. They are reminiscent of
a generation of Northern documentary starting thirty years earlier, when
direct-sound language burst out of the shell of the classical silent (voice-
over) documentary. Thanks to a Nagra or a blimp, the silenced subject
became suddenly empowered with the gift of speech. In such currents as
Quebec direct cinema, U.S. Newsreel's vérité works with urban African
Americans or blue-collar white workers, or women's documentary during
the consciousness-raising phase, one recognizes a similar eagerness of the
disenfranchised to speak out. Though the oral-culture-as-liberation method
periodically gets reenergized, as in such recent pockets of renewal as AIDS

activist video in North America or in the documentary stream of the new
black British cinema and video, in general it fell increasingly into disrepute
in the North in the late seventies and eighties: the method seemed no less
subject than any other to short cuts and standardization, abuses, manipu-
lations, and excesses. "Talking heads" became, often unfairly, a cliché
and synonym for an aesthetic rut of static framing and visual monotony;
the ideal of "letting people speak"—"*donner la parole*"—became matter
for parody (such as in Claudia Weill's denigration of documentary in the
recent Canadian "talking heads" feature documentary *Calling the Shots*
as the activity of following people around all day trying to get them to
say what you want to say). For Bill Nichols, the interview film became a
structure in which the authorial voice was disguised or abdicated or both
and in which the filmmaker became a ventriloquist hiding behind carefully
selected charismatic subjects (1985).

Such criticism of the abuses of a method, however valid, hardly
negates its undeniable and continuing achievements. For example, a
filmmaker like Sophie Bissonnette achieves through scrupulous research
and conscientious consent protocols a workable negotiation of ethical
and political accountability. An author's voice can encounter in authentic
ways and perhaps even merge with the (collective) voices. In Bissonnette's
Quel numéro what number?, comic skits are presented by her telephone
operator subjects to show their working conditions. These skits constitute
a fascinating performative variant of the "talking group" process, while
another "singing group" scene has an infectious ebullience: documentary
brings musical production numbers onto the supermarket floor! Ultimately
Nichols's ideal of self-reflexivity may be a timely summons to an authorial accountability to subjects and audience, but is it not also a culturally
bound aesthetic articulating an individualist ideology of the fetishized
authorial self? In this sense, are not Trinh's collage multilayered voice-over
soundtracks for her two West African films, for all their unsettling origi-
nality in their use of wild sound and commentary, simply new refinements
in a culture-centric silencing of the (post)colonial subject? No wonder such
tactics are absent in India and elsewhere in the Third World. Inflected by
cultures where traditional orality is still wrestling with the weight of print
and media technology, the sixties gospel of emancipatory speech has resur-
faced in a collective idiom. Functioning as a kind of cultural empowerment
with a wide range of political ramifications, the Indian direct cinema
matches the first-person plural of its subjects' dialogue with a model of
first-person plural cinematic discourse.

The overall picture of direct cinema has always been complicated
by the logistic problems raised by the recording and circulation of direct

Bombay Our City (Anand Patwardhan, 1985)

The shelter crisis within an urban megalopolis. Slum dwellers and squatters resist eviction. A matriarch and her family, assembled in front of their erstwhile hut as it is being rebuilt, articulate their experience and determination. In the five shots of this three-minute scene, the woman and her mother-in-law, their voices bolstered by other family members, describe their situation and articulate their defiance to the crew. A handheld camera moves back and forth between the speakers and the objects of their remarks.

WOMAN GARBAGE-PICKER. We work in the garbage dump. I collect hair and make wigs to sell. There was nothing in the village so we came here. If they throw us out now, where can we go? I told them "Break whatever you want. I'll just spread my sari and form a shelter. You'll be wasting your own time." That's my younger brother, that's my mother-in-law, my three children, my nephew, and my husband's brother, who's ill. (Mother-in-law, speaking Tamil in contrast to her daughter-in-law's adopted Hindi, interjects a comment, not translated by the subtitles). She says that if we had our own place at least we could die in peace instead of drying up in the sun.

FILMMAKER. Speak on, Mother.

MOTHER-IN-LAW. They come again and again and take everything away.

FILMMAKER. You're rebuilding at the same site?

WOMAN. Yes, there's no choice.

FILMMAKER. Won't they demolish again?

WOMAN. Let them. We have no alternative. It costs us one rupee for a bucket of water. My husband earns Rs 10 a day and we have a whole family to feed. We need water to drink, bathe, wash clothes—we need soap, oil. On top, the Municipality is after us, and the people here are all cowards. When the authorities come, they run. I'm left standing alone. No one dares speak up. They just run. If we stood together and fought—we could get something. But they start complaining—only after the authorities have left. In front of them no one speaks. You can't fight alone. So yesterday I also sat. My things were destroyed like everyone else's.

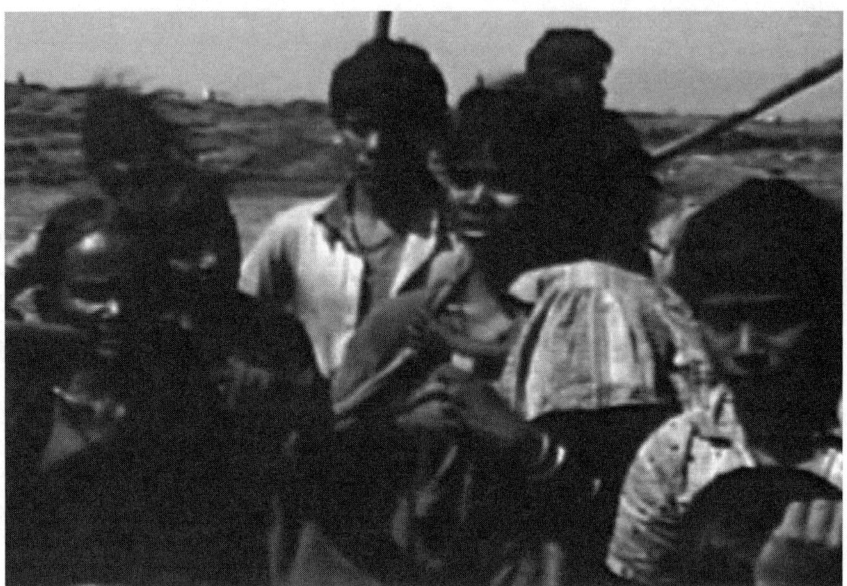

Bombay Our City (Anand Patwardhan, 1985). An extended family group of slum dwellers, represented by its matriarchs, speak of the loss of their home to the municipal wreckers and of their powerlessness.

speech in multilinguistic contexts and is all the more problematical in the semiliterate multilinguistic entities of the Third World. It is no doubt this particular issue that has forced fiction filmmakers from Sembene to Sanjinés to channel their narrative vision through modes of nonverbal communication, from gesture and dance to percussion and song rather than through classical dialogue, and this in cultures where griots, shamans, and folk poets still flourish. (In *Emitai* and *Blood of the Condor*, interestingly enough, the most dialogue-heavy sections present groups discredited by the filmmaker, Sembene's immobilized elders and conscripted colonial troops, and Sanjinés's Peace Corps imperialists speaking missionary Spanish, respectively. Significantly, when Trinh scrutinizes the same multilinguistic geographic region as Sembene, she comes up with the documentary equivalent of Sembene's and Sanjinés's nonverbal language: her tropes of architecture, music, and dance crowd out the culture of speech.)

Coming back to multilingual India, the traditional top-down solution imposed by the federal state's documentary aesthetic was the voice-of-God narration. Easily dubbed in the seventeen or so official state languages, the device had the welcome additional political advantage for Bombay-Delhi bureaucrats of the full discursive control inherent in one-way top-down communication. The Films Division never liked direct cinema. Aside from the problem of the exorbitant costs of the high-ratio shooting intrinsic to the direct method, as well as the inadaptability of the existing 35mm infrastructure, people never said what they were supposed to say. In the most famous case, a 1968 birth control film by P. Arora called *Actual Experience* was made in a direct-cinema idiom that was briefly in vogue by a few Films Divisions directors looking North. The film's purpose was to promote intrauterine contraception devices, but the women speaking in the often stiff interviews all complained about problems and side effects from the device, thus effectively torpedoing the project's goal and causing considerable embarrassment.

Independent documentarists' choice of a direct cinema method does incur a linguistic disadvantage when shown outside of its linguistic territory, regardless of whether the chosen means of translation is subtitling, dubbing, or more likely the improvised solution of live contextual interpreting (in which the live translator enters into the plurivocality of the communications system). But the disadvantage of translation is outweighed by clear political benefits: in addition to the democratic potential of multiple-directional communication, direct cinema counters the centralizing and bureaucratic effect of the Films Division voice-over with the program of regional cultural autonomy symbolized by the state languages and their countless dialects.

▶──────────────────────────────────────

A Note on Gender

Gender also enters this picture (as it always does), both behind and in front of the camera. It may be no accident that all three of my representative films privilege women as social actors; not content with the codes of silent suffering that are omnipresent elsewhere in Third (World) Cinema(s), all present groups of women responding with authority to the crisis and articulating courses of action. (It is no accident either that a women director and codirector are responsible for *Sacrifice* and *Voices*, respectively, nor that women are highly visible behind the camera across the entire sector of independent Indian documentary, regardless of whether a film is about "women's issues.") In any case the high visibility of women confirms their unchallenged and respected role as purveyors of oral culture and as wielders of matriarchal power at least within domestic or semipublic space or within homosocial public space. An exceptional "talking group" shot in yet another film, *Bhopal: Licence to Kill*, has great symbolic impart when a woman subject crosses over in front of male speakers to appropriate the microphone and the frame and to transgress the clearly defined demarcations of women's public territory.

Similar patterns of authorship and subject emerged when I rescreened a dozen or so Northern ethnographic films on Third World subjects as a kind of control group, wondering whether traditional cultures sometimes impose the "talking group" trope on Northern documentarists as a matter of course. I was not surprised that only a very few of the films included "talking group" scenes, and these—disappointingly short for all their memorable impact—suggested that Northern ethnographers rarely catch on to the apparatus's potential sensitivity to the social structure of speech in their subject societies, to the importance of *how* things are said in addition to *what*. Significantly most of these scenes involved women subjects and seem to have been constructed by woman directors or codirectors. One need not ascribe to crude gender essentialism in order to pinpoint the interface of social gender and documentary style in both North and South as a subject for urgent further research.

▶──

Camera Culture

The presence of the "talking group" engages, it goes without saying, a whole complex of cultural attitudes to the camera in the host community, including larger cultural attitudes to representation and self-representation itself. For example, when the peasant and working-class subjects of the Indian independents are isolated in close-up, they are usually awkward and inarticulate (unlike their Euro-American counterparts whom a skilled director can often get to blurt out their deepest feelings). But an Indian group confronting a camera is overtaken by a dynamic energy and an inspired gift of speech, even a pride in facing the camera together. At the same time, formal demonstration scenes, a staple of contestatory cinema in both North and South, are sometimes much stiffer in India where participants become self-conscious about prescribed behaviors like unison chanting and synchronized gestures that contradict deeper-rooted and improvisatory group conventions.

The codes of group discourse in the face of the documentary camera, as in the public arena in general, constitute a basic mechanism for a community to effectively control its own representation: this is the reason why the Indian films almost never reveal the clowning and grandstanding that characterize group scenes in the North (except perhaps by curious children) and one reason (other than the obvious material one) why the Northern code of observational vérité has had a hard time establishing itself. The observational camera provokes a palpable tension as the codes of a public face and prescribed roles of group discourse itch to take over from the unfamiliar, illusion-based discourse of "acting natural" and "don't look at the camera."

It might be assumed that the issues explored here simply arise within any culture at what Susan Sontag calls "the early stages of camera culture." Yet Sontag's analysis of Chinese attitudes to photographic representation is as Eurocentric as it is incomplete, speaking of the "characteristic visual taste of those at the first stage of camera culture, when the image is defined as something that can be stolen from its owner" (Sontag 1978, 171). As an explanation for the Chinese disinclination to capture motion or unguarded moments on film, their compulsion to pose, "camera culture" needs further consideration. For one thing, the metaphorical belief in the danger of having your image stolen is not limited to exotic primitives: judging from the evidence of the camera-shy disenfranchised and homeless crowding onto Sontag's Manhattan backyard or the Montreal police caught without name tags as they bash Mohawks or lesbians and gays or the uptight public relations official at the closing plant in *Roger and Me*—the belief in the symbolic soul-stealing power of the camera would seem to be no less widespread in Sontag's own culture. To put things differently, what is at stake whether for Chinese and Indian social actors (or for our Victorian ancestors having their portrait taken) is not a superstition that the soul is stolen by the camera but the instinctive assumption of the right to reveal one's soul on one's own terms in controlled address of the camera. The impulse to "pose," to control one's photographic representation—including the Northern post-Kodak "posing" of spontaneity—seems crosscultural to say the very least. Working-class subjects usually understand, when caught in a group, that the camera wields political power and expresses economic and cultural difference and that it must be confronted with group solidarity and control over the pose: one of Patwardhan's subjects challenges him in exactly these terms, accusing him in effect of being a poverty tourist. Similarly, in both North and South, poor and powerless groups often identify even the most ragtag camera unit as a network TV crew and consequently as an arbiter of power, either a source of redress to be petitioned or an invasive menace to be chased away. The grandstanding phenomenon in the North, teenyboppers grimacing, waving, or preening into the lens, often involves the powerless and anonymous "performing" power and individuality to the camera, petitioning the camera to confer identity on the alienated self. Caught up in the desperate postmodern cult of spontaneity and acting out the tired inheritance of romantic individualism, our camera culture seems at a rather primitive stage itself.

Is it possible to speculate about how our own social and cultural formation have inflected documentary discourse in the North? If the trope of
the "talking group" has a counterpart in Euro-American documentary, it
is surely the solitary interview, the "talking head." If our "talking head" is
also reflective of social organization, it is surely that organization Williams
called "bourgeois": "an idea of society as a neutral area within which each
individual is free to pursue his own development and his own advantage as
a natural right" (Williams 1958, 325).

The long take, intimate close-up declarations of subjects in direct-
cinema works from *Golden Gloves* to *Roger and Me*, from *Chronique
d'un été* to *Shoah*, are symptomatic of a social ideology organized
around the individual, and what is more, a religiocultural tradition
based on the confession. Politics is privatized and internalized, the self
is fetishized and dramatized. The individual confronts trauma first and
foremost in isolation. If our "talking head" embodies the culminating
point of what Brian Winston has called the Griersonian tradition of
the victim (Winston 1988; see figure on this page, *Roger and Me*), it is
also the key trope of the hybrid interview format pioneered by Emile

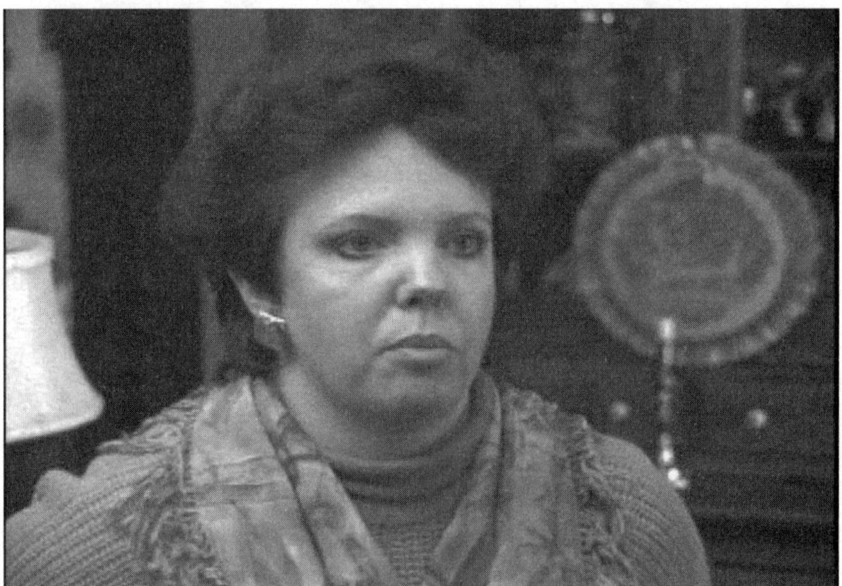

Roger and Me (Michael Moore, 1989). Janet, the desperate Amway cosmetics
"color consultant": in the Northern documentary, the confessional close-up constructs the individual as victim.

de Antonio. In this format, the "talking head" belongs more often than
not to an expert and hence becomes not confessional in its function, but
sacerdotal, administering the sacrament of absolution to the conscience
of the audience, bestowing the authority of scripture on the word of the
author. (See figure on this page, a sacerdotal expert witness, Margaret
Laurence, in *Speaking Our Peace*.)

Groups are often seen but not heard in Northern documentary. Most
often and typically, the group appears (1) in long shot and/or (2) silent,
spied upon, or otherwise disenfranchised. If heard, groups are often constructed through the common newsgathering format of the crowd on the
street, talking into a rotating, director-controlled microphone about something trivial ("How do you feel about the Expos' chances?") or, if about
something serious, in the desired monosyllabic "sound-bites" that tend to
sentimentalize ("Did you all lose everything in the hurricane?") or ridicule
("What are the cultural advantages in Flint Michigan?" [see *Roger and Me*
figure, next page]).

The exceptions prove the rule: Frederick Wiseman's preservation
of communal institutional space throughout his oeuvre usually serves
to accentuate the individual's alienated place within the unit, and that
environment's inherent dynamics of competition, miscommunication,
repression, victimization, or frustration. (Interestingly, the cameramen

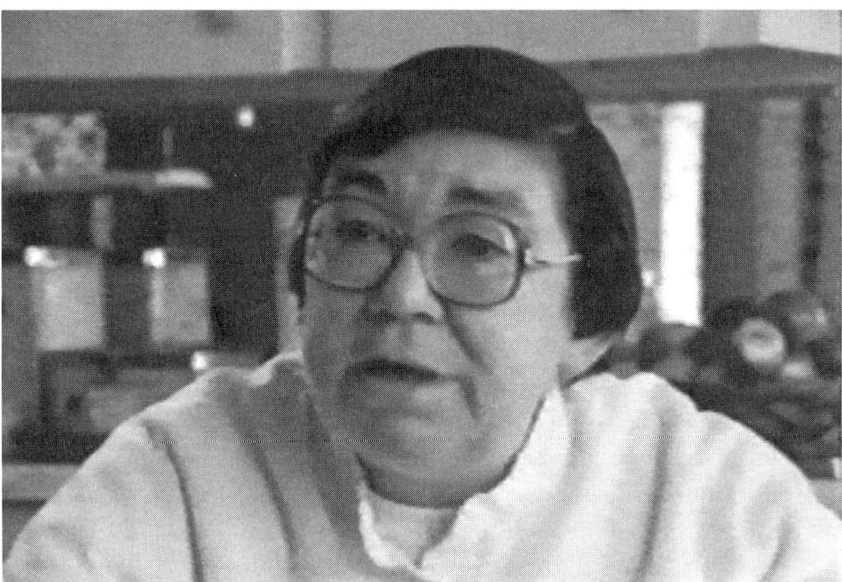

Speaking Our Peace (Terre Nash and Bonnie Sherr Klein, 1985). Famed writer
Margaret Laurence testifying as expert rather than victim: the Northern close-up
can also be sacerdotal.

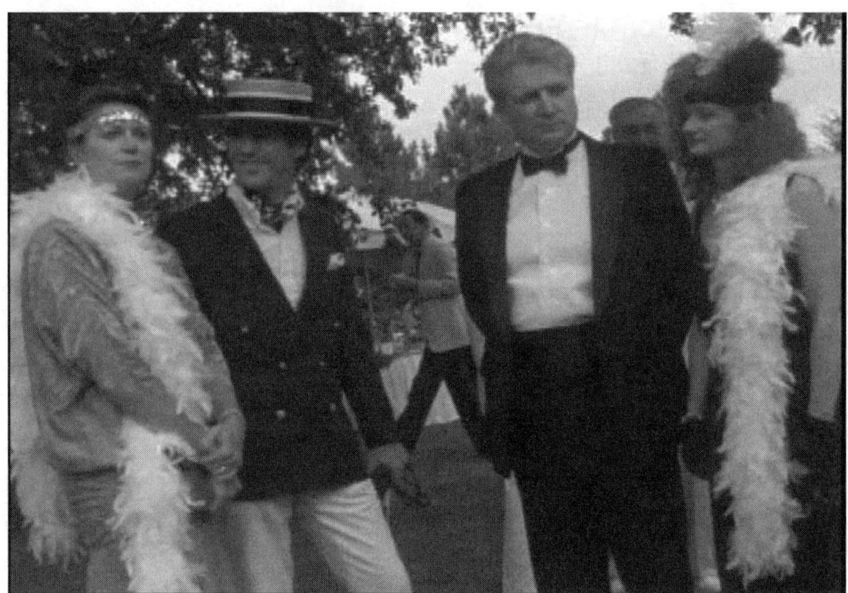

Roger and Me (Michael Moore, 1989). In Northern documentaries, the group is often constructed in a newsgathering crowd-on-the-street format that often ridicules: "What are some of those good aspects of Flint?"

responsible for the extra tight, decontextualizing close-ups of Wiseman's first two films, *Titicut Follies* (1967) and *High School* (1968), were quickly dropped from the director's crew before his habitual cameraman, William Brayne, with an eye for the individual's surroundings, came on board.)

As important further exception can be located in the radical documentary where the project of collective enfranchisement is consciously applied to cinematographic practice, most notably and consistently in women's documentary. Here, as has been noted by Julia Lesage, the principle of the consciousness-raising group is translated into documentary structure (Lesage 1984). But even in the films where this works best, as in JoAnn Elam's *Rape*, the group affiliation seems to lack an organic basis, or at least the group formation is the precarious work of the film rather than its premise, that is, constructed through, rather than "revealed by," the cinematic process (literally through the visionary device of passing the camera around the circle). The end result differs sharply from the "talking group" trope in that there is no direct address of the camera and the artificial rules of observational illusion are maintained. (This is not to mention *Rape*'s protocol of processed video image necessary to preserve anonymity for the speakers, a protocol that incidentally never occurs to Northerners shooting in the South.) In general, whatever group sensibility is affirmed in Euro-American documentary is often all too tenuous, even in women's and left cinema, with directors ever ready to yank a subject out of the collective context and to crank in for some close-up "talking head" intimacy.

Another interesting Northern experiment with talking groups is Godard/Gorin's perversely memorable sequence in *British Sounds* (1969): a group discussion by unionized auto workers about capitalism and piecework monitored by a mobile camera that in fact alights its one-shot frame everywhere around the group *except* on the speaker whose voice is carried by the lip-sync soundtrack. Godard is self-reflexively deconstructing the whole institution of sync-sound, and the alienated relationship of the individual one-shot to the group voice is interrogated in the process. Who cares if the content of the discussion is lost in the process? Elsewhere in the film, the one scene where a syntax of direct-sound group speech is respected, the scene where the militant students are dreaming up alternative revolutionary lyrics to Beatles' songs, is a cunning sendup.

The clash between the cultural foundation of "talking head" and "talking group" becomes symptomatically visible when Northern cinematographers look at the Third World. One of the three aforementioned Indian directors mentioned told me about his or her tour of the NFB where he or she had been shown rushes shot by an eminent Canadian cinematographer for a film on popular music in a Third World society. Various scenes had unfolded before the camera according to the "talking group" structure, but the rushes revealed that the Canadian cinematographer had consistently and unwittingly singled out speaking individuals within the frame, thereby distorting the social weave of the profilmic event.

India Cabaret offers an even more dramatic example, with the hybrid Northernized perspective of its emigrant director and American cameraman cemented through the mechanics of the shot and the structure of the film as a whole. The collective social images of the professional group of women cabaret dancers are the centerpiece of the film, but this primary group identification is repeatedly wrenched apart as a narrative impulse zeroes in on individual "characters"—now on Rekha's life-changing decision to leave the group through marriage (an apparently atypical dénouement for group members) and now on Rosy's staged return to her distant, long-abandoned and still unforgiving family. Interestingly, these shifts from the social grouping of the workplace to the obsolete affiliation with the (oddly occidental) nuclear family are replicated with the male customer group of the film. From this collective grouping of leering and jovial customers as well, the filmmakers separate a likely candidate and drive him home to his wife, driving home the vivid though somewhat facile theme of private family ideology contradicting public sexual entertainment.

One wonders to what extent Northern ethnographers filming preindustrial or "modernizing" cultures are guilty of similar impositions on their subject communities through the unwitting deployment of individualized cinematic syntaxes. I have already referred to my random group of direct-sound ethnographic films from the seventies and eighties, examined as a control sample, exploring from an outsider's objective and scientific perspective cultural formations within societies from Amazonia to West Africa: of these only a few showed scenes approaching the structure of the "talking group," though most employed observational vérité and "talking head" interviews. The few films that did incorporate the "talking group" did so only in incidental fragments that predictably stood out with great vividness and authenticity from the continuum of the films. Granada TV's *Asante Market Women* (1982) employed the largest number of "talking group" formations, in which speech bubbled up from every corner of the frame (determined, incidentally, by a pecking order that hardly corresponded to Gabriel's nonhierarchical ideal). The filmmakers clearly recognized the special power of a *"singing group"* scene, for they chose this as a privileged concluding episode in which the market vendors sing their product theme song. In this respect, I find myself wondering what Trinh would have done with sync sound in *Reassemblage* and *Naked Spaces: Living Is Round:* would she have had to name-drop Heidegger on the soundtrack had the image fragments of architecture, dance, and song been mortared by a fourth layer of speech? Would her long-shot silhouettes lingering in aestheticized space, her idealized vision of prelapsarian communities untouched by buses, cigarettes, plastic, and Coca-Cola have been so prevalent if the sync microphone had been part of her cinematic apparatus?

In the North, as I have intimated, the close-up has a kinship with the ritual of confession, with the filmmaker (or expert witness) as confessor. An individual is isolated and constructed as victim and his or her confession is expressed through the codes of (illusory) intimacy. In India and elsewhere in the South, where religious rituals are collective, not the solitary confession but the group *darshan*,[5] the close-up "talking head" is still present but has a specific and different function. Here, the "talking head" is usually a marker of material status rather than of spiritual or ideological role. The one-shot subject is usually shown having control over space, more clearly articulated through greater camera range and frontal compositions than in Northern conventions. A characteristic Indian locale is the chair set out on the lawn, which is perhaps the ultimate marker of privilege with its occupation of unproductive and purely decorative land. Individual control over space is usually synonymous with middle-class authority, and other favorite conventions say it all: of the bureaucrat seated behind a distancing desk, of the shopkeeper enthroned idly in front of his wares (both bureaucrat and merchant following the discursive conventions of public spatial power as well as of documentary shorthand). To be sure, one also encounters in Indian documentary, somewhat atypically, the isolated victim in the Western Griersonian sense (with a Northern-trained filmmaker as often as not behind the camera), but the testimony is usually stiff, unnatural, and unproductive.

Not that "stiff" automatically means "unnatural" and "unproductive," but it is the stiffness of the expressive group that can trigger the eloquence of direct address rather than that of the isolated and bewildered individual trapped in front of the lens. The Films Division's Mani Kaul builds his work brilliantly on the "stiff" performative convention of the musical group, facing the camera as frontally as any talking group, suggesting a commonality between Kaul and his independent compatriots that is not immediately apparent. (*Bombay* and *Baliapal* also incorporate performative material in the form of street theater, but this is usually intradiegetic rather than facing the camera so that the interaction of performers and audience is preserved.) On this side of the North-South divide, another excursion by Godard into the domain of the talking group likewise profits from the uncanny cinematic potential of the highly static, stylized, and artificial frontal performance. In *Tout va bien* (1972), a group of strikers' frontally imaged, direct-address songs and slogans are scripted and formal, rather than profiting from the structure of spontaneous collective speech. At the same time Godard has an astute sense of the frame as an index of politics, heightened without a doubt by the stylization: he assigns the boss a talking head, the sellout union bureaucrat a symmetrical three-shot, flunkies behind each shoulder, and the *spontanéiste* strikers an artfully anarchic and crowded frame, with only the designated spokesperson looking right into the lens. A poignant song spoken by a red-lipped worker to her *Monsieur Patron* [Mr. Boss]—the lens—has all the intensity the vérité games of *British Sounds* lacked. Curiously these examples of performative tropes seem to anticipate an emerging North American variation of the direct-address "talking group" trope, the rap documentary.

Tongues United: Let's Rap!

Looking at Indian independent filmmakers reminds us not only that cultural variants determine cinematic forms, even within the "international language" of direct cinema, but also that aesthetics and ethics/politics are inseparable in the (documentary) cinema. Bringing these films into circulation within our culture and analyzing their inflections of a cinematic idiom developed in our backyard, is a means not only of reversing the image flow against the grain of neoimperialism but also of reexamining how we ourselves speak and are spoken to as documentary practitioners, subjects, and consumers.

It is thus not inappropriate to end in this backyard by reflecting on the rap-umentary's resemblance to talking group tropes, both Godard's performative stylizations and the documentary collective utterances of the Bombay slum dwellers and Bay of Bengal fishermen. Take for example the

encouraging recent pair of pedagogically tilted rap performance documentaries, Marlon Riggs's video *Tongues Untied* and Alison Burns's and
Patricia Kearns's film *Let's Rap!* The two works from San Francisco and
Montreal's Studio D of the NFB respectively, derive their astonishing vigor
as much from their stylized rendition of the "talking group" as the urgency
of the enfranchisement of voices hitherto seldom heard, black gay men and
marginal/minority young women. Should it be argued that the performative mode is antipathetic to the documentary, it must be countered that
the "direct" has always had its foundation in the performative mode of
speech. Moreover the stylization of rap may well spark the Euro-American
documentary out of its TV-induced coma, in which collective speech has
lost its magic communicative and transformative power. We have to learn
to speak and listen together again. Should Riggs's and Studio D's "post
documentary" reliance on dramatization and scripting as a conduit for
improvisation be seen as symptomatic of the global simulacrum where
documentary methods and codes of truth value are irrelevant, and where
group formations and words of command are meaningless, so be it: there
are lots of other rough youthful documentaries out there, North and
South, video and film—who haven't heard the news yet either.

10

Joris Ivens and the Legacy of Committed Documentary (1999)

*This article was developed as a keynote address for a 1998 confer-
ence celebrating the centenary of Joris Ivens held in Nijmegen,
the inland Dutch city where the documentarist was born. Ivens
had been my doctoral dissertation topic in the late seventies, and
ever since his death in 1989, I had been awaiting an opportunity
to publish my dissertation. In my mind it had dated hardly at all
(and this conference confirmed as much) and was only awaiting the
DVD release of his works in order to find a new life. Meanwhile
this attempt to take stock of Ivens's legacy through the exploration
of idioms he inaugurated and shared with subsequent generations
of activist documentarists provides a felicitous essay with which to
conclude this volume. "Legacy" returns to the transhistorical, transcultural scope with which I opened this book and hopefully offers a
few finishing touches.*

*As usual, my keynote address format, stuffed with clips, trans-
lated awkwardly to the printed page, but as with all the chapters of
this book the reader is summoned to track down the original works
wherever possible in order to adjudicate my arguments, which as
usual deploy textual analysis as a point of departure. In the meantime
I hope that a few illustrative film stills will fill in the gaps. My parting
challenge to Ivens's estate to get moving and release his work to his
rightful heirs bore only partial fruit. The much delayed but fastidi-
ously and richly produced DVD box set in 2008 offered unfortunately
a partial selection of the oeuvre (some would say the noninclusion of
the entire Soviet-bloc period and much of the* How Yukong Moved the
Mountain *series from the package constitutes censorship, but logistics,*

funding, and rights issues have no doubt hampered the effort). Still with twenty films now available, one can now really talk of a "legacy" and hope for the release of the remaining thirty or more.

As a teacher of film history, I believe in always starting with the moving image. I did so in Nijmegen, and here I shall try to replicate this cinematic departure point with the following brief descriptions of the film and excerpts I showed (in chronological order):

- *Misère au Borinage* (Joris Ivens and Henri Storck, Belgium, 1933). Striking Borin miners dramatize for the camera an earlier solidarity procession, complete with a portrait of Marx at the head. Supporters line the route fists upraised. But the fictional march turns into a real one, and police are shown cycling to the scene to restore "order."
- *Indonesia Calling* (Joris Ivens, Australia, 1946). This film, one of several of Ivens's masterworks to be virtually inaccessible (myself not having seen it in almost twenty years), also resorts to dramatization, thanks to the politics and economics of its semiclandestine context. This resilient story of Australian labor militants backing

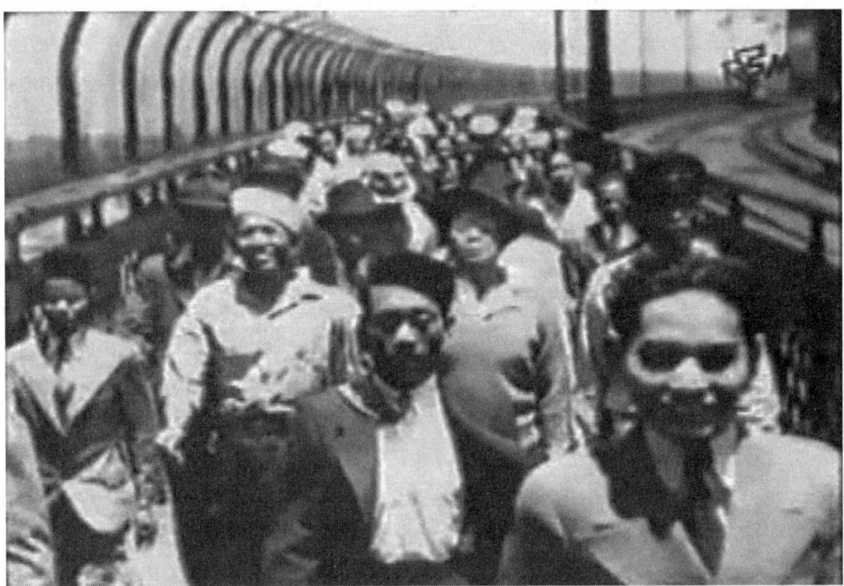

Indonesia Calling (Joris Ivens, 1946). A zero budget and forties technology mean dramatized sit-downs and marches, including this rousing climactic march over the harbor bridge.

up the effort of Indonesian nationalists to defend their newly independent homeland is full of oratory and city- and harborscapes and above all dramatized anecdotes of sit-downs and demonstrations. It culminates in the rousing march over the Sydney harbor bridge that rhetorically unites all the national contingents in this tale of international solidarity.

- *Le Joli mois de mai (C'est la révolution Papa)* (Ateliers de recherches cinématographiques, France, 1968). The Left Bank is surging with a flood of protesting students, intellectuals, and workers, flaunting banners and slogans and confronting the police. Handheld cameras capture the demonstrations, battles, and pursuits, from the center of the action with images often jostled or blurred.
- *Doctors, Liars, and Women: AIDS Activists Say No to Cosmo* (Jean Carlomusto and collective, 1988, USA) A handheld video camera records a demonstration of angry ACT UP women before the New York head office of *Cosmopolitan* magazine, which has just run an article falsely reassuring their women readers about HIV transmission risks. They then invade TV talk shows and confront both the article's author and a media hierarchy that silences "nonexpert" (i.e., women's) voices.

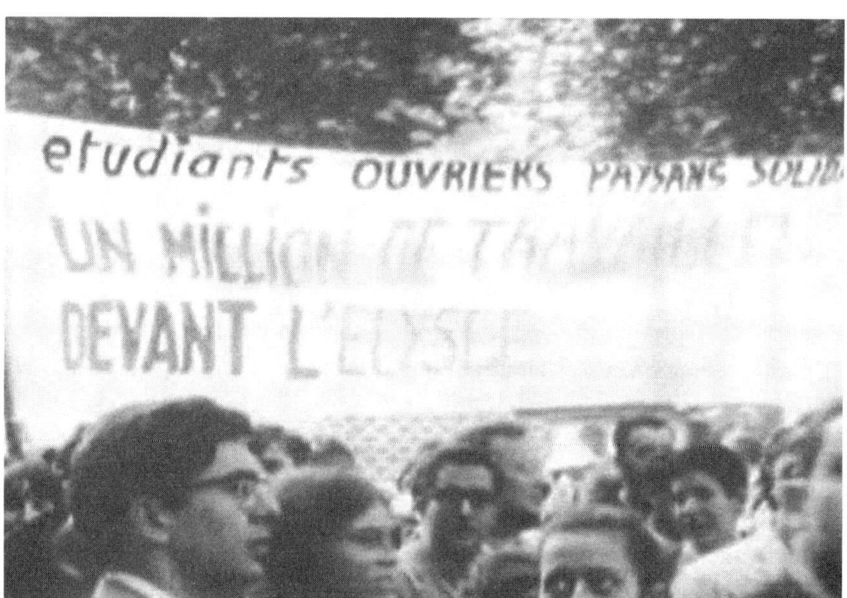

Le Joli mois de mai (C'est la révolution, Papa) (Ateliers de recherches cinématographiques, 1968). May '68: handheld 16mm cameras capture the surge of student and worker demonstrators and their clashes with police.

- *A Narmada Diary* (Anand Patwardhan and Simantini Dhuru, India, 1995). Demonstrators whose ancestral villages are threatened by the Narmada Dam superproject, financed by the World Bank, demand a meeting with the World Bank president, who is attending a fashion show in Bombay's luxurious Taj Mahal hotel and thus refuses to meet them. The villagers and camera both invade the fashion show.
- *A Place Called Chiapas* (Nettie Wild, 1998, Canada). The camera crew follows a group of unarmed Mayan refugees who have returned in a group to their original village, now occupied by paramilitary thugs. Only the camera presence prevents this public confrontation from escalating into a massacre, and the peasants are allowed (temporary?) access to their homes.

Judging from this film and these five film excerpts from six different countries and dating from the thirties, forties, sixties, eighties, and the nineties, one would think that there is nothing new in the realm of the committed documentary. And indeed there hardly is. At least that is what I shall try to argue based on the astonishing symmetry and assonance, both textual and contextual, of these sequences produced over almost seven decades. These clips may well reflect the radical disjunctures in the political and cultural history of the century and the evolving agendas and constituencies of the Left, but they testify also (selectively excerpted I admit) to the remarkable continuity in the textual and political strategies of artists intervening in that history, artists making documentaries to change the world.

If for me this sounds like a familiar tune, it is because I made a similar argument fifteen years ago when I produced an anthology on the militant or committed documentary film, called *"Show Us Life": Toward a History and Aesthetics of the Committed Documentary*, published in 1984 (see chapter 1). But before proceeding, certain misunderstandings that arose in the original discussion period in Nijmegen impel me to clarify my use of the term "committed" (originally inspired by the French "engagé"), as well as the basic assumptions underlying this committed paper about committed documentary in honor of the centenary of a committed filmmaker. By "committed" I am referring to activist cultural interventions on the Left, situated along the continuum that that ideological label evokes. "Committed" documentary has its own continuous and autonomous history of more than eighty years in the cinema, as well as its own recognizable repertory—iconographical, aesthetic, ethical, tactical, and technical. I dispute the possible insinuation offered in the Nijmegen discussion that propaganda is propaganda, Right or Left, and have demonstrated in the past (Waugh 1981, esp. 290–301, 338–52) the Left documentary's distinctiveness in relation to activist documentary on the Right (the latter notion is paradoxical, it could well be argued). This is all the more true since the history of Right documentary has, until recently perhaps, been mercifully sporadic and, with a few exceptions, inconsequential. I would be happy to demonstrate how the last decade's AIDS activist video current in the English-speaking world, exemplified above, is distinctive, and substantively so, from the pro-life, antiabortion work mentioned in the discussion, were this not a digression from the task at hand.

"Show Us Life" took stock of the vagaries of the committed tradition over several generations, from founding parents Dziga Vertov and Joris Ivens to Santiago Alvarez and Anand Patwardhan. In my 1984 preface, I undertook to affirm and analyze documentary's continued priority as radical political and cultural discourse and to inventory, historically as well as taxonomically, the forms it had taken since the heady days of the twenties, when Ivens had not yet got his feet wet. My stance was somewhat defensive in the early eighties, for those were of course years of great geopolitical stress, the Reagan Empire engaged in its genocidal war on the Sandinista revolution and its lunatic race in star wars weaponry. In academia itself, the orthodoxies of poststructuralist agnosticism and pseudo-Brechtian formalism added to the stress more than any kind of Reaganite academics, for the current attack on the humanities and the arts in North America was hardly felt yet—or at least not in Canada. As for the 1989 *New Criterion* attack on *"Show Us Life"* in terms of Soviet-style double talk, false consciousness, and the communist "infiltration" of academia—honoring me by unmasking the strange bedfellows Erik Barnouw and Annette Michelson as my coconspirators—this would only arrive much later, laughably the same year as the fall of the Soviet empire of which we were pawns and dupes (Murray-Brown 1989, 21–33).

I masked my defensiveness in 1984 by a cheery celebration of the Central American solidarity films that were then current and avoided dealing with the inescapable fact that we were in a bit of a slump. Outside of Central America, the Latin American front was eerily quiet, and the Cubans seemed to have abandoned a stirring documentary heritage. Elsewhere in the North, the New Left experiment in documentary activism of the late sixties seemed far in the distant past. In fact the legacy of May 1968 militancy had been utterly renounced in France, the country that had once been its crucible. (I discovered this when I asked for permission to reprint one of the essential balance sheets of French militant cinema for my anthology, only to find that what I would sarcastically term in my introduction the "Gallic intellectual ritual of repudiations of all former positions every leap year" had taken its toll on French *cinéma engagé* as well. Guy Hennebelle, once its high priest, couldn't believe he'd once written those things and opined that Marxism was inoperative even on the therapeutic level! [Hennebelle 1983, 168–71].) Thus in the dark years of the early eighties, political documentary once more seemed to converge on the cultural spectrum with the avant-garde, just as Ivens had declared in 1931 at the time of the release of *Philips Radio*, as he was preparing to leave for his second Soviet trip (Ivens 1931; 1933, 171). I was thus able to draw consolation from a vantage point of history that showed this and other cyclical patterns, from that hoary Marxist "certitude," as Ivens put it at the time of *Borinage*, "that a strike is never lost, that even a provisional defeat is only a stage of the struggle and that the struggle continues" (Ivens 1968, 193).

Now fifteen years later, this radical heritage seems slightly less under siege due to the academic publishing boom on documentary (two books on Emile de Antonio, for example), the international flurry of documentary festivals, the stepped-up infusion of European television money into transnational documentary, and the still proliferating video rental market—offering access to our documentary past that earlier practitioners (and myself, the young Ivens researcher of the seventies) would have died for. Yet there are clouds on the horizon: a new world media economy based on super mergers, deregulation, privatization, and the closing down of public space everywhere, as John Hess and Patricia Zimmerman have chillingly described it (Zimmerman and Hess 1997, 10–14), together with the global demoralization of the Left predicated on the alleged death of Marxism and the alleged end of history and often expressed in a postmodern cyborg aestheticism.

My recent experience on the programming committee for an international human rights documentary festival in Montreal[1] has given me an optimistic viewpoint on the matter despite working with a committee of activist filmmakers whose sense of radical film history goes back no further than Barbara Kopple, most totally oblivious to the precedents of Vertov and Ivens, let alone Newsreel and Challenge for Change.[2] The reports of demoralization are premature. I found the sense that, despite everything, there has been an extension of the legacy, however unwitting, by hundreds of eager young documentarists out there, eager to denounce injustice and change the world by the force of their art. The guard has changed, and the new shift is busily reinventing the wheel as zealously as their grandparents had done under the Popular Front and as their parents had done again in the late sixties. Haven't these green-haired multiply pierced young activists heard the news about the end of history? As for the necessity that they reinvent the wheel, no doubt this is a blessing in disguise, for, as Ivens discovered as soon as he started making political films, it is the process rather than the recipe that is the key to a significant political cinema.

This of course is a cyclical view of documentary film history that is nonteleological, noncanonical, and perhaps even nonmaterialist. It is *nonteleological* in the sense that Bill Nichols's evolutionary dynamic (which he warned at Nijmegen should not be taken too reductively as a Darwinian model of documentary evolution but which I affectionately caricature all the same as the expository mode connected to the observational connected to the interactive connected to the reflexive connected to the performative) is reflected in this trajectory not so much as shifting structural cores or discursive consensuses than as optional stylistic or technical veneers on a stable subject-centered ideal and rhetorical constant.

It is *noncanonical* in the sense that—the dead white male names I have evoked notwithstanding—we are talking of a trajectory with few auteurs and fewer masterpieces, and even fewer works available on video. As I stated in 1984, this is a trajectory of anonymous journeywork that meets few criteria of conventional aesthetics:

> Instead of meeting the criteria of durability, abstraction, ambiguity, individualism, uniqueness, formal complexity, deconstructed or redistributed signifiers, novelty, and so on, all in a packageable format, political documentaries provide us with disposability, ephemerality, topicality,

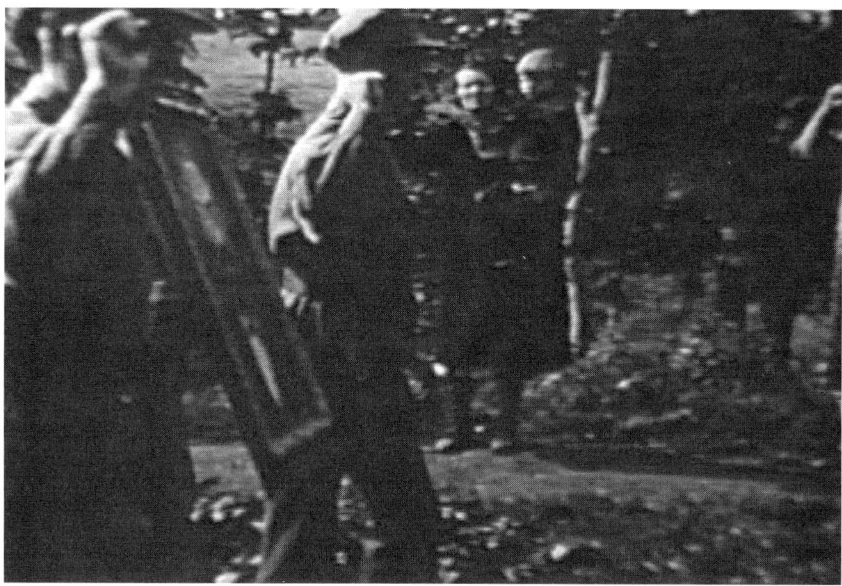

Misère au Borinage (Joris Ivens and Henri Storck, 1933). A staged demonstration becomes real: the public procession celebrating the portrait of Marx (left) sparks raised fists of passersby but also a police clampdown and beatings.

directness, immediacy, instrumentality, didacticism, collective or anonymous authorship, unconventional formats, nonavailability, and ultimately
nonevaluability. (Waugh 1984, xxii; see chapter 1)

In other words the aesthetics of political use-value, as I put it, makes
writing the history of the art form difficult and doubly so in a climate where
graduate students are understandably feeling pressured to write theses on
name-brand documentary auteurs like Frederick Wiseman, Errol Morris,
Trinh T. Minh-ha, and Chris Marker rather than the ephemeral, anonymous
variety that have constituted the common fund of our activist legacy.

It will be already obvious that I chose to show these foregoing five
clips alongside *Indonesia Calling* because they all belong to the generic
"demonstration" trope. They are flirting on the one hand with the deadli-
est, most formulaic cliché of the committed cinema. The demo is the trap
for all bad filmmakers and literal-minded sectarians (as those few of us
fortunate enough one late night at Nijmegen to rescreen Ivens's 1954
demonstration-smothered epic *Lied der Ströme* can attest) and the fodder
for parodic deconstruction and mythic intensification by filmmakers of
every political stripe, from Joyce Wieland to Woody Allen, not to mention
lapsed Leftists from Sidney Lumet and Bernardo Bertolucci to Jean-Luc
Godard himself. Yet on the other hand, these clips show that the demonstration trope is also one of this tradition's most evocative, still fresh as the

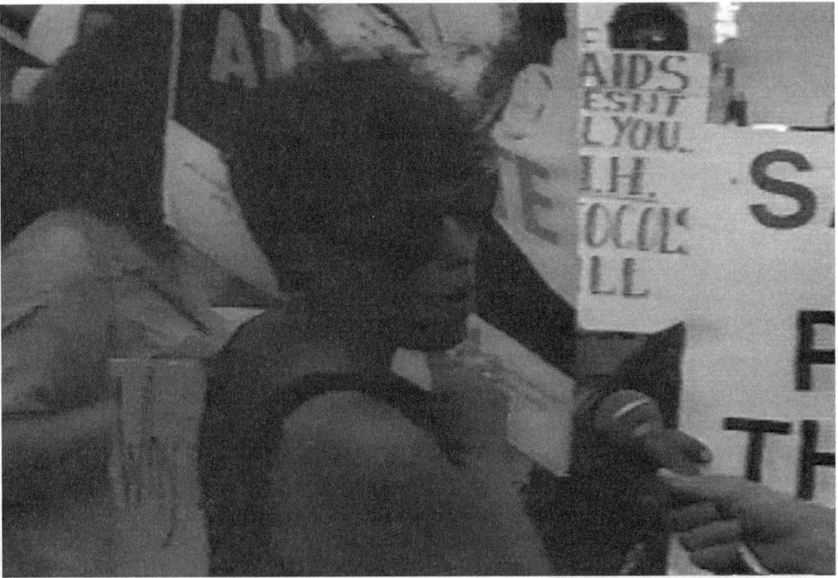

Doctors, Liars, and Women: AIDS Activists Say No to Cosmo (Jean Carlomusto
and collective, 1988). The video-captured march on the women's magazine claims
traditional public geography but also the discursive space of media.

day it was born, lending itself, no matter how formulaic, to an astonishing variety of cultural and ideological gradations and still capable of riveting us to the screen. Indeed, *Indonesia Calling*, a no-budget reconstruction of events from the immediate past, is so fresh fifty-odd years after its production because it seems like one long demonstration trope from beginning to end.

Indeed the demonstration is not only a cinematic trope but a political resource of great transformative power. For all six of these works constitute not only documents of collective actions of public defiance but also performative engagements with those collective actions, active interventions by filmmakers and consequently by spectators into the political worlds of the films. As Ivens had said of his famed demonstration scene in (or rather as his brilliant and unacknowledged ghostwriter Jay Leyda had him say): "We joined the procession with our camera . . . and the people forgot that it was for a film. Spontaneously the whole community gathered, and our staging turned into a real demonstration . . . Thus the whole concept of the film reached a new level, and we felt ashamed to remember that we had originally come here to film facts. Facts became engraved in feelings" (Ivens 1969, 92).

Or, as Jean Carlomusto said on the soundtrack of *Doctors* a half-century later, "I was torn in a way, because, being in the organizing process, I wanted to be part of the demonstration. But when you have a camera in your hand, you have to think about documenting; so part of you has to be cool. And frankly, at that point, I lost my cool . . . So you see a lot of my feet in the rough footage because my hands were up in the air and I was chanting along with everyone else."

In the camera's loss of documentary "cool," the demonstration stops being a shorthand record of dissent and becomes, as in all of these six films, a subject-centered cinematic performance of political action—of a community coming together to support a strike in Wasmes (*Borinage*), of labor and Indonesian activists symbolically staging an anticolonial coalition in Sydney (*Indonesia Calling*), of students and workers confronting the state on the Left Bank (*Joli mois*), of feminist and AIDS activists storming the New York media (*Doctors, Liars and Women*), of rural environmental refugees invading a five-star Bombay hotel to stop a dam (*Narmada Diary*), of Mexican peasants reoccupying their homes and fields (*Chiapas*). Ivens said, "Our staging turned into a real demonstration." But since demonstrations are already by definition staged, he should have said, "Our *staged* staging turned into a real *staging*." "Staging" thus loses the pejorative connotation it once had, in the mouths of *New Criterion* redbaiters and cinéma vérité apostles alike, as the interference with the experiential truth value of a documentary. Instead, "staging" acquires the innuendo of street theater, of political performance, and, by extension since theater is transformed into the real, of performativity in the public political sphere. (Eva Hohenberger's comments at Nijmegen about the different levels of staging and role-play in everyday life are extremely helpful in this regard.)

A demonstration has also to do, by definition, with public space, with territory, since the demonstration occupies the streets where the state stages its authority. The demonstration shows its force and commits ritual speech acts that perform territorial possession and liberation, however temporarily, before the cops come to chase them away or beat them up (as they do in all six films that I have shown, whether off screen as in *Indonesia Calling*, *A Place Called Chiapas*, and *A Narmada Diary*, or on screen as in *Misère au Borinage*; *Le Joli mois de mai*; and *Doctors, Liars, and Women: AIDS Activists Say No to Cosmo*). As I said, the filmic act both performs and represents the demonstration. As performer, the filmic process alters the relations of power. Often, as we have seen, it erects a protective shelter against violence around the demonstration space, or, conversely, it invites the retributive restoration of order. Or else the filmmakers are the *metteurs-en-scène* for the staged demonstration in the first place: in this sense are the women of ACT UP simply imitating Ivens from fifty-five years earlier, with the exception that their territorial claim is not only to geography but also to the discursive space of magazines and talk shows, that is, representation itself? As representer, the filmic process infinitely extends the discursive space of the original demonstration: the original speech act not only proliferates through this magnification but is also changed qualitatively. In *A Place Called Chiapas*, Nettie Wild's voice-over calls the Zapatista revolution she is filming the "first postmodern revolution" because of its shrewd use of the Internet. Perhaps. But the challenges of cinematic discursive space that Ivens already faced in the thirties are still recognizable in Wild's negotiations of cyberspace: for example, the temptations of techno-fetishism and techno-privilege; the commodification of abjection; and the sellouts and trade-offs around personal charisma and collective stakes, short-term, and long-term objectives. Are today's anguished compromises around getting foundation funding or accessing mainstream circuits ultimately any worse than Ivens's old thirties obsession with exactly the same goals, no matter how much the technology and mediascape have been transformed?

The lure of cyberspace notwithstanding, the demonstration is first and foremost about local space and its indexical recording. Wild's Mayan villagers reclaiming their homes know this all too well, looking worriedly

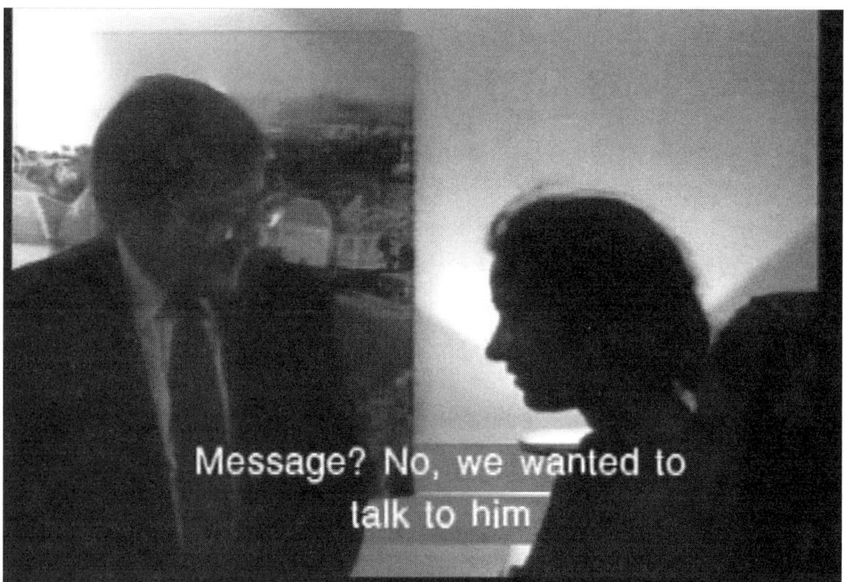

A Narmada Diary (Anand Patwardhan and Simantini Dhuru, 1995). Antidam activist Medha Patkar (right) getting the brush off from a World Bank spokesperson before protesters invade the five-star fashion show where his other World Bank colleagues are hiding.

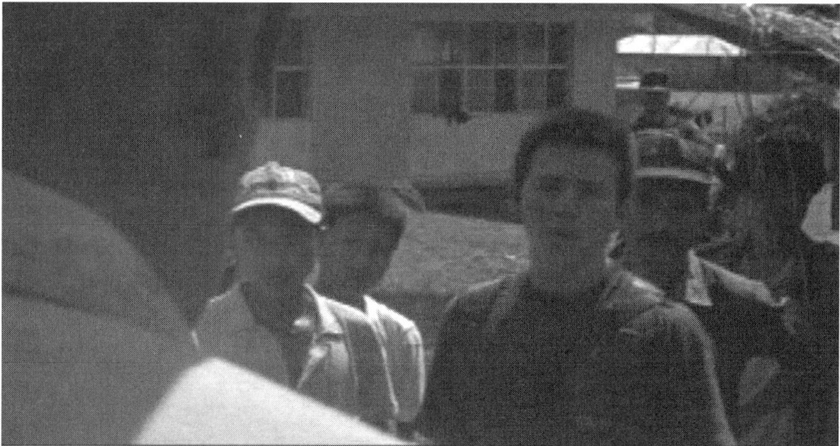

A Place Called Chiapas (Nettie Wild, 1998). Mayan villagers, rear view in foreground, march to reclaim their homes and are confronted by paramilitary goons (facing camera), but the camera forestalls violence.

back at the crew as if to remind them that the cinematic *here* is preceded, for all its postmodernity, by the staking out, penetration, reclaiming, and defense of the historic *here*. Of course film and video in their materiality capture that historic *here* so well—and that is the magic of indexical

audiovisual forms, especially when the operator loses her cool and shows
the texture of the Manhattan sidewalk, Paris paving stones, or Mexican
earth or enacts the blurry kinetics of standing the line, of nervously standing behind the front line, or of strategic flight.

Significantly, in all of my film and video examples, the reclamation of
local space is directed against the nation state, against its agents of occupation. The genre of committed documentary where the nation is synonymous
with revolution, community, or justice, as in Ivens's *Spanish Earth* or Cuban
films or in the Sandinista films I was including in 1984, or the other films
of postcolonial national liberation, has undergone a permanent eclipse
(although the cyclical view of history doesn't allow us to use the word
permanent). The discourse of local space is addressed not nationally but
globally, to transnational discursive space. "Think globally, act locally" may
well be another cliché of the Left, but it is one that these works test and verify. The filmic subjects of the South know this even better than those of the
North. The stormers of the Bombay hotel—and indeed the subjects of that
entire very lively subgenre, the antidam, antidevelopment film that thrives
from China to the Cree territory of Northern Quebec[3]—know full well the
importance of the World Bank and the other planetary webs of corporate
neoliberalism and their role in propping up the national oligarchies' desperate superprojects at the expense of local livelihoods.

I am reminded of the journals of one of Patwardhan's compatriots
and contemporaries, Manjira Datta, who like him, is fiercely committed
to the local as site of projection as well as of politics. (And I shall cite her
screening journals at length to underline the absence of voices from the
South at this centenary of the artist who founded the tradition of third
world anticolonial solidarity films in 1946.) Datta's film *Seeds of Plenty,
Seeds of Sorrow* (1992) dissects the Green Revolution and indicts the
complicity with Intellectual Property Rights that has lined pockets on the
national and corporate level and poisoned lives, communities, and soil on
the local level. The film, internationally financed by the BBC and transnational development money, had a screening on a dark and stormy night in
the South Indian state of Kerala:

> People here have heard about the Rio Earth Summit but did not know
> anything about GATT [General Agreement on Tariffs and Trade], IPR, etc.
> The screening is packed, 200 men, men only. It is held inside a shed under
> some palm trees, the film soundtrack competes with the drumming sound
> of the rain on the tin roof. Despite all this the para-dubbing by Mohan is
> loud and clear. However, towards the end he obviously gets tired and loses
> the thread completely, and misses out some of the critical portion about

global economic demands, etc. The generator starts acting up and the film speed fluctuates but there is hushed silence and total concentration from the audience.

The first question is why the disaster wrought by the Green Revolution isn't shown more visually, graphically. My reply is that, in the areas that I have visited and filmed in, the ill effects of the Green Revolution are just now being discovered by farmers. The film has been made as a warning, it has been made to generate more active discussions.

Somebody clarifies for me what has happened in Kerala re land reform . . .

Someone asks why the local political struggles weren't shown . . . why only development and environment were highlighted: local politics is very important. I replied that when I had made the film, local protests hadn't started so in that sense the film was a bit dated. Yes I agree that local struggles are very important but under the sweeping reforms of the New World Order it has become imperative to understand the strategies and tactics of global politics which are bound to influence local level politics in the future. Politics have to be addressed today at two levels—protests and movements have to be at the global level as well as at the local level. I feel it is about time people in India started talking more and more widely about the connections between development strategies and environmental effects. (Datta 1993)

The resemblances to the discussions Ivens had with his audiences in the Soviet Union in the early thirties are of course striking (Ivens 1969, 58–61): Local issues from elsewhere are filtered through lenses specific to the local reception context, for example housing and the buying power of wages, and on this basis global dialogue and alliances are formed.

In Ivens's day, the global meant the humanity that will be saved by the dictatorship of the proletariat, as the last title of *Borinage* put it. In fact the political discourse of Ivens's work right up to 1968 was shaped by an international context dominated by the institutional Left, specifically by the peripeteias of the international communist movement to which he loyally but discreetly subscribed. This may be explicit only in *Borinage* and the Cold War films among Ivens's entire oeuvre (and then often subliminal or disingenuous), but it is a structuring absence everywhere else. If *Borinage*'s intransigence was dictated by the Comintern's sectarian paranoia of the early thirties and if *Indonesia Calling*'s manic triumphalism was shaped in disavowal by the postwar rout of the communist movement in the West and the Cold War, already under way, my four post-Ivens clips testify to entirely different contexts. If the images of May 1968 are energized by the oedipal revolt against the organized and monolithic Old Left, the images of the last decade are characterized by its utter absence. The disappearance of the relation to "the Party" as a cinematic issue may thus be the single factor that distinguishes Ivens's work most from that of his grandchildren.

"The Party" is over, but, as I have said, there remain surprising constants in the way its grandchildren are articulating the relationships of local space to the global. One important way these are expressed is through the quantum proliferation of networks and constituencies for the documentary committed to radical change as we head for the next century. This is another observation I made in 1984, and *The New Criterion* took great delight in mocking the "ragbag army of malcontents" I listed at that time as the constellation of constituencies to whom the radical documentary was addressed:

> both those working within the framework of the traditional Left and workers' movements and those within the progressive mass movement of the seventies and eighties: the women's movement; minority, antiracist, and national movements; the environmental/antinuke/peace movement; lesbian and gay liberation groups; and other resistance movements enlisting prisoners, consumers, welfare recipients, immigrants, the handicapped, the elderly, the unemployed, and others on down the endless list of those disenfranchised under patriarchal capitalism. (Waugh 1984, xiii; see chapter 1)

Of course the traditional proletariat is still critically at the core of the committed documentary vocation, though their classical embodiments within the cinegenic primary resource industries or manufacturing, as in *Borinage*, are increasingly swallowed by information industries, demoralized, and marginalized as Michael Moore discovered in *Roger and Me* or else displaced to the deregulated and deunionized "free trade" zones of the South. Otherwise the army is still lively and very malcontent indeed, and I would only make some further additions to the list, thanks to the HIV pandemic, the proliferating politics of subjectivity and identity in the North, the intensification of the environmental movement, and exacerbated immiseration in both North and South. Among many urgent new rags in the bag: the infected and the medically destitute; the sexually marginalized; the drugged and psychiatrized; the poisoned, indigenous, and displaced; students and young people without jobs or hopes of jobs; intellectuals and cultural workers, increasingly marginalized and censored; and in the South, rather than the postcolonial *clients* of so-called development as seen in Ivens's *Demain à Nanguila* (1960), its *victims* as seen in the work of Datta and Patwardhan.

Some of these new constituencies have consolidated emerging or reanimated documentary genres such as the autobiographical film and the media deconstruction; new technologies have also reanimated the ideal of subject-produced nonprofessional radical culture that has been around since the agitprop trains of the Soviet Revolution. And if these new genres, constituencies, and technologies have led to the multiplication of potential distribution outlets and formats, none of this has fundamentally altered the structural relations of producer to constituency, the disappearance of centralized Party networks notwithstanding. This is the wheel that the green-haired youths have been constantly reinventing: not the relations of cultural commodification but the specifically subject-centered political relations of analysis and mobilization, of linking local space to global solidarity.

I worried earlier that my sense of film history in this paper might turn out to be a nonmaterialist one, as any panhistoric juxtaposition of images threatens to be. But in fact it is the materiality of subject-centered film distribution, of the relationship of image producer to image receiver, of receiver as producer, that also binds my six instances together, beyond the iconography of the demonstration that I have highlighted. My three excerpted works of the eighties and nineties have deployed a wide range of distribution tactics, from the classical Ivensian models of parallel theatrical release and the local shed-and-generator community screening method, to public television. But most promising may be the video blanket approach shared by the Indian independents and ACT UP alike. This approach consists of blanketing constituency networks, both preexisting and customized according to the issue at hand, with cheap or free copies of the work, on cassette—or increasingly on the Internet. Intellectual Property Rights are the latest weapon of international corporate capital, and it hardly behooves committed filmmakers to play their game. These tapes are made for pirating!

Perhaps this is a fitting note for a conclusion. Upon the centenary of a committed filmmaker whose relevance continues to amaze and inspire, I call on the Ivens estate to profit immediately from the example of ACT UP and the Indians and to reconsider the cautious inertia that has held back the circulation of Ivens's work since his death. The 2008 DVD set is a wonderful first step and I call on the guardians of the hoard to build on it by immediately releasing cheap if not free copies of twenty of Ivens's most immediate political works to the community networks who are his proper constituency and heirs. The young practitioners of committed documentary who are reinventing the wheel deserve full access to the works of this founder of their art form. At one hundred, the youthful Ivens belongs not to the archivists and lawyers but to the green-hairs and the whole ragbag army of malcontents.

Preface

The occasional idea or formulation in this preface developed out of brainstorming with my colleague and research collaborator, video documentarist Liz Miller.

1. This jeremiad arose out of my 2006 attendance at Toronto's chic Hot Docs festival. "Foreword: Documentary, Lies, and Truth," *Nouvelles vues sur le cinéma québécois* 5 (Spring 2006): 1–6, http://www.Cinema-quebecois.net.
2. Among excellent sources on artists' video as documentary are Michael Renov, "Video Confessions," in *Resolutions: Contemporary Video Practices*, Michael Renov, and Erika Suderburg, ed. (Minneapolis: University of Minnesota Press, 1996), 78–101; Catherine Russell, *Experimental Ethnography: The Work of Film in the Age of Video* (Durham, N.C.: Duke University Press, 1999); and Frances Guerin and Roger Hallas, ed., *The Image and the Witness: Trauma, Memory and Visual Culture* (London: Wallflower, 2007).
3. Greg Youmans argues, and I take his interesting point, that this inextricability of "Left" and "queer" of the nineties may not have been as seamless as I retroactively perceive: "The rise of the AIDS pandemic helped to cast a lot of queer work as de facto Left without . . . needing to define any given film's 'social commitment' by the bullet-point criteria . . . put forth in [chapter 1]" (e-mail, April 14, 2008).
4. Jonathan Kahana has inspired this reading of Gaines's conciliatory role between her two confrères Nichols's and Renov's canonical documentary paradigms of sobriety and desire respectively (e-mail, April 19, 2008).
5. I hoped this masturbatory nuance would go undetected, but Jonathan Kahana (e-mail, April 19, 2008) and Ross Higgins, loyal readers, know me too well.

1. Why Documentary Filmmakers Keep Trying to Change the World

1. Genre studies is a useful theoretical framework for the study of documentary, though more properly speaking, documentary is not so much a genre as a genre family that coincides with a distinct mode of filmic and nonfilmic discourse and practice.
2. The concept of "political modernism" originates with Fredric Jameson (1977) and is developed by Sylvia Harvey (1978).
3. I am thinking for example of the Cubans' shift away from self-reflexive works like *The Adventures of Juan Quin Quin* (1967) toward conventional political melodramas like *El Brigadista* of a decade later.

2. Dziga Vertov, 1930s Populism, and *Three Songs of Lenin*

1. The exception is John MacKay's enterprising and thorough article (2006).
2. We were seeing of course the 1970 "restoration" of *Three Songs of Lenin*, released as part of the sixties "Thaw"-era rehabilitation of Vertov that also saw his writings published in 1966. However "provenance" was never on the agenda of our discussions at that time. See MacKay 2006 for a summary of the history of versions of the film.
3. In reediting this piece I remembered that it was at this point that I discovered the Vertov quote that would morph into the title for my first book almost a decade later, *"Show Us Life."*

4. Michelson has continued occasional publications on Vertov, including a major article on *Three Songs of Lenin* ([1987] 1990). The latter reads the film in relation to the tradition of the Russian icon and Freud's theory of mourning and is valuable in terms of the author's awakened interest in affect and, dare I say it, cultural studies. But I continue to find her approach problematical in its selective understanding of the film's textuality as well as its historical and cultural context.

5. For the former, see Honarpisheh (2005) as well as MacKay (2006); for the latter, see my further recycling of seventies research, a forthcoming update and expansion of my 1981 doctoral dissertation on Joris Ivens.

6. Although my original paper offered my own English translation of citations from the French edition of Vertov's writings, for the purpose of this publication I substitute here and hereafter what has become de facto the official English translation of these texts, *Kino-Eye* (Vertov 1984). However, notwithstanding my ignorance of both Russian and Vertov's original texts, I can't squelch my intuitive worry about the linguistic politics of O'Brien's matter-of-fact use of the masculine gender to translate Vertov's apparent inclusive masculine throughout his writings (to refer to artists, workers, viewers, etc.); and similarly of his choice of "folk" to translate *narodnoe tvorchestvo* ("folk creation") and related concepts rather than other more politicized and possibly more accurate options evoking "popular" or "people's cultural expressions," as he puts it in his translator's note, "in the Marxist sense" (p. 183). I have also resisted his and Michelson's 1984 change in the English translation of the title of Vertov's second feature film (1926), and have followed Yuri Tsivian's example in respecting the traditional formulation, *Stride, Soviet!* (2008).

7. Trotsky, as paraphrased in Michelson's introduction to Vertov (1984, xxxiii).

8. My 1975 choice of this formulation is obviously not an uncanny anticipation of postmodern theory, rather an effort to categorize the movement of Vertov, Ivens and many others from the modernist avant-gardes of the twenties toward what I would characterize as populist documentary culture, which Ivens would helpfully also characterize as the "avant-garde" ([1931] 1979, 98–100).

9. See the epigraph to chapter 1 for this citation in full.

10. Joris Ivens's autobiography contains a vivid recollection of such a situation during his stay in the Soviet Union in the early thirties: "An invitation to show my films and to lecture at the club house of the Metro construction workers turned out to have a great influence on my future work. The workers had been in Moscow about two months. An audience of about eight hundred people filled the small auditorium. Although I had seen my films about two hundred times during the tour and wanted to stay outside the hall, I had become aware that it was insulting to an audience not to see the films with them. When the show started, a man in the middle of the audience stood up and began to read the Russian titles aloud—very loud. Surprised, I asked my interpreter what this meant. 'Oh that's all right,' she said, 'you see, about half these people cannot yet read or write so this comrade is reading the titles for his fellow workers'" (1969, 57).

11. Shub's film has recently been "revived" in the West (at the 2007 Visible Evidence Conference in Bochum, Germany) by Michael Chanan, who discovered one of his ancestors therein.

12. I have not had the opportunity to see Vertov's 1937 sound feature *Lullaby*, which began appearing at festivals outside of Russia long after the other major works of the twenties and thirties had become familiar.

3. Bread, Water, Blood, Rifles, Planes

1. *Heart of Spain* apparently used Ivens's outtakes of civilian evacuation from Madrid as well as many of his shots of aerial combat and battle casualties that appeared in *Earth*.

2. Of course the Left was not alone in introducing characterization into documentary film and journalism: from Robert Flaherty to *The March of Time* the strategy was the same, though the former lacked the theory and the latter the principle of the Leftists.

3. Benjamin is of course discussing Brecht's epic theater but elsewhere had the insight to discuss Ivens and Vertov together in similar terms (1936).

4. Acting to Play Oneself

1. The term "social actors" designating "real-life" characters playing their own social roles in nonfiction film and presumably having an extratextual autonomy has been standard in documentary studies since Bill Nichols's influential *Ideology and the Image* (1981).

2. For example, the scope of a 1986 McGill University symposium on docudrama included a range of NFB productions: a TV movie–style fictionalized reconstruction (*Canada's*

Sweetheart: The Saga of Hal C. Banks); an archival compilation interpolated with cabaret-style theatrical sketches (*The Kid Who Couldn't Miss*); several documentaries incorporating fictional episodes (such as *Mourir à tue-tête*, *Le Dernier glacier*, or *Passiflora*); and a scripted fiction feature constructed on improvisational performances by nonprofessional actors (*90 Days*). Cf. the author's "Thunder over the Docudrama: Symposium Highlights NFB's World-Class Role," *Cinema Canada*, no. 128 (March 1986): 26.

3. Julia Lesage has often discussed the importance of consciousness-raising as a deep structure of feminist discourse in documentary, most concentratively in Lesage 1984.

5. Beyond Vérité

1. Michelson's declaration, "I am saying, then, that filmmaking and the theory and criticism of film, must, in their most intense and significant instances, ultimately situate themselves in relation to the work and thinking of these two artists, and I will infer, correlatively, that failure to do so may be seen most indulgently as provincialism, must more exactly be termed unseriousness," (70) led to many debates at grad student potlucks as to whether provincialism was better than unseriousness, what were the criteria for each, and who among us merited each epithet the most—a high camp politics of shame before its time.

2. The allusion is to the now-forgotten paean to the counterculture, Charles A. Reich, *The Greening of America: How the Youth Revolution Is Trying to Make America Livable* (New York: Random House, 1970).

3. The Movement was how insiders referred to the confluence of the antiwar movement and the New Left at its heyday in the late sixties and early seventies.

4. Twenty-first-century readers probably do not need to be reminded that the Symbionese Liberation Army was the Bay Area radical group that kidnapped heiress Patty Hearst in 1974.

5. The allusion here is to Costa-Gavras's *State of Siege*, a political thriller about a U.S. diplomat kidnapped by Uruguayan revolutionaries, which had been released in 1972.

6. The *Village Voice*'s damning words appeared in the "Openings" centerfold of the edition of May 10 (the day after *Underground*'s release) and were then repeated in the consumer guide arts listings of subsequent editions. It was my conviction of the time that the tone of the blurb (signed "FMcD"), and perhaps more significantly the absence of a standard review, effectively killed the career of *Underground* in New York, and consequently elsewhere in the United States.

7. I am indebted to Randolph Lewis (2000) for this information as well as other background facts, 214.

8. Nichols's definition does not have to do with reconstruction and dramatization (1994, 92–106), strictly speaking, but rather refers to relationships between artist and audience and the real. But the fact that the vast majority of his examples of performative documentaries build on dramatization confirms that the common elision between "performativity" and "performance" is a creatively productive one. See chapter 8.

9. De Antonio had of course been visible in the mirror, along with his codirector Mary Lampson and cinematographer Haskell Wexler, throughout *Underground*, but his titular performance and persona in *Mr. Hoover and I* are clearly of a different valence.

6. Sufficient Virtue, Necessary Artistry

1. A total of 63 French-language films and 145 English films are listed in the NFB catalog as of February 2008, but this figure includes several English-versioned French films and French-versioned English films.

2. The following is the official breakdown as of February 2008: 33 French titles are available on DVD and 18 on VHS out of a total of 63, compared to only 30 English titles on DVD and 54 on VHS out of a total of 145. As of 2010, almost fifty titles are available for online streaming at nfb.ca, as a tie-in with the publication of Waugh, Baker, and Winton 2010, but the streaming facility preserves the linguistic "two solitudes" that dogged the original distribution of the corpus.

3. Another American's consideration of the project (Lansing 1990), offers some interesting insights in relation to "the current reappraisal of anthropological knowledge," undermined by the author's inability to distinguish between Labrador and Newfoundland, between Canada and the province of Newfoundland and Labrador, and between film and video.

4. The author and his collaborators ran into this myth yet again in 2007–8 as we were developing a plan for a rerelease package of CFC/SN classics.

5. Now a luxury condo complex on a prime riverside site, Habitat '67, designed by hotshot Israeli architect Moshe Safdie, would thereafter become a symbol more of urban monumentalism and elite consumption than of the populist ideal of affordable housing.

6. Honored by official municipal historians, Saulnier is remembered differently by ecological and community activists, not to mention Quebec nationalists, for his determining role in Montreal's legacy of decimated neighborhoods gashed apart by expressways and paved-over green spaces. Among other things Saulnier called in the federal army to control the city during the "apprehended insurrection" of the October crisis of 1970.

7. The "slumming" dynamic was described to me by an anonymous CFC producer who came in at the end of the program. October 25, 2007.

8. Carrière went on to make one more feature-length SN work *De grâce et d'embarras* (1979) at the tail end of the program, another work confronting the realities of rural Quebec.

9. Other work that had feature fiction "versions" arguably included the Fogo Island series, translated almost two decades later into the bitter nostalgia of Gordon Pinsent's *John and the Missus* in 1987.

10. Akwesasne Chief Mike Mitchell was the de facto director of the film, though Montreal NFB director Mort Ransen was somehow credited as such, and Mitchell also appears onscreen as one of the leaders of the demonstration. Akwesasne is situated at the three-way convergence of Ontario, Quebec, and New York state, straddling the St. Lawrence River.

11. Christina Pochmursky, *Challenge for Change* (National Film Board and the Documentary Channel, Michael Burns, producer, 2006, 55 min.). Apart from the well-earned celebration, the gloomy consensus of the participants—Bonnie Sherr Klein, Dorothy Hénaut, Adam Symansky, George Stoney, Mike Mitchell, Tony Ianzelo, Robert Forget, and Boyce Richardson—that the loss of production funds at the end of the seventies dried up the entire political process that had been sparked is the work's main fodder for reflection.

7. Lesbian and Gay Documentary

1. On an early-eighties issue of the Canadian Broadcasting Corporation's *The Journal*, Troy Perry, head of the Metropolitan Community Church, was invited to debate about AIDS with Jerry Falwell. *Pink Triangles* includes a television clip of a California "moral majority" leader advocating capital punishment for gays.

2. Susan Saxe was a poster woman for U.S. radical lesbian activism in the seventies, having figured on the FBI "most wanted" list for much of the decade and been sentenced to eight years in jail after pleading to a lesser charge in connection with a 1970 bank robbery.

3. For a gay/lesbian perspective of John and Rose Kastner's CBC documentary *Sharing the Secret*, see Waugh and Rock 1981.

4. For an excellent discussion of Hammer's work, see Zita (1981) and Weiss (1981). The same special section on lesbians and film also includes a discussion of the autobiographical work of another well-known lesbian filmmaker, Jan Oxenberg.

5. Edward Jackson provides an account of the dispute in his discussion of *Before Stonewall*, *The Body Politic* (Toronto), no. 108.

6. Until the eighties, Barbara Hammer restricted her films to women's audiences; lifting that restriction has greatly extended dialogue between the lesbian constituency and other oppositional groups. Other lesbian cultural workers, including a well-known Montreal video collective, continue this restrictive practice. Sara Halprin (Barbara Martineau) discusses her exhibition experiences in Halprin (1984). For a profile of Réseau Vidé-Elles, the Montreal group referred to, see Waugh (2006), 496–97.

7. Halprin (1984) discusses the problem of expert testimony.

8. Walking on Tippy Toes

1. I remember not including the "breakthrough" *Word Is Out* (Mariposa, 1977) in "Show Us Life" because I then agreed with ideological criticisms of the film's assimilationist agenda and its soft pedaling of activism and transgression. The lesbian-authored short I included was *Heroes* (Barbara Martineau, now Sara Halprin, 1983).

2. To my knowledge, prior to *Framed Youth* (Lesbian and Gay Youth Video Project, 1983) and *Orientations* (Richard Fung, 1984), the only titles in the corpus by directors or codirectors outside of the white Euro-American demographic mainstream were *Word Is Out* (collective member Andrew Brown, 1977); *Public* (Arthur Dong, 1981); *L'Aspect rose de la chose* (Chi Yan Wong, 1980); and *Susana* (Susana Blaustein, 1980).

3. My notion of performance as self-expressive behavior carried out in awareness of the camera, with either explicit or tacit consent and/or in collaboration with the director, needs to be distinguished from what Nichols calls *virtual performance*, the rich repertory of behavioral expression that constitutes social interaction in real life and is recorded by the documentary camera as an unmistakeable generic marker since its very beginning. Nichols's concept

is apparently derived from sociologist Ervin Goffman's idea of the performance of self in everyday life (Nichols 1991, 122).

4. Although Butler later disavows the "reduction of performativity to performance" and Sedgwick's reading of the centrality of drag as metaphor and paradigm in *Gender Trouble*, Butler seems to leave the options open by using terms like "mime," "theatricality of gender," "hyperbolic gesture," and "acting out" (Butler 1993, 17–32).

5. Throughout this chapter I use the politically incorrect first person plural to evoke the experience I lived as a (colonized Canadian) member of the heterogeneous (and no doubt hegemonic) discourse community of North American and European lesbian and gay filmmakers, critics, users, and specialized documentary audiences during the seventies and into the eighties and the nineties.

6. "Zaps" were a characteristic gay lib strategy of public political theater in the early seventies, grafting camp and theatricality onto civil rights tactics like the sit-in, later to be reinvented and perfected by ACT UP–style AIDS activists.

9. "Words of Command"

1. The awkward expression "Third (World) Cinema(s)" is used in this essay to avoid the fruitless semantic quibble between "third world cinema" and "third cinema," both terms having certain usefulness despite their imprecision and the cultural decontextualization they usually imply. Other terms expressing versions of the traditional cultural and political dichotomies, such as the UNESCO-preferred "North" and "South," will also enter my discussion, sometimes where appropriate, sometimes according to whim, and sometimes well ensconced in quotation marks, as a reminder of the still provisional status of the terminology in this rapidly shifting interdisciplinary field. As the dust is still settling, scholars must be all the more vigilant in establishing contexts and distinctions and avoiding the idealizations rampant in the territory without at the same time entirely immobilizing descriptive and generalizing possibilities. Looking at national third (world) "cinemas," one must insist on the local vertical gradations of the entertainment industries, the state-sponsored "art/auteur" cinemas, and the "third" oppositional cinemas; at the same time this must be balanced by a perspective of structural and political analogies between Rio and Bombay, Ecuador and Senegal, ICAIC and the Shanghai Film Studio, Montreal's Alanis Obomsawin and Manila's Nick DeoCampo, and this can surely be done without mystifying obvious cultural and political particularities of each context. Even cross-cultural auteur canons have their place, if only because the marketplace in which we all have to work is most responsive to them, even though we can surely do better than Willemen's masculinizing pantheon of "masters" in *Questions of Third Cinema* (Willemen 1989). As for the critical neglect of third world documentary, Julianne Burton's new anthology on *The Social Documentary in Latin America* (1990) promises to fill in some of the gaps, taking over from the seven articles in my own anthology *"Show Us Life,"* which previously seemed to be the most systematic tour of the field (Waugh 1984).

2. Barnouw and Krishnaswamy's account of this contradictory and anomalous situation is the most accessible of several (1980).

3. As this volume was being submitted in 2008, Anand Patwardhan's nth suit against Doordarshan prevailed at the appeal level and his prizewinning *War and Peace* (2001) hit the airwaves.

4. Another German festival, Mannheim, made up in 1990 for this lapse by awarding a prize to Anand Patwardhan's *In Memory of Friends*, a work on the Punjab crisis that, true to form, includes a requisite number of "talking group" scenes.

5. In Hindi, this literally means "seeing" but more loosely means "unveiling," "revelation," or "presence."

10. Joris Ivens and the Legacy of Committed Documentary

1. Les Rencontres Internationales du Documentaire de Montréal, December 2–6, 1998, became an annual festival.

2. Two production operations that epitomize the activist documentary aspirations of the North American New Left of the late sixties, in the United States and Canada (the National Film Board), respectively (see chapter 6).

3. Two superb non-Indian examples I have in mind are *The Damned* (Lee de Bock, Belgium, 1998, on China's Three Gorges project) and Magnus Isacsson's and Glen Salzman's *Power* (Canada, 1997, on the Great Whale project in Northern Quebec).

Filmography

À bientôt j'espère (See you soon I hope), Chris Marker, France, 1968
Acadiens de la dispersion, Les (The Acadians of the Dispersion), Léonard Forest (National Film Board (NFB)), Canada, 1968
Actual Experience, P. Arora, India, 1968
All My Babies, George Stoney, U.S., 1953
America Is Hard to See, Emile de Antonio, U.S., 1970
American Family, An (TV series), Alan Raymond and Susan Raymond, U.S., 1973
American Revolution Two, Howard Alk, U.S., 1969
Antonia: A Portrait of the Woman, Jill Godmilow, U.S., 1974
Army of Lovers (Revolt of the Perverts) (Armee der Liebenden oder Revolte der Perversen), Rosa von Praunheim, West Germany, 1978
Asante Market Women (TV), Claudia Milne, UK, 1982
Aspect rose de la chose, L' (The pink side of things), Chi Yan Wong, France, 1980
Atlanta Child Murders, The (TV miniseries), John Erman, U.S., 1985
Atomic Café, The, Jayne Loader, Pierce Rafferty, and Kevin Rafferty, U.S., 1982
Attica, Cinda Firestone, U.S., 1974
Au chic resto pop, Tahani Rached (NFB), Canada, 1990
Audience, Barbara Hammer, U.S., 1982
Aventuras de Juan Quin Quin, Las (The Adventures of Juan Quin Quin) Julio García Espinosa, Cuba, 1967
Backbreaking Leaf, The (Candid Eye series), Terence Macartney-Filgate (NFB), Canada, 1959
Banks and the Poor (TV), Morton Silverstein, U.S., 1970
Batalla de Chile (The Battle of Chile) Patricio Guzman, Cuba/Chile/France, 1975
Before Stonewall: The Making of a Gay and Lesbian Community, Greta Schiller and Robert Rosenberg, U.S., 1985
Best Boy, Ira Wohl, U.S., 1980
Bethune, Donald Brittain (NFB), Canada, 1964
Bhopal: Beyond Genocide, Suhasini Mulay and Tapan Bose, India, 1986
Bhopal: Licence to Kill, Shoba Sadogopan, Reena Mohan and Ranjan Palit, India, 1986
Bigger Splash, A, Jack Hazan, UK, 1974
Black Panther, San Francisco Newsreel, U.S., 1969
Blackstar: Autobiography of a Close Friend, Tom Joslin, U.S., 1977
Blockade, William Dieterle, U.S., 1938
Blood of the Condor (Yawar Mallku), Jorge Sanjinés, Bolivia, 1969
Bombay, Our City, Anand Patwardhan, India, 1985
Bowling for Columbine, Michael Moore, U.S., 2002
Breaking the Silence, Melanie Chait, UK, 1984
Brigadista, El (The Teacher), Octavio Cortázar, Cuba, 1977
Bright Eyes, Stuart Marshall, UK, 1987
British Sounds, Jean-Luc Godard and Jean-Henri Roger, UK, 1969
Burroughs, Howard Brookner, U.S., 1983
Caffé Italia Montréal, Paul Tana, Canada, 1985
Calling the Shots, Janis Cole and Holly Dale, Canada, 1988

Chapaev, Georgi Vasilyev and Sergei Vasilyev, USSR, 1934

Chelsea Girls, Paul Morrissey and Andy Warhol, U.S., 1966

Chez nous c'est chez nous (Our home is our home), Marcel Carrière (NFB), Canada, 1972

Chicken Ranch, Nick Broomfield, U.S., 1982

Childhood of Maxim Gorky (*Detstvo Gorkogo*), Mark Donskoy, USSR, 1938

Choosing Children, Debra Chasnoff and Kim Klausner, U.S., 1984

Chronique d'un été (*Chronicle of a Summer*), Edgar Morin and Jean Rouch, France, 1961

City Centre and Pedestrians, Michel Régnier (NFB), Canada, 1974

Comedienne, Katherine Matheson, U.S., 1983

Comedy in Six Unnatural Acts, Jan Oxenberg, U.S., 1975

Coming Home, Bill Reid (NFB), Canada, 1973

Confort et l'indifférence, Le (Comfort and Indifference), Denys Arcand, Canada, 1981

Corporation, The, Mark Achbar and Jennifer Abbott, Canada, 2003

Coup pour coup (*Blow for Blow*), Marin Karmitz, France, 1972

Damned, The, Lee de Bock, Belgium, 1998

Dark Circle, Judy Irving, Chris Beaver, Ruth Landy, U.S., 1972

Dark Lullabies, Irene Lilienheim Angelico and Abby Jack Neidik, Canada, 1985

Darwin's Nightmare, Hubert Sauper, Austria, 2004

Daughter Rite, Michelle Citron, U.S., 1978

Day after Trinity, The, Jon Else, U.S., 1981

Days before Christmas, The (Candid Eye series), Terence Macartney-Filgate, Stanley Jackson, and
 Wolf Koenig (NFB), Canada, 1958

Demain à Nanguila (Tomorrow in Nanguila), Joris Ivens, France, 1960

Democracy on Trial: The Morgentaler Affair, Paul Cowan (NFB), Canada, 1984

Dernier glacier, Le (*The Last Glacier*), Roger Frappier and Jacques Leduc (NFB), Quebec, 1984

Doctors, Liars, and Women: AIDS Activists Say No to Cosmo, Jean Carlomusto and collective, U.S.,
 1988

Don't Bank on Amerika, Peter Biskind, U.S., 1970

Double Strength, Barbara Hammer, U.S., 1978

Edvard Munch, Peter Watkins, Norway, 1974

Eleventh Year, The, (*Odinnadtsatyy*), Dziga Vertov, USSR, 1928

Emitai, Ousmane Sembene, Senegal, 1971

Enthusiasm (Symphony of the Donbas) (*Entuziasm: Simfoniya Donbassa*), Dziga Vertov, USSR, 1931

Erotikus, Tom de Simone, 1972

Eye of the Mask, Judith Doyle, Canada, 1985

Eyes of Stone, Nilita Bachani, India, 1989

Face in the Crowd, A, Elia Kazan, U.S., 1957

Far from Poland, Jill Godmilow, U.S., 1984

Finally Got the News, collective, U.S., 1970

Fires Were Started, Humphrey Jennings, UK, 1943

Flow: For Love of Water, Irena Salina, U.S., 2007

Forbidden Love: The Unashamed Stories of Lesbian Lives, Lynn Fernie and Aerlyn Weissman (NFB),
 Canada, 1992

Forest of Bliss, Robert Gardner, U.S., 1986

Four Hundred Million, The, Joris Ivens, U.S., 1938

Frame Up: The Imprisonment of Martin Sostre, Pacific Street Collective, U.S., 1973

Framed Youth, Lesbian and Gay Youth Project, UK, 1983

¡Fuera de aquí! (Get out of here), Jorge Sanjinés, Bolivia, 1977

Gai savoir, Le (*The Joy of Learning*), Jean-Luc Godard, France, 1969

Gandhi, Richard Attenborough, UK and India, 1982

Gay U.S.A., Arthur J. Bressan Jr., U.S., 1978

General Line, The (*Staroye i novoye*), Grigori Aleksandrov and Sergei Eisenstein, USSR, 1929

Gimme Shelter, Albert Maysles and David Maysles, U.S., 1970

Golden Gloves, Gilles Groulx (NFB), Canada, 1961

Greetings from Washington, Lucy Winer, U.S., 1981

Grey Gardens, David and Albert Maysles and Ellen Hovde, U.S., 1976

Grierson, Roger Blais (NFB), Canada, 1973

Haircut, Andy Warhol, U.S., 1964

Halfmoon Files, The, Philipp Scheffner, Germany, 2006

Happy Mother's Day, A, Joyce Chopra and Richard Leacock, U.S.,1963

Harlan County, U.S.A., Barbara Kopple, U.S., 1976

Harvest of Shame, Edward Murrow and Fred W. Friendly, U.S., 1960

Heart of Spain, Herbert Kline and Geza Karpathi, U.S., 1938

Hearts and Minds, Peter Davis, U.S., 1974

Heroes, Sara Halprin (formerly Barbara Martineau), Canada, 1983

High School, Frederick Wiseman, U.S., 1969

Histoire de vent, Une (*A Tale of the Wind*), Joris Ivens, France, 1988

Home Movie, Jan Oxenberg, U.S., 1983

Hookers on Davie, Holly Dale and Janis Cole, Canada, 1984

Hora de los hornos: Notas y testimonios sobre el neocolonialismo, la violencia y la liberación, La (*Hour of the Furnaces*), Octavio Getino and Fernando E. Solanas, Argentina, 1968

House Salad (*Salata Baladi*), Nadia Kamel, Egypt, 2007

Housing Problems, Edgar Anstey and Arthur Elton (John Grierson, producer), UK, 1935

How Yukong Moved the Mountains (*Comment Yukong déplaça les montagnes*) (series), Joris Ivens and Marceline Loridan, France/China, 1976.

Hunger in America, Martin Carr and Peter Davis, U.S., 1968

I Don't Think It's Meant for Us, Kathleen Shannon (NFB), Canada, 1971

I. F. Stone's Weekly, Jerry Bruck, Canada and U.S., 1973

If You Love This Planet, Terre Nash (NFB), Canada, 1982

In Black and White, Michael McGarry, Canada, 1979

In Memory of Friends (*Un Mitron Ki Yaad Pyaari*), Anand Patwardhan, India, 1990

In the Best Interests of the Children, Frances Reid and Elizabeth Stevens, U.S., 1977

In the King of Prussia, Emile de Antonio, U.S., 1982

In the Year of the Pig, Emile de Antonio, U.S., 1968

Inconvenient Truth, An, Al Gore, U.S., 2006

India Cabaret, Mira Nair, India and UK, 1985

Indian Story, An, Suhasini Mulay and Tapan Bose, India, 1981

Indonesia Calling, Joris Ivens, Australia, 1946

Industrial Britain, Arthur Elton and Robert J. Flaherty, UK, 1933

Inside North Vietnam, Felix Greene, U.S., 1967

Interviews with My Lai Veterans, Joseph Strick, U.S., 1971

Introduction to Arnold Schoenberg's Accompaniment to a Cinematic Scene (*Einleitung zu Arnold Schoenbergs Begleotmusik zu einer Lichtspielscene*), Jean-Marie Straub and Danielle Huillet, Germany, 1973

Introduction to the Enemy, Haskell Wexler, U.S., 1974

It Is Not the Homosexual Who Is Perverse, But the Situation in Which He Lives (*Nicht der Homosexuelle ist pervers, sondern die Situation, in der er lebt*), Rosa von Praunheim and Martin Dannecker, Germany, 1971

Jane, Richard Leacock, U.S., 1962

John and the Missus, Gordon Pinsent, Canada, 1987

Joli mois de mai, Le (C'est la révolution Papa) (The merry month of May/It's the revolution, Papa), Ateliers de recherches cinématographiques, France, 1968

Journal inachevé, Un (*Unfinished Diary*), Marilú Mallet, Canada, 1982

Journeys from Berlin/1971, Yvonne Rainer, U.S., UK, and Germany, 1980

Juarez, William Dieterle, U.S., 1939

Kid Who Couldn't Miss, The, Paul Cowan (NFB), Canada, 1982

Kino Pravda (series), Dziga Vertov, USSR, 1922–1925

Kino-Glaz (*Kino Eye*), Dziga Vertov, USSR, 1924

Komsomol: Leaders of Electrification, Esfir Shub, USSR, 1932

Land, The, Robert Flaherty, U.S., 1942

Lavender, Colleen Monahan, U.S., 1972

Leninist Film-Truth (*Kino Pravda No. 21*), Dziga Vertov, USSR, 1925.

Let's Rap! (*Five Feminist Minutes*), Alison Burns and Patricia Kearns (NFB), Canada, 1990

Life and Times of Rosie the Riveter, The, Connie Field, 1980

Life of Emile Zola, The, William Dieterle, U.S., 1937

Little Burgundy, Bonnie Sherr Klein (NFB), Canada, 1969

Loads, Curt McDowell, U.S., 1980

Loin du Vietnam (*Far from Vietnam*), Joris Ivens, William Klein, Claude Lelouch, Agnès Varda, Jean-Luc Godard, Chris Marker, and Alain Resnais, France, 1967

Lonely Boy, Wolf Koenig and Roman Kroitor (NFB), Canada, 1961

Looking for Langston, Isaac Julien, UK, 1988

Louisiana Story, Robert Flaherty, U.S., 1948

Man of Aran, Robert Flaherty, UK, 1934

Man with a Movie Camera (*Chelovek s kino-apparatom*), Dziga Vertov, USSR, 1929

March of the Penguins, Luc Jacquet, France, 2005

Marjoe, Howard Smith and Sarah Kernochan, U.S., 1972

Masculine Mystique, The, John N. Smith and Giles Walker (NFB), Canada, 1984
McGraths at Home and Fishing, Colin Low (NFB), Canada, 1967
Mental Mechanisms (series), NFB, 1947–50
Methadone: An American Way of Dealing, Julia Reichert and Jim Klein, U.S., 1974
Michael, A Gay Son, Bruce Glawson, Canada, 1980
Middletown (series), collective, U.S., 1982
Milestones, John Douglas and Robert Kramer, U.S., 1975
Millhouse: A White Comedy, Emile de Antonio, U.S., 1971
Misère au Borinage (Poverty in the Borinage), Joris Ivens and Henri Storck, Belgium, 1933
Missiles of October, The (TV), Anthony Page, U.S., 1974
Moana, Robert Flaherty, U.S., 1926
Mother Tongue, Derek May (NFB), Canada, 1979
Mourir à Madrid (*To Die in Madrid*), Frédéric Rossif, France, 1963
Moving Pictures, Colin Low (NFB), Canada, 2000
Mr. Hoover and I, Emile de Antonio, U.S., 1989
Murder of Fred Hampton, The, Howard Alk and Mike Gray, U.S., 1971
My Dinner with André, Louis Malle, U.S., 1981
Naked Spaces: Living Is Round, Trinh T. Minh-ha, U.S., 1985
Nanook of the North, Robert Flaherty, Canada/U.S., 1922
Narmada Diary, A, Anand Patwardhan and Simantini Dhuru, India, 1995
Native Land, Leo Hurwitz and Paul Strand (Frontier Films), 1942
Negro Soldier, The, Stuart Heisler, U.S., 1944
Night Mail, Basil Wright and Harry Watt (GPO Film Unit, John Grierson, producer), UK, 1936
Nightcleaners, The, Marc Karlin and James Scott, UK, 1975
Noce est pas finie, La (*The Wedding's Not Over*), Léonard Forest (NFB), Canada, 1971
Northern Lights, John Hanson and Rob Nilsson, U.S., 1978
Not a Love Story: A Film about Pornography, Bonnie Sherr Klein (NFB), Canada, 1981
Not a Pretty Picture, Martha Coolidge, U.S., 1976
Not Crazy Like You Think, Jacqueline Levitin, Canada, 1984
Occupation, Bill Reid (NFB), Canada, 1970
On est au coton, Denys Arcand (NFB), Canada, 1970
One Day in People's Poland, Maciej J. Drygas, Poland, 2005
One-Sixth of the World (*Shestaya chast mira*), Dziga Vertov, USSR, 1926
Orientations, Richard Fung, Canada, 1985
Our Family, K. P. Kayasankar and Anjali Monteiro, India, 2007
P'tite Bourgogne, La (*Little Burgundy*), Maurice Bulbulian (NFB), Canada, 1968
Painters Painting, Emile de Antonio, U.S., 1973
Paris Is Burning, Jennie Livingston, U.S., 1990
Paris qui dort, René Clair, France, 1925
Passiflora, Fernand Bélanger and Dagmar Gueissaz-Teufel (NFB), Canada, 1985
Paul Tomkowicz: Street-Railway Switchman, Roman Kroitor (NFB), Canada, 1954
People of the Cumberland, Elia Kazan, U.S., 1937
People's War, The, John Douglas and Norman Fruchter, U.S., 1970
Pink Triangles, Cambridge Documentary Films, U.S., 1982
Place Called Chiapas, A, Nettie Wild, Canada, 1998
Plow that Broke the Plains, The, Pare Lorentz, U.S., 1936
Point of Order, Emile de Antonio, U.S., 1963
Portrait of Jason, Shirley Clarke, U.S., 1967
Portrait of the Artist—As an Old Lady, Gail Singer (NFB), Canada, 1982
Pour la suite du monde (*For the Ones To Come*), Pierre Perrault (NFB), Canada, 1963
Power and the Land, Joris Ivens, U.S., 1940
Power, Magnus Isacsson and Glen Salzman, Canada, 1997
Primary, Richard Leacock, U.S., 1960
Prince Edward Island Development Plan, Roger Hart (NFB), Canada, 1969
Prostitute, Tony Garnett, UK, 1979
Public, Arthur Dong, U.S., 1980
Pumping Iron II: The Women, George Butler, U.S., 1985
Pumping Iron, Robert Fiore and George Butler, U.S., 1976
Québec-Haïti, Tahani Rached (NFB), Canada, 1985
Queen, The, Frank Simon, U.S., 1968
Quel numéro what number?, Sophie Bissonnette, Canada, 1985
Quiet One, The, Sidney Meyers, U.S., 1949

Race d'ep: Un Siècle d'homosexualité (The Homosexual Century), Lionel Soukaz and Guy Hoc-
   quenghem, France, 1979
Radiant City, Jim Brown and Gary Burns, Canada, 2006
Rape, JoAnn Elam, U.S., 1977
Rate It X, Lucy Winer and Paula de Koenigsberg, U.S., 1985
Reassemblage, Trinh T. Minh-ha, U.S., 1983
Revanche, La (Revenge), Maurice Bulbulian (NFB), Canada, 1974
Richmond Oil Strike, Newsreel, U.S., 1970
Right Candidate for Rosedale, The, Bonnie Sherr Klein (NFB), Canada, 1979
River, The, Pare Lorentz, U.S., 1937
Roger and Me, Michael Moore, U.S., 1989
Rush to Judgment, Emile de Antonio, U.S., 1967
Sacrifice of Babulal Bhuiya, The, Manjira Datta, India, 1989
Saint-Jérôme, Fernand Dansereau (NFB), Canada, 1968
Salesman, Albert and David Maysles, U.S., 1969
San Francisco State on Strike, Newsreel, U.S., 1969
Sans soleil (Sunless), Chris Marker, France, 1983
Sant Tukaram, Vishnupant Govind Damle and Shivram Fatehlal, India, 1936
Sari Red, Pratibha Parmar, UK, 1988
Sea in the Blood, Richard Fung, Canada, 2000
Seeds of Plenty, Seeds of Sorrow, Manjira Datta, India, 1992
Seeing Red: Stories of American Communists, Jim Klein and Julia Reichert, U.S., 1983
Self Health, Catherine Allen, Judy Irola, et al., U.S., 1974
Selling of the Pentagon, The, Peter Davis, U.S., 1971
Seventeen, J. De Mott and J. Kreines, U.S., 1982
Shoah, Claude Lanzmann, France, 1985
Siddheshwari, Mani Kaul, India, 1989
Silent Pioneers, Lucy Winer, U.S., 1984
Silverlake Life: The View from Here, Peter Friedman and Tom Joslin, U.S., 1993
Sixième face du Pentagone, La (The Sixth Face of the Pentagon), Chris Marker, France, 1968
Smattes, Les (The Wise Guys), Jean-Claude Labrecque (NFB), Canada, 1972
Soldier Girls, Nick Bloomfield, Joan Churchill, U.S., 1981
Soleil pas comme ailleurs, Un (A Sun Like Nowhere Else), Leonard Forest (NFB), Canada, 1972
Some American Feminists, Nicole Brossard, Margaret Wescott, and Luce Guilbeault, Canada, NFB,
   1977
Some of Your Best Friends, Kenneth Robinson, U.S., 1971
Sorrow and the Pity, The (Le Chagrin et la pitié), Marcel Ophüls, France, Switzerland, and Germany,
   1969
Spanish Earth, The, Joris Ivens, U.S., 1937
Speaking Our Peace, Terre Nash and Bonnie Sherr Klein (NFB), Canada, 1985
State of Siege, Costa-Gavras, France, 1972
Stop Making Sense, Jonathan Demme, U.S., 1985
Store, The, Frederick Wiseman, U.S., 1983
Story of Louis Pasteur, The, William Dieterle, U.S., 1936
Storytelling, Kay Armatage, Canada, 1984
Strange Victory, Leo Hurwitz, U.S., 1948
Stravinsky, Wolf Koenig and Roman Kroitor (NFB), Canada, 1965
Streetwise, Martin Bell, Mary Ellen Mark, and Cheryl McCall, U.S., 1984
Stride, Soviet! (Shagay, sovet!), Dziga Vertov, USSR, 1926
Striptease, Kay Armatage, Canada, 1980
Sugar Cane Alley (Rue cases nègres), Euzhan Palcy, France and Martinique, 1983
Superdyke Meets Madame X, Barbara Hammer, U.S., 1978
Susana, Susana Blaustein Munoz, Argentina, 1980
Sync Touch, Barbara Hammer, U.S., 1981
Taboo: The Single and the LP, Curt McDowell, U.S., 1980
Tarnation, Jonathan Caouette, U.S., 2003
Taxi zum Klo (Taxi to the Toilet), Frank Ripploh, Germany, 1981
Teorema, Pier Paolo Pasolini, Italy, 1968
That's Where the Action Is, Emile De Antonio, U.S. 1965
Thin Blue Line, The, Errol Morris, U.S., 1988
Things I Cannot Change, The, Tanya Ballantyne Tree (NFB), Canada, 1967
Thousand Days and a Dream, P. Baburaj and C. Saratchandran, India, 2006
Three Songs of Lenin (Tri pesni o Lenine), Dziga Vertov, USSR, 1934

Times of Harvey Milk, The, Richard Schmiechen and Rob Epstein, U.S., 1984
Titicut Follies, Frederick Wiseman, U.S., 1967
Tongues Untied, Marlon Riggs, U.S., 1989
Tout va bien (Everything's All Right), Jean-Luc Godard, France, 1972
Track Two, Harry Sutherland, Gordon Keith, and Jack Lemmon, Canada, 1982
Triumph of the Will (*Triumph des Willens*), Leni Riefenstahl, Germany, 1935
Trop tôt, trop tard (*Too Soon, Too Late*), Jean-Marie Straub and Danièle Huillet, Germany, 1982
Tupamaros, Jan Lindkvist, Uruguay, 1974
Turlute des années dures, La (*The Ballad of Hard Times*), Richard Boutet and Pascal Gélinas, Quebec, 1983
Twentieth Century (TV series), CBS, U.S., 1957–1970
24 (Vingt-quatre) heures ou plus (24 hours or more), Gilles Groulx (NFB), Canada, 1972
Two Laws, Carolyn Strachan, Australia, 1980
Underground, Emile de Antonio, U.S., 1976
Union Maids, Julia Reichert and James Klein, U.S., 1976
Universe, Roman Kroitor and Colin Low (NFB), Canada, 1960
Up against the System, Terence Macartney-Filgate (NFB), Canada, 1969
Vie est à nous, La (*Life is Ours*), Jean Renoir and collective, France, 1936.
View from a Grain of Sand, Neena Samji, U.S., 2006
Voices from Baliapal, Ranjan Palit and Vasudha Joshi, India, 1989
VTR Rosedale, Len Chatwin (NFB), Canada, 1974
VTR St-Jacques (*Opération boule de neige*), Bonnie Sherr Klein (NFB), Canada, 1969
Waiting for Fidel, Michael Rubbo (NFB), Canada, 1974
War and Peace (*Jang aur Aman*), Anand Patwardhan, India, 2001
War at Home, The, Glen Silber and Barry Alexander Brown, U.S., 1979
Warrendale, Allan King, Canada, 1967
Waves of Revolution, Anand Patwardhan, India, 1974
Ways of Seeing, John Berger, UK (BBC), 1972
We All Have Our Reasons, Frances Reid and Elizabeth Stevens, U.S., 1981
What Harvest for the Reaper? (TV), Morton Silverstein, U.S., 1969
What Sex Am I? Lee Grant, U.S., 1984
What You Take for Granted, Michelle Citron, U.S., 1983
When the Mountains Tremble, Pamela Yates and Thomas Sigel, U.S., 1983
Who Happen to Be Gay, Dale Beldin and Mark Krenzien, U.S., 1979
Winds of Fogo, The, Colin Low (NFB), Canada, 1969
Winter Soldier, Fred Aronow, Nancy Baker, et al., U.S., 1972
Witches, Faggots, Dykes, and Poofters, One in Seven Collective/Digby Duncan, Australia, 1979
Wobblies, The, Deborah Shaffer and Stewart Bird, U.S., 1979
Woman's Film, The, Louise Alaimo, Judy Smith, et al., U.S., 1971
Women I Love, Barbara Hammer, U.S., 1976
Woodstock, Michael Wadleigh, U.S., 1970
Word Is Out: Stories of Some of Our Lives, Mariposa Film Collective, U.S., 1978
Year of the Tiger, Deirdre English, Dave Davis, and Steve Talbot, U.S., 1974
You Are on Indian Land, Mort Ransen and Mike Mitchell (NFB), Canada, 1969
Young Mr. Lincoln, John Ford, U.S., 1939
Young Social Worker Speaks Her Mind, A, Terence Macartney-Filgate (NFB), Canada, 1969
Youth of Maxim (*Yunost Maksima*), Grigori Kozintsev and Leonid Trauberg, USSR, 1935

Bibliography

Alexander, William. 1981. *Film on the Left: American Documentary Film from 1931 to 1942*. Princeton, N.J.: Princeton University Press.

Anderson, Elizabeth. 1999. "Studio D's Imagined Community: From Development (1974) to Realignment (1986–1990)." In *Gendering the Nation: Canadian Women's Cinema*, ed. Kay Armatage, Kass Banning, Brenda Longfellow, and Janine Marchessault, 41–61. Toronto: University of Toronto Press.

Armes, Roy. 1987. *Third World Film Making and the West*. Berkeley: University of California Press.

Atwell, Lee. 1978–79. "*Word Is Out* and *Gay U.S.A.*" *Film Quarterly* 22, no. 2: 50–57.

Babuscio, Jack. 1977. "Camp and the Gay Sensibility." In *Gays and Film*, ed. Richard Dyer, 40–57. New York: Zoetrope.

Bakker, Kees, ed. 1999. *Joris Ivens and the Documentary Context*. Amsterdam: Amsterdam University Press.

Barnouw, Erik. 1974. *Documentary: A History of the Nonfiction Film*. New York: Oxford University Press.

Barnouw, Erik, and S. Krishnaswamy. 1980. *Indian Film*. New York: Oxford University Press.

Barsam, Richard Meran. 1992. *Nonfiction Film: A Critical History*. Bloomington: Indiana University Press.

Bazin, André. (1957) 1985. "On the *Politique des Auteurs*." In *Cahiers du Cinéma: The 1950s, Neo-Realism, Hollywood, New Wave*, ed. Jim Hillier, 248–59. Cambridge, Mass.: Harvard University Press.

Benjamin, Walter. (1934) 1973. "The Author as Producer." In *Understanding Brecht*, ed. Stanley Mitchell, 85–104. London: New Left Books.

———. (1936) 1969. "The Work of Art in the Age of Mechanical Reproduction." In *Illuminations*, ed. Hannah Arendt, 217–52. New York: Schocken.

Biskind, Peter, and Marc Weiss. 1975. "The Weather Underground: Take One." *Rolling Stone*, November 6.

Boyle, Deirdre. 1999. "O Canada! George Stoney's Challenge." *Wide Angle* 21, no. 2: 48–59.

Bruzzi, Stella. 2006. *New Documentary*. 2nd ed. New York: Routledge.

Bulbulian, Maurice. (2003) 2006. "Propos recueillis par Diane Cantin et Isabelle Lavoie." *Nouvelles vues sur le cinéma québécois* 5: 1–11. My translation.

Burch, Noël. (1969) 1973. *Theory of Film Practice*. New York: Praeger.

Burch, Noël, and Jorge Dana. 1974. "Propositions." *Afterimage* (UK) 5 (Spring): 40–66.

Burnett, Ron. 1995. "Video Space/Video Time: The Electronic Image and Portable Video." In *Mirror Machine: Video and Identity*, ed. Janine Marchessault, 142–83. Toronto: YYZ Books.

———. 1996. "Video: The Politics of Culture and Community." In *Resolutions: Contemporary Video Practices*, ed. Michael Renov and Erika Suderberg, 283–303. Minneapolis: University of Minnesota Press.

Burton, Julianne. 1985. "Marginal Cinemas and Mainstream Critical Theory." *Screen* 26, no. 3–4: 2–22.

———, ed. 1990. *The Social Documentary in Latin America*. Pittsburgh, Penn.: University of Pittsburgh Press.

Butler, Judith. 1990. *Gender Trouble: Feminism and the Subversion of Identity*. New York: Routledge.

———. 1993. "Critically queer." *GLQ* 1, no. 1: 17–32.

Cahiers du cinéma. 1972. "Préface." In *Dziga Vertov, Articles, journaux, projets,* trans. Sylviane Mossé and Andrée Robel, 7–13. Paris: Inédit Cahiers du cinéma.

Campbell, Russell. 1982. *Cinema Strikes Back: Radical Filmmaking in the United States, 1930–1942.* Ann Arbor, Mich.: UMI Research Press.

Ciment, Michel, and Bernard Cohn. 1970. "Entretien avec Emile de Antonio." *Positif* 113 (February): 28. My translation.

Cinéaste. 1973. "Radical American Film? A Questionnaire." *Cinéaste* 5, no. 4: 15.

Corneil, Marit Kathryn. 2010. "Winds and Things: Towards a Reassessment of the Challenge for Change/Société nouvelle Legacy." In *Challenge for Change: Activist Documentary at the National Film Board of Canada,* ed. Thomas Waugh, Michael Brendan Baker, and Ezra Winton, 389–403. Montreal: McGill-Queen's University Press.

Crowdus, Gary, and Irwin Silber. 1971. "Film in Allende's Chile: An Interview with Miguel Littin." *Cinéaste* 4, no. 4: 7.

Cvetkovich, Ann. 2003. *An Archive of Feelings: Trauma, Sexuality, and Lesbian Public Culture.* Durham, N.C.: Duke University Press.

Dansereau, Fernand. 1977. "Saint-Jérome: The Experience of a Filmmaker as Social Animator." In *Canadian Film Reader,* ed. Seth Feldman and Joyce Nelson, 128–31. Toronto: Peter Martin.

Datta, Manjira. 1993. Unpublished screening diary. Courtesy of the author.

Dick, Ronald. 1986. "Regionalization of a Federal Cultural Institution: The Experience of the National Film Board of Canada 1965–1979." In *Flashback: People and Institutions in Canadian Film History,* ed. Gene Walz, 107–33. Montreal: Film Studies Association of Canada/Mediatexte Publications, Inc.

Downing, John. 1987. *Film & Politics in the Third World.* New York: Autonomedia.

Drobachenko, Sergei. 1966. "Der Sowjetische documentärfilm: Ein historischer abriss." No reference available.

Druick, Zoë. 2007. *Projecting Canada: Government Policy and Documentary Film at the National Film Board.* Montreal: MQUP.

Dyer, Richard. 1990. *Now You See It: Studies on Lesbian and Gay Film.* London: Routledge.

Eisenstein, Sergei M. 1942. *Film Sense.* New York: Harcourt Brace.

Ellis, Jack, and Betsy McLane. 2005. *A New History of Documentary Film.* New York: Continuum.

Epstein, Rob. 1981. "*Word Is Out:* Stories of Working Together." *Jump Cut* 24–25: 9–10.

Evans, Gary. 1991. *In the National Interest: A Chronicle of the National Film Board of Canada from 1949 to 1989.* Toronto: University of Toronto Press.

Fanon, Frantz. (1961) 1968. *The Wretched of the Earth.* New York: Grove.

Feldman. Seth. 1984. "'Cinema Weekly' and 'Cinema Truth': Dziga Vertov and the Leninist Proportion." In *"Show Us Life": Toward a History and Aesthetics of the Committed Documentary,* ed. Thomas Waugh, 3–20. Metuchen, N.J.: Scarecrow.

———. 2007. "Vertov after Manovich." *Canadian Journal of Film Studies* 16, no. 1: 39–50.

Gabriel, Teshome. 1982. *Third Cinema in the Third World: The Aesthetics of Liberation.* Ann Arbor, Mich.: UMI Research Press.

———. 1989. "Towards a Critical Theory of Third World Films." In *Questions of Third Cinema,* ed. Jim Pines and Paul Willemen, 30–52. London: BFI.

Gaines, Jane M. 1996. "The Melos in Marxist Theory." In *The Hidden Foundation: Cinema and the Question of Class,* ed. David E. James and Rick Berg, 56–71. Minneapolis: University of Minnesota Press.

———. 1999. "Political Mimesis." In *Collecting Visible Evidence,* 84–102. Minneapolis: University of Minnesota Press.

———. 2007. "Documentary Radicality." *Canadian Journal of Film Studies* 16, no. 1: 5–24.

Gans, Herbert. 1975. *Popular Culture and High Culture: An Analysis and Evaluation of Taste.* New York: Basic Books.

Gauthier, Guy. (1995) 2002. *Le documentaire: un autre cinéma.* Paris: Nathan.

Gever, Martha, John Greyson, and Pratibha Parmar, eds. 1993. *Queer Looks: Perspectives on Lesbian and Gay Film and Video.* New York: Routledge.

Giddins, Gary. 1968. "Wanted by the FBI [Review of *Mr. Hoover and I*]." *The Village Voice,* April 24, 68.

Goldsmith, David A. 2003. "Interview Bonnie Sherr Klein." In *The Documentary Makers: Interviews with 15 of the Best in the Business,* 64–73. Mies, Switzerland: RotoVision.

Gorky, Maksim. 1946. "Extracts from a Paper Read to the First All-Union Congress of Soviet Writers." In *Literature and Life: A Selection from the Writings of Maxim Gorki.* London: Hutchinson International Authors.

Grierson, John. 1966. *Grierson on Documentary,* ed. Forsythe Hardy. Berkeley: University of California Press.

Gross, Larry, John Katz, and Jay Ruby, eds. 1988. *Image Ethics: The Moral Rights of Subjects in Photographs, Film, and Television*. New York: Oxford University Press.

Guerin, Frances, and Roger Hallas. 2007. *The Image and the Witness: Trauma, Memory, and Visual Culture*. London: Wallflower Press.

Hall, Stuart, and Paddy Whannel. 1965. *The Popular Arts*. New York: Pantheon.

Halprin, Sara (Barbara Halpern Martineau). 1984. "Talking about our Lives and Experiences: Some Thoughts about Feminism, Documentary, and 'Talking Heads'" In *"Show Us Life": Toward a History and Aesthetics of the Committed Documentary*, ed. Thomas Waugh, 252–73. Metuchen, N.J.: Scarecrow Press.

Harvey, Sylvia. 1978. *May '68 and Film Culture*. London: BFI.

Hénaut, Dorothy Todd. 1969. "In the Hands of Citizens: A Video Report (with Bonnie Klein)." *Challenge for Change Newsletter* 4: 2–6.

———. 1991a. "The Challenge for Change/Société Nouvelle Experience." In *Video the Changing World*, ed. Nancy Thede and Alain Ambrosi, 48–53. Montreal: Black Rose Books.

———. 1991b. "Video Stories from the Dawn of Time." *Visual Anthropology Review* 7, no. 2: 85–101.

Hennebelle, Guy. 1984. "French Radical Documentary after May 1968." In *"Show Us Life": Toward a History and Aesthetics of the Committed Documentary*, ed. Thomas Waugh, 168–71. Metuchen, N.J.: Scarecrow.

Honarpisheh, Farbod. 2005. "The Oriental 'Other' in Soviet Cinema, 1929–1934," *Critique: Critical Middle Eastern Studies* 14, no. 2: 185–201.

———. 2006. "*You Are on Indian Land*." In *The Cinema of Canada*, ed. Jerry White, 81–90. London: Wallflower Press.

Hurwitz, Leo. (1934) 1979. "The Revolutionary Film: Next Step." In *The Documentary Tradition* (2nd ed.), ed. Lewis Jacobs, 91–93. New York: Norton.

Ivens, Joris. (1931) 1979. "Quelques réflexions sur les documentaries d'avant-garde." In *Joris Ivens: 50 Years of Film-Making*, ed Rosalind Delmar, 98–100. London: BFI.

———. 1933. "Mijn lezing in Parijs." *Filmliga* 6, no. 6: 171.

———. 1940. "Collaboration in Documentary." *Films* 1, no. 2: 30–42.

———. 1969. *The Camera and I*. New York: International Publishers.

Jameson, Fredric. 1977. "Afterword." In Ernst Bloch, *Aesthetics and Politics*, ed. Ronald Taylor. London: NLB.

———. 1986. "Third-World Literature in the Era of Multinational Capitalism." *Social Text* 15: 65

Johnston, Claire, and Paul Willemen. 1975. "Brecht in Britain: The Independent Political Film (on *The Nightcleaners*)." *Screen* 16, no. 4: 105–18.

Jones, G. B. 1981. *Movies and Memoranda: An Interpretive History of the National Film Board of Canada*. Ottawa: Canadian Film Institute.

Katz, John Stuart, ed. 1978. *Autobiography: Film/Video/Photography*. Toronto: Art Gallery of Ontario.

Kellner, Douglas, and Dan Streible, ed. 2000. *Emile de Antonio: A Reader*. Minneapolis: University of Minnesota Press.

Khouri, Malek, and Darrell Varga, eds. 2006. *Working on Screen: Representations of the Working Class in Canadian Cinema*. Toronto: University of Toronto Press.

Kleinhans, Chuck. 1984. "Forms, Politics, Makers, and Contexts: Basic Issues for a Theory of Radical Political Documentary." In *"Show Us Life": Toward a History and Aesthetics of the Committed Documentary*, ed. Thomas Waugh, 318–42. Metuchen, N.J.: Scarecrow Press.

Kracauer, Siegfried. 1947. "Supplement: Propaganda and the Nazi War Film." In *From Caligari to Hitler*, 275–307. Princeton, N.J.: Princeton University Press.

Kurchak, Marie. (1972) 1977. "What Challenge? What Change?" In *Canadian Film Reader*, ed. Seth Feldman and Joyce Nelson, 120–28. Toronto: Peter Martin.

Lane, Jim. 2002. *The Autobiographical Film in America*. Madison: University of Wisconsin Press.

Lansing, J. Stephen. 1990. "The Decolonization of Ethnographic Film." *SVA Review* 6, no. 1: 13–15.

Lesage, Julia. 1984. "Feminist Documentary: Aesthetics and Politics." In *"Show Us Life": Toward a History and Aesthetics of the Committed Documentary*, ed. Thomas Waugh, 223–51.Metuchen, N.J.: Scarecrow Press.

Lewis, Randolph. 2000. *Emile de Antonio: Radical Filmmaker in Cold War America*. Madison: University of Wisconsin Press.

Leyda, Jay. 1973. *Kino: A History of the Russian and Soviet Film*. New York: Collier.

Lissitzky-Kippers, Sophie, ed. 1968. *El Lissitzky, Life, Letters, Texts*. Greenwich, Conn.: New York Graphic Society.

MacKay, John. 2006. "Allegory and Accommodation: Vertov's *Three Songs of Lenin* (1934) as a Stalinist Film." *Film History* 18 (Spring): 376–91.

MacKenzie, Scott. 2004. *Screening Quebec*. Manchester: Manchester University Press.

Marchessault, Janine. 1995. "Amateur Video and the Challenge for Change." In *Mirror Machine: Video and Identity*, ed. Janine Marchessault, 13–25. Toronto: YYZ Books.

Manovich, Lev. 2001. *The Language of New Media*. Cambridge, Mass.: MIT Press.

Marcorelles, Louis. (1970) 1973. *Living Cinema: New Directions in Contemporary Film-Making*. New York: Praeger.

Marsolais, Gilles. (1974) 1997. *L'Aventure du cinéma direct revisitée*. Laval, Québec: Les 400 Coups.

Maslin, Janet. 1983. "*King of Prussia* with Berrigan Brothers." *New York Times*, February 13, 57.

Michelson, Annette. 1972. "*Man with the Movie Camera*: From Magician to Epistemologist." *Artforum* 10 (March): 60–73.

———. 1973. "Eisenstein, Brakhage." *Artforum* 11 (January): 30–81.

———. (1987) 1990. "The Kinetic Icon and the Work of Mourning: Prolegomena to the Analysis of a Textual System." *October* 52 (Spring): 16–51; Rpt. in *The Red Screen: Politics, Society, Art in Soviet Cinema*, ed. Anna Lawton, 113–31. London: Routledge.

Millard, Peter. 1983. "In Search of Our Own Morality." *The Body Politic* 97 (October): 32–33.

Murray-Brown, Jeremy. 1989. "False Cinema: Vertov and Early Soviet Film." *The New Criterion* 8, no. 3: 21–33.

Newsreel. 1968. "Newsreel: A Montage of Programmatic Comments by Newsreel Filmmakers." *Film Quarterly*, no. 22 (Winter): 45.

Nichols, Bill. 1976. "Documentary Theory and Practice." *Screen* 17, no. 4: 34–48.

———. 1981. *Ideology and the Image: Social Representation in the Cinema and Other Media*. Bloomington: Indiana University Press.

———. 1983. "The Voice of Documentary." *Film Quarterly* 36, no. 3: 17–29.

———. 1991. *Representing Reality*. Bloomington: Indiana University Press.

———. 1994. *Blurred Boundaries: Questions of Meaning in Contemporary Culture*. Bloomington: Indiana University Press.

Noriega, Chon. 1996. "Talking Heads, Body Politic: The Plural Self of Chicano Experimental Video." In *Resolutions: Contemporary Video Practices*, ed. Michael Renov and Erika Suderburg, 206–28. Minneapolis: Minnesota University Press.

Olson, Ray. 1979. "Gay Film Work: Affecting, but too Evasive." *Jump Cut* 20 (May): 9–12.

Patwardhan, Anand. 1984. "The Guerilla Film, Underground and in Exile: A Critique and a Case Study of *Waves of Revolution*." In *Show Us Life*, ed. Thomas Waugh, 444–64. Metuchen, New Jersey: Scarecrow.

Perovic, Lydia. 2007. "A First for Film Studies." *Books in Canada* 36, no. 1: 13–14.

Pevere, Geoff. 1986. "Projections: Assessing Canada's Films of '85." *The Canadian Forum* 65, no. 2: 39.

Plummer, Kenneth. 1995. *Telling Sexual Stories*. New York: Routledge.

Ramirez, John. 1984. "The Sandinista Documentary: A Historical Contextualization." In *Show Us Life*, ed. Thomas Waugh, 465–79. Metuchen, New Jersey: Scarecrow.

Renov, Michael. 1996. "Video Confessions." In *Resolutions: Contemporary Video Practices*, ed. Michael Renov and Erika Suderburg, 78–101. Minneapolis: University of Minnesota Press.

———. 2004. *The Subject of Documentary*. Minneapolis: University of Minnesota Press.

Renov, Michael, and Erika Suderburg, ed. 1996. *Resolutions: Contemporary Video Practices*. Minneapolis: University of Minnesota Press.

Robin, Régine. 1986. *Le Réalisme socialiste: une esthétique impossible*. Paris: Payot.

———. 1992. *Socialist Realism: An Impossible Aesthetic*. Trans. Catherine Porter. San José: Stanford University Press.

Rosenbaum, Jonathan. (1990) 2000. "The Life and File of an Anarchist Filmmaker." In *Emile de Antonio*, ed. Douglas Kellner and Dan Streible, 335–44. Minneapolis: University of Minnesota Press.

Russell, Catherine. 1999. *Experimental Ethnography: The Work of Film in the Age of Video*. Durham, N.C.: Duke University Press.

Russo, Vito. 1981. *The Celluloid Closet: Homosexuality in the Movies*. New York: Harper.

Sadoul, Georges. 1971. *Dziga Vertov*. Paris: Éditions Champ Libre.

Sarris, Andrew. (1967) 1971. "The New York Film Festival." In *Confessions of a Cultist: On the Cinema, 1955/1969*, 314–18. New York: Simon and Schuster.

Sedgwick, Eve Kosofsky. 1993. "Queer Performativity: Henry James' *The Art of the Novel*." *GLQ: A Journal of Lesbian and Gay Studies* 1, no. 1: 1–18.

Seitz, Michael H. (1983) 2000. "Swords into Plowshares," *The Progressive* (Madison, Wisc., April); Rpt. in *Emile de Antonio: A Reader*, ed. Douglas Kellner and Dan Streible, 319–22. Minneapolis: Minnesota University Press.

Sheldon, Caroline. 1977. "Lesbians and Film: Some Thoughts." In *Gays and Film*, ed. Richard Dyer, 5–26. London: BFI.

Sitney, P. Adams. (1977–78) 1978. "Autobiography in Avant-garde Film." *Millennium Film Journal* 1, no. 1: 60–106; Rpt. in *The Avant-garde Film: A Reader of Theory and Criticism*, ed. P. Adams Sitney. 199–246. New York: New York University Press.

Solanas, Fernando. 1969. "Cinema as a Gun." *Cinéaste* 3, no. 2: 20.

Sontag, Susan. 1978. *On Photography*. New York: Delta.

Taylor, Richard. 1998. "Three Songs of Lenin." In *Film Propaganda: Soviet Russia and Nazi Germany* (rev. ed). ed. Richard Taylor, 74–84. London: I. B. Tauris.

Thede, Nancy, and Alain Ambrosi, eds. 1991.*Video the Changing World*. Montreal: Black Rose Books.

Time. 1938. Review of *The Spanish Earth*. August 23.

Turvey, Malcolm, and Annette Michelson, eds. 2007. "New Vertov Studies." *October* 121: 3–110.

van Dongen, Helen. 1965. "Robert J. Flaherty, 1884–1951." *Film Quarterly* 18, no. 4: 4.

Vertov, Dziga. 1920. "A Film-Show in a Village." Trans. Masha Enzenberger. *Screen* 13, no. 4.

———. 1962. "The Writings of Dziga Vertov." Translated by Val Telberg and S. Brody. *Film Culture* 25 (Summer): 50–65.

———. 1972. *Articles, journaux, projets*. Translated by Sylviane Mossé and Andrée Robel. Paris: Inédit, *Cahiers du cinéma*.

———. 1984. *Kino-Eye: The Writings of Dziga Vertov*. Edited by Annette Michelson. Translated by Kevin O'Brien. Berkeley: University of California Press.

Watson, Patrick. 1977. "Challenge for Change." In *Canadian Film Reader*, ed. Seth Feldman and Joyce Nelson, 112–19. Toronto: Peter Martin.

Waugh, Thomas. 1979. "Report on the 1979 Alternative Cinema Conference." *Jump Cut* 21: 37–40.

———. 1980. "Lawn Mowers and Harlequins: Two Trigger films, Brad and Jenny." *The Body Politic* 63 (May): 32.

———. 1981. *Joris Ivens and the Evolution of the Radical Documentary, 1926–1946*. PhD diss., Columbia University.

———. 1982. "Men Cannot Act in Front of the Camera in the Presence of Death: Joris Ivens's *The Spanish Earth*." *Cinéaste* 12, no. 2: 30–33.

———. 1984. "Joris Ivens's *The Spanish Earth*: Committed Documentary and the Popular Front." In *"Show Us Life": Toward a History and Aesthetics of the Committed Documentary*, ed. Thomas Waugh, 105–32. Metuchen, N.J.: Scarecrow Press.

———. 1988. "Lesbian and Gay Documentary: Minority Self-imaging, Oppositional Film Practice, and the Question of Image Ethics." In *Image Ethics: The Moral and Legal Rights of Subjects in Documentary Film and Television*, ed. Larry Gross, et al., 248–72. New York: Oxford.

———. 1995. "Men's Pornography: Gay vs. Straight." In *Out in Culture: Gay Lesbian and Queer Essays on Popular Culture*, ed. Alex Doty, 307–27. Durham, N.C.: Duke University Press. Originally published in *Jump Cut* 30 (Spring 1985): 30–36.

———. 2006. *The Romance of Transgression in Canada: Queering Sexualities, Nations, Cinemas*. Montreal: McGill-Queen's University Press.

———. 2006. "Foreword: Documentary, Lies, and Truth." *Nouvelles vues sur le cinéma québécois* 5 (Spring): 1–6. www.Cinema-quebecois.net.

Waugh, Thomas, and Joyce Rock. 1981. "Gays Set the Record Straight." *Cinema Canada* 73: 32–33.

Waugh, Thomas, Michael Brendan Baker and Ezra Winton, eds. 2010. *Challenge for Change: Activist Documentary at the National Film Board of Canada*. Montreal: McGill-Queen's University Press.

Weiner, Bernard. 1971. "Radical Scavenging: An Interview with Emile de Antonio." *Film Quarterly*, 25: 3.

Weiss, Andrea. 1981. "*Women I Love* and *Double Strength*: Lesbian Cinema and Romantic Love." *Jump Cut* 24/25: 30.

———. 1981a. "Filmography of Lesbian Works." *Jump Cut* 24/25: 22.

———. 1992. *Vampires and Violets: Lesbians in the Cinema*. London: Jonathan Cape.

White, Jerry. 2006. "The Winds of Fogo." In *The Cinema of Canada*, ed. Jerry White, 73–80. London: Wallflower Press.

Wiesner, Peter K. 1992. "Media for the People: The Canadian Experiments with Film and Video in Community Development." *American Review of Canadian Studies*, Spring, 65–99.

Willemen, Paul. 1989. "The Third Cinema Question: Notes and Reflections." In *Questions of Third Cinema*, ed. Jim Pines and Paul Willemen, 1–29. London: BFI.

Williams, Raymond. 1958. *Culture and Society 1780–1950*. New York: Harper & Row.

Winston, Brian. 1988. "The Tradition of the Victim in Griersonian Documentary." In *Image Ethics: The Moral Rights of Subjects in Photography, Film and Television*, ed. Larry Gross, Jay Ruby, and John Katz, 34–57. New York: Oxford.

Wong Chi Yan. 1981. "*L'Aspect rose de la chose* (Interview)." *Cinémaction* 15: 97–98.

Youdelman, Jeffrey. 1982. "Narration, Invention and History: A Documentary Dilemma." *Cineaste* 12, no. 2: 8–15.

Zimmerman, Patricia, and John Hess. 1997. "Transnational Documentaries: A Manifesto." *Afterimage*, January/February, 10–14.

Zita, Jacquelyn. 1981. "Films of Barbara Hammer: Counter-currencies of a Lesbian Iconography." *Jump Cut* 24/25: 26–30.

Publication History

Chapter 1 has appeared previously in Thomas Waugh, *"Show Us Life": Toward a History and Aesthetics of the Committed Documentary* (Metuchen, N.J.: Scarecrow Press, 1984), xi–xxvii.

Chapter 3 was originally published in Kathleen Vernon, ed., *The Spanish Civil War and the Arts* (Ithaca, N.Y.: Cornell University Western Societies Program Occasional Papers, Number 24, 1990), 14–24.

Chapter 4 has appeared previously in Carole Zucker, ed., *Making Visible the Invisible: An Anthology of Original Essays on Film Acting* (Metuchen, N.J.: Scarecrow Press, 1990), 64–91.

The first two parts of chapter 5 originally appeared respectively as "Emile de Antonio and the New Documentary of the Seventies" in *Jump Cut* October 11 (1976) and "Emile de Antonio's *Underground*," *Jump Cut*, December 13 (1977) and are archived online at http://ejumpcut.org.

Chapter 7 has appeared previously in Larry Gross, John Stuart Katz and Jay Ruby, ed. *Image Ethics, the Moral and Legal Rights of Subjects in Documentary Film and Television* (New York: Oxford University Press, 1988), 248–72. Used by permission of Oxford University Press.

Chapter 8 has appeared previously in Chris Holmlund and Cynthia Fuchs, eds., *Between the Sheets, In the Streets: Queer, Lesbian, Gay Documentary* (University of Minnesota Press, 1997), 107–24. Copyright Regents of the University of Minnesota.

Chapter 9 has appeared previously in *CineAction!* (Toronto) no. 23 (Winter 1990–91), 28–39.

Chapter 10 has appeared previously in Kees Bakker, ed., *Joris Ivens and the Documentary Context* (Amsterdam: Amsterdam University Press, 1999), 171–82.

Index

THOMAS WAUGH is professor of film studies and interdisciplinary studies in sexuality at Concordia University, Montreal, Quebec.